TOWARD A MODERN CHINESE BUDDHISM

TOWARD A MODERN CHINESE BUDDHISM
Taixu's Reforms

Don A. Pittman

University of Hawai'i Press
Honolulu

© 2001 University of Hawai'i Press

All rights reserved

Printed in the United States of America

01 02 03 04 05   5 4 3 2 1

Library of Congress Cataloging-in-Publication Data

Pittman, Don Alvin.
    Toward a modern Chinese Buddhism : Taixu's reforms / Don. A. Pittman
        p. cm.
    Includes bibliographical references and index.
    ISBN 0–8248–2231–5 (alk. paper)
    1. Buddhist renewal—China. 2. Ta'i-hsü

BQ4570.R4 P58 2001
294.3'0951'09041—dc21
                              00–061603

University of Hawai'i Press books are printed on acid-free paper and meet the guidelines for permanence and durability of the Council on Library Resources.

Printed by The Maple-Vail Book Manufacturing Group

For Nancy

*and in memory of
Joseph Mitsuo Kitagawa
(1915–1992)*

CONTENTS

Acknowledgments ix
A Note on Romanization xi

Introduction: In Search of a New Buddhism 1

1 Defending the Dharma in a Revolutionary Age 13
2 The Sound of the Tide for a New China 61
3 An Ecumenical Vision for Global Mission 105
4 Mahāyāna and the Modern World 153
5 A Creative Recovery of Tradition 196
6 Taixu's Legacy 255

Notes 299
Glossary of Chinese Characters 353
Selected Bibliography 363
Index 379

ACKNOWLEDGMENTS

This book on modern Chinese Buddhism evolved over a number of years, and in its preparation I benefited from the help of many people. Those who read all or part of the manuscript and offered valuable comments include Joseph M. Kitagawa, who first suggested to me a study of Taixu's reforms when I was a doctoral candidate at the University of Chicago, Frank E. Reynolds, Judith A. Berling, Liu Qingqian, and Venerable Master Shengyan. Richard C. Bush, Jr., was kind enough to loan me his set of *Taixu dashi quanshu* (The Complete Writings of the Venerable Master Taixu) until I could purchase my own. Hong Jinlian and the staff of the Chung-Hwa Buddhist Institute, the library staff of the Fa-Kuang Buddhist Institute, and Shen Jiaqi of the School History Office and Chinese Catholic Museum of Fu Jen University, all in Taipei, kindly answered questions and provided me with helpful materials.

Appreciation must also be expressed to Venerable Master Xingyun and the staff of Foguang Shan, who invited me to participate in the 1990 Foguang Shan International Buddhist Conference on "Buddhism in the Modern World" and to deliver a paper on Taixu. In connection with that conference, I would also like to thank John R. McRae, the coordinator for the English-language section, as well as the Office of Graduate Studies and Research, Texas Christian University, which provided me with a faculty travel grant. For the encouragement offered in recent years by President I-to Loh and my colleagues at Tainan Theological College and Seminary, Tainan, Taiwan, I am also very grateful.

For permission to publish the photographs of Venerable Master Taixu and Venerable Master Yinshun, I would like to thank the Yinshun Cultural and Educational Foundation (Yinshun wenjiao jijin hui) in Xinzhu County, Taiwan. For providing the photograph of Venerable Master Xingyun, I would like to thank Venerable Master Juemen, Executive General of Foguang Shan, Kaohsiung County, Taiwan. For the photograph of Venerable Master Shengyan, I want to thank the staff of the Nongchan si near Taipei, and for that of Venerable Master Zhengyan, the staff of the Buddhist Tzu Chi Philanthropic Foundation (Fojiao Ciji shan shiye jijin hui) near Hualian, Taiwan.

Several research assistants in the United States and Taiwan labored to help me find and interpret relevant materials. Therefore, I want to thank Jin Gu, Pamela G. Holt, Chen Wenshan, and Lin Mingzhen. I also wish to thank Patricia Crosby, senior editor of the University of Hawai'i Press, and her editorial staff for their patient assistance during the publication process, as well as the two anonymous readers whose critical reviews of the first draft prepared for the press were very helpful in making final revisions. Of course, any errors of fact or judgment in the book are my responsibility alone.

Finally, I wish to thank my entire family. Without their constant love and support—especially that of my wife Nancy and my daughters Debra, Katheryn, and Merillat—the sustained effort required of this extended period of research and writing would not have been possible.

D. A. P.

A NOTE ON ROMANIZATION

No single romanization system for Chinese names and terms is satisfactory in all respects. The Wade-Giles system or some variant of it was used in virtually all the English-language resources cited in this study. However, because the *pinyin* romanization system, often referred to as the United Nations' Mandarin Phonetic Symbol System, is increasingly used in both scholarly and popular literature, I have chosen to adopt it in this book. Therefore, romanizations within quoted material have been edited to conform to this system, unless otherwise noted.

A few exceptions have been made for certain personal or place names that are commonly recognized in the West, such as Chiang Kai-shek (rather than Jiang Jieshi) and Taipei (rather than Taibei). For clarification, the Wade-Giles romanization is included in parentheses following the *pinyin* romanization for all personal names in the Glossary of Chinese Characters.

Chinese authors whose works have been published in English are cited under their own chosen romanizations (e.g., Yu-yue Tsu), except in a few cases where the authors were significant participants in the events of the period and are mentioned as such in the text; an example is Hu Shi, whose English publications bear the romanized name Hu Shih.

All romanizations within the titles of published works in English have been retained. Also preserved are the self-selected romanized names of certain Buddhist institutions or organizations that are internationally known, such as Tzu Chi (*pinyin:* Ciji).

INTRODUCTION

IN SEARCH OF A NEW BUDDHISM

The chaotic Republican period in China (1912–1949) was one of intense self-criticism, ideological polarization, military conflict, and change. The corrupt Manchu dynasty had been overthrown, yet the forging of a new social order proved far more difficult than anyone had imagined. It was a time of grand utopian dreams and of harsh, unyielding realities. Foreign intrusions, famine, civil war, and constant struggle in social, political, and religious spheres among conservatives, progressives, and radical modernists characterized the period.

Striving to recover from the anti-Buddhist paroxysms of the violent Taiping Rebellion (1851–1864) and deeply concerned with spiritual revitalization, the Buddhist community was not exempt from bitter clashes between traditional and reformist visions of an appropriate response to the post-dynastic context and the secularizing influences of modernity. Moreover, against external threats of confiscation, the sangha had to defend its institutional holdings in China and assert its right to self-regulatory propagation.* The numerous Chinese Buddhist associations chartered during the Republican period tried to present their institutional concerns to governmental authorities

---

* In this study, the term "Sangha" with an initial capital letter refers to the entire Buddhist community, including monastic and lay practitioners, whereas the term "sangha" in lowercase refers more narrowly to the monastic community.

and counter the arguments and actions of hostile anti-religionists. They sought to affirm their ancient religious tradition as an enduringly valuable part of the Chinese cultural heritage, to improve the public image of Buddhism through various devotional, educational, and social service activities, and to present an effective challenge to Christian missionaries from Europe and North America.

A pivotal figure among Chinese Buddhist reformers in the quest for a new, modern form of Buddhism was the monk Taixu (1890–1947). An energetic, intelligent leader whom many Buddhists came to revere highly, he was nevertheless judged by most of the Chinese monastic community as a teacher far too radical in his insistence on religious change. More concerned with establishing a pure land on earth than in achieving rebirth in the Western Pure Land of Amitābha, Taixu called for a revitalization of Buddhism through institutional reorganization, modern education, compassionate social action, and ecumenical cooperation in global mission. Conservative teachers in the sangha, such as the respected Pure Land master Yinguang (1861–1940), responded by portraying Taixu as a gifted but dangerously strident and disruptive voice within a Chinese Buddhist community that did not need innovation but only rededication to its ancient patterns of spiritual discipline.

Taixu's own assessment of his ultimate failure to convert the majority of the sangha to his point of view about the need for a complete "Buddhist revolution" *(fojiao geming)* referred not to the extremity of his ideas but to his unfortunate inability to inspire and lead people in a difficult and divisive time.[1] Holmes Welch, however, in *The Buddhist Revival in China,* asserts that Taixu's most serious failing was that he did not seem "to have pondered deeply enough on whether, if Chinese Buddhism was reformed in the manner he proposed, it would still be Buddhist or even Chinese." In Welch's opinion, had Taixu's modernizing, secularizing reforms been fully carried out, "most of the identifiably Buddhist, specifically religious institutions and practices would have faded away."[2]

Although I prefer not to speculate about the validity of this latter hypothesis, I would suggest that Taixu did seriously consider the direction of his proposed reforms. In fact, his specific intention was to facilitate a transition toward a modern form of Buddhism *and beyond*. His teachings, which he sought to ground in Mahāyāna scriptures and traditional paradigms, were intended to address directly the pressing social and spiritual problems of the twentieth century in keeping with what he understood to be the ultimate goals of institutional Buddhism—goals that lay beyond the preservation of institutional Buddhism itself. Indeed, in forging his unique response to the issues that the Sangha confronted in the Republican period, Taixu can be said to represent within the Chinese Buddhist community a "classical" figure, in Joachim Wach's sense.[3] That is to say, he represents a "type" of spirituality which exemplifies religious trends that John Randall, Joseph Kitagawa, and others have identified as prominent in the modern period: namely, an ethicization of religion and a this-worldly soteriology.[4] In essence, he represents a particular form of religious piety.

TAIXU AS "ETHICAL PIETIST"

To appreciate Taixu's particular form of piety and the nature of the "Buddhist revolution" to which he called his religious community, a brief preliminary discussion of the heuristic model that I employ in this study is appropriate. Without imposing an overly rigid analytical framework on Taixu's life and work, I want to be clear about my use of comparative terminology in characterizing his teachings and contribution to modern Chinese Buddhism. Thus, in this particular study, I use the term "truth" in its most comprehensive, transformative sense, to refer to a disclosure of the way things are in actuality in relation to the way things ought to be ideally. "Religious" truth refers to such a disclosure or revelation that is specifically linked to compelling experiences of transcendent realities or verities. Nonreligious ideologies often present comprehensive and functionally similar pictures of present realities and future possibilities without explicit references to transcendence. Yet in both cases, truth includes both a visionary and an ethical dimension.[5]

By "visionary," I intend to convey the idea that what a perspectival tradition enables one to "see" is precisely the ultimate context for human existence. What is apprehended are those realities or values that are of central significance for life, and to which all other realities and commitments should be subordinate. Religious or ideological communities, therefore, support identity formation as individual people come to realize who they are in relation to all things. Expressions of visionary experiences—through forms of art, music, dance, poetry, mythic narrative, sacred history, highly systematized doctrinal apology, and so forth—map reality and locate persons in terms of past, present, and future verities. Defining normative ways of thinking, they orient one to the nature of ultimacy, the spatio-temporal universe, and the human being in community, as Table 1 shows.

The "ethical" dimension of truth, as employed in this study, refers broadly to a tradition's normative modes of action that integrally and creatively relate to aspects of the visionary dimension of truth.[6] That is, religious or ideological perspectives are most comprehensively founded not only on realizations of who each person is in relation to all things, but on intuitive apprehensions of what each one should do to live within reality-as-it-is in greater congruity with reality-as-it-should-be. As a result, creative interactions between disparate visionary and ethical experiences of truth may contribute to significant perspectival changes within a tradition—and to redefinitions of what it is most important to teach and how truth should be embodied in contemporary contexts.

Within specifically religious communities, primary apprehensions of salvific modes of action are often expressed in at least four basic types of norms, or sets of ideal rules, roles, themes, and images:

Norms for cultic performance—requirements for proper liturgical practice in both ordinary and extraordinary times;

Norms for self-cultivation—personal disciplines for spiritual maturation, including dietary, hygienic, meditational, educational, and other transformational practices;

Norms for the organization of the holy community—structural expectations for optimally productive forms of intracommunal religious

Table 1. Transformational Truth

	Experiential Aspect	Expressional Aspect	
Visionary Dimension	Immediate, holistic apprehensions of reality, of the way things are in actuality in relation to the way things ought to be ideally; the realization of personal identity in relation to all things	Shared understandings of the ultimate context for human existence; theoretical articulations that map reality and locate persons in terms of past, present, and future verities; normative ways of thinking	Understandings of the nature of ultimacy Understandings of the spatio-temporal universe Understandings of the human being in community
Ethical Dimension	Intuitive apprehensions of what one must do to live within reality-as-it-is in greater congruity with reality-as-it-should-be	Shared understandings of how most appropriately to live in light of the total context and conditions that shape human identity and destiny; normative ways of acting	Norms for cultic performance Norms for self-cultivation Norms for the organization of the holy community Norms for social responsibility (morality)

interchange and for appropriate relations with other communities, sacred and secular; and

Norms for social responsibility—basic moral guidelines that contribute to spiritual progress and the realization of the ideal social order.

Any particular valued or devalued action may, of course, be related to more than a single norm. For example, religious practices such as fasting, praying, preaching, healing the sick, and hunting could be described in relation to all four of these types of ethical norms.

Religious traditions are dynamic realities, of course, which in varying degrees and contexts validate competing forms of piety and different emphases with regard to truth. By the term "piety," I refer to a disposition of thought and action that is both the means and the end, or goal, of transformational discipline. Historians of religions and students of comparative religious ethics are naturally interested in understanding the multiple ways—even within single traditions—that link the visionary and ethical dimensions of truth. Historians of religions have been especially interested in studying the historical development of different forms of spirituality and the dynamics of intra-religious as well as interreligious conflict.

In relation to this bidimensional characterization of religious truth, important features of many religious traditions may be illuminated by identifying two basic forms of religious piety: visionary piety and ethical piety. Advocates of a visionary piety may be said to emphasize the attainment of mental dispositions, the "seeing" of the true nature of things. For them, being religious primarily means believing certain things, trusting in the verity of certain comprehensive visions. Ethical expressions of truth deemed most important for sustaining such visions without obstructing them are given priority. Ethical pietists, in contrast, tend to emphasize transformation through normative activities—that is, the doing of truth. For them, being religious primarily means acting according to prescribed rules and roles. Regardless of the ethical norms emphasized, what are highlighted are those aspects of the tradition's vision that undergird such practices without apparent contradiction or unnecessary complication.

In addition to the differences in orientation between these two basic forms of piety, strong disagreements frequently occur within pieties. Individuals and groups within a religious community may vigorously debate which aspects of their shared vision or ethical norms ought to be judged of the highest priority for spiritual attainment. For example, some religious people who can be fundamentally characterized as ethical pietists may be drawn to emphasize cultic performance. For them, religious practice means, essentially, participation in rites. Other ethical pietists within the same community may locate the essence of their spiritual life in actualizing norms for social responsibility, while giving minimal attention to cultic participation.

Religious debate can also be related to the tension between different expectations about experiential intensity or expressional clarity. A central issue may be to what extent it is necessary or even possible to describe the content of religious experiences. Many practitioners may question to what degree such intellectual efforts constitute spiritually centripetal or centrifugal activities—that is, whether they draw one closer to ultimate transformation or propel one farther away from it. A "mystic," for example, may assert that other seekers within his or her own tradition have lost the transforming immediacy of their religious experience due to excessive concern with producing systematized doctrines or with advocating prescribed ethical systems. Yet those who make such charges may themselves be criticized as seekers so absorbed in the immediacy of the sacred that they are unable or unwilling to share such experiences with clarity and thereby foster the creation of community.

These distinctions help us understand Taixu's significance within his own religious community and, even more broadly, the significance of his particular type of piety in the history of religions. I hope to demonstrate, first, that Taixu was an ethical pietist. While he was concerned about explicating the Buddhist vision, and accordingly devoted considerable attention to reviving interest in the complex idealistic philosophy of the Weishi (Consciousness-Only) school, Taixu believed that religious actions were at the very heart of the spiritual life. In a new bodhisattva's process of religious transformation, the Chinese reformer gave priority to selfless modes of action that both expressed and produced profound insights into emptiness. For those struggling along the bodhisattva's path toward full enlightenment, Taixu emphasized that wisdom could not be attained apart from compassionate actions in the world. This was a truth, he asserted, that far too many Mahāyāna Buddhist practitioners, both monastic and lay, seemed to have forgotten, to their peril.

Second, I hope to show that, in the course of stressing enlightenment through the doing of truth (i.e., the concrete embodiment of religious truth within the world), Taixu also emphasized those ethical norms of the Buddhist heritage especially related to social responsibility. He was concerned with norms for cultic performance, self-cultivation, and organizational efficiency, yet his principle concern was, clearly, human morality. Furthermore, he affirmed a soteriology that understood personal metanoia as intrinsically related to the transformation of the entire social order. Unlike many of his contemporaries within the sangha, he understood action within the socio-political sphere to be a primary means to complete enlightenment, not an obstacle to it.

THE STRUCTURE OF THIS STUDY

Chapter 1 summarizes the historical context in which Taixu's controversial leadership emerged. China in the late nineteenth and early twentieth centuries was marked by political and intellectual revolution, by conflicting responses to the West and what it represented. The goal of virtually all civic leaders was the creation of a "new people" *(xin min)*, yet there was much disagreement on the necessary and appropriate means to that end. Some leaders were optimists who hoped for a slow, evolutionary transformation of Chinese society; some were warlords who sought to dictate the direction of change; some were cultural iconoclasts with more energy for tearing down than building up; some were utopian dreamers who envisioned completely new forms of socio-political order. Buddhist leaders were determined to protect their religious community during this turbulent period and to promote its role in a new China. Yet they faced a formidable task. Thus I review key elements of the crises of the late Qing and Republican periods and of the efforts of Chinese Buddhists to defend the Dharma in light of complex internal and external challenges.

In Chapters 2 and 3, I offer a biographical sketch of Taixu's career as a Buddhist master, from his introduction to the religion as a young boy to his eventual status as the most internationally recognized leader within the Chinese Buddhist community of his day. Chapter 2 looks at Taixu's early career, including his spiritual formation and initial efforts to reenliven the Chinese Sangha. Thus this chapter highlights his concerns as a Chinese patriot immediately before and after the historic 1911 revolution and his relationships with known socialists, anarchists, and Buddhist radicals; it also reviews his plans for reorganizing and reforming the monastic community, and for promoting its closer ties to lay groups interested in reform. In Chapter 3, I summarize Taixu's religious activities both in China and abroad in the latter half of his career, as he sought to foster interreligious and intercultural understanding, Buddhist ecumenical cooperation, and global mission.

Chapters 4 and 5 present a synopsis of Taixu's teachings about his "new Buddhism" *(xin fojiao)*. Of particular interest is the way he shaped his presentation of the Mahāyāna heritage so as to highlight the tradition as potentially, if not in actual practice, the most scientifically respectable and socially responsible religious force within human society. In Chapter 4, I examine Taixu's basic perspectives on the role of Mahāyāna Buddhism in the contemporary world, summarizing his description of what he judged to be the fundamental dilemma of the modern, secularized age—namely, the catastrophic loss of any adequate foundation for moral action. Taixu argued that the development of modern science, however beneficial, had effectively discredited all god-language, had undermined both theological and philosophical ethics, and had fueled a consumerism that threatened to destroy all civility. In response, the Chinese master prescribed what he considered the only effective antidote to the spreading global poison of egocentrism and violence: a "Buddhism for human life" *(rensheng fojiao)*.

In the context of this human-centered Buddhism, Taixu pursued concrete solutions to real human problems, both spiritual and political. He sought to restate and refocus traditional Chinese Buddhism as he simultaneously encouraged a reconstitution of the Chinese social world. The most politically involved of all the major Buddhist leaders in the Republican period, he clearly thought of himself as a patriot working toward practical religio-cultural syntheses of new and old. His concern was to demonstrate the relevance of Mahāyāna Buddhism for the creation of a "moral culture" that could heal the wounds of a deeply divided China as well as those of an increasingly polarized and violent global community.

Chapter 5 presents a more detailed account of the bodhisattva's pilgrimage toward complete enlightenment and the religious community's potentialities. Taixu's characteristic descriptions of the path to buddhahood, though in accord with Mahāyāna understandings, were still expressive of his particular form of piety. Through what might be termed a "creative recovery of tradition," he sought to distance himself from those masters who stressed dependence on great celestial buddhas and bodhisattvas. Rather, he emphasized what could actually be accomplished in this world through the self-sacrificial work of thousands of average bodhisattvas dedicated to building a pure land here and now. Indeed, beyond merely recommending the unified practice of the Six Perfections *(liu du)*, Taixu was willing to explore practical plans for realizing a communal utopia on earth. His complementary plans for reorganizing and reducing the size of the Chinese sangha proved to be highly controversial and were widely ridiculed. Although many aspects of his parallel efforts to modernize monastic education for "new monks" *(xin seng)* were gradually accepted, many Buddhist leaders actively discouraged students from attending Taixu's seminaries.

Nevertheless, despite conservative Buddhist critiques that Taixu was rashly dangerous, secular humanist conclusions that he was completely irrelevant, and Christian missionary charges that he was spiritually misguided, the reformer's sense of direction remained unaltered. In response to ardent advocates of Pure Land devotionalism who spoke of declining abilities in the final Dharma age *(mofa)*, Taixu asserted that their pessimism about this world was not in keeping either with the spirit and needs of the modern world or with the primary thrust of Mahāyāna. In response to secular humanists, Taixu argued that their position was fundamentally relativistic and that they had misjudged the beneficial contribution that a modern form of Buddhism could make to China's reconstruction and to an emerging global culture. In response to Christian evangelists, he claimed that a theistic faith was no longer tenable in the modern, scientific world and that the particular form of civilization that Christianity had spawned was destructive of human community everywhere.

Chapter 6 discusses Taixu's legacy after 1949 within the Chinese Sangha, especially his influence on the revival of Buddhism in contemporary Taiwan. As Frank Millican remarked in 1923, "Taixu and modern Buddhism are inseparable. You can no more write intelligently about modern Buddhism and ignore Taixu than you could about the [Protestant] Reformation and leave [Martin] Luther out."[7] Developments in the last seventy-five years have only reinforced Millican's prescient judgment, made when Taixu was only thirty-three. Today, the teachings of the charismatic master from Zhejiang continue to shape aspects of a revitalized Buddhism in East Asia. In the People's Republic of China there is renewed interest in his career, despite his close ties to the Guomindang government, and in Taiwan important masters such as Yinshun, Xingyun, Shengyan, and Zhengyan have all advanced dimensions of his modernization. Taixu may have felt that his "Buddhist revolution" failed, yet his work remains the basis for intellectual, humanitarian, and missionary-minded expressions of the religion around the world. Contemporary Buddhism within the Chinese cultural sphere simply cannot be fully understood apart from his efforts at reform.

Taixu interpreted Mahāyāna Buddhism as a religion that was both in harmony with Śākyamuni's teachings and appropriate to the special needs and spirit of his time. In so doing, he exemplified trends found within many religious traditions in the late nineteenth and twentieth centuries. His efforts have much in common with those of other Asian Buddhist leaders who have advocated a socially engaged Buddhism and joined liberation movements against all forms of human oppression. Much like advocates of the liberal Christian Social Gospel and of Reform Judaism, Taixu simplified and radicalized his religious heritage, defining the essence of the religion in a way that emphasized the role of selfless bodhisattvas in, but not of, the world.

As a realist, Taixu acknowledged the complexities of the human condition in an increasingly interdependent and dangerous global community. As a utopian, he sought to paint with bold colors intriguing images of an enlightened realm of justice and equanimity, a future pure land on earth. Optimistic about human potential for attaining final buddhahood, his goal was progress toward a fully modern form of Buddhism and beyond.

CHAPTER 1

DEFENDING THE DHARMA IN A REVOLUTIONARY AGE

In the late nineteenth century, long before the 1911 revolution that forced the abdication of Puyi (1906–1967), the last emperor of the Qing dynasty (1644–1912), Chinese intellectuals were engaged in a reevaluation on an unprecedented scale of the very foundations of their ancient culture. The primary reasons for this intense introspection, and the sometimes polarizing, divisive debate that it occasioned, were serious dynastic decline and the growing influence in China of western civilization.[1] Local revolts and regional rebellions against Manchu rule caused significant upheaval and dislocation. Many issues that contributed to the general unrest and sense of insecurity, such as official corruption, taxation policies, and governmental treatment of minority groups, were essentially unrelated to the presence of westerners in China. Other critical issues, however, were either directly or indirectly related to western influences on a society that for centuries had been minimally affected by developments elsewhere in the world.

Westernization was largely a consequence of the Chinese empire's forced political and economic concessions to foreign powers that began with the Opium War (1839–1842). China's military defeat by Great Britain and the subsequent infusion of western personnel and ideas into the country had created a piercing awareness of a fundamental disequilibrium between civilizations that had to be addressed.

Not only had China's sovereignty been compromised, but the previously confident self-perception of the Chinese people had been seriously challenged. The precise nature of the imbalance between East and West and the identity crisis that it precipitated were differently evaluated. Yet on one resolution virtually all Chinese could agree: in view of these untoward circumstances, creative, energetic leadership was needed to reconsider the country's past and reenvision its future in a changing global environment. The solution to China's internal problems, many judged, was intrinsically related to an appropriate response to the new external pressures. As a result, as Joseph Levenson has suggested, two sharply contrasting responses emerged to this crisis of identity vis-à-vis the West: the abandonment of tradition by iconoclasts on the one hand, and its petrifaction by traditionalists on the other. Significantly, both these responses, the iconoclastic as well as the traditionalistic, demonstrated "a Chinese concern to establish the equivalence of China and the West."[2]

For several millennia, the Chinese people had considered their country, Zhongguo (the "Middle Kingdom"), to be the center of the world. They thought of their domain not so much as one nation among others but as the sole civilized world surrounded by peoples of less developed societies. Attempts to enforce a tributary system, in which countries that desired relations with China were required to acknowledge their inferior status, reflected this ethnocentric worldview. During the Ming dynasty (1368–1644), the ceremonies associated with a unified tributary system became highly structured, and the formal procedures for establishing and maintaining relations with China were very complicated and expensive.[3]

By the late sixteenth century, elements of a more bilateral model for foreign relations were introduced through interchange with the Manchus and Mongols. However, western nations encountering the country's hierarchical political ideology in the seventeenth and eighteenth centuries responded to all aspects of the tributary system with considerable resentment. Prior to 1800, all but one of the leaders of the trade missions to China from western powers were forced to accede to demands to kowtow before the Qing emperor in accordance with the rituals of the system.[4] Yet by the early nineteenth century, the governments and commercial agents of the western nations refused to recognize or comply fully with Chinese expectations. As Immanuel C.Y. Hsü notes:

> The traders wanted greater freedom of action, and the Western governments, newly released from the Napoleonic Wars and greatly strengthened by the Industrial Revolution, would not suffer the tributary treatment. They insisted on international relations according to the law and diplomacy of Europe; but the Chinese would not sacrifice their cherished system. In effect, they said, "We have not asked you to come; if you come you must accept our ways," to which the West's reply was "You cannot stop us from coming and we will come on our own terms."[5]

The English defeat of the Chinese in the Opium War dramatized and reinforced that sharp reply. Furthermore, it opened China to increased western trade based on a series of unequal treaties that not only were extremely advantageous to the western nations but substantively undermined Chinese sovereignty as well. Five treaty ports were authorized by the Treaty of Nanjing in 1842, and that number increased dramatically in the last half of the nineteenth century through other treaty concessions. By 1911, westerners from a number of nations resided with extraterritorial privileges in forty-eight Chinese cities. Governed by their own national laws rather than those of the empire, such treaty-port communities were established on a combination of commercial self-interest and Christian evangelical zeal.[6] Indeed, many westerners interpreted their presence and work in China as a part of a divinely ordained vocation, in Max Weber's sense.[7] Many related their individual calling to the manifest destiny not only of Christianity but of capitalism throughout the world. Given this rationalization of their place on Chinese soil, it surprised no one that these "foreign devils," as they were commonly called, often displayed arrogance and disdain, whether or not consciously intended, for the Chinese people and their ways of life.[8]

The Manchu's authority to rule the empire was increasingly challenged from within the country as well as from without. Their right to govern was jeopardized not only because of the bureaucracy's inability to respond effectively to the aggressive exploitation of China by foreign powers, but also because of widespread poverty among the rural peasants, unemployment and crime in urban areas, excessive taxation, and notable government corruption and mismanagement. The Mandate of Heaven on which Qing authority rested was widely questioned, and in mid century, civil strife erupted throughout the empire. The Taiping (1851–1864), Nian (1851–1868), and Moslem (1855–1873) rebellions were suppressed only with tremendous bloodshed and loss of life.[9] In the 1860s and 1870s, as a result, the Qing government was forced to adopt a reform agenda in a self-strengthening movement known as the Tongzhi Restoration (Tongzhi zhongxing). However, as Mary Clabaugh Wright has shown, the "restoration" only momentarily reduced growing social conflict and alienation with the Manchus.[10]

During the final quarter of the nineteenth century, debate between ideological conservatives and advocates of modernization intensified. The fundamental flaw in the initially attractive proposal of selective innovation championed by Zhang Zhidong (1837–1909) and others —and captured in the famous phrase *"Zhongxue wei ti, Xixue wei yong"* (Chinese learning for essential values, Western learning for practical values)—came to be recognized by all.[11] The Chinese "essence" was increasingly devalued as wholly irrelevant for achieving the practical objectives of economic and technological advancement required for parity with the West. At the same time, western imperialism and Japanese aggression continued to increase throughout Asia, with numerous spheres of interest and leased territories in China being exploited for foreign gain, accompanied by a corresponding increase in xenophobia and anti-Christian sentiment among the Chinese people. Political decentralization also accelerated, in part because of governmental corruption, in part because of local militarization and the formation of regional armies.[12] The reform program initiated by the emperor Guangxu (1871–1908) in the wake of China's humiliating defeat in the Sino-Japanese War (1894–1895) was immediately countermanded by the powerful empress dowager Cixi (1835–1908).[13] Incarcerating the emperor in the palace and continuing to blame all China's problems on foreign intervention, the dowager's court chose furtively to support the anti-foreign paroxysms that characterized the Boxer Rebellion of 1899–1900.[14]

With the death of the empress dowager in November 1908, and the mysterious death the previous day of the emperor Guangxu, the dowager's three-year-old grandnephew Puyi succeeded to the Dragon Throne as the Emperor Xuantong. His father, who was selected to assume the responsibilities of regent during the emperor's minority, was at first perceived to be receptive to a transition toward a true constitutional monarchy. Yet he immediately disappointed reformers, both by rejecting petitions calling for the convening of a parliament and by appointing a preponderance of Manchu advisers to his cabinet. Optimism quickly waned about any significant change under Qing rule, and the political momentum swung sharply toward revolutionary leaders like Sun Yat-sen (1866–1925). Chairman of the Chinese United League (Tongmeng hui), a revolutionary organization founded in 1905, Sun succinctly formulated the three primary goals of the radicals: nationalism *(minzu)*, democracy *(minquan)*, and economic livelihood *(minsheng)*. The manifesto of the Chinese United League called explicitly for the overthrow of the tyrannical Manchu dynasty, the restoration of China to control of the Chinese, the establishment of a republican form of government elected by the people, and the equalization of land ownership in a socialist state.[15]

When an anti-Manchu revolt in Wuchang in October 1911 precipitated multiple declarations of provincial independence from Beijing, Sun Yat-sen was in the United States pursuing diplomatic support for revolution. Upon his return to China, provincial delegates to a revolutionary assembly convening in Shanghai immediately elected him provisional president of the Republic of China, a position he officially assumed in Nanjing on January 1, 1912. Yuan Shikai (1859–1916), the powerful governor-general of Hunan and Hubei, was finally persuaded by Sun, through assurances of future power, to throw his support behind the burgeoning revolutionary movement. With that critical political and military development, the position of the Qing court, which had also pleaded desperately for Yuan's continued support, became untenable. On February 12, 1912, the young emperor Xuantong's abdication was formalized, ending 268 years of Manchu rule, and the long dynastic history of China came to an end. Taixu, the politically active young Buddhist monk from Zhejiang who was advocating a parallel religious revolution, was then twenty-two years old.[16]

A NEW REPUBLIC IN TURMOIL

Yuan Shikai was elected the first president of the Republic when Sun Yat-sen stepped aside for tactical reasons. However, at the time there was no one reform agenda—or leader—to which a majority of the Chinese people were clearly committed. As James Sheridan has described this transitional period,

> There was little sense of a national community, little cooperative effort toward a national end. The orientation [of the revolution] was anti-Manchu, anti-imperialist, and strongly provincialistic. There was no national hero or leader who could become the symbol of national aspirations, and thereby stimulate nationalist feelings. Sun Yat-sen did not have the capacity for that role, and in any event Sun was not a central figure in 1911, except to his own United League. . . . But the most important limitation on Chinese nationalism was the limited involvement of the mass of the Chinese people. Peasants joined the revolt, of course, but their participation was localized in character and restrictive in goals. For most, the revolution ended with provincial secession. That is why, despite the bloodshed that did occur, the revolution seems curiously bland. In 1911, Chinese nationalism was only skin deep.[17]

Yuan Shikai's own rather limited reform commitments were immediately obvious when he became engaged in bitter struggles with Sun Yat-sen's more progressive colleagues who were active within the newly formed Nationalist Party (Guomindang). In part this stemmed from Yuan's basic judgment that the Chinese people were not actually prepared for democracy, a view in which he was encouraged by numerous conservative advisers who favored a monarchy. With the help of provincial warlords, Yuan soon betrayed the republican movement altogether, dissolving the Guomindang in 1913 and brashly attempting to assume imperial powers. The ill-conceived bid was ultimately unsuccessful; Yuan died in the summer of 1916 as his political authority was disintegrating into the political confusion and bitter civil warfare that was to characterize the next twenty years.

With the death of the Republic's first president, chaos reigned. In the power vacuum, warlords rushed into battle with each other for control. For a brief time Kang Youwei (1858–1927) and others sought vainly to restore the last emperor Puyi to an imperial throne, while Sun Yat-sen reestablished his military government at Guangzhou (Canton) in order to protect the fragile Republican constitution. Discouraged by his lack of success and in failing health, Sun died in Beijing nine years later, in 1925, during efforts to negotiate peace and unification between his Republican government in the south and the warlord government that had succeeded that of Yuan Shikai in the north. It was not until 1927 that Nationalist forces under the direction of general Chiang Kai-shek (1887–1975) succeeded in unifying the country with an extensive military expedition against the northern warlords.

That successful unification, however tentative and superficial, was also in part the result of an uneasy coalition forged between the Guomindang and the fledgling Chinese Communist Party (Gongchandang), founded in Shanghai in 1921 through the efforts of intellectuals such as Chen Duxiu (1879–1942) and Li Dazhao (1889–1927). With the guidance of Bolshevik emissaries, the Chinese Communist Party initially committed itself to a radical Marxist utopianism and the advancement of socialism without any collaboration with bourgeois-democrats. Ultimately, however, Lenin counseled a strategic accommodation with the Guomindang until the communist movement had an opportunity to develop greater popular support throughout the country. A first united front agreement for the purpose of seeking national unification was thus reached with leaders of the Guomindang in 1924. As Derek Waller has suggested, the Communists thought a united front would provide an opportunity for taking eventual control of the Guomindang, whereas Nationalist leaders thought they could contain the Communists while making use of the economic aid and military weaponry provided by their Russian supporters.[18] As a part of the first united front agreement, three Communists were elected to the Central Executive Committee of the Guomindang. The young political radical from Hunan, Mao Zedong (1893–1976), was made an alternate member.

Fundamental tensions, however, between the aims of the Guomindang and the more radical revolutionary goals of the Communists could not long be peacefully mediated. By 1927, Chiang Kai-shek was prepared to terminate the united front and deal militarily with the Communists, their Russian patrons, and their left-wing sympathizers within the Guomindang. His army's swift and ruthless massacre of Communist Party members and supporters in Shanghai, which had become a center for their activities under the leadership of Zhou Enlai (1898–1976), marked the end of the united front. Within days, the party's structure was almost totally destroyed and its future viability in China seriously jeopardized. In the wake of the Shanghai disaster, it was Mao Zedong who was increasingly recognized as the Communist Party's visionary leader. An advocate for the advancement of communism through the organization and ideological education of peasants in the countryside, Mao argued forcefully that rural bases, or "soviets," would provide opportunities for effective land reform and guerrilla warfare against the Guomindang. Moreover, they would be far less vulnerable to attack than urban proletariat organizations.

In the early 1930s, Chiang Kai-shek directed four "encirclement and annihilation" campaigns designed to eliminate the Communists. Mao was eventually forced to abandon his principal base in Jiangxi in 1934 and flee on a torturous year-long "Long March" to Shaanxi, on which many thousands of his followers perished. At the same time, with Chiang's political fortunes apparently on the rise, the Guomindang tried to instill in the populace the expectation of a forthcoming period of peace and prosperity for China. Government leaders encouraged an increased measure of optimism about the creation of a new people and about the salvation of the country. In a campaign initiated in 1934 and known as "the New Life Movement" (Xin shenghuo yundong), Chiang advocated a form of militaristic personal discipline and hygiene for the entire citizenry. Such appeals for reform through personal discipline were only partially successful, however, and ultimately failed to inspire the confidence and passion of the masses to the same extent as Mao's continuing call for change through systematic class struggle.

From 1937 to 1945, to counter Japanese aggression during the second Sino-Japanese War, the Guomindang and the Communist Party were led of necessity to forge another united front, although the truce was never faithfully observed. The Communists used the time during World War II to gain considerable popular support, military strength, and territorial control. By the end of the war in 1945, they were well-positioned for the final, bitter days of civil war, despite the Nationalists' confidence that they themselves could win a military confrontation. Attempts by the United States to moderate discussions of a possible coalition government between the Communists and the Nationalists quickly failed. The military struggle that ensued ended only four years later, with Mao Zedong's declaration in Beijing, on October 1, 1949, of the founding of the People's Republic of China, and his rejection of Chiang's desperate proposal for a division of the country at the Yangzi River, the lines of the former Sung dynasty. The brief and turbulent Republican period in China, a period only thirty-eight years long, came abruptly to a close. For some Chinese as well as outside observers, it ended as suddenly and unexpectedly as the long dynastic history of the country ended in the 1911 revolution. For many, it was viewed as equally inevitable.

ICONOCLASM AND THE INTELLECTUAL RENAISSANCE

The late Qing and early Republican years in Chinese history were aptly characterized by Wu Yue, a revolutionary from Anhui, as a "season of assassins."[19] It was an age of violent terrorism and valiant heroism. Yet it was also a time of significant intellectual creativity and achievement. The creation of a new social order—indeed, of a new humanity—was the common goal of all the intellectuals of the age.[20] As Jerome Grieder has commented, prior to the 1911 revolution, Chinese intellectuals, whether monarchists or republicans, had an ebullient, naive optimism that political change would quickly translate into a much broader and efficacious socio-cultural transformation.[21] Following the revolution, disappointments about the lack of change led to a sweeping critique of traditional Chinese civilization and the cultural ethos that informed such individual and collective resistance to progress. Within many circles, attention came to be focused less on new political structures and more on the development of a new culture. Reversing the logic of most pre-revolutionary arguments, many intellectuals began to maintain that a distinctly new and modern Chinese culture would eventually provide an adequate foundation for the creation of a more efficient and just political order.

"The New Culture Movement" (Xin wenhua yundong) refers to the decade or so of intense intellectual activity, usually dated from 1915, that was directed toward a comprehensive reappraisal of Chinese cultural traits and practices. Labeled "the Chinese Renaissance" (Zhongguo wenyi fuxing) by the scholar Hu Shi (1891–1962), the period was marked by a critical, iconoclastic spirit. It was a time in which intellectuals systematically doubted everything in order, finally, to believe in something. Challenging Chinese intellectuals not to shy away from a penetrating examination of their nation's history and culture, Chen Duxiu declared boldly in 1915:

> We indeed do not know which of our traditional institutions may be fit for survival in the modern world. I would rather see the ruin of our traditional "national quintessence" than have our race of the present and future extinguished because of its unfitness for survival. Alas, the Babylonians are gone; of what use is their civilization to them now? As a Chinese maxim says, "If the skin does not exist, what can the hair adhere to?" The world continually progresses and will not stop. All those who cannot change themselves and keep pace with it are unfit for survival and will be eliminated by the processes of natural selection.[22]

As Chen's statement suggests, the concepts of evolution and natural selection fired the imagination of Chinese intellectuals in the early twentieth century. According to James Reeve Pusey, it was the work of Charles Darwin, rather than that of Immanuel Kant, G. W. F. Hegel, or Karl Marx, that first revolutionized Chinese concepts of history: "It was Darwin who 'proved' progress, who brought 'scientific proof' that the world was 'evolving' and, more important, 'evolving upwards.'"[23] Hu Shi argued that the idea of social evolution was compelling to Chinese intellectuals because it resonated with their humanistic optimism that the course of events could be altered and a brighter future realized despite China's desperate circumstances.[24] Interest in social evolution was fueled by important translations of western literature by Yan Fu (1853–1921) and other literary scholars. Works such as T. H. Huxley's *Evolution and Ethics,* Herbert Spencer's *A Study of Sociology,* J. S. Mill's *On Liberty,* and Montesquieu's *De l'espirit des lois* became widely available.[25] Those students who had returned from studies in Japan, the United States, and Europe were able to interpret the unique Chinese story within the broader context of an evolving human story. Most returned to China with an empowering sense that they could actively create history and help save their country from extinction.[26]

Education at the feet of "Mr. Science" and "Mr. Democracy" was thought by most to be the key for the creation of a new people. Accordingly, there were new initiatives in the field of adult vocational education, in order to train workers for positions in modern industry, and a new focus on higher education at the university level. The respected scholar Cai Yuanpei (1876–1940) returned in 1916 from four years in Germany and France to assume the chancellorship of the National University of Beijing. He took immediate steps to restructure the university on a European model, recruiting a diverse and qualified faculty who were promised academic freedom and participation in curricular decisions. Both the American philosopher and educator John Dewey (1859–1952) and the English philosopher Bertrand Russell (1872–1970) accepted invitations to become visiting lecturers for a year. University enrollment increased markedly as professors and students considered together creative new possibilities for cultural syntheses between the East and the West. Despite opposition from some literary scholars and translators like Yan Fu and Lin Shu (1852–1924), most educators affirmed the need for a literary revolution and the adoption of the vernacular form of Chinese *(baihua)* for all contemporary literature. In fact, in 1920, following an appeal by the National Alliance of Educational Associations, the Ministry of Education ordered that all textbooks written in the ancient classical language *(wenyan)* be abandoned in public schools.

University iconoclasts associated with the New Culture Movement also proceeded to sharply attack the Confucian heritage, traditional Chinese family relationships, and popular religious superstitions. Numerous prominent scholars denounced Confucianism as the product of an agrarian and feudal society of the ancient past. Confucianists, they argued, merely encouraged submission to superiors instead of critical thinking and independent action; emphasized family patterns and expectations rather than individual potentialities; valued hierarchy and inequality rather than egalitarianism; and reinforced tradition while suppressing innovation. As John K. Fairbank has commented,

> The attack on the old Confucian order of hierarchy and status denied the validity of the ancient "three bonds," the subordination of subject to ruler, of son to father, and of wife to husband. It denounced the three corresponding virtues—loyalty to superiors, filiality, and female subjection—as props of despotism in both state and family. The anti-Confucianists attacked the tyranny of parents, their arrangements of marriages, and the subordination of youth to family.[27]

In a stinging rebuke of tradition, the popular writer Lu Xun (1881–1936), for example, declared that "Chinese culture is a culture of serving one's masters who are triumphant at the cost of the misery of the multitudes."[28] Thus convicted, intellectuals extended their reexamination and "reorganization of the heritage" *(zhengli guogu)* to virtually every field of academic endeavor, from literary criticism and the arts to history, philosophy, science, and so forth.

Yet although many of the scholars involved in the debates of this period were influenced by the West, they were certainly not uncritical of western civilization. The horrors of World War I in Europe, they pointed out, prevented any simplistic exaltation of all things western. As Guy S. Alitto has observed, Liang Qichao (1873–1929), Zhang Jiasen (or Zhang Junmai, who published in English under the name of Carsun or C. S. Chang; 1886–1969), and Liang Shuming (1893–

1977) all articulated a more conservative position vis-à-vis the adoption of western culture.²⁹ Such intellectuals feared that any "cultural synthesis" might ultimately destroy the uniquely valuable elements of traditional Chinese culture, elements that indeed had universal significance for humankind. Liang Shuming's *Dong Xi wenhua ji qi zhexue* (Eastern and Western Cultures and Their Philosophies) became a classic statement of the problem from a conservative perspective.³⁰ Liang argued that China was not simply "behind" the West in its historical development but on an altogether different and more efficacious cultural track. Wu Zhihui (1864–1953), Guomindang leader and a longtime friend of Cai Yuanpei, responded unequivocally by characterizing Liang Shuming as a "useless creature of the 17th century."³¹

Most intellectuals of the New Culture Movement summarily dismissed religious beliefs and practices as worthless remnants of a prescientific feudal society or unfortunate survivals from humanity's psychological childhood. Accordingly, Chinese popular religion as well as Daoism, Buddhism, Islam, and Christianity were all devalued in the forging of a new national and global culture. Nevertheless, as Chow Tse-tsung has indicated, in the earliest years of the reform movement, religion was not a primary target of attack.³² A negative view of religious commitments was implicit in many criticisms leveled in 1913 against the attempt to make Confucianism the state religion during the presidency of Yuan Shikai. Again, in 1916, anti-religious sentiments surfaced when Kang Youwei urged the parliament and President Li Yuanhong (1864–1928) to adopt a similar Confucian proposal in order to unify the country. On both occasions, a number of intellectuals took the opportunity to characterize religion as primitive superstition based on fear and ignorance and to describe religious adherents as dogmatic and divisive. Chen Duxiu, for example, while claiming that "the value of a religion is in direct proportion to the extent of its benefit to the society"³³ and urging the Chinese people "to cultivate the lofty and majestic character of Jesus,"³⁴ also finally charged that "all religions are useless as instruments of government and education. They are to be classed with the other discarded idols of a past age."³⁵

Cai Yuanpei's public lecture on religion at the National University of Beijing in 1917 set the tone for many intellectuals. Cai argued that the Chinese mentality was not favorable to the attitudes and sentiments of religion and that the religious institutions of the world had only obstructed the progressive development of the human race. As Hu Shi has indicated, Cai ventured to propose a more acceptable substitute for religious commitment:

> He thought that religion was essentially a product of the instinctive love for beauty and sublimity, and that it might be replaced by a universal education in aesthetics, a training which should lead men to love the beautiful and the sublime in human conduct as well as in nature.[36]

In the midst of continuing controversy about the place of religion in Chinese society, the convening in Beijing in the spring of 1922 of the World's Student Christian Federation sparked an intense anti-Christian campaign as well as a more organized nationwide anti-religion movement. A "Great Federation of Anti-Religionists" (Fei zongjiao da tongmeng) was established with leadership from both the left wing of the Guomindang and the fledgling Communist Party.[37] The Federation sponsored educational efforts that sought to label all forms of religious belief and activity as fundamentally irrational and to identify the Christian religion, in particular, as both un-Chinese and unscientific. As Levenson observes, in the seventeenth century Christianity was widely rejected by the Chinese for not being traditional and Confucian enough; ironically, in the early twentieth century it was rejected for not being scientific and modern enough.[38] Many intellectuals charged not only that Christianity was a foreign spiritual tradition ill-suited to the Chinese people, but that it represented a naive theistic worldview increasingly rejected by scientific minds everywhere.

In concert with more organized efforts to eliminate religious practice came more specific attacks on both Christian teaching and the institutional church. According to Zhang Jiasen, doctrinally, Christianity was seen as too unscientific because of its teachings on miracles and the resurrection of Jesus from the dead. It was contrary to logic because of its intractable theodicy problem (i.e., a good Creator

God and an evil world). Christian faith was contrary to modern social theories because its spiritual emphasis on reliance on God and on heavenly rewards neglected human capabilities for social reformation and advancement within this world. Finally, it was not suitable for Chinese culture because Christianity's foreign character was an unnatural and potentially dangerous basis for a national renaissance.

Institutionally speaking, according to Zhang, the Christian church was portrayed as a hypocritical organization with a terrible history of contributing to human oppression and war while preaching that one "love thy neighbor." Thus it was seen as supporting unbridled capitalism in China and throughout the developing world, but maintained little interest in more just and sustainable solutions of social and economic reconstruction. The church was interpreted as an agent of western colonialism both because of its past function as a religious vanguard for imperialistic governments and because of its continuing insensitivities to the national integrity of the Chinese people. It was understood to be given to corrupt methods of proselytization because of its various ingenious ways of tricking and seducing poor and uneducated people into converting to Christianity. And finally, according to Zhang, the church was said to be made up of persons of low moral standards because of its many "rice Christians," who professed faith merely for personal gain.[39] Chen Duxiu, for example, while complaining about the numerous "rice Christians," also queried critically in 1920:

> Jesus said, "Every one that listens to this teaching of mine and does not act upon it may be compared to a foolish man who built his house on the sand. The rain poured down, the rivers rose, the winds blew and struck that house, and it fell; and great was its downfall" (Matt. 7:26–27).
>
> Are the Christians of the world all like the foolish man or not? We need not speak about those who look upon preaching as a means of livelihood. In every country there are many professed Christians. Why do they not oppose the unchristian acts of militarists and the moneyed? And why do they, instead, connive at the injustices practiced by them? They see the "House of Prayer for all the nations" turned into "a den of robbers," and are indifferent. They hold tenaciously to frivolous traditions as if they were the weightiest doctrines. In my view, these fool-

ish men, and not the anti-Christian scientists, are the real destroyers of Christianity. The responsibility for its destruction should be on their shoulders.[40]

Some intellectuals in the Republican period, of course, were willing to acknowledge that western Christian missionaries had accomplished a modest measure of good in China and could continue to contribute to national reconstruction. However, a far greater number concluded that Christianity was tainted beyond redemption by western imperialism; that it was inappropriately emphasized in the curriculum of too many mission schools, to the detriment of the overall educational needs of the students; and that, with the advances of modern science, the outdated theistic religion would ultimately disappear in the Middle Kingdom, as elsewhere in the world. The long-term outlook for Buddhism, Christianity's major religious competitor in China, was commonly judged to be even bleaker.

ASSESSING THE VITALITY OF CHINESE BUDDHISM

The study of Buddhist philosophy was something of a vogue in intellectual circles in the late Qing, as the scholar-reformer Liang Qichao testified.[41] Nevertheless, the religion as popularly practiced was often subjected to harsh criticisms. Even for many intellectuals for whom the challenging subtleties and intricacies of Chinese Buddhist philosophy held some appeal, Buddhism as an institutional religion offered very little. A moderate number of educated persons were appreciative of the Buddhist heritage and hoped expectantly for Buddhist reform and revitalization, but many more concluded that there were few Chinese Buddhist masters of ability anymore, that the average monk had little education or moral virtue, and that institutional Buddhism was effectively and justifiably moribund. Most members of the Chinese sangha were seen to be primarily engaged in performing rites for the dead for personal financial gain and were judged largely incapable of contributing much of significance toward national goals.

Accordingly, in the waning years of the Qing dynasty, some political reformers proposed that the considerable assets of Buddhist monasteries be appropriated by the government for use in modernization efforts. Zhang Zhidong, for example, in his 1898 *Quan xue pian* (Exhortation to Learning), suggested that the Qing court confiscate Buddhist monasteries and Daoist temples—up to 70 percent of their property—to support general educational reform. He even argued that this action would serve in the long run to benefit Buddhism and Daoism. Zhang reasoned that because the property confiscations would reinforce Confucianism as the guiding political ideology for the country, the more stable central government that resulted could subsequently protect and encourage the revitalization of all religious traditions, including Buddhism and Daoism.[42]

Liang Qichao, who studied Buddhist philosophy with his friend Tan Sitong (1865–1898), is typical of the intellectuals who expressed mixed feelings about Buddhism's potential place in a modern China. If Buddhism, he suggested, could distance itself from superstition and emphasize its rational temper and beneficial spirit toward the world, it could actively contribute to the nation's future. If not, its influence could only be a detrimental one. Acknowledging Buddhism's historically important position within Chinese society, Liang commented:

> In this unclean and evil world, men developed all sorts of vexation, frustration, grief, and sorrow; seeking a refuge that could offer security of life and peace of mind, men with some spiritual proclivity naturally fled to Buddhism. Buddhism, by nature, was neither renunciatory nor negativistic, but men who studied it faithfully and could truly maintain it with a positive spirit [were so few] that it would have been difficult to find even one or two, apart from Tan Sitong. . . .
>
> The Chinese had always been quite badly tainted with the poison of superstition; as Buddhism became prevalent, all sorts of belief in evil spirits and unorthodox doctrines as well as methods for public deception and popular delusion were revived in its wake. . . . If this [trend] continues unchanged, then Buddhism will become a great obstacle in our intellectual world, and even those of us who have always treated Buddhistic teachings with respect will henceforth be tongue-tied and afraid to discuss it any more.

Jiang Fangzhen has said: ". . . Our country's new turning point hereafter should also develop from two directions: one, the emotional, which [involves] a new literature and a new art, and the other, the rational, which [involves] a new Buddhism." I very much agree with his words. There is no doubt that Buddhism in China, which could not be suppressed or eradicated even by those who hated it intensely, will always be an important factor in our social thinking; whether this is beneficial or baneful to our society depends solely on whether the new Buddhists appear.[43]

In the late nineteenth and early twentieth centuries, social reformers of many different persuasions wondered with Liang Qichao whether "new" expressions of Buddhism would appear. They openly questioned whether or not the ancient religion had enough vitality left to respond to the changes being wrought in the modern world. Throughout its long history in China, from the middle of the Han dynasty (206 B.C.E.–220 C.E.) forward, the Sangha had experienced numerous cycles of growth and decline. Significantly, from the Ming period on, in times of crisis and decay it had been most notably the Buddhist laity who activated renewal movements. Of course, accomplished Buddhist masters had continued to achieve broad attention, to be widely revered, and to help stimulate and guide lay activities and organizations. The health of monastic and of lay Buddhism were always closely interrelated.[44] However, associations of devoted lay followers had come to play an increasingly important role in Buddhist life.

Throughout the Tang period (618–907), lay associations in China commonly emphasized the planning of Buddhist festivals, the preservation of scripture, and sūtra recitation, but by the time of the Northern Song dynasty (960–1127), the primary focus of most lay associations was the communal recitation of the Buddha's name. As Chün-fang Yü has explained, "During their periodic meetings members recited together the name of the Amitābha Buddha and transferred the merits thus accrued to their speedy rebirth in the Western Paradise. The members also engaged in philanthropic activities, but invocation of the Buddha *(nian fo)* was the main purpose."[45]

In contrast to their earlier prototypes, these groups were more frequently comprised of commoners than members of the upper class. Moreover, they tended to be rather informally constituted and loosely organized. By late Ming times, however, lay Buddhist groups were usually much more highly structured. As Edward Ch'ien comments,

> Organization and group consciousness also characterized the highly syncretic lay Buddhist world of late Ming, during which lay Buddhist associations proliferated in number.... These associations were rather unlike their earlier counterparts, which consisted of an indeterminate number of people meeting at unspecified times. By contrast, the lay Buddhist associations of late Ming were formally established institutions with definite rules for both group conduct and individual behavior.... Lay Buddhist associations grew numerically and organizationally, involving both the common people and also the educated literati-gentry elite, who, though steeped in the Confucian tradition, embraced with all seriousness certain Buddhist principles and practices in their daily lives.[46]

In the Ming and Qing dynasties, while large numbers of Buddhists explored doctrine and ritual practice within these lay associations, many other Chinese became familiar with elements of the religion through popular literature, syncretic religious traditions, or millenarian sects and secret societies. Chinese novels such as *Jin Ping Mei* (Golden Lotus), *Xiyou ji* (Journey to the West), and *Shuihu zhuan* (Water Margin) gave both readers and illiterate listeners opportunities to learn about Buddhist values, practices, and personalities. Simply written morality books *(shan shu)* offering ethical maxims, lists of good and evil deeds, and expected merits and demerits reinforced Buddhist understandings of karma and of merit-making possibilities for the laity.

Beyond the unreflective syncretism of Chinese popular religion, more sophisticated syncretic religious groups such as the Three Teachings Sect (San jiao) of Lin Zhaoen (1517–1598) contributed to the broadening of a sinicized Buddhism.[47] Lin's own goal was to develop a single method of mind cultivation that effectively integrated the insights of the Confucian, Buddhist, and Daoist traditions. Finally, many sectarian religious groups, such as the Maitreya Society (Mile tuan), the White Cloud Sect (Baiyun zong), and the White Lotus Sect (Bailian jiao) extended Buddhism's appeal. Devotionally focused and highly syncretic, these sects made adherents familiar with certain elements of the Buddhist tradition, especially Maitreyan eschatology.[48] The White Lotus Sect, for example, synthesized accounts of a deity known as Xi Wang Mu (Mother Ruler of the West) with traditional Buddhist expectations about transmigration, the decline of the Dharma through three periods of history, a paradisaical Western Pure Land, and the Buddha of the Future, Maitreya. In similar ways, members of most Chinese secret societies encountered diverse elements of Buddhist practice and belief. Rites of the Triad Society, for example, so named for its ideal of harmony between Heaven, Earth, and humankind, included explicit references to various Buddhist deities.

IN THE DAYS OF THE LAST DYNASTY

During the Qing era, Lamaism (Lama jiao), a form of Tantric Buddhism integrated with elements of indigenous Tibetan religion, expanded its influence in China through special court patronage. It had once been recognized as the state religion by the Mongol rulers of the Yuan dynasty (1280–1368). Largely for political reasons, support for the tradition had also been extended by Ming rulers. As the monk Dongchu has observed, the Qing emperors also aimed to maintain good relations with the Mongols and Tibetans by showing courtesies to the Dalai Lama and other venerated "living buddhas." Governmental assistance was provided for the construction of numerous Tibetan temples throughout the country, including the large and important Huangjiao si in Beijing, constructed in 1651 to house four hundred Lamaist monks.[49] Also generally favored by the court was Chan Buddhism, especially the Linji school. Nevertheless, virtually all the Qing emperors were interested in promoting religious harmony and encouraging the ecumenical impulses evident within post-Tang Buddhism. Chan remained the dominant tradition, but Pure Land devotionalism was widely practiced in monasteries associated with all Buddhist schools.

Lay Buddhist associations continued to be important in the mid and late Qing, with their lay leaders enjoying even greater freedom from sangha control.[50] Yet in many parts of China, the Buddhist monastic establishment struggled in light of declining popular support for its operations. The Qing government sponsored a new printing of the Chinese Buddhist canon, completed in 1738, as well as its translation into Manchu, completed in 1790. At the same time, facing new financial exigencies itself, the court was becoming considerably less generous with institutional Buddhism than had been true under the benevolent paternalism of Ming and early Qing emperors. Moreover, the government sought more strictly to control ordination and to reduce the number of Buddhist monks and Daoist priests, charging that most were not authentic spiritual seekers but mere social parasites. For example, the fourth Qing emperor, Qianlong (1711–1799), declared in a 1739 edict:

> The ruling princes of old often issued decrees calling for the screening of monks and Daoist priests. Certainly this was because there was indiscriminate mixture of the good and bad among the Buddhist and Daoists. Those among them who shut themselves from the world to practice secretly the monastic discipline probably number but one or two in a hundred, while those who are idlers and loafers, joining the sangha under false pretenses just to seek for food and clothing, and those who are criminals and draft dodgers, fearing punishment and concealing themselves to escape the clutches of the law, are probably countless.
>
> If one male does not farm, some people will starve; if one female does not weave, some people will be cold. The addition of one new monk means the decrease of one farmer. This group does not farm but it still eats, it does not weave but it still wears clothes. Moreover, it consumes choice foods and wears elegant clothing shamelessly, as if these were its proper due. Therefore, the income of two or three hard-working farmers is not sufficient to satisfy the needs of one monk or priest. Since these monks and priests waste the wealth of the people and contaminate the customs of the land, and since they are parasites in society and a disgrace to their religion, certainly they should not be permitted to

increase in numbers without cease. However, since these religions have been transmitted for a long time and their followers are numerous, it is difficult to proscribe them at once. Therefore we command that the system of issuing monk certificates be again practiced, so that there may be an investigation and registration of the monastic order now, for the ultimate purpose of gradually decreasing their numbers in the future. This is our purpose in administering this business.[51]

In addition to encountering more hostile government policies on religion, the sangha faced two other significant challenges in the late Qing. The first was monastery reconstruction following the devastating Taiping Rebellion. The rebellion was led by Hong Xiuquan (1814–1864), a visionary from Guangdong who was influenced by Confucian utopianism and Protestant Christianity. In 1851, after claiming to have experienced revelations of his true identity as the son of God and younger brother of Jesus, Hong formally declared his revolutionary intention to establish in China a "Heavenly Kingdom of Great Peace" (Taiping tianguo).[52] Serving as "the Heavenly King" (Tian wang), Hong soon organized a theocratic state that unified religious, civil, and military command. Basing his utopian teachings on his readings of Christian scriptures, he ordered the communalization of all privately owned land and property. The equality of the sexes was advanced, cohabitation restricted, and strict ethical codes formulated that prohibited opium, tobacco, wine, prostitution, foot-binding, slavery, gambling, and polygamy. The reading of Confucian classics was forbidden and a new civil service examination system designed around the Christian Bible and other Taiping literature. An intemperate crusade against ancestor veneration and idol worship was undertaken. In the process, Daoist and Buddhist monks were threatened and killed, and monuments and monasteries defaced and destroyed. Yang Xiuqing (d. 1856), commander of the Taiping Grand Army, issued a proclamation in 1853 that read, in part:

> With regard to the temples and monasteries, where the Buddhist and Daoist monks stay, together with property possessed by brothels and gambling houses, it is much better that it should be distributed among the poor people of the villages. At present we are seizing the Buddhist

and Daoist monks throughout the country and having them beheaded, and we are inquiring into those who have been foremost in the building and repair of Buddhist temples, that we may have them apprehended likewise.[53]

Before the Qing government was able finally to end the rebellion in 1864, with the cooperation of western governments—a rebellion in which perhaps twenty million people died—the Taipings controlled an extensive area in south-central China, the very heartland of Chinese Buddhism. Citing the report on the region by the Hunanese scholar-general Zeng Guofan (1811–1872) that, because of the Taipings, "there is no Buddhist, Daoist, or city god temple that has not been burned and no idol that has not been destroyed," Dongchu concluded that the Taipings inflicted on Buddhism an almost fatal blow. In Guangdong and Guangxi, in particular, he stated, "not a Buddhist temple or Buddhist image was fortunate enough to escape damage."[54]

Buddhism's second major challenge was that presented by the Christian church. Christian missionaries posed a threat not to the external paraphernalia of institutional Buddhism but to its internal spirituality and popular support. The Italian Jesuit Matteo Ricci (1552–1610) and his colleagues had labored under difficult circumstances to provide a foundation for Christian missionary endeavors in China. As Chan Kim-kwong has noted, hoping to appeal to the ruling elite and Confucian literati, Ricci's mission strategy was to commend Confucianism as a philosophy compatible with Christianity while repudiating Daoism and especially Buddhism.[55] The strategy had limited success because it remained in conflict with the popular understanding of the complementarity of Confucianism, Daoism, and Buddhism. Nevertheless, despite firm and widespread opposition, especially among the intelligentsia, to any potential expansion of foreign Christian missions, the eventual edict of Qing emperor Kangxi (1654–1722) seemed to promise an atmosphere of respect and toleration. As the court declared in 1692,

> The Europeans are very quiet; they do not excite any disturbances in the provinces, they do no harm to anyone, they commit no crimes, and their doctrine has nothing in common with that of the false sects in the

empire, nor has it any tendency to excite sedition.... We decide therefore that all temples dedicated to the Lord of heaven, in whatever place they may be found, ought to be preserved, and that it may be permitted to all who wish to worship this God to enter these temples, offer him incense, and perform the ceremonies practiced according to ancient custom by the Christians. Therefore let no one henceforth offer them any opposition.[56]

This spirit of goodwill, however, did not survive the so-called Rites Controversy of the early eighteenth century, when the Roman Catholic pope and the Chinese emperor each attacked the authority of the other to determine the character of the Christian mission in China.[57] As a result of the pope's decision to denounce any accommodation with ancestor veneration and all rituals associated with it, as well as the Chinese emperor's corresponding decision to expel missionaries who refused to accept such accommodations, the early Roman Catholic mission in China was virtually abandoned. When the first Protestant missionary Robert Morrison (1782–1834) reached the southern port city of Guangzhou in 1807, he was able to begin only very slowly, after language study and without legal status, to spread the gospel to the Chinese people in the area.

Morrison's pioneer successors in mission continued to push the limits of government toleration. Karl F. A. (Charles) Gützlaff (1803–1851) of the Netherlands Missionary Society made several missionary voyages along the coast of China from 1831 through 1833. A subsequent attempt to travel inland via the Min River was repelled by the Chinese military. It was only after the treaty of Nanjing, at the close of the Opium War, that foreigners were able to penetrate the previously inaccessible interior of the mainland. As mission historian Stephen Neill has commented on these developments,

> Little was said in the treaty about religion, but it was clear that missionaries no less than merchants could take advantage of the privileges accorded to foreigners. On the whole, while deploring the war and doubting the wisdom of the treaty, missionaries took the view that what was deplorable in itself had been overruled by divine providence with a view to the opening up of China to the Gospel. This manifestation of

western aggressiveness was bitterly resented at the time by the Chinese, and the feelings it aroused have never quite died away. That Christian work seemed so plainly to enter in the wake of gunboats and artillery was to be a permanent handicap to it in China.[58]

In the second half of the nineteenth century, almost every missionary society in Europe and the United States began organizing for a major new evangelization effort in China. Early missionary endeavors were limited and primarily restricted to the coastal areas. As late as 1865, Protestant missionaries were located in only seven of the eighteen provinces. However, in that year the English missionary James Hudson Taylor (1832–1905), who had himself served in China from 1853 through 1860, founded the China Inland Mission (now the Overseas Missionary Fellowship), which became extremely influential in shaping an effective approach to mission in the Chinese context. Taylor called for a mission that would be conservative theologically but interdenominational; that would enlist for mission work in China all Christians of good character willing to serve, rather than only highly educated professionals; that would be directed primarily from the mission field in China, rather than from distant home offices in Europe or the United States; that would encourage missionaries in the field to dress according to Chinese custom and to identify as much as possible with the indigenous culture of the people; and that would be more concerned with personal evangelism than other forms of Christian education and service.[59] By the turn of the century, the China Inland Mission and other missionary organizations were able to report considerable success both in recruiting personnel for overseas service in China and in establishing fledgling mission churches throughout the mainland. By 1906, there were more than seventy different independent Protestant mission societies at work in China, with nearly four thousand foreign missionaries.[60]

From its inception, an important dimension of the modern mission to China was the publication of Christian books and tracts to be used in preaching, evangelism, and education. Perhaps not surprisingly, many of those materials not only described classical Christian teaching (calling people to "the Way, the Truth, and the Life") but offered pointed criticisms of other religious beliefs and practices of the Chinese people (calling people away from falsehood and perversion). As Ralph R. Covell observes, an analysis of the content of the most widely distributed missionary publications among the nearly eight hundred that were produced from 1810 to 1873 reveals that Buddhism was the religious tradition that the majority of Christian writers most explicitly wished to condemn. "The Protestant missionaries," writes Covell, "were one with the Jesuits in finding nothing of any help in the teaching of Buddhism. It was a foreign intrusion into the religious scene and was worthy only of condemnation."[61]

Only a very few Christian missionaries in the 1800s, like the English Baptist Timothy Richard (1845–1919), articulated a more inclusive theology. Arriving in China in 1869, Richard sought to define an approach to mission that was based more on the striking continuities between Buddhism and Christianity than on their often highlighted discontinuities. Indeed, he preferred to think of Mahāyāna as "not Buddhism, properly so-called, but an Asiatic form of the same Gospel of our Lord and Savior Jesus Christ, in Buddhist nomenclature."[62] Richard once stated:

> Let no man conclude . . . that I think lightly of Buddhism. On the contrary I hold it to be one of the noblest efforts, on one of the grandest scales the world has ever seen, of men trying to solve some of the greatest problems of human existence. I hold also that in its search after a better life it has given comfort to untold millions of our race by that light of nature which the Apostle Paul says is from God. . . . Notwithstanding its weak points it has its strong ones too. Its aims to save all mankind and even all living beings; its doctrines of repentance, faith, love and self-sacrifice; its teaching of the utter vanity of the best in this world, as compared with the future, and an unfailing recompense of our deeds, whether good or ill; its teaching of the supreme importance of union with the One Mind of the universe, though often vague and almost forgotten, are still truths dear to every Christian heart. If we can see them more clearly than the Buddhists, we should pity them, because they have not had the same privileges as ourselves. Although Buddhism has not succeeded in its great purpose, yet owing to its experiments the world is much richer today than it was.[63]

The vast majority of Protestant missionaries, in contrast, maintained an exclusivist theological perspective and saw little of value in Buddhism. As Whalen Lai points out, having already derisively condemned Roman Catholic monks and nuns as uncaring and immoral, it was easy for Protestant missionaries to excoriate Chinese Buddhist monastics.[64] Gützlaff thought Chinese Buddhism's "orgies of idolatry" repulsive and referred to its sacred island of Putuo Shan, which he visited in 1833, as an "infamous seat of abomination."[65] And although Ernest J. Eitel, one of the first missionaries to study Chinese Buddhism in any systematic way, was somewhat appreciative of its scriptural injunctions to be compassionate to other beings, he judged the religion to be fundamentally abhorrent, an "unnatural and monstrous" tradition, and its priesthood among the most ignorant, indolent, and "wretched specimens of humanity, more devoted to opium smoking than any other class in China."[66] Writing in 1884, Eitel concluded straightforwardly:

> Whether we look upon Buddhism as a system of religion, morality or philosophy, we cannot help observing everywhere fundamental errors directly antagonistic to a healthy development of either the intellectual or moral faculties of mankind. . . . Buddhism is intellectually defective. It arose from a feeling of spiritual bankruptcy and never recovered its mental equilibrium. It is therefore essentially a religion of sullen despair, based on the total obliteration of a healthy faith in the actual constitution of things, penetrated by a spirit of morose abandon, mental and moral. . . . Buddhism is in fact a system of religion without hope and strictly speaking even without God, a system of morality without a conscience, a system of philosophy which wears either the mask of transcendental mysticism or of nihilistic cynicism. Again, Buddhism is further intellectually weak because of its prodigious fondness for the miraculous. . . . [It] is utterly incapable of comprehending or appreciating the claims of reality and the demands of the present.
>
> Morally also Buddhism is found sadly wanting. Though professing to destroy self, its system of morality is pervaded by a spirit of calculating selfishness, its social virtues are essentially negative and strikingly unfruitful in good works. . . . It is a science without inspiration, a religion with-

out God, a body without a spirit, unable to regenerate, cheerless, cold, dead and deplorably barren of results. Can these dry bones live?[67]

Among the more widely respected of the many Christian mission leaders who concurred with the negative answer implied in Eitel's rhetorical question was Joseph Edkins, a missionary-scholar first associated with the Evangelical Missionary Society of Basel and later with the London Missionary Society. Edkins claimed that, despite Buddhism's long influence on the Chinese, its intellectual vigor was dead beyond any hope of resurrection. Buddhism's superstitions and idolatry, he argued, would continue to be an effective barrier against its civilized advance and true illumination. Therefore, he concluded in 1893, "Buddhism is not so powerful in China as to cause alarm to the Christian missionary, in view of the coming struggle which he anticipates.... Buddhism makes no effort that can for a moment compare with the work which Christianity has done for mankind."[68] The ancient religion had served merely as a *praeparatio evangelica* for the Christian gospel. Although Buddhism was a part of China's past, Edkins maintained, it had no capacity for being a religion of China's future. Reflecting on his own experience in thirty-five years of mission work in China, Arthur H. Smith similarly concurred that Buddhism had long ago "degenerated into a mere form." "Its priests," he wrote in 1908, "like those of Daoism, are for the most part idle, ignorant, vicious parasites on the body politic. The religion, like many of its temples, is in a condition of hopeless collapse."[69]

TAKING UP THE CHALLENGES

In the waning years of the Qing dynasty, the Buddhist community struggled to respond both to the disruption and devastation brought about by the Taiping Rebellion and to the piercing criticisms by Christian missionaries of the religion's doctrines, spiritual practices, and institutional forms. Unquestionably, the most important attempt to respond to these challenges was that of the remarkable lay Buddhist leader Yang Wenhui (1837–1911), also known by his courtesy name of Renshan. Yang was an energetic young man who one day, at the age of twenty-six, happened to purchase a copy of *Dasheng qixin lun* (The Awakening of Faith in Mahāyāna). The text sparked his interest in Buddhism, and he soon began to study other popular Mahāyāna literature enthusiastically, including the *Jingang jing* (Diamond Sūtra) and *Lengyan jing* (Sūraṅgama Sūtra). His granddaughter, Zhao Yang Buwei, later reported that Yang so immediately became preoccupied with his Buddhist studies that his family was concerned that he might ultimately choose to become a monk.[70]

In 1864, immediately after Qing forces commanded by Zeng Guofan took control of the Taiping capital of Nanjing, Zeng appointed Yang Wenhui supervisor for the construction of the Zongli Yamen (Office for the Management of the Business of All Foreign Countries) in the city. Thus it was in Nanjing that he settled permanently, and that he and other Buddhist friends eventually established the important Jinling Scriptural Press (Jinling kejing chu). Yang was convinced that any adequate response to the challenges that Buddhists were facing first required that they become more knowledgeable about the tradition's sacred literature. Unfortunately, many of the great Buddhist libraries in south-central China had been destroyed by fire during the Taiping Rebellion. The monasteries themselves were being actively restored, but the libraries needed to be replaced and their contents made more accessible if Buddhism was to continue to be a vital force in modern China. As Welch aptly observes,

> What motivated Yang was not the sight of monasteries in decay (because many of those he saw were just being rebuilt), but the traditional wish to gain merit by filling the shortage of Buddhist books.
>
> But if Yang and his friends had little reason to consider Buddhism decaying, they must have become increasingly aware of the contrast offered by Christianity, more and more of whose evangelists they could see about them after the treaties of 1858 and 1860. It is a significant coincidence that 1866, the year Yang began his printing venture, was also the year when the first party of the China Inland Mission took advantage of the newly won right of Europeans to live in the interior rather than in the treaty ports. Letter-perfect in the gospel, they expounded it not intramurally to other clerics, but on street corners to

audiences of common people. How many Buddhist monks knew their scripture so well? And of the few that did, how many were expounding it to lay audiences? Yet one of their traditional obligations was to spread the Dharma among all sentient beings. Such thoughts must have reinforced Yang's determination to make the scriptures available.[71]

The Jinling Scriptural Press ultimately published more than a million copies of Buddhist works. During the early years of the press's existence, Yang Wenhui provided most of the operational funding himself by working at his official post during the day. In the evenings, Dongchu states, "Yang studied Buddhism devotedly. In addition, he collated and prepared scriptures for publication and distribution. He chanted scriptures, recited the Buddha's name, or sat in silent meditation, often until he fell asleep in the early hours of the morning."[72] In 1878, Yang accepted an appointment extended by Zeng Guofan's son, Zeng Jize (1839–1890), to serve as a staff member during his term as ambassador to Great Britain. During two separate tours at the embassy, Yang spent a total of about five years in London, where he enjoyed the opportunity to learn more about western technology and civilization. He also established important contacts with scholars interested in Chinese Buddhism, such as Max Müller, the renowned professor of comparative philology and religion, and Nanjio Bunyiu, Müller's able Japanese student, who later helped Yang retrieve from Japan Buddhist texts that were not included in the Chinese Tripiṭaka.

After Yang Wenhui returned to China from England in 1888, he was introduced by Timothy Richard to the Anagarika Dharmapala (1864–1933), the revered lay Buddhist leader from Ceylon who had founded the Maha Bodhi Society in Columbo in 1891.[73] Following Dharmapala's participation in the World's Parliament of Religions held in Chicago in September 1893, the Ceylonese leader was visiting Japan and China in the hope of gaining support for his plan to restore Buddhist holy sites in India and to organize a cooperative international Buddhist mission to India.[74] Dharmapala thought it should be a grave concern of Buddhists everywhere that since the fifteenth century the ancient Indian religion had almost vanished in the land of its origin. In a late December meeting that the Christian missionary-scholar Joseph Edkins had helped arrange with monks at the Longhua si near Shanghai, Dharmapala stated to those assembled:

> Today there are nearly four hundred and seventy five millions of people who acknowledge the Buddha as their Teacher. A thousand years ago almost the whole of Asia was under the benign sway of the gentle teachings of this great Teacher.
>
> About seven hundred years ago Buddhism was totally destroyed in India by the Mohammedan conquerors; and as long as they were in power, Buddhism had no place in the land. Thousands of priests were killed, temples and sacred books destroyed, and those who escaped from these persecutions fled into the mountain countries of Nepal and Tibet and also to China. . . .
>
> Now there is no Buddhism in India, and my object in coming to this great country is to inform my Chinese co-religionists of this fact and to ask their support and sympathy for the rehabilitation of this religion. India gave you her religion and now I appeal to you to help her in her hour of need.
>
> The Christians, Mohammedans and Hindus (Brahmans) have their respective sacred places in Jerusalem, Mecca, and Puri under their guardianship; but to our sorrow, I find that the Buddhists have entirely forgotten their holy land.
>
> The Blessed Buddha addressing Ananda soon before his final passing away, said: "Ananda, there are four places, which my Bhikkhus, Bhikkhunīs, Upāsakas and Upāsikās should visit, and these places are, where the Tathāgata was born, where he attained anuttara-samyak-saṁbodhi, where he preached the Dharma-cakra, where he attained Nirvāṇa. A visit to these places will bring joy into their minds, and after their death they will be born in heaven."
>
> To restore these sacred sites, to station Bhikkhus from all Buddhist countries in these places, to train them as Buddhist missionaries to preach Buddhism to the people of India, to translate again from Chinese the Buddhist scriptures into the Indian languages, is our object, and to carry out this great scheme, we have formed a great Buddhist Society, called the Maha-Bodhi-Society, on an international basis. All the Buddhist countries, viz. Japan, Siam, Burma, Tibet, Ceylon, Chitta-

gong and Arakan have joined us in our work, and now I make this appeal to the Buddhists of China, whose illustrious predecessors, the great Faxian, Xuanzang and Yijing, have shed a lustre by their heroic devotion to Buddha and by their pilgrimages to the sacred land—the land of the Buddhas.[75]

Otto Franke, a representative from the German consulate who, along with Timothy Richard, accompanied Dharmapala to the monastery to serve as interpreter, reported that the visit was unproductive and discouraging.[76] The monks were curious about the Buddhist relics that Dharmapala brought with him, but hesitant about participating in any type of religious "society" that might appear suspicious to the Chinese government. Initially they offered to print and distribute a Chinese translation of Dharmapala's appeal. Eventually, however, as Whalen Lai has noted, the monks at the Longhua monastery became "so scared of being impeached by the government for 'illicit association' that they begged to be relieved of their initial promise to help."[77] Rather than recruit Chinese missionaries willing to go to India, Yang Wenhui recommended to Dharmapala an alternate plan more likely to succeed. Indian Buddhists could be recruited for advanced studies in China in order to prepare them for subsequent mission work among their own people. In the process of discussing such innovative ideas, both lay leaders expressed their wish that Buddhism be revitalized in Asia "in order to spread it throughout the world."[78]

By this time, Yang Wenhui was already attracting a number of able students, among them the gifted young political activist Tan Sitong, who later praised his teacher as one "who was widely versed in Buddhist texts and history."[79] Several years later, in 1898, to expand his work, Yang purchased a large estate in Nanjing that came to be known as "the Jetavana Hermitage" (Zhihuan jingshe). The property was acquired to house the Jinling Scriptural Press and also, in response to Dharmapala's appeal, an innovative school for the education of monks for global mission.[80] Eventually, a basic three-year curriculum of full-time studies was designed in Buddhist scripture, history, literature, and foreign language training, with the possibility for further advanced work.[81] Especially remarkable was the fact that knowledgeable laypeople actually offered instruction in many subjects to ordained monks. A Buddhist Research Association (Fojiao yanjiu hui) was later founded that sponsored weekly public lectures, principally by Yang himself.

Because of financial difficulties, Yang Wenhui's innovative school survived only the 1908–1909 academic year. Yet even a partial list of those who were teachers or students there reveals the significance of the layman's efforts. Among faculty members were Dixian (1858–1932), the eminent Tiantai master and later abbot of Guanzong si, who served as dean of students *(xuejian)*, and Su Manshu (1884–1918), the poet, translator, and anti-Manchu revolutionary, who taught English.[82] Among the twenty-four students (twelve monks and twelve laymen) were Zhiguang (1889–1963), later the respected abbot of Dinghui si on Jiao Shan; Ouyang Jingwu (1871–1943), the brilliant lay Buddhist educator and leader of the revival of interest in the Weishi (Consciousness-Only) school; Mei Guangxi, who would later become one of Ouyang Jingwu's major financial supporters; and the controversial reformist monk Taixu.[83] Remembered as a model of lay Buddhist piety and as the principal initiator of the revitalization of Buddhism that began in the late Qing, Yang Wenhui died just before the Republican revolution in October 1911.[84]

In the early Republican period, the monastery rebuilding program that had begun to gain momentum in the last quarter of the nineteenth century continued, although it varied considerably by region. Lewis Hodous, writing in 1923, commented in particular on the newly completed monasteries in Fujian, and on the construction projects then underway in Zhejiang and Jiangsu, as well as in many large cities, including Beijing.[85] He also noted that there were a number of monasteries, especially in the Yangzi valley and in southern and western China, that still stood in ruins as a result of the Taiping Rebellion. From Shaanxi in the northwest to Sichuan in the west and Guangdong in the far south, many monasteries were either abandoned or poorly staffed and in a state of disrepair.

This is in basic harmony with the assessments of James B. Pratt and Johannes Prip-Møller. In a paper delivered before the Chinese

Social and Political Science Association in 1924, Pratt reported that in the southern city of Guangzhou, for example, most temples had been confiscated by the government and were being used by the military as barracks. A few lay Buddhist societies were active in the city, but their membership and activities were limited. North of the Yangzi valley, especially in Shandong, the Buddhist temples were often in poor condition and generally reflected as much Daoist as Buddhist influence and devotional practice. In Beijing, most temples and monasteries were in fair to excellent condition, but Pratt discovered few well-educated monks and little evidence of significant interaction between the monastic community and the laity.

In the northwest, in Shanxi, except for the sacred pilgrimage site of Wutai Shan, Buddhism appeared to be in no better condition than in Guangdong. In the provincial capital, Taiyuan, the only Buddhist temple was closed nearly all the time. Concluding with a pointed question, Pratt commented:

> In the smaller towns and villages one finds Daoist temples, but the Buddhist temples have either been made into schools or are falling to pieces. All over central Shanxi, in short, Buddhist temples and the Buddhist faith are quietly decaying. The most marked architectural features of the region are the great bottle-shaped tombs of former Buddhist abbots, mute witnesses to the fervor of the Buddhist faith in this region in a day long past. In some places one can count a score of these great tombs. They mark the graves of dead abbots; do they also mark the grave of a dead religion?[86]

In Shaanxi, according to Pratt, the poor conditions of Buddhist institutions did not differ greatly from those of Shanxi, except perhaps in the provincial capital of Xi'an.

In the central region of China in the 1920s and 1930s, in contrast, Buddhist monasteries were being actively repaired, rebuilt, and newly constructed. This work represented a considerable capital investment. In addition, the number of people active in the practice of Buddhism appears to have been considerable, and the communication and cooperation between the monastic and lay communities generally quite good. Pratt reported that from Sichuan in the west, with its impressive Emei Shan, eastward to Hubei, Hunan, Anhui, Jiangxi, Jiangsu, Zhejiang, and Fujian, the Buddhist temples and monasteries were largely well cared for and well populated.[87] "Hankou and Wuchang," he remarked, "are perhaps the most important centers of the so called Buddhist revival; while Nanjing, Suzhou, Hangzhou, Ningbo and all the adjacent regions of Jiangsu and Zhejiang are filled with very living Buddhism. New temples are being constructed, old ones repaired and pilgrimages carried on, young monks are studying and old monks meditating, throughout all this region."[88]

Prip-Møller, reporting on his own studies of Buddhist monastic architecture between 1929 and 1933, explained the necessity of conducting research in central China by contrasting the vitality of Buddhism in that region to its condition elsewhere in the country. He further noted that virtually all the monasteries in the lower Yangzi valley bore witness to the extensive destruction caused by the Taiping rebels. As a result, a great many of the facilities were being totally or substantially rebuilt, although, according to Prip-Møller, only in a very few cases were they being restored "with anything like the same splendour as before."[89] In line with these reports highlighting Buddhist activity in the central region of the country, Welch notes that, by 1930, based on statistics said to have been compiled by the Chinese Buddhist Association, "there were twenty times more monks per capita in central China than in most of the northern and southern provinces."[90]

The Buddhist community maintained no effective organizational structure that bound together the independent monasteries and the individual abbots who were in charge of them. The vast majority of the five hundred thousand some monks in China during the Republican period lived in small hereditary temples *(zusun miao)* whose ownership remained within a "family" of monks that was created through tonsure, the ceremonial head-shaving by a master that initiated the monastic life.[91] The large public monasteries *(shifang conglin)*, which were owned by the entire sangha and whose leadership selection transcended tonsure relationships, represented only a small percentage of the approximately 100,000 temples and monasteries in which monks resided. In addition, about 225,000 nuns lived in more than 130,000 nunneries—most of which were, obviously, very small, and provided for by particular families. Thus the total size of institutional Buddhism, along with its lack of a unified organizational structure, made it quite vulnerable to localized anti-religious activity and to governmental attempts to confiscate property in order to support educational or military aims.

In the early Republican period, especially during the first united front between the Guomindang and the Communist Party, the government often acted with no concern for the rights or interests of Buddhist communities. Government troops frequently damaged and looted monasteries, destroyed images, and converted temples into schools and other institutions. According to E. H. Cressy's research in Wuchang, for example, by the early 1930s, 65 of the city's 165 religious institutions—39 percent of its Buddhist and Daoist temples and monasteries—had been converted by the government to nonreligious purposes.[92] On the basis of a study of temples and monasteries in west China, D. S. Dye concluded in 1931 that only about 2.3 percent of the temples were being used exclusively for religious purposes; 2.9 percent had been demolished; 58 percent were being used at least in part for public projects such as hospitals or government bureaus; and 36.8 percent had been converted to private uses such as residences, factories, and business concerns. Dye reported:

> In many of these temples now diverted to other uses idols are still *in situ* and incense may be burned. Priests may be found in ones and twos in many, while in a few temples some tens of priests may still be found.
>
> The writer ventures a shrewd guess without data to support, that the functioning priest population of Chengdu temples does not exceed 30 percent of that which existed in March, 1911—two decades ago.[93]

Not infrequently, both Christian missionaries and Buddhist modernists exaggerated the severity of the sangha's problems for their own purposes. However, their parallel observations about the state of Chinese Buddhism did identify many issues that a broad spectrum of Buddhists leaders acknowledged as critically important. The Norwegian missionary Karl Ludvig Reichelt (1877–1952), for example, whose fair-minded attitude led Welch to refer to him as "the leading champion of Chinese Buddhism's good repute,"[94] described in 1934 the generally poor condition of institutional Buddhism, while also outlining features of developing reforms that showed the vitality of the religious community:

> Turning to Buddhism in China, as it is at the present time, the first thing to be said is that *externally,* that is in regard to temple buildings, processions, the grandeur of public festivals, etc., Buddhism is decidedly on the decline. In all the provinces many temples and monasteries have been ruined or badly damaged by the soldiers or by the young people.... In many places the temple fields and the other sources of revenue have been confiscated by the authorities and the funds used for educational purposes. In consequence the monks are hustled back into some of the corner buildings where it is impossible for them to conduct religious ceremonies in a decent way. In some districts the temples seemingly stand intact, but even there a marked decrease in income is noticed and the monks have to struggle hard to secure the most necessary means of living. The result is that many of the inmates are driven to the big cities, where they join the despised crowds of "business monks," who operate in rented houses in bigger or smaller teams, as exorcists or as common priests, chanting masses for departed souls or practicing all kinds of obscure divining methods.
>
> Under such circumstances much of the temple paraphernalia is missing and there are no rules or discipline. The moral standard is very low. The financial stringency in general naturally affects the whole Buddhist society also. There has been, therefore, a remarkable decrease in the number of monks during recent years. Even at the big Buddhist centers and holy mountains the financial difficulties are very great. For that reason many of the best monks have to go out with subscription lists in order to collect the most necessary funds for the repair and maintenance of the monasteries. The low ebb in spiritual and religious life at these places must be considered in the light of this general depression.
>
> This decline in connection with present-day Buddhism in China is so apparent that it does not take much ability to observe it. Consequently the judgment passed by most people is this: Buddhism is vanishing; the monks are disappearing more and more; and the temples and monasteries are on the decline.

> How important it is that [Christian] missionaries at least know the truth about these things which is, that the picture of the external decline, as given above, does not mean that Buddhism as a religion is either dying out or going back in China. To those who live in close contact with the new religious movements in modern China it is apparent that in some ways Buddhism is going forward. There are revivals and activities such as never were. Buddhism is taking a new and strong grip on circles which were not seriously interested before.[95]

Indeed, central to the agenda of the Chinese Buddhist community throughout the Republican period was organizing for self-protection and local mission. A number of the fledgling organizations were designed to honor the Dharma by upholding the ancient Vinaya regulations—that is, by clarifying and enforcing proper standards for ordination and monastic discipline. Some societies were established to improve educational opportunities for both monastic and lay followers. A few were especially interested in funding publication efforts such as new editions of the Tripiṭaka, scriptural commentaries, and periodicals such as *Fojiao congbao* (Buddhist Miscellany) and *Fojiao yuebao* (Buddhist Monthly). Other Buddhist organizations aimed to promote moral cultivation, social service, or institutional effectiveness. In the post-dynastic era, progress on all of these fronts was deemed necessary not merely for spiritual renewal but for the Sangha's survival in an increasingly secularized modern society.

The most important and broad-based of these organizational ventures was the Chinese General Buddhist Association (Zhonghua fojiao zonghui), founded in Shanghai in 1912 by the revered old Buddhist master Jichan, also known as Eight Fingers (Bazhi Toutuo) because of his devotional sacrifice of one finger from each hand. The organization was established in immediate response to the founding in Nanjing of the Chinese Buddhist Association (Zhongguo fojiao hui) under the leadership of Ouyang Jingwu, the radical lay disciple of Yang Wenhui, who at the time of his teacher's death was given charge of the Jinling Scriptural Press. Numerous other societies were begun about the same time, including the Buddhist Confederation (Fojiao gonghui); the Buddhist Moral Endeavor Society (Fojiao jinde hui); the Buddhist Research Society (Foxue yanjiu she); the Young

Buddhist Study Association (Fojiao qingnian xuehui); the Chinese Yellow Swastika Society (Zhonghua huangwanzi hui), which engaged in emergency relief work similar to that of the International Red Cross; the Association for the Advancement of Buddhism (Fojiao xiejin hui), which Taixu founded in January 1912 at the Pilu si in Nanjing; the Buddhist Society of the Great Vow (Fojiao hongshi hui), which Taixu founded in February 1913 at Ningbo's Yanqing si; and the League for the Support of Buddhism (Weichi fojiao tongmeng hui), which Taixu announced in March 1913 from the Guanyin si in Beijing.[96]

Very few of these Buddhist organizations were functionally effective or long-lived. Initial inspiration was rarely matched by sustained commitment to action. Many were merely announced but never actually formed, while others vanished soon after they were established. As Yu-yue Tsu reported,

> As a reaction to external circumstances enthusiasm surged high at first, but there was nothing within the Order to uphold it, and so, when the first impetus had spent itself, the movement fell to pieces. One by one the activities such as educational and charitable institutions, lectures and magazines were given up, and the various societies, which had sprung up like mushrooms, disappeared as quickly.[97]

Even the Chinese General Buddhist Association of 1912, impressive because of its proposals for representational accountability, could not long maintain its initial momentum. At its first annual conference in March 1913, soon after its charter had been approved by the government, it was able to claim twenty-two provincial branches and more than four hundred local chapters, coordinated from national offices in the Jing'an si in Shanghai.[98] Yet even though the eminent Chan master Yekai (1852–1922) was elected to serve as president and a basic national structure was rapidly developed, the association failed to operate effectively within the year. Its new periodicals, which Taixu had been appointed to edit, ceased publication for lack of adequate funding.[99] Apathy within the sangha, factional distrust, organizational inexperience, and general economic difficulties were all contributing factors.

The Chinese General Buddhist Association was resuscitated briefly in 1915 to defend the community from the potentially destructive consequences of a bill entitled "Regulations for the Control of Monasteries and Temples" (Guanli simiao tiaoli). Although adopted by the parliament, it became meaningless in the political chaos that prevailed after Yuan Shikai's failed bid to become emperor in the spring of 1916 and his sudden death in June of that year. A more formal effort in 1917 to resurrect the association with an amended charter was terminated in 1919, when questions about the legality of the organization led the Ministry of the Interior to order its dissolution. Several other attempts failed at creating a lasting representative structure prior to the modest success of the Chinese Buddhist Association (Zhongguo fojiao hui), which was founded in Shanghai in April 1929 and reorganized after World War II by Taixu and other prominent monks.

At the same time that the monastic community struggled to organize institutionally, it sought to address pressing economic problems, support lay Buddhist activity, improve monastic education, and monitor political events while cultivating sympathetic officials within the government. The sangha had always served as a "field of merit" for the Buddhist laity, who had historically given generously to those Chinese monastic institutions that exemplified selflessness and proper discipline. Most large public Buddhist monasteries, therefore, owned a considerable amount of property. The rent income from donated farmlands provided the principal funding with which the monasteries were operated. A second important source of capital for many of the large monasteries—and the primary source for most of the small hereditary temples—was the income from fees collected for ceremonies for the dead.

Direct monetary donations from lay patrons was a third source,[100] although a distressed national economy that was severely disrupted by civil strife and warfare throughout the Republican years, Guomindang land reform policies that restricted the rights of landowners, the anti-superstition attack on Buddhist funerary rites, and the harsh anti-bourgeois rhetoric of the progressively influential Communist movement all curtailed the monasteries' ability to collect rent and to receive other donations. Few monasteries were substantially enough endowed with land and other resources not to be constantly dependent on lay patronage. Therefore, to ensure financial stability, monastic leaders found it increasingly important to foster closer ties with the lay societies.

The fact was that committed lay Buddhists in China—namely, those who had formally taken refuge in the Three Jewels of the Buddha, Dharma, and Sangha *(guiyi sanbao)*—made up only perhaps 1 percent of the country's population. Given the traditionally syncretic patterns of Chinese religious practice, a great number of people occasionally worshipped at Buddhist temples, employed the services of monks at family funerals, and even read Buddhist literature without ever seriously considering taking the five vows *(wu jie)* required to become a lay disciple.[101] Religious harmony remained highly valued and religious eclecticism quite common, as illustrated by the success in the Republican period of sects like the United Goodness Society (Tongshan she), the Apprehension of Goodness Society (Wushan she), the Court of the Dao (Dao yuan), the Six Sages True Dao Union Society (Liu shen zhen Dao tongyi hui), the Study of Morality Society (Daode xue she), the Temple of Five Religions (Wujiao Dao yuan), the Way of Unity (Yiguan Dao), and others. Such religious groups flourished in the period by offering syntheses of Chinese popular religion, Confucianism, Daoism, Buddhism, Christianity, and other forms of spirituality.[102] Nevertheless, the Buddhist revival movement did succeed in leading many people to develop, far more intentionally than before, their own religious identities *as Buddhists.*

This development was in part the result of a genuine spiritual renewal movement within the Buddhist community and in part a response to strident expressions of Christian theological exclusivism, which heightened a sense of interreligious competition. Many Chinese were, in fact, experiencing new religious insecurities in light of Christian preaching that explicitly or implicitly devalued their own traditional patterns of spirituality as excessively syncretistic and otherworldly. Thus it was in response to both internal enthusiasms and external critiques that lay Buddhist societies sought to redouble their own social service efforts in the areas of public health, welfare, and disaster relief work, as well as to deepen religious commitment through scriptural study and devotional practice.

Several lay associations even provided residential facilities for members who wished to engage in reading and contemplation in a tranquil setting. Laypeople who practiced vegetarianism and celibacy were at times permitted to reside in monasteries for periods of study and meditation with the monks. Likewise, monks benefited from programs specifically designed for educated lay Buddhists, as they did by enrolling in classes at Ouyang Jingwu's Chinese Metaphysical Institute (Zhina neixue yuan) in Nanjing, which emphasized Weishi philosophy. Established in 1919, the Institute operated continuously until the Japanese invasion of Nanjing in 1937, offering learning opportunities that served to underscore some of the inadequacies in both lay and monastic education.

A few ambitious masters within the Chinese sangha were committed to experimental projects for improving monastic education. Perhaps 70 or 80 percent of monks were literate, compared to the 1926 estimate of a 20 percent literacy rate among the general population. However, their educational opportunities were limited largely to a small number of traditional texts and practical manuals.[103] After renouncing the lay life in a hereditary temple, a monk's basic training in monastic life was customarily provided by his tonsure master and tonsure family. This education might extend over several years before a monk was encouraged to seek ordination *(shou jie)*. Although after 1911 ordination was no longer controlled by the government through a limited number of monasteries authorized for such actions, ordinands generally continued in the Republican period to travel to the large public monasteries that provided "Vinaya schools" or structured programs of monastic discipline. Education for monks in such centers focused on the practice of the 250 vows of the Prātimokṣa *(sifen jieben)* and concluded ceremonially with the "bhikṣu vows" *(biqiu jie)*, the 58 "bodhisattva vows" *(pusa jie)*, and the burning of "incense scars" *(xiang ba)* in the monk's scalp with moxa *(shao ba)*.

According to the monk Zhenhua (b. 1922), completing the standard educational program was a difficult endeavor, particularly so in the largest and most famous ordination center in central China, Baohua Shan, east of Nanjing. Recalling the intensity and severity of the monastery's Vinaya school, Zhenhua wrote:

> From the time classes were opened at the beginning of the session to the burning of ordination scars at the end, we lived a life of "trembling dread, like skirting an abyss or treading on thin ice." From the beginning to the end, the features of the ordination masters were hardened into forbidding masks. For the entire fifty-three day session, I never once saw them give a kind look or say a civil word to an ordinee. Never once did I see an encouraging smile.... The ordination instructors at Baohua Mountain had excellent deportment and were dedicated to teaching monastic rules, but they were overly severe. In fact, they were severe to the point of cruelty. This made the ordinees feel more resentment than respect, more enmity than gratitude.[104]

Ordained monks who were interested in expanding their understanding of doctrine or ritual techniques would subsequently travel around to different monasteries to find sound teachers. Most often they would travel on foot, finding shelter when they could in the public monasteries that were obligated to grant them hospitality, however meager. Some of the most serious and zealous monks would eventually seek to become disciples of a particular Dharma master *(fashi)* recognized for knowledge of a particular text or tradition. Well-known teachers, such as the eminent Chan master Xuyun (1840–1959) or the venerable Tiantai master Dixian, had large numbers of monastic students and lay followers. The anti-sectarian spirit within the Buddhist community at the time made it easy for monks to belong to one particular lineage but also to broaden their knowledge beyond it. One could be tonsured by a Chan master of the Linji lineage, yet also extensively study Tiantai, Huayan, or Tantric texts and engage in Pure Land practice. As the memoir of the monk Zhenhua suggests, regionalism, factionalism, and personalism often limited one's access to learning and spiritual advancement, but many dedicated monks persevered.

Distinctively new in the Republican period were monastic schools that attempted to reform pedagogical methods and to expand the scope of education beyond traditional Buddhist studies. In many schools, modern instructional methods such as the use of the blackboard and the graded evaluation of demonstrated learning were gradually introduced. In some monastic schools, lay teachers were even employed. Among the most notable institutions were Huayan University (Huayan daxue), founded in Shanghai in 1912 by Yuexia; the Academy for Spreading the Dharma (Hongfa xueyuan), founded at the Guanzong si in Ningbo in 1918 by Dixian; the Wuchang Buddhist Institute (Wuchang foxue yuan), founded in that city in 1922 by Taixu; the South Fujian Seminary (Minnan foxue yuan), founded in Xiamen (Amoy) in 1925 by Taixu; and the Tianning Buddhist Institute (Tianning foxue yuan), founded in 1931 in Zhangzhou and led by Deyi, Minzhi, and others who favored educational modernization.[105]

Most of the new monastic schools, however, were poorly funded and short-lived. Altogether, they attracted probably no more than 1 or 2 percent of the Republican sangha. Most monks seemed to think that the traditional educational system was more than sufficient for their needs. In Dongchu's judgment, the new efforts at monastic education in the Republican period were a failure for three basic reasons: first, because sangha leaders did not sufficiently manifest the required spirit of self-sacrifice and persistence in the face of difficulties; second, because the schools were usually not organized according to sound educational principles; and, third, because students were sometimes permitted to concentrate on peripheral secular subjects and to neglect the fundamental moral disciplines emphasized in traditional monastic training. This third element, he concluded, led not a few young Buddhist monks of talent and promise to become so secularized in outlook that they ultimately abandoned their religious practice. Perhaps not wishing to appear overly critical in this respect of Taixu and the monastic schools established under his leadership, Dongchu tempered his remarks by acknowledging that the reformer did consistently offer appropriate and compassionate counsel to young monks who chose to return to lay life. According to Dongchu, Taixu advised them to remain active laypersons within the Buddhist community rather than become completely secularized citizens without commitments to the Dharma.[106]

Besides seeking ways to achieve financial stability and improve monastic education, the Chinese sangha was concerned during the Republican period with forecasting the political weather in order to detect potentially destructive storms brewing on the horizon. The historic principles that discouraged monks from direct involvement in political matters did not deter monastic leaders from pursuing relationships with, and currying favors from, national and local officials in the hope of preventing new attempts to confiscate Buddhist property or intervene in sangha affairs. The 1898 and 1904 Qing appropriations of Buddhist monasteries and farmlands for the support of educational reforms, both of which had been rescinded after Buddhist protests, had not been forgotten. In those cases, prominent monks had appealed to the throne for a reconsideration of the policies, asserting in part that the sangha was also promoting modern educational reform.

After the 1904 action, some monasteries had also tried to protect themselves through temporary affiliations with the Japanese Buddhist Higashi-Honganji sect, which was engaged in missionary work in China.[107] This more radical strategy of seeking shelter under a Japanese institutional umbrella, first proposed by two Japanese priests, Mizuno Baigyō and Itō Kendō, apparently caused some consternation at the Qing court. Imperial concerns that such protective relationships with Japanese institutions might begin to increase may actually have contributed to a 1905 edict that provided the Buddhist community with temporary relief from extensive governmental confiscations.

During the Republican years, most Guomindang leaders concluded that the Buddhist community constituted no significant political threat. Therefore, although the sangha was closely supervised, it was allowed to function with relative freedom. Nevertheless, under the provisions of the Regulations for the Control of Monasteries and Temples, promulgated in 1915 during Yuan Shikai's presidency, all monks and nuns, monasteries and temples were to be registered with the government. In addition, Buddhist properties could not be alienated without state approval, and religious activities and public preaching were to be monitored and regulated.[108] An organized Buddhist protest and lobbying effort against the legislation soon led to Yuan's retaliatory order to close the Chinese General Buddhist Association. Although the regulatory law of 1915 was never enforced, most of its provisions were revived in December 1929 with the adoption of "Regulations for the Supervision of Monasteries and Temples" (Jiandu simiao tiaoli). While the 1929 law did recognize the representative authority of the Chinese Buddhist Association that had been founded in Shanghai that year, the organization was placed under the direct control of the Ministry of the Interior to ensure its patriotic allegiance to the state.

Throughout the Republican era, Buddhist properties were the target of military or local government confiscations. Condemning such actions, Buddhists remained especially indignant that the large and historic Longhua si in Shanghai, visited by Dharmapala in 1893, was occupied by one military force after another from 1911 on.[109] The editors of *The Young East* reported in September 1928 that Japanese Buddhists were again offering to help by lodging an official protest because the Christian General Feng Yuxiang (1882–1948) and other leaders of the Nanjing government had "shown a disposition to confiscate all landed properties belonging to Buddhist temples throughout China."[110] Zhenhua testified that by the time he set out from his home in Henan in 1945 in search of spiritual instruction in the south, "Buddhism in Henan had been crushed by the 'Christian General' Feng Yuxiang, and ... ninety percent of the province's pristine, solemn places of truth had already become vacant and dilapidated temples. ... The better temples were changed into schools and army camps, their scriptures and images vandalized with impunity and the temple lands divided and taken."[111] Such appropriations and property damages increased notably after 1937, when the war of resistance against the Japanese began. In fact, sangha leaders found it increasingly difficult to cultivate effective friends in high places. Guomindang officials were far more concerned with achieving critical military and political goals than with not offending Buddhists.

Moreover, an increasing number of government officials were either influenced by anti-superstition campaigns and antagonistic toward all religious faiths or were Christian converts with strong anti-Buddhist prejudices. According to Kenneth Scott Latourette, vigorous Christian missionary efforts in the early Republican years had established a growing community of about 3.5 million church members by 1927—three times the number in 1900.[112] Although this still represented an extremely small percentage of the total population of China, Christians were often educated people who held important positions of leadership in education, commerce, and government. Sun Yat-sen was a professing Christian who had once been banished from his home village as a youth for breaking a finger off an image of a deity associated with Chinese popular religion. Chiang Kai-shek was baptized a Christian in Shanghai in 1930, after his marriage to a Chinese convert, Soong Meiling (b. 1897), a member of a prominent Chinese family.[113]

Buddhist leaders were accustomed to encountering Christians in large coastal cities with sizable foreign communities, such as Shanghai, and even in small, isolated mission stations in the interior. They were aware of "the Mountain of the Logos Spirit" (Dao Feng Shan), the special mission station devoted to Christian-Buddhist encounter that Karl Reichelt founded at Shatin, near Hong Kong, in 1927.[114] Yet they were not accustomed to confronting unsympathetic Christians holding important positions in public institutions and government offices. Most leaders of the sangha began to realize that both secular humanism and Christianity would present Buddhism with ever more serious challenges in the years ahead.

A VOICE OF REFORM

It was in the context of these many efforts to reinvigorate the Buddhist community and to defend the Dharma in an era of social change and civil strife that Taixu, a young Buddhist monk from Zhejiang, rose to prominence as a religious reformer. Sometimes expansively referred to as "the Saint Paul of Chinese Buddhism"[115] and "the Buddhist Pope of China,"[116] he was a person of considerable energy, intelligence, and charisma. Taixu believed that, given a constantly changing world, Chinese Buddhism must change, too; were it to cling rigidly to a form shaped by past realities and experiences, he observed, it would wither and vanish. For Chinese Buddhism to achieve its historic mission, its monastic and lay communities needed to reorganize and reorient themselves for the radical demands of the bodhisattva path in the modern world. As an ethical pietist, Taixu called for an engagement with, rather than a withdrawal from, the issues of the socio-political world. Emphasizing the moral demands of bodhisattvahood, he called for compassionate social service both as a necessary result of and as a means to an experience of complete enlightenment.

It may be argued that Taixu manifested what has been termed a "utopian propensity."[117] That is, he hoped through his teachings to encourage within the Buddhist community a new measure of religious imagination, to provoke an exploration of things that had never been but that could be. Indeed, he was often so intently focused on shaping Buddhism's future that he appeared to be insensitive to and dismissive of its present and its past. Like all utopian thinkers, Taixu repudiated much of his tradition's contemporary expression in his desire to outline a more ideal, perfect future way. He was confident that his modernist Buddhist perspectives were in harmony with processes of religious evolution that would ultimately lead all sentient beings to Buddhism and beyond, and that would one day make of this very world a pure land.

Despite the many disciples who followed and revered him, the reformer's views were not widely accepted within the sangha. Taixu had many ardent detractors. According to Weihuan, most established masters would not let their students go to Taixu's Wuchang Buddhist Institute for fear that they would become "new monks" and return to "revolutionize their old life."[118] It has been said that "utopians are almost always tragic or tragicomic figures who die unfulfilled."[119] This was indeed Taixu's ultimate fate. He died thinking that he had been a failure. What he tried to accomplish, how he hoped to defend and advance the Dharma, where he thought the future was leading, and why he thought himself a failure are the subjects of the chapters that follow.

CHAPTER 2

THE SOUND OF THE TIDE FOR A NEW CHINA

To understand the mental universe of many religious leaders, it is important to know something about the fabric of their lives. In such cases, interpretation requires a sense not only of the person's historical context but of how he or she experienced and engaged it. Thus biographical accounts and autobiographical reflections are crucial to appreciating the diverse forms of piety represented by spiritual guides such as Augustine (396–430), Nichiren (1222–1282), Moses Mendelssohn (1729–1786), Mohandas Gandhi (1869–1948), Dietrich Bonhoeffer (1906–1945), and the Ayatollah Ruhollah Khomeini (1902–1989). The modern Buddhist reformer Taixu was also such a figure.

The Chinese monk lived and taught in a time of revolution and renaissance, a complex and turbulent period of change for China and the entire world. During Taixu's lifetime, the Chinese people experienced the end of dynastic rule and the beginning of a republican experiment. They entertained grand dreams for the country's future and suffered the grim nightmares of social, political, and economic upheaval. They engaged in bitter civil strife and were enveloped in a devastating global war. Taixu sought to serve as a transformative agent within that context. He heard "the sound of the sea tide" (i.e., the Buddha's voice) calling for a new Buddhism for a new China. He firmly believed that the propagation of that modern form of Buddhism held the keys not only to the salvation of his country but to the emergence of a just and peaceful global civilization. Accordingly, he commended to the Mahāyāna community an ethical form of piety that centered bodhisattva practice not on exercises of religious philosophy, sitting meditation, or ritual observance but on expressions of enlightened social responsibility within the world. Highlighting the reformer's religio-historical context, Frank Millican once commented:

> To understand Taixu we need to see him as a lad among a group of droning priests at Tiantong Monastery, situated in the seclusion of the beautiful hills of Zhejiang, near Ningbo city. Here he lived under the shadow of the images of Buddha and the many Buddhist worthies and learned to chant his prayers, make his prostrations, and share in the daily routine of a typical monastery. There must have been in his veins some blood different from that of his fellow priests, or, to speak in the language of the school of thought in which he was trained, the person of a previous existence whose "karma" was reborn in him must have lived a life which merited much, that he alone of hundreds should have risen above the humdrum existence of his fellow priests and have emerged as interpreter of Buddhism to this age.[1]

There were, of course, many other influential and competent voices within the Chinese sangha interpreting the Dharma in relation to the challenges of the modern world. Yet because of the force of Taixu's charismatic personality, the breadth of his academic interests, the timeliness of his ecumenical concerns, and the scope of his vision for a reenergized and missionary form of Buddhism, he left a lasting impression on many both within and outside of his own religious community. Just as the firebrands of the late Qing and early Republican years called for a thoroughgoing political revolution and the creation of a "new people" *(xin min),* so in a parallel manner did Taixu call for a "Buddhist revolution" *(fojiao geming)* and the creation of "new monks" *(xin seng).* To achieve this end, he proposed a reorganization of the sangha through broad structural, educational, and economic reforms, called for closer ties between the monastic and lay communities, and proposed new measures of cooperation in global mission. Sometimes his ideas were rejected; sometimes what was rejected was Taixu the man. His critics perceived not only errors in judgment but personality flaws; his disciples rarely acknowledged either.

Taixu's story, therefore, consists of both ideas and events, concepts and confrontations, opinions and opponents. Despite the fact that Taixu was never recognized as a brilliantly original Mahāyāna theoretician, the contours of his map of the bodhisattva path in and through the modern world continue to inform the practice of many Buddhists in East Asia and around the world. Taixu is remembered most for his unique embodiment of one compelling perspective on what it might mean to be a Chinese patriot, a Buddhist devotee, and a global citizen.

SPIRITUAL FORMATION AND EARLY EDUCATION

Taixu (original school name: Lu Peilin) was born in the village of Chang'an in the Haining county of northern Zhejiang province on January 8, 1890, in the fifteenth year of the Qing emperor Guangxu's reign. His father was a bricklayer who died when his son was only a year old. Two years later, when his mother remarried into the Li family, he became the responsibility of his maternal grandmother. A devout woman who was well versed in poetry and literature, she cared for the young boy and introduced him to Buddhism through frequent visits to nearby temples. Although Taixu suffered from remittent fevers and was frequently ill, his maternal uncle, a local schoolteacher, made certain that he received a sound primary education in the Chinese classics.

When Taixu was eight, his grandmother began to take him on pilgrimages to some of the more famous Buddhist centers in the sacred mountains of east-central China. He was fascinated with the rituals performed by the monks of Anhui's Jiuhua Shan and the large and impressive Jin Shan monastery near Zhenjiang in Jiangsu prov-

VENERABLE MASTER TAIXU

Source: Yinshun Cultural and Educational Foundation (Yinshun wenjiao jijin hui), Xinzhu County, Taiwan.

ince. Eventually he also accompanied his grandmother to the famous Buddhist center on Putuo Shan on the coast of Zhejiang, as well as to the Yuwang (Asoka) and Tiantong monasteries near Ningbo. These religious pilgrimages were formative journeys during which Taixu began to develop an interest not only in Buddhism but in the ideals and daily rhythms of the monastic life.

In 1901, Taixu accepted a business apprenticeship in Chang'an, but this was soon interrupted by the unexpected death of his mother and further health problems of his own. Although in time he returned to his duties as a shop clerk, recurring illnesses presented considerable difficulties for both his professional responsibilities and personal study. According to Yinshun, in 1903, for the very first time, Taixu "began to long for the carefree life of the Buddha's way."[2]

Just a year later, in the spring of 1904, as the impoverished Qing government was authorizing the confiscation of monastic property to support new educational ventures, Taixu was actively contemplating joining the sangha. At the age of fourteen, influenced by his grandmother's piety, grieved by the death of his parents, and anxious about his physical health and stamina, he decided to renounce lay life. His original plan was to travel by river boat to Putuo Shan via Shanghai. However, when he realized that he had mistakenly boarded a boat heading to Suzhou, he got off at Pingwang and walked to the nearby Xiao Jiuhua si, which he and his grandmother had visited briefly when on a pilgrimage to temples near the city of Zhenjiang, at the intersection of the Grand Canal and Yangzi River.[3]

Judging his karma to be in harmony with his ultimate aim, Taixu presented himself to Master Shida, the prior of the monastery *(jian yuan)*, and explained his intent. The prior received him, but because the Xiao Jiuhua si was a public monastery *(shifang conglin)* that was not permitted to tonsure and train novices, he soon arranged to conduct the young man's tonsure ceremony at a small hereditary temple in Suzhou. There Shida gave him the Dharma name Weixin (Mind Only). Remembering the occasion at a later date, Taixu confessed, "I renounced the lay life, longing for the supernatural powers of the immortals *(xian)* and Buddhas *(fo)*." In fact, he noted, "still not distinguishing between the immortals and the Buddhas, but thinking of attaining their supernatural powers, I entered the sangha."[4]

Several months later, Shida escorted the novice to meet the Buddhist Master Zhuangnian, who was the head monk of the Yuhuang temple near Ningbo. It was Master Zhuangnian who gave the young monk the style or courtesy name Taixu (Supreme Emptiness) to forever remind him that he "existed in the midst of supreme emptiness."[5] The elderly master also provided the herbal medicines that finally helped cure the novice of his persistent fevers. In the late fall of 1904, Zhuangnian accompanied Taixu to the Tiantong si at Ningbo, where he officially took the Buddhist precepts and was ordained under the revered old Chinese master and poet Jichan, also widely known as Eight Fingers (Bazhi Toutuo).[6]

In light of Taixu's intellectual promise, Eight Fingers soon recommended that he begin studies with the respected Buddhist master Qichang, abbot of Ningbo's nearby Yongfeng si. Master Qichang undertook to instruct Taixu in meditational disciplines using the *hua tou* ("critical phrase") method of Chan, posing enigmatic questions for contemplation.[7] He also guided the young monk's introduction to Buddhist history and literature. In his studies of famous Buddhist texts such as the *Zhiyue lu* (Record of Pointing at the Moon) and *Gaoseng zhuan* (Record of the Lives of Eminent Monks), Taixu proved himself an earnest and able pupil.

In his early studies of the Chinese Tripiṭaka, Taixu was especially attracted to the *Lengyan jing* (Śūraṅgama Sūtra) and *Fahua jing* (Lotus Sūtra), the study of which helped him recognize the fundamental differences between Buddhist and Daoist teachings. It was during this initial period of Buddhist training that Taixu first met Yuanying (1878–1953), a disciple of Eight Fingers who came to visit Master Qichang in the summer of 1906.[8] Twelve years Taixu's senior, Yuanying would become an important leader within the sangha and serve as the first president of the Chinese Buddhist Association of 1929. Acknowledging their common interests, Taixu and Yuanying established a friendship and pledged to work with each other for a revitalized religious tradition in China. Because of differences of opinion and personal style, it would turn out to be a difficult relationship to maintain. Many years later, in fact, Taixu wrote in his autobiography, "Although afterwards he and I were constantly engaged in conflict, when I think back on those days of scriptural studies, . . . I shall always remember his friendship."[9]

Taixu benefited not only from Qichang's instruction but also from private interviews with Eight Fingers at the Tiantong si nearby, as well as from opportunities to meet other respected Chinese Buddhist masters who visited the Ningbo area monasteries, including the Venerable Daojie (1866–1932), another of Eight Fingers' disciples.[10] Yet in the fall of 1907, inspired by lectures on the scriptures given by Daojie and strongly encouraged by Yuanying, the young monk bid farewell to Qichang and departed for Cixi to pursue more advanced studies at the Xifang si, which maintained one of the larger Buddhist libraries in Jiangsu. It was there, while concentrating on the Prajñāpāramitā (Perfection of Wisdom) literature, that Taixu had a powerful religious experience that was to prove a milestone in his spiritual progress. For Taixu, this represented the arising of the thought of enlightenment *(bodhicitta)* and was the real beginning of his bodhisattva career. He testified that it enabled him to slough off the "pollution of the world" and gave him "new life."[11] He later recalled, "After some time, knowledge of the Buddha came to me like a pearl, lost and found again, and as with a mirror, I was enabled to see clearly through the changes of this life and the world."[12]

In the spring of 1908, when Taixu was eighteen years old, the reformist monk Huashan came to the Xifang si, where Taixu was staying. According to Yinshun, Huashan was actually "the first person to start modernizing the sangha."[13] Impressed with Taixu, Huashan told him about those working for revolutionary political and social changes within China, asserting that the monastic order itself must modernize and promote educational reform. Initially, Taixu was uncertain about Huashan's ideas; indeed, the two monks argued for more than ten days about what such modernization efforts would require. Challenging Taixu to broaden his reading, Huashan gave him a wide variety of provocative books with which he was unfamiliar, including

Kang Youwei's utopian classic *Datong shu* (The Book of the Great Community), Liang Qichao's *Xinmin shuo* (On New People), Zhang Taiyan's (1868–1936) *Gao fozi shu* (Letter to Followers of the Buddha) and *Gao baiyi shu* (Letter to Lay Buddhists), Yan Fu's *Tianyan lun* (On Evolution), and Tan Sitong's *Renxue* (An Exposition on Benevolence).

Deeply influenced by these writings, Taixu soon aligned himself with Huashan's modernist stance. Committed to both political reform for the nation and religious reform for the Buddhist community, he formalized a special alliance of friendship with Huashan and began to consider how in practical terms a "new Buddhism" could be created in China to parallel the creation of a new nation. Writes Yinshun, "Because of Taixu's great resolve to save the world through Buddhism, he moved forward from that point and could never again restrain himself. Turning from the kind of religious path that seeks to transcend the human realm in order to enter the Absolute, rather he chose to distance himself from the Absolute in order to confront the world of humankind."[14] The vow to pursue this kind of path to transform the world, Taixu stated, was a direct result of his close relationship with Huashan.[15]

Soon thereafter, at the Xiao Jiuhua si near Pingwang, Taixu met Qiyun, the revolutionary monk from Hunan. Qiyun was a former student of Eight Fingers who, during studies in Japan, had become an early member of the Tongmeng hui (Chinese United League) founded by Sun Yat-sen in 1905. An iconoclastic spirit, Qiyun was associated with Xu Xilin (1873–1907), Qiu Jin (1879?–1907), and other revolutionaries intent on the overthrow of the Qing government.[16] Yinshun notes that, according to the demands of each particular situation, Qiyun wore either western clothes with leather shoes or Buddhist monastic garb. When Taixu first encountered him, he was wearing the monastic robes that permitted him to hide from government officials in the monastery. It was through Qiyun's influence that Taixu was first encouraged to read political materials such as Sun Yat-sen and Zhang Taiyan's *Minbao* (People's Journal), Liang Qichao's *Xinmin congbao* (New People's Review), and Zou Rong's (1885–1905)

Geming jun (Revolutionary Army). Influenced deeply by Sun's three principles of the people *(sanmin zhuyi)*, he became filled with optimism about revolutionary proposals for broad Chinese political and social reforms. Comments Yinshun, "This was the beginning of Taixu's associations with political partisans *(dangren)*."[17]

In the fall of 1908, Taixu went to Ningbo to work with Eight Fingers. The elderly master was serving as director of the Ningbo Sangha Educational Association (Ningbo seng jiaoyu hui), which he had founded earlier that year. When Taixu learned that Qiyun had been arrested on suspicion of involvement in subversive activities, he immediately sought Eight Fingers' help in pleading for Qiyun's release. After the monk was freed from prison, Taixu, Yuanying, and Qiyun assisted Eight Fingers with the promotion of his newly established educational association. The association in Ningbo was only one of a number of ideas for expanding monastic education that had been developed since the Qing government had suspended the imperial examination system in September 1905. That governmental decision had resulted in renewed efforts to confiscate Buddhist property by many local officials throughout China, because each locality faced the daunting expense of creating new educational institutions at which students could become qualified for official service. Buddhist leaders intended to counter such confiscations of property in part by highlighting their own attempts to improve education within the sangha.

Taixu's introduction to such efforts through the Ningbo Sangha Educational Association gave him a glimpse of the promise of educational reforms not only for enhancing the public image of the sangha but for advancing broad reforms of Buddhist thought and practice. Moreover, the organization gave Taixu some of his first opportunities to lecture on contemporary trends within Chinese society and religion, as well as to test the support for his views among the established leaders of the sangha. Thus, observed one commentator, by design and good fortune, Taixu had by his eighteenth birthday already made the acquaintance of "the most celebrated Buddhists in China and obtained a profound view of Buddhism."[18]

In the spring of 1909, Yuanying and Zhuangnian recommended that Taixu go to Jin Shan to practice meditation. Nevertheless, Taixu later confessed, "By that time my thoughts were already directed toward modern studies."[19] Thus he traveled instead to Nanjing, with the encouragement of Huashan and Qiyun, to begin studies at the Jetavana Hermitage (Zhihuan jingshe) operated by Yang Wenhui, later often called "the father of the Buddhist revival."[20] As noted in Chapter 1, Yang was a well-educated Buddhist layman who had devoted himself to publishing and distributing Buddhist literature through his Jinling Scriptural Press. In addition, as an aspect of his special alliance with the Ceylonese lay devotee Anagarika Dharmapala, he had founded a new kind of school on his estate for all those interested in Buddhism's global mission. Yang himself lectured on the Buddhist scriptures, especially on the Śūraṅgama Sūtra, which he judged to be especially compatible with modern science.

Otto Franke reported that the bylaws for the school were carefully articulated in thirty-five articles.[21] The school was designed to have three levels of education, with a total curriculum of eight years of academic work. At each level, there were requirements in Buddhist textual studies, modern Chinese literature, and English language and literature, with a minimum of forty-two hours of class time each week. The bylaws called for a limitation of enrollment to twenty-four students, monks, and laymen. All those selected for admission were to have as their ultimate goal the propagation of Buddhism throughout the world. Although Yang's innovative school was forced to close for financial reasons at the end of the academic year, Taixu's brief experience at the Jetavana Hermitage further fueled his optimism about possibilities for real social, political, and religious reformation in China.

By this time, Yuanying had become head monk of the Jiedai si at Ningbo, while Daojie had assumed similar responsibilities at the Fayuan si in Beijing. On Huashan's recommendation, Taixu served for a semester on the faculty of the Huayu Primary School at Putuo Shan. Staying at the famous monastery gave him an opportunity to meet many leaders within the sangha whom he did not know, including the Pure Land master Yinguang, whose conservatism would always set the two at odds.²² Although Taixu returned to the Xifang si in Cixi to continue his studies of the Tripiṭaka, only a month later, early in 1910, he accepted Qiyun's invitation to help him organize in Guangzhou an Association for the Education of Monks (Seng jiaoyu hui), as encouraged by his friend Yuebin, the head monk of the Shuangxi si, which was located on White Cloud Mountain (Baiyun Shan) outside the city. At the time, Guangzhou was a major center for anti-Qing revolutionary activity. In fact, during the period when Taixu was in Guangzhou, radicals staged an unsuccessful uprising in the city, while in Beijing others plotted the assassination of the prince regent.

In the summer of 1910, Taixu, Qiyun, and Yuebin were all invited to lecture at the Hualin si in Guangzhou. While there, Taixu visited the Shizi lin (Lion's Grove), where he helped organize a new center for Buddhist studies *(fojiao jingshe)*. Because several of his lectures at the Shizi lin were eventually edited and published, Yinshun claims that "this was the beginning of Taixu's scholarly writing."²³ Indeed, it was Taixu's first opportunity to publish some of his ideas about the path of a modern-day bodhisattva and the necessity for a comprehensive reformation within the sangha. For example, stressing the need for developing an attitude that is open to religious change, he wrote in "Jiao guan zhuyao" (An Introduction to Buddhist Teaching and Meditation), "The good student of Buddhism relies on his heart and mind, not on ancient tradition, relies on the essential meaning of words, not on the words themselves. The good student is constantly adapting to circumstances and cleverly provoking people to think."²⁴ And in "Fojiao shi lue" (An Outline of Buddhist History), Taixu asserted that Buddhism's failure to remain a vital force in modern China was due to the otherworldliness of the sangha and the tendency of Buddhists to hold onto the externals of their religion without understanding its essence. Claimed Taixu, "China has entered the era of a world community. Government, religion, and science have all changed. Therefore Buddhism must change or it will definitely not survive!"²⁵

CONFLICTS AND COMMITMENTS

Although Taixu was only in his early twenties, he was already beginning to be recognized within the Chinese Buddhist community for his personal charisma and modernist positions. Indeed, because he was respected by many prominent government officials and gentry in Guangdong and Jiangxi provinces, Taixu was selected in the fall of 1910 to undertake for the first time in his career the heavy responsibilities of a head monk *(zhuchi)*. When his colleague Yuebin resigned as head monk of the Shuangxi si near Guangzhou, Taixu was called to the position. Within a year, in which he was constantly lecturing both in the monastery and in the city of Guangzhou, Taixu prompted the transformation of the monastery into a "Great Lecture Center" (Mohe jiangyuan). His educational goal was to emphasize the equality of all Buddhist schools and yet the special characteristics of each.[26]

In the months preceding the successful revolt at Wuchang in October 1911, which led to the downfall of the Qing dynasty, Taixu cultivated his many close relationships with known socialists and revolutionaries in Guangdong. Among his friends were political radicals such as Pan Dawei, Liang Shangtong, and Mo Jipeng, the latter "a well known anarchist of this period who was associated with the 'assassination teams' that specialized in killing government officials in South China."[27] Together they read the controversial works of Peter Kropotkin (1842–1921), Mikhail Bakunin (1814–1876), Pierre-Joseph Proudhon (1809–1865), and Karl Marx (1818–1883). In discussing China's political future, they debated a broad spectrum of views proposed by advocates of anarchism, socialism, democracy, and constitutional monarchy. Although there is no evidence of Taixu's participation in any overtly subversive activity, it was said that he met almost daily in secret with radicals plotting revolution. Their common anxiety about being discovered was justified when Qiyun was arrested again in April 1911. Soldiers were soon dispatched to the Shuangxi si to arrest Taixu as well. According to Yinshun, when Qiyun was taken into custody, a eulogy that Taixu had written in memory of the revolutionary martyrs who had died in the unsuccessful 1910 Guangzhou uprising was discovered among Qiyun's papers. Taixu was able to escape by hiding at the newspaper offices of his associate Pan Dawei. Because of these difficult circumstances, he decided to return to Zhejiang as soon as possible.

Accordingly, Taixu resigned as head monk of Shuangxi si that summer, then traveled to Ningbo to consult with Zhuangnian and Eight Fingers before going on to Putuo Shan for the remainder of the season. In the early autumn, he responded to Eight Fingers' urgent request to return to the Tiantong si at Ningbo. At the time, new attempts to confiscate Buddhist property by force had led Buddhist leaders in Shanghai to ask the elderly master to carry a petition to Beijing in protest. Taixu helped write the petition beseeching the Qing government to help protect Buddhist institutions. He even planned to accompany Eight Fingers to the capital to present the plan, hoping to have an opportunity to explain his own ideas about the revitalization and reform of Buddhism, but revolutionary activities along the rail line made the long trip to the capital too dangerous.

Taixu soon decided, however, to travel up the coast as far as Shanghai to meet with the gifted revolutionary monk Zongyang (1861–1930?), who was then at work on a major publication project designed to contribute to the education of the sangha: a newly edited edition of the entire Chinese Tripiṭaka.[28] Zongyang was a close associate and supporter of Sun Yat-sen, with whom he had become friends during an earlier period of residence in Japan. At this time he was living as a layman and using his lay name, Huang Zongyang.[29] He was settled at Hardoon Gardens (Ai li yuan), the large estate in the French Concession of Shanghai owned by his devoted and wealthy follower, Mrs. Silas Hardoon (Luo Jialing). It was there that Taixu heard the exciting news of the Wuchang revolt that precipitated the fall of the Qing dynasty. Jubilant at the reports, he considered with colleagues the future of the country and the precarious situation of Buddhism.

At the time of the 1911 revolution, Taixu noted that some monks actually organized monastic troops *(seng jun)* to support and participate in the military struggle against the Manchus.[30] According to Yinshun, in addition to the monk Quefei, who organized monastic troops at the Yufo si in Shanghai, "Tieyan of the Kaiyuan si in Shaoxing [in Zhejiang province] used monastic assets for troop provisions, organized monastic forces, and appointed Dixian, the head monk of the Jiezhu si in Shaoxing, as commander."[31] In Wuhan, Welch reports, sangha troops were actually formed by order of revolutionary military commanders, although such quasi-military activities by Buddhist monks were, without exception, short-lived and insignificant.[32]

The Republic of China was officially founded in January 1912, when Sun Yat-sen accepted the provisional presidency in Nanjing. Taixu, who had spent the previous few months visiting monasteries in Zhejiang, also traveled to Nanjing to organize an Association for the Advancement of Buddhism (Fojiao xiejin hui). With help from associates in the Socialist Party, he obtained permission from the office of the president to initiate operations from the Pilu si. As Taixu was just beginning his organizational efforts, the radical monk Renshan (1887–1951), whom Taixu had known as a fellow student at Yang Wenhui's Jetavana Hermitage, came to Nanjing and met with him.[33] The discussions between the two monks bent on reform were significant because the immediate result would soon become widely known as "the invasion of Jin Shan" *(danao Jin Shan)*. Indeed, the dramatic events that subsequently unfolded at the famous Jin Shan monastery marked a most important chapter in Taixu's career. As he later declared, "From this incident, the reputation of my Buddhist reformation spread, and since then it has been either respected, feared, despised, or admired by the people."[34]

Renshan had come to Nanjing with the intention of petitioning the Ministry of Education to change the well-endowed Jin Shan monastery—a large and traditionally conservative monastic institution—into a modern school for monks. When he heard about Taixu's plans for an Association for the Advancement of Buddhism, Renshan told him that there were many monks and lay devotees who resided in nearby Zhenjiang, just down the Yangzi River from Nanjing, who would be interested in a modern program of Buddhist education. Thus he encouraged Taixu to travel with him to Jin Shan to open and establish such an association there. When they reached the monastery, they stayed at the Guanyin ge, a hereditary temple in the large Jin

Shan complex where Renshan had first entered the sangha. With the knowledge of Abbot Qingquan, Prior Yinping, and Guest Prefect Shuangting, Renshan and Taixu prepared to hold the opening conference of the new association in the meeting hall. They printed and sent out invitations to the monks in Zhenjiang, Yangzhou, Nanjing, and as far away as Shanghai. Invitations were also sent to potential lay supporters, who were members of the army, government officials, merchants, or scholars in the Zhenjiang area.

When the conference opened, Taixu estimated that there were two to three hundred monks in attendance plus three to four hundred lay guests. Many of the latter were reportedly members of the Socialist Party in Zhenjiang. Taixu was chosen to serve as chairman, and he set forth briefly his basic principles of religious reform. As Howard Boorman summarizes,

> He [Taixu] believed that Buddhist land holdings were the common property of all followers of the religion and should be dedicated to the promotion of social welfare, particularly education. In a statement that aroused strong controversy, he advocated the adoption in religious communities of the principle that each person should be judged by his abilities and rewarded according to his work. Moreover, he argued for the redefinition of Buddhist doctrine because he believed Buddhism to be a religion for this world.[35]

Taixu also discussed the aims and purposes of the new association at Jin Shan and read its proposed bylaws. After Renshan made a supporting speech, a monk from Yangzhou named Jishan offered a sharply critical response. Angered, Renshan replied by recounting in detail the autocratic ways of Qingquan, Jishan, and other monks. Furthermore, he proposed that the entire Jin Shan monastery be turned into a modern school by using its considerable resources to cover the school's operating expenses. At this, according to Taixu, most of the guests clapped enthusiastically. However, shouting between opposing forces ensued, and the whole crowd became agitated. Renshan's proposal was ultimately accepted, and he and Taixu were elected to transform the Jin Shan monastery into the headquarters of the Association for the Advancement of Buddhism with a modern monastic school. Taixu later acknowledged that the struggle certainly did not end there:

> That evening Renshan led more than twenty fellow students into the monastery to designate rooms for the association's offices. The next morning, when the association began to function, they went into the monastery's business office to examine its financial ledgers, and then into the meditation hall to announce the opening of the school. However, Qingquan, Yinping, Shuangting, Jishan and others had already left the monastery and were posting notices and even making appeals to government offices in order to oppose and stop the association. . . .
>
> Entrusting affairs in Zhenjiang to the care of Renshan, I went to Nanjing. . . . One night thereafter, Shuangting and others led more than ten workmen in fighting their way into the association's offices. Renshan and a number of others were wounded with knives and clubs. Afterwards, they initiated legal action, and in several months it was decided that Qingquan, Shuangting, plus five or six others be imprisoned for terms ranging from several months to several years. Because of this whole incident, the association's activities as well as the operation of the Jin Shan monastery were equally disrupted and the result was a confused situation that could not be straightened out.[36]

As Yinshun points out, Taixu maintained throughout his life that his intent at Jin Shan was only the very worthy one of providing modern educational opportunities for the monks of the Zhenjiang area. Taixu later wrote, "The association's bylaws did contain the revolutionary socialist idea of utilizing Buddhist property to operate a public Buddhist enterprise, but [what was] intended were peaceful, progressive steps."[37] He also stated, "It was with a peaceful attitude that I announced the preparation for these events."[38] Naturally, however, staunchly conservative opponents to modernization efforts within the sangha, as well as many moderates, fully sympathized with the monks of Jin Shan. While eschewing the violence, many Buddhists thought that the convicted monks had acted only to defend their monastery from an illegal takeover attempt that was substantially no different than those encouraged by hostile military and government officials.

Among traditionalists, therefore, Taixu soon came to represent the radical modernism and aggressive tactics that they feared and resisted. At the same time, he was embraced by the more progressive spirits within the Buddhist community as a promising young leader for reform.[39] Comments Welch, "Whatever the motives of its perpetrators, the 'invasion of Jin Shan' epitomizes the shock with which the Republican era burst upon the Buddhist establishment. It drastically foreshadowed the long conflict ahead between conservatives and radicals in the sangha."[40]

On April 1, 1912, less than two months after the abdication of the child Xuantong emperor later known as Puyi, Taixu responded to a call from Eight Fingers and traveled to Shanghai to participate in the establishment of the Chinese General Buddhist Association (Zhonghua fojiao zonghui). The old master had been very upset by the intemperate actions of the progressive young Buddhist leaders that had led to the serious events at Jin Shan. He was also concerned about the threateningly far-reaching charter of the Chinese Buddhist Association (Zhongguo fojiao hui), founded in Nanjing some weeks earlier by several radical Buddhist laymen who had little respect for the monastic order. The most prominent among these lay leaders was the scholar Ouyang Jingwu, who had been Taixu's fellow student at Yang Wenhui's Jetavana Hermitage.[41] The charter of the Chinese Buddhist Association claimed for itself extensive and unprecedented religious authority: the right to superintend all Buddhist properties, to reorganize and promote all Buddhist financial affairs, and to arbitrate all disputes within the Buddhist community. According to the monk Weihuan, the association's charter promised the government, in return for such broad powers and organizational independence, that the association would not sanction activities beyond the religious sphere proper to Buddhism. The charter was actually submitted to and approved by Sun Yat-sen, the provisional president of the Republic, in the early months of 1912.[42]

Welch asserts that Ouyang's organization never actually represented more than the audacious plans of a small group of his close friends and colleagues.[43] Nevertheless, it did challenge Eight Fingers to seek the help of Yuanying, Dixian, Xuyun (1840–1959), Taixu, and other monastic leaders to organize a more representative and responsible Buddhist association that was supportive of the sangha.[44] Hoping to promote reconciliation and harmonious order, Eight Fingers persuaded Taixu to cease any further promotion of his own Association for the Advancement of Buddhism in order to merge it with a new organization, the Chinese General Buddhist Association.[45] He invited monks from seventeen provinces to convene at Shanghai's Liuyun si for the inaugural meeting of a new association. The result was the first truly broad-based national Buddhist organization established in China.

The Chinese General Buddhist Association proposed to improve the quality of the sangha through the close supervision of ordination, educational standards, leadership selection, and social work activities. Some monks wanted the new association to pursue special agreements with the military to guarantee protection for Buddhist property in exchange for direct financial contributions. Taixu persuasively opposed the plan, however, arguing that "it is the government's natural responsibility to protect the sangha's property. With regard to the sangha contributing directly to the military, that is rather an obligation of all the citizenry. The sangha ought not use its contributions to obtain the government's protection, and the government should not use protection of property as a way to elicit direct financial support from the sangha."[46]

Such a potentially powerful national Buddhist organization had never existed before, requiring all Chinese monks and nuns to join and to abide by its regulations. Yet the leaders of the sangha believed that the times called for new measures. Because the proposed organization was basically the product of moderate voices within the sangha, it received wide support. Xuyun states that he accompanied Eight Fingers to Beijing to present the charter of the Chinese General Buddhist Association to representatives of Yuan Shikai's newly established government.[47] According to Yu-yue Tsu, the charter's basic provisions included the following:

1. This society is formed by the union of all Buddhist monks.
2. With branches all over the country, it exercises supervision over all the monasteries and monks.

3. All monks, formally admitted into the Order, are given certificates attesting to their membership in the society.

4. No monk is permitted to receive any pupil [candidate for the Order] unless the candidate is a bona fide applicant and of good family.

5. No monastery is permitted to alienate any of its property without authorization from the society.

6. Observance of monastic rules should be strictly enforced; for violation of the same rules, monks are to be punished.

7. Seminaries for the training of candidates for the Order are to be established, and in them Buddhist scriptures and Chinese classics are to be taught.

8. Persons under twenty years of age are not to be admitted into the Order; also those who have not had three years' theological training.

9. For monks to hire themselves out for the performance of funeral services, especially appearing in funeral processions, is considered derogatory to the dignity of the monastic order, and so the practice is to be strictly prohibited.[48]

Although Eight Fingers was rudely rebuffed by officials of the Ministry of the Interior, the charter was eventually ratified, even as Ouyang Jingwu's rival association ceased to exist. Before the charter's ratification, however, the elderly master became ill and died in Beijing's Fayuan si, on November 10, 1912, believing that he had failed in his mission.[49] Taixu was deeply grieved by the death of the teacher whom he respected so much. Moreover, without Eight Fingers' strong leadership within the sangha, the new association for which the master worked so hard during the last year of his life functioned for only two short years. Yet the continuing need to defend Buddhist property and to address the infighting between the more conservative and radical factions within the Buddhist community contributed to the creation of more than a dozen other Buddhist organizations through the 1920s. Taixu himself was soon promoting the Buddhist Society of the Great Vow (Fojiao hongshi hui) from Ningbo's Yanqing si. To facilitate reform, he also considered trying to organize a specifically Buddhist "Tongmeng hui" (Buddhist Chinese United League), which he named the League for the Support of Buddhism (Weichi fojiao tongmeng hui).[50]

Speaking at Eight Fingers' memorial service at Shanghai's Jing'an si in February 1913, Taixu spoke of the urgent need for three revolutions: an organizational revolution *(zuzhi geming)*, an economic revolution *(caichan geming)*, and an intellectual revolution *(xueli geming)*. In consonance with these three revolutions, Taixu argued, in the founding policy statement of the League for the Support of Buddhism, for five essential elements that he judged would be absolutely necessary for the revivification and preservation of the Buddhist faith in China: first, a religious community freely organized; second, a spirit as fearless as that of sacrificial animals; third, a desire to learn and to seek education; fourth, a plan for putting into actual practice compassionate action toward all; and fifth, a dedication marked by peace of mind and a sense of vocation.[51]

When the first national assembly of the Republic began meeting in Beijing that year, Taixu was arguing publicly that religious practice founded on such elements deserved freedom of expression. In a petition to members of the assembly, he declared boldy that, "based on the principle of religious freedom, we should recognize in practice the separate jurisdictions of government and religion."[52] At the same time, he emphasized to members of the Buddhist community that the struggle for religious freedom from government intervention was something about which they could never become complacent. Indeed, that struggle would be joined again soon because of the expansive new regulations of the Buddhist establishment approved by Yuan Shikai's government in 1915.

In early 1913, Taixu took up residence at the Qingliang si in Shanghai, where the editorial offices of the Chinese General Buddhist Association were located. There he helped with the editing responsibilities for the association's new journal, *Fojiao yuebao* (Buddhist Monthly). Along with like-minded colleagues at the Qingliang si and Jing'an si, the site in Shanghai of the official headquarters of the association, Taixu considered the possibilities for Buddhist reforms and the divisive political debates within the fledgling Chinese republic. The summer months brought the national turmoil of what became known as "the second revolution," as a number of provinces declared independence from the Republic in the clash between parliament and the provisional president Yuan Shikai. Although the rebellion was quickly crushed by Yuan's army, attempts to check presidential powers continued well into the fall, when Yuan actually dissolved the Guomindang and assumed dictatorial authority.

New intrusions into Buddhist monasteries were reported in relation to the fighting. Taixu and his friends Zongyang, Yuexia (1857–1917), and others considered the dangers of their political radicalism in view of Yuan's reactionary style of leadership.[53] In response to the heated political debates on China's future at the time, Taixu himself asserted, "The political perspectives of anarchism and Buddhism are very close, yet beginning from the stage of democratic socialism we can make gradual progress toward anarchism."[54] In the fall of 1913, the *Fojiao yuebao* ceased publication because of lack of funds. At age twenty-four, Taixu had reached what he later considered to be a pivotal point in his life.

CONTEMPLATION IN SEALED CONFINEMENT

In the summer of 1914, Taixu elected to travel to Putuo Shan near the coast of the East China Sea, where he stayed at the Xilin temple. World War I, with its disillusionment about human capacities for progress and mutuality, had just begun in Europe. In addition, the distrust and enmity aroused by the Jin Shan incident remained acute in certain circles of the sangha. According to the monk Xuming (1919–1966), upon recognizing the failures of his own reformist endeavors within the Chinese Buddhist community and the war-torn state of his country and the world, Taixu actually began to have doubts about Buddhism's ability to be an effective and universal healing force.[55] Unwilling and unable to back away from his long-term aims, Taixu nevertheless considered a period of strategic retreat appropriate. He was later to recall:

> The wish gradually formed within me of applying the law of Buddha for the harmonizing of the philosophies of ancient and modern times and of the east and the west, and of leading the nations of the whole world to follow the teachings of Śākyamuni. Since then, during the past decade, through circumstances favorable and unfavorable, whether traveling abroad or staying at home, whether engaged in mundane affairs or retired in lonely hermitage, this wish has not for one moment been permitted to leave my mind.
>
> Then the European War broke out. Added to the rottenness of the inward life of man, was the brutal struggle of the outward world. I was convinced of the magnitude of the human calamity, which like a wagonload of hay on fire could not be extinguished with a cupful of water.
>
> Since it was ordained that I should wait until the ripe time to carry out my wish, I decided to make use of the waiting to exercise my religion [contemplation], and so I "shut myself" on Putuo Island for three years.[56]

In October, Taixu entered a voluntary three-year period of isolated study and meditation known as "sealed confinement" *(biguan)*. Such self-isolation was a highly respected religious practice of self-discipline for Chinese monks, during which they were released from the usual expectations associated with communal living and permitted to read and meditate on their own. Small cells or huts for monks so dedicated were often erected and provided for as an act of merit-making by lay supporters. The initiation of *biguan* was normally accompanied by elaborate rituals in which the monk's quarters were sealed with bright red banners announcing his inspirational example of commitment to the Dharma.[57] In Taixu's case, it was the Venerable Yinguang who presided over the formal ceremonies that sealed Taixu in his cloister.

The Christian missionary Karl Ludvig Reichelt, who became well acquainted with the monk, describes Taixu's surroundings at Putuo Shan in his book *The Transformed Abbot,* a biography of one of Taixu's disciples who eventually converted to Christianity:

The idea of *biguan* is that a monk may be given opportunity to rehabilitate himself by concentrated meditation and thorough study of the Buddhist scriptures. Long meditations were not according to Taixu's mind but studies were simply life to him and he looked forward to having time for writing too. From the monastic library he had brought Buddhist writings. Paper and Chinese ink he regularly obtained through the little trap-door that opened and shut whenever food was pushed in for him. In the cell were a bed, a bench to sit on, a table with writing instruments and chopsticks, an extra table for books and a small altar in one corner with an image of Buddha. In the yard, just large enough to allow him a little exercise, were a small flower-bed and a few water jars. The water supply came through a long bamboo pipe from the mountain stream beyond. A couple of poles were set up with a string for laundry and in one corner of the yard the necessary "little room" had been erected.[58]

According to Reichelt, the silence and tranquillity of the place were accentuated by the sound of the sea tide as it rushed in and out among the sandbanks of Putuo Island. The profound influence of this setting on the development of Taixu's career, he points out, was reflected in the title of the most significant and long-lasting Buddhist periodical originating in the Republican period, namely, *Haichao yin* (The Sound of the Sea Tide), which Taixu founded in 1920.

During his three years of sealed confinement, Taixu devoted himself to an extensive reading program. In his autobiography, he claims that he kept firmly to a daily schedule that called for meditation and veneration of the buddhas *(li fo)* upon arising; the study of Buddhist literature in the morning; additional reading and writing in the afternoon, with attention not only to the Chinese classics but to modern literature as well; and, each evening, veneration and a final period of meditation before retiring.[59] Within his broad-ranging program of studies, Taixu was especially intrigued by the writings of Zhang Taiyan and the scholar-translator Yan Fu, both of whom maintained an active interest in Buddhism.[60] His reading included works in western history, philosophy, and science, although he spent most of his time studying the sacred scriptures of Buddhism, with special attention given to the *Lengyan jing* (Śūraṅgama Sūtra), *Dasheng qixin lun* (*Mahāyāna-śraddhotpāda Śāstra), and *Cheng weishi lun* (Vidyā-mātra-siddhi Śāstra).

During his period of confinement, Taixu wrote such diverse pieces as "Fofa daolun" (An Introduction to the Buddhist Dharma), "Jiaoyu xinjian" (New Conceptions of Education), "Zhexue zhengguan" (Proper Perspectives on Philosophy), "Lun Xunzi" (On Xunzi), "Lun Zhouyi" (On the *Book of Changes*), and "Lun Hanyu" (On Hanyu). Throughout his various works he called for a globalized form of modern education, individual freedoms in the context of a community committed to the welfare of all, and Buddhist wisdom and compassion as the basis for a new world civilization. According to Yinshun, in many of these works readers could easily see how "Taixu blended socialism *(shehui zhuyi)* with Buddhist teachings."[61]

Although in seclusion for three years, Taixu continued to monitor political developments in China and overseas. In May 1915, Yuan Shikai, hoping that affairs with foreign governments would not interfere with his bid for presidential powers that extended beyond even the extraordinary privileges granted in the revised constitution of May 1914, accepted the infamous Japanese "Twenty-one Demands." As Immanuel C.Y. Hsü notes, these called for "(1) recognition of Japan's position in Shandong; (2) special position for Japan in Manchuria and Inner Mongolia; (3) joint operation of China's iron and steel industries; (4) nonalienation of coastal areas to any third power; and (5) control by Japan of China's several important domestic administrations."[62] Additional agreements were signed with Russia and Great Britain for their special interests in Outer Mongolia and Tibet, respectively. These humiliating actions, along with Yuan's shocking announcement in December 1915 that he would assume the full powers of a monarch, led to a series of revolts throughout the country.

Taixu was also made aware while in seclusion of the adoption by the parliament in October 1915 of the Regulations for the Control of Monasteries and Temples (Guanli simiao tiaoli) promulgated through the parliament with Yuan's full support. The regulations were not only more restrictive than those adopted by the Ministry of the Interior in 1913, but extended supervision well beyond the Qing codes. As Tsu comments, the act was particularly troublesome for Buddhism:

> While these regulations were supposed to apply to Buddhist and Daoist institutions without discrimination, it was clear that owing to the fact that Buddhist institutions far outnumber those of the Daoist faith and that Daoism has no monks anyway, the regulations would fall more heavily upon the Buddhists—in fact, that was the intention of the government. The government justified itself by arguing that temples and monasteries are public institutions and many of them are of historic and artistic importance, and so supervision was necessary to prevent their falling into private hands. The chief features of the regulations are: (1) registration of temples and monasteries, monks and nuns; (2) taxation of temple property; (3) non-alienation of temple property; (4) subjection of religious activities and preaching services to police regulation.[63]

Welch notes that the final sweeping element of the policy aimed to limit any public statements by monks and nuns "to doctrinal exegesis, moral exhortation, and 'stimulating patriotic thoughts.'"[64] The government also reasserted its right to monitor and control ordination through required certificates issued by the Ministry of the Interior. Yet it went even further, claiming the authority to dismiss abbots for infractions not only of the civil code but of monastic rules as well. Paul Callahan reports that these actions resulted in vehement opposition in China "from both Buddhists and Christians." On the sangha's reaction, he remarks:

> The Buddhist National Society [Chinese General Buddhist Association (Zhonghua fojiao zonghui) founded in Shanghai in 1912] set up a lobby, a preaching hall, near the National Assembly and worked zealously to influence the populace and delegates against the government. In retaliation, the government declared the society inimical to public safety and closed it. Though Yuan's schemes failed and the Society was reorganized after his fall, it was again closed by the government in 1917.[65]

The confrontations with the government that continued during Taixu's period of sealed confinement eventually led him to reflect further on the Sangha's relation to the world and its inability to speak with one voice. He came to believe that these issues were not unrelated to the diversity within the Buddhist community itself. Thus he began to argue that those pursuing the bodhisattva path needed to understand deeply—and actually integrate—the different emphases and diverse forms of piety associated with what he had customarily spoken of as two basic approaches to the Dharma: the intuitive approach of Chan, which was not founded on special scriptures *(buli wenzi)*, and the teaching approach adopted by the Vinaya (Lü), Tiantai, Huayen, Yogācāra (Weishi, or Mind-Only), Pure Land (Jingtu), and Tantric (Zhenyan) schools.

Taixu came to claim that since no one school encompassed the entire canon and none was without a sound foundation in the Buddha's Dharma, practitioners would benefit from a synthetic approach to enlightenment based on a broad study of scripture and tradition. Nevertheless, Xuming observes, while the reformer began to advocate forging a new religio-philosophical synthesis and was convinced that each school's perspectives were grounded in a "pure mind" *(jing xin)*, he was always extremely appreciative of the idealistic philosophical perspectives that he discovered in the Weishi tradition. Thus, on the one hand, as Xuming asserts, it was most clearly in the terms of this tradition that Taixu "grasped the fundamental principles of Chinese Buddhism."[66] On the other hand, as Shengyan indicates, his stance was clearly that of a Chan master:

> Taixu studied Chan in his early years; and although Taixu later judged the eight schools to be of equal importance, he did state, "When one reaches understanding, one naturally comes to the Prajñā (Sanlun) School and the Chan School of Bodhidharma." . . . He emphasized the application of Yogācāra philosophy and constantly used its terminology to explain Buddhist texts. Hence, he often has been mistaken for a scholar of the Yogācāra School, when in fact he only borrowed its terminology as a matter of expediency.[67]

Concurring that Taixu came to stress the unity of Buddhism early in his monastic career, Gao Yongxiao argues that one can discern in the monk's writings three distinct stages of reflection on the issue of the unity and diversity of Buddhist teaching *(fofa de panshe)*.⁶⁸ In the first period of the reformer's religious life, Gao says, from about 1908 to 1914, Taixu followed the traditional method of distinguishing between a *zong,* or "lineage," and a *jiao,* or "school." A *zong* primarily emphasized the transmission of enlightenment experiences, while a *jiao* focused on certain highly prized scriptures and the transmission of enlightened understandings about the human situation and the nature of reality.

During the second phase of Taixu's career, from 1915 to 1923, after extensive studies of the Chinese Tripiṭaka during his *biguan,* the monk began to emphasize the fundamental interrelationship between Nikāya Buddhism and Mahāyāna Buddhism.⁶⁹ Indeed, notes Gao, Taixu began to highlight the teaching of the *Lotus Sūtra* that in fact "there is only one Dharmic vehicle, not two or three."⁷⁰ The Śrāvakayāna *(shengwen sheng),* the Pratyekabuddhayāna *(yuanjue sheng),* and the Bodhisattvayāna *(pusa sheng)* were just expedient expressions of the one Buddhayāna *(fo sheng).* The eight schools of Buddhism, Taixu thought, represented only different aspects of the one true Dharma, which is adapted according to the various needs of its hearers. Shengyan observes:

> According to Taixu, "There are many tributaries of the Dharma, yet the source is one." True Suchness, being the essence of the Dharma, is one and undifferentiated. Differences among the treatises are for promoting the effect of preaching. Taixu divided the teachings into the Prajñā (Sanlun [Mādhyamika]) School emphasizing "Selectivity," the Yogācāra [Weishi] School emphasizing "Existence," and the True Suchness Schools (Chan, Tiantai, Xianshou [Huayan], and Esoteric [Zhenyan]) emphasizing "Emptiness." He also explained these three emphases in terms of the three natures noted in Yogācāra: the Prajñā School emphasizes the nature of wrong discrimination, the Yogācāra School emphasizes the nature of dependence on others, and the True Suchness Schools the nature of perfect knowledge. All three are perfect teachings, despite their different functions.⁷¹

John Blofeld once remarked, after a conversation with Taixu about the great diversity of traditions within the Buddhist household,

"I comfort myself with the words of the Venerable Taixu who declared that the various sects are like beads in the same rosary and that each one of them is the best approach for certain individuals."⁷² Although Taixu acknowledged that every person must begin his or her pilgrimage through earnest study of one particular school's teaching about the truth, he judged that all practitioners would finally realize that the same goal could be reached by different routes. Thus, he concluded, "Upāya *(fangbian)* has many gates, but in returning to the origin *(gui yuan)*, there are not two roads."⁷³

According to Gao, during the third phase of Taixu's career, from 1923 to 1947, he "distinguished between 'schools' *(jiao)*, 'doctrines' *(li)*, and 'actions' *(xing)* in order to organize a comprehensive presentation of Śākyamuni's transmission of Dharma."⁷⁴ As Chou Hsiang-kuang shows in outlined detail, in his teaching Taixu used "schools" as a category for explaining the historical development of the various Nikāya, Mahāyāna, and Vajrayāna traditions, as well as for introducing Pali, Chinese, and Tibetan, the languages that he judged to be most critical for advanced Buddhist studies. Under the category of "doctrines," Taixu explored with his students basic Buddhist teachings about karma, saṃsāra, nirvāṇa, and conditioned origination, as well as the more difficult Mahāyāna doctrines of buddha-nature, mind-only, and so forth. The category of normative Buddhist "actions" provided Taixu with a framework for a detailed discussion of Buddhist morality in terms of the five vows *(wu jie)*, the ten forms of good action *(shi de)*, and the great career of the bodhisattva in wise and compassionate service to all.⁷⁵

As Yang Huinan points out, it was also in this third period, after 1923, that Taixu began frequently to refer to an important threefold distinction within Buddhism to embrace the scope of its doctrine—namely, the Dharma common to the Five Vehicles, the Dharma common to the Three Vehicles, and the distinctive Dharma of the Great Vehicle (Mahāyāna).⁷⁶ As discussed in Chapter 4, his central points were that the basic moral precepts required of all beginners on the path toward enlightenment remain significant for more advanced followers, and that reliance on only one part of the teachings is unproductive.

Just as Taixu had entered sealed confinement in 1914 with a certain amount of fanfare, so he came out of seclusion on February 4, 1917 with more than the usual attention. Reichelt says that, on the appointed day for the monk's return to society, a number of abbots, Buddhist scholars, and dignitaries gathered at Putuo Shan, formed a procession, and proceeded to Taixu's cloister. "Salvoes of firecrackers were discharged," he writes, "and a solemn mass was offered in front of his cell. Then the red seal was removed by the abbot and the hero was led out and acclaimed with enthusiasm."[77] Acutely aware of the great conflagration that raged on in Europe, of China's own instability, and of disorder within the sangha, the twenty-seven-year-old Taixu immediately began traveling to important monasteries throughout central China and visiting colleagues among the more conservative monastic leaders, such as Yuanying, as well as the more radical, like his old colleague Renshan.

Invigorated by the experience of confinement and more determined than ever to make a difference in advancing the Dharma in an age of confusion, Taixu also accepted invitations to travel to Japan and Taiwan (then a Japanese colony) to consult with other Asian Buddhist leaders about the present and future condition of their religion. He talked constantly about the dilemmas of a war-weary world, the bankruptcy of western culture, the certain demise of Christianity, the problems of Buddhist sectarianism, and the possibilities for the development of a "new Buddhism." Yet as Xuming has emphasized, Taixu never used the term "new" in any popular sense of the term (i.e., to mean "western," "foreign," "ultramodern," or "anti-traditional"). Rather, he claims, the reformer always intended "new" in the sense of the true, original essence of Chinese Buddhism, which needed to be rediscovered.[78]

That rediscovered essence of wisdom and compassion, embodied by the bodhisattva, was for Taixu the hope of all sentient beings. History had shown that neither western humanism nor western religion could adequately support the creation of a global culture. Yet Mahāyāna Buddhism, Taixu confidently proclaimed, could provide the foundation for a lasting world peace that would be an Asian gift to the rest of the world. As he concluded in a lecture at the Yunhua tang, in the city of Zhanghua in central Taiwan, in October 1917:

> Buddhism is representative of East Asian civilization. Now Christianity, which is representative of contemporary Western civilization, has already at this point lost its religious power in Europe and America. Europeans and Americans have thus lost their basis for a secure life and the fulfillment of their destiny. It is because of this fact that the great World War is now taking place. We ought to proclaim our East Asian good word of peace and spread Buddhism universally throughout the world in order to change their murderous perversions and save all beings from great disaster.[79]

ORGANIZING AND EDUCATING "NEW MONKS"

After his travels through Japan and Taiwan, and after consultations with Zhang Taiyan and Wang Yiting, Taixu instigated his reformist movement with the founding in Shanghai, in August 1918, of the Bodhi Society (Jue she).[80] During his *biguan,* Taixu had spent considerable time on imaginative plans for reorganizing the Chinese sangha, a project he considered as necessary as it was difficult. The first of several versions of his *Zhengli sengqie zhidu lun* (The Reorganization of the Sangha System) was written in 1915, in response to the threat presented by the Regulations for the Control of Monasteries and Temples. Yet Taixu recognized that the ultimate reception of such a controversial proposal would require the establishment of bases of monastic and lay support that could serve as effective organs for propaganda. The Bodhi Society—so named, said Taixu, "because of my long-cherished hope that the world could be saved through Buddhism"—was to be one such base.[81] According to Xuming, the founding of the organization constituted "the beginning of Taixu's new Buddhist movement."[82] With its creation, the number of the reformer's followers began to increase rapidly. The society's explicit purposes, noted

Taixu, were "to publish research, edit collected works, sponsor lectures on Buddhism, and encourage religious cultivation."[83] The monk himself later recalled:

> The next year [1918], I was invited to visit the South Sea Islands [where there are colonies of prosperous Chinese emigrants]. I formed the idea of building a National Monastery. My observation leads me to feel that the monastic institutions in our country have fallen away from ancient pure ideals and are corrupt beyond reform. If I could raise the funds from people abroad, I would build the national monastery [as a model of renewed and purified monasticism]. If I should fail to attain my object I would reconcile myself to the life of a wandering mendicant and, leaning upon Buddha's mercy, thus travel to my life's end.
>
> When I was at Putuo, some of my earnest devotees requested me to lecture on "Weishi lun.". . . I talked to them about my wish to reform monastic institutions and my plan to go south. They also saw the works I have written. They strongly advised against the southern trip at the time as the European War was at its height, and it would be difficult to raise money there, but urged me to publish my works and to organize a society for the promotion of Buddhism in China as the first step of my larger plans. And so we organized the "Bodhi Society" in Shanghai.[84]

The initial announcement of the Bodhi Society reveals the organization's aim to promote "self-enlightenment and the enlightenment of others" and its rules designed to nurture those on the bodhisattva path. The basic bylaws read as follows:

I. Purpose:
   A. To set forth the true principles of Mahāyāna Buddhism to cause those who slander the truth to repent, those who doubt to have faith and understanding, those who believe and understand to put their faith into action, and those who understand and practice their religion to witness to others; to transform fools and common people, radicals and ultraconservatives into sages, saints, and buddhas.
   B. To proclaim the true principles of Mahāyāna Buddhism to turn those who are cruel and evil into benevolent people and

those who are greedy and belligerent into righteous people; so that the wise will rejoice in the way and the strong will honor morality; to turn this war-torn and suffering world into a place of peace and happiness.

II. Regulations for members . . . :
   A. Rules for self-cultivation:
      1. Required practices:
         a. To take refuge in the Three Jewels of Buddha, Dharma and Sangha and take the four universal vows of a bodhisattva to make definite one's faith and resolve.
         b. To observe the ten great precepts for the laity as found in the *Brahmajāla Sūtra*. If a member is not immediately able to observe all of the precepts, then he should select one or two of them and gradually increase the number until he is in compliance with all the right actions.
         c. To reflect on perfect knowledge, investigate the essence of the mind, study the Buddhist scriptures, and practice bodhisattva behavior in order to develop your own wisdom.
      2. Special regular practices:
         a. To reflect on the [teachings of the] Chan school,
         b. To support the teachings of the Zhenyan school,
         c. To chant the Mahāyāna scriptures,
         d. To recite the name of Amitābha,
         e. To practice one form of meditation *(zhiguan),*
         f. Or to engage in several of these practices simultaneously.
      3. Things to be done at one's convenience: to worship, offer repentance, and make donations. Practice all these

things properly as opportunities arise in all times and places.

B. Regulations about group activities for the entire membership . . . :

1. On the eighth day of the fourth month, members should gather for one day to observe the birthday of Buddha by fasting, offering penance, releasing living beings, making donations, and doing other meritorious deeds.

2. Beginning on the evening of the eleventh day of the eleventh month, and continuing for seven days, members should hold a meeting for reciting the name of Buddha *(nian fo hui)*. The time should be limited so as to attain a oneness of mind without confusion.

3. Each year, from the first to the eighth day of the twelfth month, members should hold a meeting for meditation *(can chan hui)*. The time should be limited so as to become enlightened to the original Mind from which all things arise.[85]

Late during the next year, following the Beijing demonstration in May 1919 at which students protested the government's humiliating policy toward Japan and the outcome of the Versailles peace negotiations, the headquarters of the Bodhi Society were moved from Shanghai to Hangzhou, as Taixu moved to the Jingfan yuan near the West Lake. Shortly thereafter, in early 1920, the *Jueshe congshu,* the organization's quarterly magazine that Taixu edited, was renamed *Haichao yin* and became a monthly publication. In a relatively short time, it was to become the most important and widely read Buddhist periodical of the Republican period. Its goal was the exploration of models for the organization and education of "new monks." Although Taixu was obviously directing events to achieve his long-range goals, his own recollection, not surprisingly, is self-deprecating. He wrote in 1920:

> Lately I have been living in Jingfan yuan monastery, on the side of the Western Lake, Hangzhou. Here I had desired to live quietly for the practice of contemplation, but the members of the Bodhi Society have asked me to edit a new magazine, called *Haichao yin* [The Voice of Sea Waves] to meet the needs of the time. I have consented to do it for one year, as the work is congenial to my original wish, and so for this year, I have decided to lay aside other work and devote myself to editing the magazine. But at the close of ten thousand years, the Tathāgata will surely raise up men to establish the Law and spread it throughout the world of the living.[86]

The society's publishing effort—for which Taixu was able to secure financial assistance from interested laypersons—aimed both at religious instruction and institutional reform. The ultimate goal of *Haichao yin* was no less than a modernizing transformation of Chinese Buddhist piety and of the institutional structures that could encourage and support an expression of that piety. Observed Tsu:

> It aims to lift the voice of Mahāyāna Buddhism for the guidance of mankind tossed as it is by the waves of modern thought. The magazine contains (1) exposition of Buddhist doctrines, as for instance a new commentary of "Mahāyāna-śraddhotpāda-śāstra" (Awakening of Faith); (2) apologetics or defense of the faith in face of modern criticism; (3) advocacy of reformation, as reorganization of the monastic order; (4) testimonials: stories of conversion experience, lives of saintly devotees, etc.; (5) critical review of works on religion and philosophy, especially on Buddhism. It is of high quality and is edited by Taixu Fashi himself.[87]

The significance of the appearance of the innovative Chinese Buddhist periodical was soon acknowledged by the Japanese editors of the international journal, *The Eastern Buddhist*, who wrote:

> The Kaichoou *(Haichao yin)*, a Buddhist monthly, published at Wuchang under the editorship of Rev. Taixu is full of interest and information. This we wish to be the real beginning of a general re-awakening of interest in Buddhism throughout the length and breadth of the Middle Kingdom, which produced in the past so many saintly souls and spiri-

tual leaders contributing to the ever-upward progress of Eastern civilization, and where Buddhism, fully assimilated by the native genius and mode of feeling, has resulted in the creation of its special form now designated as Zen or Chan.[88]

One of the first articles published in 1920 in *Haichao yin* was from Taixu's *Zhengli sengqie zhidu lun* (The Reorganization of the Sangha System), composed in first draft during his period of sealed confinement. According to Callahan, the essay "took the Chinese Buddhist world by storm."[89] Although the specifics changed slightly in later revised versions, as discussed in Chapter 5 below, Taixu's plan called for Chinese Buddhism to be reshaped institutionally with new model monasteries, benevolent organizations, and educational ventures. It required higher levels of education for all monks and nuns in view of the increasing levels of education in the general populace. It proposed productive physical labor by all able-bodied monastics so that the community could be self-supporting, eliminating the need for the decadent commercialism of masses for the dead. Taixu also envisioned monasteries and temples more as places of study and meditation than as centers for esoteric rites. Accordingly, an exemplary national monastery was to be established, complete with a massive library and a museum of Buddhist art and artifacts open for research. Affiliated with it would be a network of related institutes for Buddhist studies, as well as centers for Dharma proclamation and meditation.

As Taixu refined his plan in the years that followed, he chose to address not only the issue of the sangha's functional organization but the question of how many monastics were needed to propagate Buddhism in China. His recommendations eventually called for drastic reductions in the size of the monastic community, while redefining the sangha's role vis-à-vis society to reflect his own form of ethical piety. Under his controversial scheme, a moderate number of professional monks would perform good works for the benefit of society as a whole (such as operating schools, orphanages, and hospitals) under the direction of a small cadre of highly educated scholar-monks who were experts in Buddhist doctrine, and complemented by an almost equally small number of elderly monks who specialized in spiritual cultivation through meditation and chanting. The great majority of monks, who Taixu thought shouldn't really be called monks at all, would engage in manual labor to support the propagation of the religion by those most able to do so in a modern society. Welch comments:

> Between 1915 and 1947 he produced seven more versions [of his plan for reorganizing the sangha], each representing an evolution over the last. None was ever put into practice: they were, in fact, so impracticable and so grandiose that it is hard to see how they could have been taken seriously. Rather, as if he were a child deploying regiments of toy soldiers, Taixu divided up the sangha into departments, each with its own specialty. For example, according to one of his later schemes, China was to have ten thousand scholar monks, who earned academic degrees in four grades according to the number of years they spent at study. The highest grade would consist of eight hundred monks with the Ph.D., each of whom had studied for nine years. Twenty-five thousand monks were to engage in good works (nine thousand teaching Buddhism, seven thousand running hospitals, orphanages, and so on). Finally, a small number of elders would run sixty centers of religious cultivation *(xiu lin)*, at which a thousand monks would meditate and recite Buddha's name. This accounted for only thirty-six thousand of China's half a million monks. What would have happened to the rest is unclear. Perhaps Taixu expected that many of them would disrobe to avoid manual labor and military service, both of which he is said to have favored for monks. With the sangha reduced to scholars and functionaries, there would not have been funerary specialists to perform rites for the dead, but this objection carried no weight with Taixu, for such rites were something of which, by now, he tended to disapprove. Indeed, he seems sometimes to have had grave doubts about monkhood itself.[90]

Taixu, with his "utopian propensity," was convinced that Buddhism could revitalize itself in the twentieth century through educational modernization, social service, and international cooperation. His greatest accomplishment in the area of monastic education was the Wuchang Buddhist Institute (Wuchang foxue yuan), founded in 1922. According to Earl Herbert Cressy, Taixu moved in that year from Hangzhou in Zhejiang province to the Wuchang and Hankou area in Hubei province because "he found the monasteries in Hangzhou too conservative to welcome his more up-to-date attitude."[91] In Hankou, in contrast, his lectures on modern Buddhist reform soon inspired the establishment of a new lay organization, the Right Faith Buddhist Society of Hankou (Hankou fojiao zhengxin hui), for which Taixu served as "Guiding Master" *(daoshi)*. The society soon built a large three-story complex for its publishing and educational activities, and by 1933 claimed a membership of thirty thousand.[92] Still, Taixu's principal concern at the time was the creation of his new type of monastic school across the Yangzi River in the neighboring city of Wuchang. Cressy reports:

> Upon the arrival of the Monk Taixu in Wuchang, in 1922, there was an emphasis upon securing better educated leaders for Buddhist monasteries and associations. Accordingly a college was established which had a plant consisting of three main buildings and ample accommodations for classrooms, service departments, and living quarters for faculty and students.
>
> About $60,000 was expended in establishing the school. For the first two years it was conducted on a modest basis, but later it was divided into a number of departments. The writer visited this school in 1925 and interviewed Taixu, its head. The seventy students in residence were middle-school graduates and were a very intelligent and keen group of young men.[93]

With the generous support of lay Buddhist leaders Li Yinchen, Chen Yuanbai, Wang Senpu, Li Kaicheng, and others, Taixu's seminary in Wuchang became a pioneer in Buddhist education. The school adopted the western educational format of lecture and discussion classes. It employed monastic and lay instructors, provided blackboards for use by teachers and students, and required academic course work not only in Buddhist studies and languages but in secular subjects, such as history, literature, and psychology, as well.[94] Its excellent library was renowned for a collection that eventually included more than forty thousand books. Because of the success of Taixu's innovations, the Wuchang Buddhist Institute gained recognition as an educational model for Buddhist seminaries throughout China. James B. Pratt, who visited the seminary in 1923, reported attending one of the lectures after a pleasant private interview with the master:

> At the lecture were sixty-three students, all but five of them being monks. Taixu lectured without notes and very easily, making constant use of the black board. Each student had a copy of the sūtra that was being expounded, and followed the lecture eagerly, taking careful notes. I gathered from what my interpreter told me that his lectures were less abstruse than those of Mr. Ouyang [Jingwu]. His influence must be considerable. If sixty monks, or half that number, can be sent out every year with his impress upon them, there is still hope for Chinese Buddhism.
>
> Taixu's aim, he told me, is chiefly to make Buddhism known as it really is. He is the more hopeful that his effort in this direction will bear fruit, because it is in response to a real demand. Chinese students are returning every year from Europe and America, or graduating from colleges in China, and demanding to know what Buddhism is. The question, he insists, must be answered from Chinese sources—from the great Mahāyāna sūtras—and in a scholarly and philosophical way. His primary aim is, therefore, scholarly and philosophical. Solid knowledge and solid thinking must form the basis of anything lasting in the way of a Buddhist revival. Only indirectly does he hope to spread Buddhism among the common people.[95]

Taixu's modernization extended well beyond the five seminaries that eventually came under his direct authority. Conservative leaders disparaged the broader scope of education available in Taixu's seminaries, maintaining that it served only to distract monks and nuns from the more essential elements of a uniquely Buddhist style and content to learning. Yet many Chinese Buddhists found a more comprehensive form of education especially relevant given the intellectual challenges in the wake of the "May Fourth Movement" and the anti-religion activities of the 1920s. While others debated his methods, Taixu never altered his course or wavered in his insistence that students seek to understand the Dharma in relation to the social and political issues of the day. Nevertheless, after 1934, financial difficulties forced the closure of the groundbreaking school at Wuchang, and the plant was occupied by soldiers, as it had been for a brief period in 1929. Attempts to revive the school by transferring it to Beijing ultimately failed to continue its operation beyond 1937, when the war with Japan made funding extremely scarce.

Meanwhile, Taixu founded and directed other monastic schools, each theoretically a part of his World Buddhist Institute. The seminary in Beijing at the Bolin si (Bolin si jiaoli yuan), which, like the Wuchang Buddhist Institute, was to specialize in English-language studies, functioned only for the 1930–1931 academic year.[96] Taixu's important South Fujian Seminary (Minnan foxue yuan) in Xiamen (Amoy), which specialized in Japanese-language study, functioned from 1925 to 1939. His seminary in Chongqing, Sichuan (Han Zang jiaoli yuan), specializing in Tibetan studies, was in operation from 1932 to 1949. And in Xi'an, Shaanxi, the seminary that he established at the Daxingshan si (Bali sanzang yuan), specializing in Pali studies, functioned for only a short period after its founding in 1945.[97]

Taixu was not only a pioneer administrator concerned with new structures for monastic education but a popular Buddhist lecturer who was able to adjust the tone and content of his messages to the special character of different audiences. On the one hand, he could explicate for his students in the classroom the difficult metaphysical theories of Weishi idealism. On the other hand, though he viewed Buddhist devotionalism as a *upāya* (skillful means), he could speak impressively for the laity on the glories of the pure lands. In fact, when Taixu had been appointed head monk of the West Lake's Jingci si in the spring of 1921, he had urged the transformation of the traditional meditation hall *(chan tang)* into a "horned tiger hall" *(jiaohu tang)*, "so as to continue the complementary practice of Chan and Pure Land Buddhism that was the custom of Yongming Yanshou [904–975]."[98] Moreover, Taixu and his seminarians from Wuchang effectively used Protestant-style worship services in brightly illuminated street chapels to attract potential followers. Describing Taixu's accomplishments in Hankou in the 1920s, Reichelt commented:

> A new and interesting scene was revealed when darkness fell. A door had been opened wide and people from the street poured in to the preach-

ing-chapel where an imposing image of Amitābha stood at the rear. The niche where the image was set up was brilliantly illuminated by electric bulbs. The radiant figure of Amitābha and the music from the organ soon had their effect and the hall became completely filled. A sermon began, followed by short "testimonies" from the students. Taixu had impressed upon his assistants that on such occasions it was best to concentrate upon the message of the Pure Land School, because this was all the ignorant people could understand. In this way Buddhists could compete better with Christians who had made so much progress in China especially through evangelism in street chapels.[99]

Taixu was good at planning for his mission ventures and often sent disciples ahead of his scheduled visits to different areas to prepare the community for his preaching and teaching activities. In addition, his disciples frequently engaged in mission trips of their own when the master could not be present. For example, A. J. Brace, a YMCA official in Chengdu, reported that efforts to increase membership in his own Christian organization had been "seriously hurt" by the visit to the city in 1922 of some of Taixu's students. Providing us with a helpful picture of the new form of missionary endeavors that the Buddhist reformer actively encouraged, Brace wrote:

> In the summer of 1922 disciples of the famous monk Taixu journeyed from Shanghai to Chengdu in Sichuan Province to bring the modernized message of Buddhism as taught by their master. Their coming was the occasion of great rejoicing, and a real revival of Buddhism was the result. They had been heralded for more than a year and their way was prepared by a wide circulation of Taixu's popular magazine, "Haichao yin"—"The Voice of the Sea," or "The Sound of the Tide." Very carefully edited articles had prepared the people for the visit of the missionaries, and the new message found a ready response even before their arrival. It brought a message of peace for the troubled days, and the magazine clearly stated that the new message was destined to lift the sublime teachings of the Mahāyāna Doctrine for the help of the people tossed about in the sea of modern doubt. The message was essentially spiritual and taught, or stood for, three propositions, (1) a real

desire to reform monasticism, (2) a plan to reconstruct Buddhist theology along lines of modern philosophy, (3) to use the teachings of Buddha to elevate the people and improve social conditions.

On the arrival of the missionaries, they were welcomed officially by the Governor of the Province. The sixteen daily papers all joined in a welcome, and gave columns to the new teaching, thus supplying a liberal supply of advertising. The opening meetings were attended by large crowds who listened attentively to the new program, and large numbers voluntarily enrolled themselves for the daily course to be given. In fact, a real program was gotten out, much like a university course, or a summer school curriculum, and fees charged for the course. Then daily the large hall in the Public Garden of the Manchu City was thronged with auditors to hear the public addresses, and the class rooms were filled with eager students to listen and follow the course throughout.

A thorough course was given in the history of Buddhism, what it had done for the world, and how it had become encrusted with many superstitions. Now all was changed. The old simple story of the Enlightened One and how he found the way of salvation was declared. Idolatry was opposed, and in bygone days it was only tolerated as an accommodation to the weakness of the ignorant people. Now education was to be stressed, the priests had always been ignorant. A Buddhist university was to be established. The monks were to be encouraged to be busy as learners and servants of the people rather than follow the lazy lives of the past. The mercy of Buddha was taught and enjoined so that the wicked might be led to kindness, the selfish to righteousness, the hungry to find satisfaction in the doctrine. Most emphasized were the daily hours for fasting and meditation.

A real revival was effected along these lines, and many of the foremost business and professional men took the vows and followed the course of meditation regularly. Many men who had not been interested in religion came under the sway of the new-found faith, and personally told me of the value of the hours of meditation and how their faith had been strengthened. The course on reading was followed widely. The students burnt incense daily as they read and meditated. At the meetings singing was indulged in, and often tunes quite similar to Christian tunes were used, and one song with the refrain, "Take the name of Buddha with you." They even organized a Young Men's Buddhist Association which is going strong.[100]

Taixu also began enthusiastically to involve his seminarians and lay supporters in social service ministries. He asserted that the non-differentiation of self from others was the very basis of a bodhisattva's compassionate activities in the world, and that helping another person was coterminous with helping one's self. As a result, after Taixu's weekend sermons in Hankou, his students would commonly usher people in need of health care to rooms where physicians, who were among his lay disciples, provided free treatment and medicine, exemplifying a long tradition of Buddhist concern for healing.[101] He helped his disciples Miaoji and Hualin establish a modern school for children and a welfare program for the diseased, destitute, and jobless. It was reported that they "used to go around to the sick with medicines, dressing wounds and distributing articles to the needy."[102]

The previously mentioned Right Faith Buddhist Society of Hankou became one of the most socially active lay Buddhist associations in the country. In accord with Taixu's emphasis on social responsibility, the society operated a clinic that provided free medical treatment for the poor, administered a free primary school for children of low-income families, donated coffins to families who could not afford them, funded a non-Buddhist social service agency that provided assistance to indigent widows, distributed food to needy families on holidays, served meals in fire catastrophes, and rescued people and animals in flood crises.[103] Most of the major cities of China developed similar lay Buddhist organizations, with laity *(jushi)* active in a variety of religiously motivated pursuits, in order "to propagate the Dharma and to benefit humanity."[104] Seeking to characterize the type of lay believers who were often attracted to Taixu's teachings and whose devotion was a driving force in aspects of the effort at Buddhist revitalization, John Blofeld once wrote:

> The jushi [lay devotees] are often men of considerable learning as well as faith and piety, they sometimes exhibit a more profound understand-

ing of Buddhist philosophy than many of the monks and nuns. To this learning they add active observance of the teaching that the utmost compassion should be shown to all sentient beings. . . .

The jushi is usually a cultured person. He prefers to wear the dignified Chinese gown of blue, gray or bronze-coloured silk, and by his habits and gestures, exhibits his fondness for and understanding of the traditional culture of his country. He is often a poet or painter as well as a philosopher and metaphysician, and may be something of a historian or possess a knowledge of Chinese herbal medicine in addition. . . . They often show themselves to be far above the vulgar superstitions which have done much to lower the tone of the great moral and metaphysical system created by the Indian sage Gautama.[105]

In the early 1920s, Taixu also initiated a new program of Buddhist visitation to prisons, encouraging students at his seminary in Wuchang to minister to the incarcerated. It was recognized as an innovative program by most Buddhists, although the charter of the 1912 Chinese General Buddhist Association, founded in Shanghai, had at least called for prison visitation.[106] Perhaps Taixu's program was interpreted as new because there had been little or no actual response to this element of the association's 1912 charter. Emphasizing the Christian precedents for such activities and describing Taixu's program as merely imitative, the missionary-scholar Reichelt comments:

> Taixu had noticed that Christian missionaries and some Chinese evangelists had obtained permission from the authorities to visit the public gaols in order to speak to the prisoners. It was even described in the newspapers because quite a number of prisoners had become converted and had left the gaols as new men. This challenged Taixu. Why should not Buddhists do the same? He placed the matter before his students, and of course everybody offered for service. Taixu applied to the authorities and permission was given. . . .
>
> Prisoners used to gather in a large room and young Buddhist monks in their dignified robes performed with the greatest eloquence as "teaching masters" to this mixed audience. They too were "written up" in the newspapers.[107]

After a time, enthusiasm waned among students at the Wuchang Buddhist Institute, and the prison program lost much of its momentum. Yet despite Taixu's eventual disappointment with this development in Wuchang, the idea of prison ministries did spread to other Buddhist groups and to other parts of China.[108]

Through all these educational and human service activities, Taixu sought to respond to the demands of the time while recalling what he considered to be the true nature of his religious tradition. He wanted Chinese Buddhists to build on an essential dimension of their Mahāyāna heritage that had been overlooked and inadequately developed. In view of criticisms by Christians who facilely contrasted their own tradition's social consciousness with the blatantly self-centered spirituality of Buddhists, the reformer tried to present those on the bodhisattva path as members of a socially responsive and morally responsible religious community.

In large measure, of course, Taixu shared with Christian missionaries a critical outlook on "real" Chinese Buddhism—that is, the religion as "commonly practiced" in the Republican period. At the same time, however, he envisioned an "ideal" Chinese Buddhism that could change forever not only the future of Asia but that of the entire world. Indeed, it was to the task of articulating more clearly aspects of that projected global religion that Taixu was to give much of his time and energy during the last half of his monastic career.

CHAPTER 3

AN ECUMENICAL VISION FOR GLOBAL MISSION

During the last thirty years of his life, in addition to his efforts in the field of monastic education, Taixu devoted considerable energy to the establishment of regional and world Buddhist organizations. Xuming asserts that the reformer's growing interest in the 1920s in the global organization of Buddhists reflected a definite strategic decision on his part. At first, Taixu believed that the reorganization and reform of the monastic and lay communities within the Chinese Buddhist household would lead, rather naturally and directly, to the spiritual transformation of the nation and, eventually, of the entire world. However, given the failures and obstacles related to this internal Chinese reformation, Taixu began to think more expansively about organizing an ecumenical Buddhist movement on a global scale. Thus, while continuing efforts at institutional reform within the Chinese sangha, he hoped to find a way to bring together progressive-minded monks and laypeople from many nations who were prepared to commit themselves to a Buddhist mission to the world. It would be the conversion of the Christian West that would facilitate the thorough revitalization of Buddhism in East Asia and the shaping of a global Buddhist culture in which the enlightenment of every living being would be possible.[1]

Yet except for his brief visits to Taiwan and Japan in 1917, it was not until after 1923 that the Chinese master had any concrete opportunities to extend the horizon of his reformist activities beyond China. Therefore, although Xuming is perhaps correct about Taixu's strategic reasons for involving himself in new efforts in Buddhist ecumenism and global mission, Welch is equally right to point out that Taixu's "international debut" was not, in fact, the result of a carefully conceived master plan, but of a fortunate unfolding of events.[2]

THE WORLD BUDDHIST FEDERATION

In 1922, one of Taixu's lay disciples, Yan Shaofu, had committed himself to restoring the ancient Buddhist center, then in ruins, on famous Lu Shan in Jiangxi province—once the home of the revered fourth-century master Huiyuan.[3] As Taixu reports with dismay in his autobiography, Buddhism in the area was in decline, whereas Christian missionary activities were on the increase.[4] Therefore, in the summer of 1923, the Buddhist master went to Lu Shan's old Dalin si to encourage a limited restoration through a summer lecture series. In mid-July, before Taixu arrived, Yan posted a sign outside the lecture hall that read "World Buddhist Federation" (Shijie fojiao lianhe hui).

Soon thereafter, Inada Ensai, the influential Buddhist layman and scholar from Ōtani University in Japan, came to the monastery to visit with Taixu. Noting the intriguing sign, Inada engaged the Chinese master in a conversation about the possibilities of an active World Buddhist Federation, with a view toward a collaborative Chinese-Japanese mission to the West. It was an idea in which Taixu was very interested and one in which he was subsequently encouraged by Edo Sentaro, the Japanese consul in Jiujiang, who worked with Taixu to obtain permission from both governments for an international conference in China the following year.

The initial lecture series that first summer, held from July 23 to August 11, 1923, was fairly well attended. According to the Christian missionary Karl Reichelt, whom Taixu invited to lecture on "The Relation Between Christianity and Buddhism," about a hundred monks and lay devotees, including several Japanese and other foreign visitors, attended all or part of the program.[5] Linking modern Buddhist education, a socially engaged spirituality, interreligious dialogue, and global mission, Taixu outlined for Reichelt his aims for future conferences:

1. To stir up deeper interest in religious thinking and to promote a deeper spiritual life among ourselves.

2. To lead Buddhism in China to conform with and influence the life of society as never before.

3. To come in contact with sincere religious people of other religions, and to talk over religious problems with them to our mutual help.

4. We especially feel that Christians misunderstand us. Many of them only come in contact with ignorant and immoral Buddhist monks, strolling around in the streets. They think all Buddhists are of this type and that we are all given over to dark superstitions and do not really cultivate religion. We have started this conference movement to show you that this is not true.

5. Finally I will not conceal the fact that we hope through you to influence western countries, where Buddhism is not very well known. We think that Buddhism has something very valuable to give the world.[6]

Given the response to the lecture series and the exciting possibilities for the future, plans proceeded for a more representative conference of the "Federation" the next summer.

The first actual conference of the World Buddhist Federation was held on Lu Shan, July 13–15, 1924. According to Dongchu, Taixu summarized its purpose as threefold: "first, to unite Buddhists from each province in China; second, to unite Buddhists from each country of East Asia; and, third, to transmit the truths and spirit of East Asian Buddhism to each country of Europe and to the United States so that the Federation could become in actual fact a World Buddhist Federation, something that at the time was only an ideal."[7] The Chinese were represented by ten delegates from six provinces, including Liaochen from Hubei, Xingxiu from Hunan, Changxing from Zhejiang, and Zhu'an from Anhui. The Japanese were represented by Saeki Teien, Kimura Taiken, and Mizuno Baigyō. Although invited representatives from Mongolia, Tibet, Burma, Sri Lanka, and other countries were not able to be present, Taixu claimed that there were also Buddhist participants in attendance from Ceylon, England, Germany, Finland, and France.[8] Nevertheless, Dongchu states bluntly, "Since only the Japanese sent a delegation, the designation of the conference ought to have been changed to that of the 'Chinese and Japanese Buddhist Federation.'"[9] Despite the limited representation, the well-known Chinese monk Changxing, the scholar Kimura Taiken from the University of Tokyo, and others lectured on the need for Buddhist cooperation.[10]

In his plenary address, Taixu focused on the contrast between the "tool-making culture" of the West and the "culture of perfecting human nature" of East Asia.[11] His principal point, notes Dongchu, was that "Western culture is a culture that harms all living beings and East Asian culture is one that benefits them."[12] As an expression of their solidarity in global mission, the Chinese and Japanese delegations jointly declared:

> Since the essence of Buddhism is the teaching of anātman (no-ego; *wu wo*), there can be no talking of *my* country and *my* family. Indeed, we must understand the whole world as our country, without boundaries. Thus, Chinese and Japanese Buddhists cannot be but intimately related. The current plan to unite Chinese and Japanese Buddhists hopes to establish a common purpose and single determination for disseminating the universal Buddhist Dharma to the entire world.[13]

At the conclusion of the conference, a ten-point constitution for the Federation was adopted. It called for continued efforts, through an office soon to be established, to engage Buddhist scholars from many countries in joint research projects, lectures, and discussions on the future of Buddhism. Furthermore, plans were drawn up for an East Asian Buddhist Conference (Dongya fojiao dahui) to be held in Tokyo the following year.[14] In April 1925, in accord with the adopted constitution, Taixu set up offices in the Guangji si in Beijing for a Chinese Buddhist Federation (Zhonghua fojiao lianhe hui), as the national chapter of the World Buddhist Federation. Through these offices, permission was eventually obtained from the Ministry of the Interior for official Chinese delegates to be sent to the forthcoming Tokyo gathering of the world organization. Taixu continued to ponder how to organize effectively both monastic and lay Buddhists in a single national association with local chapters.[15]

The East Asian Buddhist Conference convened in Tokyo, November 1–3, 1925, as planned the previous year.[16] The Chinese delegation of twenty, led by Daojie and Taixu, included Chisong, Hongsan, Wang Yiting, Hu Ruilin, and others.[17] Buddhist representatives also attended from Korea and Taiwan. The only non-Asian Buddhist in attendance was the Mahāyāna scholar Bruno Petzold. Taixu began his major address with an assessment of global tensions and divisions. Asserting that only the compassionate spirit of Buddhism could save the modern world from continuing warfare and strife, he observed that some people simplistically associated these evils with capitalism and imperialism, which they sought to resist. However, he claimed, these calamities were more profoundly related to the blatantly materialistic desires that provided the foundation for all contemporary technological and consumer societies. Only Buddhism, with its teachings of no-self, the ten basic precepts, and perfect enlightenment, can constitute an effective antidote to the spiritual poison of modern materialism, Taixu concluded.

Commenting on the significance of Taixu's participation in the conference, the Japanese editors of the international journal *The Eastern Buddhist* later quoted the Chinese reformer as declaring:

> The world today stands in urgent need for some means of salvation and I think only Buddhism can save the world, because various kinds of remedies have been tried and found wanting. Socialism has been proposed as a means to cure the evils of capitalism, and anarchism as an antidote to Imperialism. Thus far they have, however, failed to effect any cure of the social and international troubles from which the present world is suffering. In order to understand the reason for this failure, one must remember that these "isms" have been worked out by minds which have not been perfectly free from the three basic evils: Avarice, Hate, and Lust. These evils, if unchecked, will always manifest them-

selves in such crimes as robbery, murder, and adultery. Any remedy or means of cure for the present troubled world worked out by minds which are not yet perfectly free from such evils will tend only to increase the troubles instead of checking or preventing them.

To use the teachings of the ancient sages like Confucius or the precepts of the Prophets like Jesus Christ or Muhammad as a means of cure for the troubles of the present world is also inadequate, because the teachings of these ancient worthies have lost their hold on man's mind in the present materialistic world; for the religious beliefs of the Christians or Moslems have been shaken and the doctrines of these prophets about the Creator, the God, etc., have been disproved in the light of modern scientific discoveries. For the present skeptical world, only Buddhism with its teachings about the ten virtues as the starting point and Nirvāṇa and "Perfect Enlightenment" as the ultimate object can be an effective remedy for the evils of the present world.[18]

Taixu grounded his appeal for ecumenical cooperation in East Asia in a frank evaluation of the strengths and weaknesses of both Chinese and Japanese Buddhists. His principal argument was that each partner needed the other, and that what virtues Chinese Buddhists lacked might be prevalent among Japanese Buddhists, while certain virtues found wanting among Japanese Buddhists might be evident among the Chinese. Thus he declared that "as the Chinese and Japanese Buddhists now come in close touch with each other, they should learn each other's good points and work together for the propagation of the Buddhist religion."[19]

With regard to the major weaknesses of Chinese Buddhist monks, Taixu charged that historically they had had little interest in social service or educational ministries; that they had been so divided among different lineages and schools that they had failed to accomplish many important common goals; that they had generally been recluses without interest or involvement in community or national affairs; and that because they had not valued a modern, scientific education and an awareness of current events, they had not been able to contextualize their preaching to appeal to contemporary minds. Paradoxically, Taixu averred, the primary virtues of Chinese Buddhist monks represented the other side of the same coin. The community's most respected monks, he stated with appreciation, had always led lives of devotion and austerity, giving themselves to study and contemplation. Although the community had divided into different traditions, Chinese Buddhists at their best had maintained a tolerant and liberal perspective. Like the Buddha, they had displayed a universal outlook, viewing all persons as members of the same family. Finally, they had retained the principal features of primitive Buddhism, despite transformations since the religion's introduction into China.

With regard to the good points and shortcomings of the Buddhist monks in Japan, Korea, and Taiwan, Taixu asserted in a parallel fashion:

> Of their good points there are four: (1) They organize themselves into bodies, which by cooperation are capable of doing charity work or carrying out large scale education campaigns for the benefit of the public; (2) Japanese monks are better trained for the work of propagating the Buddhist religion; (3) they are patriotic and often render useful, though worldly, services to the country and the community; and (4) their minds being more susceptible to Western thoughts and ideals, they are capable of making the Buddhist teachings acceptable to the modern mind. Regarding their shortcomings: (1) they are less devout in their religious life and unable to undergo the austerities of a religious recluse, as can their brethren in China and Tibet; (2) they are more sectarian and have no unity among the different sects; (3) they are too patriotic and nationalistic to pay much attention to the Buddha's teachings of universal brotherhood; and (4) they learn too much of modern scientific studies as to tinge the Buddhist teachings they preach with a touch of Modernism.[20]

In conclusion, cognizant of heightening concerns throughout East Asia about Japanese expansionism—and perhaps aware that some in his own delegation remained suspicious of their hosts' motives—Taixu implored members of the Buddhist assembly not to permit nationalism to divide them or governments to co-opt their religious tradition and institutions for their own purposes.[21] Indeed, he called for new measures of ecumenical cooperation to explore together appropriate means for preaching the Dharma and increasing popular devotion and morality. He advocated the establishment of an international Buddhist university and also encouraged the organization of compassionate social services for the general public. These included programs for famine and disaster relief work, aid to the aged and disadvantaged, promotion of new industries, and construction and maintenance of roads, bridges, and utilities. If all these new programs could be established, Taixu asserted, the Buddhists' critically important global mission might be advanced throughout the world. The immediate task of Asian Buddhists, he argued, was to modernize their own tradition, to bring the "Supreme Light" to the present world of darkness, and "to propagate the Buddhist religion among the Europeans and Americans whose civilization has been responsible for bringing about a world in which sensual desires and animal passions were reigning supreme."[22]

Taixu considered the trip to Japan a successful one for the Chinese delegation. It also presented him with the opportunity to travel around the country for several weeks after the conference to meet with prominent Japanese scholars such as Nanjio Bunyiu, Takakusu Junjirō, and D. T. Suzuki. The editors of *The Eastern Buddhist* subsequently remarked, "The visit of Chinese Buddhists in such a number and under such a management never took place in the history of both countries, Japan and China, and this was surely a great event to be recorded in big red letters in the annals of Eastern Buddhism."[23] Taixu's leadership even prompted Mizuno Baigyō, who had worked closely with the Japanese Foreign Ministry in arranging the conference, to proclaim:

> For Taixu the Buddhists of Japan are new colleagues and good partners for future efforts to spread East Asian culture throughout the world. Let us hope that Buddhists of both countries will take Taixu as their central paradigm and mutually hold on to their strong points and rectify their shortcomings in order that we might look forward to the propagation of Buddhism in all the world.[24]

Declaring a third international Buddhist conference "a desideratum for world peace for humanity," a standing committee for future international conferences was appointed. Selected to represent China were Ma Jinxun, director-general of the China Buddhist Federation, Beijing, and Hu Ruilin, former governor of Fujian and the new director of the Chinese Buddhist Federation, Beijing. Appointed for Japan were Kubokawa Kyokiyo, director-general of the Japan Buddhist Federation, Tokyo, and Mizuno Baigyō, president of the *Shina Jiho* (China Times). A small committee for cooperation in promoting Buddhist social welfare work was also appointed, consisting of Wang Yiting, manager of the Chinese Chamber of Commerce, Shanghai, and Watanabe Kaikyoku, member of the Board of Directors of the journal *The Young East*.[25]

Then thirty-five years old, Taixu was pleased with the accomplishments that these events represented in relation to his goal of increased international Buddhist cooperation. At the same time, according to Xuming, he was well aware that his enthusiasm for Buddhist ecumenism was not shared by all and that a new strategy was needed for promoting his Buddhist reform movement. Accordingly, after 1925, while continuing to promote Buddhist ecumenism in preparation for a more unified global mission, the Chinese master thought it increasingly important to address directly intellectual and religious leaders in the West. Xuming states that this new approach was reflected in the reformer's assertion that "if we want to constitute a new society based on right faith in the Buddhist Dharma, we should spread Buddhism as an international culture. And the preliminary step we have to take is to change the thinking of western intellectuals."[26] What seemed a rather distant possibility for a Chinese Buddhist master who spoke no European languages became distinctly more real when, after the 1925 Tokyo conference, Dr. W. H. von Solf, a German scholar serving at the time as ambassador to Japan, invited Taixu to visit Germany—an invitation that, within a few years, the reformer was actually able to accept.

As significant as these mid-1920s international conferences were for Taixu's dream of an ecumenical Buddhist reform movement and a reenergized global mission, Welch's caution against an overly generous evaluation of the actual accomplishments of the World Buddhist Federation is well taken. As a viable organization, both the national and world federations functioned for only two years. A subsequent international conference, initially planned for Beijing, was never convened. Welch observes that, from the very beginning, the Federation was always greater on paper than in reality:

> Elected to the council of the World Buddhist Federation in 1924 was Reginald Johnston, who had once published a book about Chinese Buddhism, but was hardly a Buddhist himself. In fact, he had refused to attend the conference in 1923, as had Liang Qichao, who was also listed as a council member—an honor of which he was perhaps unaware at the time. It seems almost certain that three other council members (Dixian, Yinguang, and Ouyang Jingwu) had not authorized the use of their names, since they were not on good terms with Taixu.
>
> In brief, the World Buddhist Federation fell somewhat short of representing either Buddhism or the world. It was essentially a meeting between the Japanese and Taixu. Yet it was a significant step ahead in his career, for it showed that he had learned how to create organizations on paper and how to think on a global scale.[27]

THE "PORTABILITY" OF CHINESE BUDDHISM

In the years immediately following the 1925 Tokyo conference, Taixu became increasingly discouraged by the ongoing bloody civil war in China. In fact, the warfare temporarily forced both his Wuchang Buddhist Institute and the Right Faith Buddhist Society of Hankou to cease functioning in October 1926, when the Nationalist army took Wuhan.[28] Taixu was further disheartened by the aggressive, insensitive pursuit of economic and political interests in China both by Japan and by western nations. In reaction to foreign domination of Chinese interests, rising winds of Chinese nationalism swept the country in the mid-1920s. Growing popular resentment toward all forms of imperialism contributed to nationwide protests and occasional strikes, as in the May Thirtieth Incident of 1925, complicating cooperative ventures with the Japanese.[29]

Taixu was troubled, of course, by the failure of the World Buddhist Federation to maintain its promising ecumenical work. He was disappointed as well by the poor response to his efforts with the World Buddhist New Youth Society and its proposed World Propaganda Team (Shijie xuanchuan dui), neither of which was successful.[30] His cooperative work with Zhang Taiyan, Wang Yiting, and others to establish an All-Asia Buddhist Education Association (Quanya fohua jiaoyu she), later renamed with the less ambitious title of the Chinese Buddhist Education Association (Zhonghua fohua jiaoyu she), also came to nothing.[31] These ecumenical failures contributed to Taixu's conviction that he needed to direct some of his energies toward finding ways to engage western intellectuals directly in considering the religio-philosophical heritage of Mahāyāna Buddhism.

As noted earlier, to Taixu the West represented a form of human civilization that was simultaneously fascinating and open to severe criticism. He wanted very much to visit Europe and the United States, not only to experience firsthand the vitality and ethos of western technological societies, but also, through his presentations in the West, to counter preconceptions about Chinese Buddhism that were prevalent there. Prejudicial views of the religion, he argued, were the result of Christian triumphalism, oversimplifications, and simple misunderstandings. Their attitudinal and relational consequences were quite hurtful to Chinese Buddhists and harmful to chances for world peace. Indeed, Reichelt once observed that, when discussing such misconceptions, "the voice and burning eyes of Taixu were witness to a very real pain and grief."[32] Therefore, an important aim for the reformer became spreading the news throughout Europe and the United States about Chinese Buddhism's modern revival—and about the possibility of a new global Buddhist movement that could ultimately transform not only East Asia but the entire world.

In a remarkable 1927 interview with Clarence H. Hamilton, Taixu shared his dream of a modern Buddhist mission to the West. During the discussion, the monk asked Hamilton to state his own perspective on an issue that Lewis Lancaster has in recent years referred to as the "portability" of Chinese Buddhism.[33] Taixu had been contemplating the difficulties of cross-cultural mission and how to distinguish Chinese Buddhism's cultural "Chineseness" from its Buddhist essence. After describing Taixu's appearance—his full mustache and horn-rimmed spectacles, round cheeks and boyish countenance, medium height, robust build, and "dark, thoughtful eyes"—Hamilton recounts a quite interesting dialogue:

> "Do you think," he [Taixu] said, "that Buddhism will penetrate and spread in the West?"
>
> The question came as a surprise. I did not know that Taixu included the West in his purposes, though I had long known of the universal claims of Buddhism itself. But after all, it was natural, considering that he is an ardent propagandist as well as reformer. I essayed an answer.
>
> "If the truth that is in Buddhism," I said, "can be put in a form that the Western mind can understand it has a chance of spreading, as does all truth eventually." Then I thought of the images and elaborate ceremonies I had witnessed in the temples and added: "But I do not believe that the forms and rites of the religion as these have been developed in the Orient can ever be taken over by the West any more than it is likely that purely Western forms of Christianity will survive in the East."
>
> "Forms and ceremonies," the monk replied, "are but incidental. It is the truth that matters.". . .
>
> Then he told us that at the present time in Beijing National University where he had given a series of lectures there are seven or eight young men who are carefully studying Western knowledge and languages with the dominant purpose of fitting themselves to lecture on Buddhism before the people of the West. When I said in reply that Buddhism as a philosophy is already studied in Western university centers, that even as a religion it has some temples in California, and that Japanese monks have already been known to lecture there he replied eagerly, "Yes, that is well known to me. But Buddhism in California is for the Asian peoples residing there. Our purpose is not to spread the doctrine of the Buddha before those who already know it, but to carry it far and wide among the people of the West who yet are ignorant, particularly of the Northern Buddhism such as we have in China and Japan."
>
> "But you say," he went on, his thought still busy with his first question, "that the truth of Buddhism must be made comfortable to the

Western mind. Let me ask if you think that the Western mind is by nature favorable or unfavorable to Buddhist truth." . . .

"I do not think," I said to Taixu, "that the dominant values cherished by the Western mind are very favorable to Buddhism as I understand it. The West values striving, achievement, reformation in the concrete outer world of nature and human affairs. But Buddhism seems to me to exalt contemplation, meditation, the quest for inward peace and poise—a type of achievement indeed, but one which is subjective and mystic, which tends to still the restlessness of endeavor in the external world. That Buddhism could appeal to a majority in the West is most doubtful. There are those, however, in the West who find its dominant tendencies too much for them. Such find the thought of ceaseless striving a burden and long for peace and rest. Such are likely to have the mystic taste most sensitive to the values of Buddhism."

A graver look deepened on the thoughtful countenance of the monk when my words were interpreted to him, as though some oft-recurring but not very happy reflection were stirred. "But has not Western striving," he said, "resulted in a European War? It would seem to me that after such an experience a larger proportion of the Western people must feel the need for something like Buddhism. Surely after such a catastrophe they will the more willingly listen to us. Mere striving cannot be the final word."[34]

While Taixu considered these matters and contemplated how to present the Dharma to western intellectuals, he was able to arrange a meeting with Chiang Kai-shek in Nanjing on June 23, 1928, seeking his support for a national organization of Buddhist monks and laymen. Chiang had just returned from a confrontation with Japanese forces at Ji'nan in Shandong province as the Northern Expedition advanced on Beijing against the last remaining warlord, Zhang Zuolin (1873–1928). By the time of their meeting, the Nationalist forces had captured Beijing, and Zhang had been killed trying to escape. Chiang believed that he was finally in a position to consolidate his power, unite China, and progressively establish his country as a world power. The general, who would soon marry Soong Meiling in a Christian ceremony, and who became a Christian convert himself in

1930, listened attentively to Taixu's assertions that a modernized, reformed Buddhism had a major role to play in China and the world. The Mahāyāna Buddhist master stated:

> Buddhism is an expression of the highest ideals of the people of the world. In particular its devotion to saving the world has no equal among other forms of learning or religion. [Yet] it must adapt to the ideas of our time and to the contemporary life of our country. Then and only then can the religion be promoted without any obstacles. This time of beginning political tutelage is a time of reform. The best idea is to establish a single Buddhist organization able to unify both monastic and lay followers so that it may benefit the citizens' prosperity, the country's strength, the government's orderly rule, and common goodness.[35]

Chiang commended Taixu for his remarks and introduced him to other government officials, who at that point were not at all encouraging about a specifically "religious" association *(zongjiao hui)*. According to Yinshun, they suggested instead a more "timely" consideration of a Buddhist "study" organization *(foxue hui)*. As a result, on July 28, 1928, Taixu established the Chinese Buddhist Study Association (Zhongguo foxue hui), hoping that it might develop into a truly representative national body. Although this did not happen,[36] soon after his meeting with Chiang Kai-shek and other Guomindang officials, Taixu was able to use these contacts, as well as his ambassadorial invitation to visit Germany, to obtain official support for a major tour of Europe, the United States, and Japan. He departed in August 1928 and did not return until late April 1929.

A MISSION TO THE WEST

As Dongchu points out, the tour did give the reformer an opportunity to tell interested westerners about the Buddhist revival in China and to discuss his proposal for a World Buddhist University (Shijie fohua daxue), later renamed the World Buddhist Institute (Shijie foxue yuan), an idea that Taixu had first put forth in 1925. Similar proposals had been made by others about the same time, including

Bruno Petzold, who at the 1925 East Asian Buddhist Conference in Tokyo had also urged the creation of an "Institute of Mahāyāna Buddhism" designed "to investigate Mahāyāna Buddhism and explain it to the Western world."[37] Similarly, the German diplomat-scholar W. H. von Solf, acknowledging the need for westerners to learn more about eastern Buddhism and its potential contribution to human community, proposed "a comprehensive Mahāyāna institute in Tokyo or Kyoto."[38] The structure of Taixu's proposed educational institution was first outlined as shown in Table 2. Xuming notes that the idea was later refined, and the hoped-for institute restructured, as indicated in Table 3.

The editors of *Taixu dashi huanyou ji* (A Record of the Venerable Master Taixu's World Travel) have documented how Taixu was warmly greeted as an important dignitary by diplomats of the Chinese legations in Europe and the United States. He was photographed with government and civic leaders and provided with funds for donations to host organizations. On September 15, 1928, he was first welcomed to Paris, where he was to spend more than thirty days. On September 27 he addressed a group of scholars who had invited him to speak on the relationship of Buddhism to science, philosophy, and religion. He took the opportunity to begin his assault on the many misconceptions of Buddhism that he judged to be prevalent in the West. During his speech, Taixu remarked:

> Common people consider Buddhism to be concerned with a negative emptiness. However, this is really not so. Buddhism is concerned with developing our perspectives on human life until they become perfect. Thus, it concerns the never ending development and progress of our cosmological nature. Therefore, Buddhism is most complete, while the final result of the theories of all non-Buddhist schools will, on the contrary, come to nothing.
>
> If we are able to understand the truth concerning the whole universe—that there is neither birth nor death, beginning nor end—then we will recognize that if the Absolute is a divine spirit *(shen)*, then we are also divine spirits; if a god *(shangdi)*, then we are also gods; if a Buddha *(fo)*, then we are also buddhas.[39]

Table 2. The World Buddhist University

World Buddhist University
(Shijie fohua daxue)

Secular Studies		Religious Studies	
Western Studies	East Asian Studies	Doctrinal Studies	Ethical Studies
Science Department	Religious Studies Department	Nikāya Studies Department	Vinaya Studies Department
Philosophy Department	Political Science Department	Wisdom Studies Department	Meditation Studies Department
Arts and Literature Department	Arts and Literature Department	Yogācāra Studies Department	Mantrayāna Studies Department

Source: Dongchu, *Zhongguo fojiao jindai shi* (A History of Modern Chinese Buddhism), 1: 302.

Table 3. The World Buddhist Institute

World Buddhist Institute
(Shijie foxue yuan)

Religious research	Doctrinal research	Practical studies	Attainment studies
The collection and study of religious implements used in Buddhist practice in various countries	Nikāya Buddhist studies, based primarily on Indian and Southeast Asian sources	Vinaya studies, focusing on the bodhisattva precepts	Studies of faith
The editing and study of historical materials on Buddhism from various countries	Mahāyāna Buddhist studies, based primarily on Indian and Tibetan sources	Meditational studies, focusing on the Chan tradition	Studies of morality
The examination and editing of Buddhist texts from various countries	Chinese Buddhist studies, based on the synthetic schools of China and Japan	Esoteric studies, with extensive research into mantras	Studies of concentration (samādhi)
The preparation of Buddhist literature from various countries for publication	Studies of new European and American forms of Buddhism	Pure Land studies on various heavens and pure lands	Studies of wisdom

Source: Xuming, *Taixu dashi shengping shiji* (A Record of the Life of the Venerable Master Taixu), 26–27, and Manzhi and Mochan, eds., *Taixu dashi huanyou ji* (A Record of the Venerable Master Taixu's World Travel), 141–142.

During the final days of September and the early days of October, Taixu focused on his forthcoming lectures but also accepted several invitations to meet with diplomats, with local Buddhist leaders concerned with how better to organize themselves in France, and even with the Roman Catholic archbishop, who wanted to discuss the developing anti-religion movement in China and issues related to religious freedom. On October 14, he delivered an important lecture at the Musée Guimet, sponsored jointly by the Association Franco-Chinoise and Association Française des Amis de l'Orient, entitled "Le Bouddhisme dans l'histoire: Ses nouvelles tendances" (A History of Buddhism and Its New Movements; Ch. Foxue yuanliu ji qi xin yundong), at which he was introduced as "Son Eminence Taixu, Président de l'Union Bouddhiste Chinoise."[40]

On October 20, a meeting of interested friends was convened at the Musée Guimet for an initial conference about his ideas for a "World Buddhist Institute" (Shijie foxue yuan). According to Yinshun, Taixu donated 5,000 French francs at the time to support its consideration.[41] The subsequent public announcement of the "Projet d'Organization d'un Institut International Bouddhiste" highlighted the universal charity and moral discipline of Buddhism's nearly five hundred million adherents. It emphasized the historic and continuing role of the Buddhist community in Asia, as well as the new hope that surrounded Taixu's great efforts to spread the Dharma in the West.

Buddhism's foundational principles of wisdom and compassion, the announcement claimed, would help alleviate human suffering throughout the world and eliminate evils such as war, poverty, prostitution, and alcoholism. The bulletin also revealed that although a permanent site had not yet been selected for the headquarters of the new institute, which already had branches in Nanjing and Singapore, they would eventually be located in "une grande capitale, centre cosmopolite intellectuel et artistique."[42] Taixu had been successful in fostering some excitement and international competition for the site of the institution's headquarters. The provisional committee that was announced for Paris included some prominent scholars, such as Alfred Foucher, Marcel Granet, René Grousset, Louis Laloy, Sylvain Lévi,

Jean Przyluski, and Louis Renou, although questions were soon raised about the legitimacy of the list.[43] The Paris chapter of the World Buddhist Institute, which was to become "Les Amis du Bouddhisme," was subsequently established with Grace Constant Lounsbery (1877–1965) as its founding president.[44]

On October 22, Taixu delivered another major lecture, sponsored by the Société Théosophique de France, entitled "Exposé concis des principes du Bouddhisme Chinois." As with earlier presentations in France, Taixu's effectiveness was severely hampered by a translator apparently ill-prepared to deal with the master's thick Zhejiang dialect, frequent extemporaneous remarks, and Buddhist technical vocabulary.[45] Moreover, the Chinese reformer clearly underestimated the level of sophistication in Buddhist studies of the majority of those in his audiences. Most of his listeners were interested in a carefully crafted description of, and thoughtful reflection on, the practice of contemporary Chinese Buddhism. Taixu's principal aim was to present the essence of Mahāyāna to western audiences in their own religio-philosophical terms, highlighting the religion's compatibility with modern, scientific patterns of thought while downplaying its coincidental East Asian cultural garb. As a result, the perception of many in the audience was that Taixu was more concerned with impressing westerners with his knowledge of science and philosophy—which surely he was—than in discussing in detail, as they had hoped, the theoretical, cultic, and institutional dimensions of the revitalization of Buddhism in China.

Nevertheless, Taixu was able to offer a brief synopsis of his vision for a modern form of Buddhism that could effectively serve as the unifying ideology for a global civilization. Even in his October 14 Paris lecture at the Musée Guimet, with its rather elementary review of the history of Buddhism and its development in China—which would surely have bored an informed audience even if the translation into French had been felicitous—the Chinese reformer did speak briefly of his own efforts at Buddhist reform and mention his plans for a World Buddhist Institute. Emphasizing Buddhism's norms for social responsibility, he claimed that the ancient religion could become the foundation of a modern global culture by synthesizing the traditional eastern emphasis on developing human sentiments and the traditional western emphasis on developing human reason:

> I have devoted myself to the study of Buddhism for more than twenty years. After ten years of study and examination, I attained the marvelous enlightenment mind of the buddhas, which allowed me to understand thoroughly all of the schools of Mahāyāna and Nikāya Buddhism, as well as all of the theories of religion, philosophy, and science. From a universal and profound study of the realm of human ideas, I know the great usefulness of the whole of Buddhism, which used to be overshadowed by each separate people's prejudices and unique practices so that it would not be realized as a universal culture.
>
> However, now because of the trend of the world's uniform, mechanized culture and the developments in communication, we ought to be able to propagate clearly and distinctly a Buddhism which advances beyond all kinds of racial and tribal obstacles of a territorial era and is able to blend thoroughly every people's culture in both East and West so as to make Buddhism a guide for all human thought and action....
>
> Moreover, we may consider that now all the people of the world are living in a time of great interdependence, when all in the world are compatriots, born into one body, as nearly everyone already knows. So if you benefit another person, then you will have benefited both of you. If you harm another person, then you will have harmed both of you. If you use force to destroy the world's peace in striving for your own private victory, not only is this not benevolence *(ren)*, it is also the height of ignorance. Therefore, I wish to explicate the true Buddhist doctrines of no-ego and mutual becoming, so as to enlighten all the peoples of the world, and change their thoughts of competing with one another in order to struggle for survival into thoughts of helping one another in order to attain coexistence, co-prosperity, and peace. Consequently I have begun to expand a new Buddhist movement for the entire world.[46]

During his visit to England, which began on October 23, 1928, Taixu spoke with a number of scholars interested in East Asian culture and in aspects of the Buddhist tradition, such as the humanist philosopher Bertrand Russell, who had spent almost a year, in 1920–1921, in China. On November 4, Taixu delivered a lecture at the

London chapter of the Maha Bodhi Society entitled "The Relation of Nikāya to Mahāyāna Buddhism"; the next evening he regaled the Buddhist Lodge in London on "The Necessity of Cooperation in Buddhist Research." In a subsequent London address, he spoke of the need for the World Buddhist Institute to explore the importance of a scientific Buddhism *(kexue de foxue)* that is in accord with the advanced knowledge of modern science, an experientially verified Buddhism *(shizheng de foxue)* that actually demonstrates its truths, a human-centered Buddhism *(rensheng de foxue)* that is concerned with the progressive improvement of human life, and a global Buddhism *(shijie de foxue)* that is intent on becoming, through mission, the single visionary and ethical guide for all people.[47]

After a brief visit to Belgium, from November 6 through 15, Taixu traveled to several cities in Germany for a series of meetings and lectures. Not surprisingly, one of his concerns there was to speak out against extreme expressions of nationalism. He was alarmed by insensitive, belligerent forms of nationalism that could pull the world into another global war. Although he made no direct reference to the government or to the political situation in Germany at the time, which would have been offensive to some of his hosts, Taixu was surely aware of the timeliness of such a message in view of the growing Nazi movement in the country fueled by Adolf Hitler's *Mein Kämpf*, published just a few years earlier. In contradistinction to a divisive, fanatical nationalism, Taixu called for the type of nationalism that he claimed Sun Yat-sen had advocated—that is, a nationalism stressing equality, peace, and cooperation among all peoples of the earth. This one specific type of nationalism *(minzu zhuyi)*, he asserted, was essentially the same as internationalism *(shijie zhuyi)* and was a principal aim of the world Buddhist movement.[48] When discussing World War I with an official of Germany's Ministry for Foreign Affairs, Taixu also remarked:

> In the past, Europe's foundation has been religious faith, which has nurtured morality. However, because of the advancement of contemporary scientific knowledge, the religion in which Europe formerly had faith [i.e., Christianity] is now difficult to maintain. Therefore, from the per-

spective of a scientific intellect, Europe ought to attain the highest and most perfect Buddhist Dharma as the new faith of a modern Europe, so as to press forward in the cultivation of morality.[49]

Taixu's major address at the China Institute in Frankfurt, on December 14, 1928, was announced as "Die Historischen und Modernen Richtungen im Buddhismus" and later published as "Buddhistische Studien der Buddhismus in Geschichte und Gegenwart." It was virtually the same address as his October 14 lecture in Paris. After detailing Buddhism's development in three primary cultural centers even after its disappearance from India—namely, in Ceylon and Southeast Asia, in Tibet, and in China, Korea, and Japan—Taixu spoke of the exciting potential that existed for Buddhists to reach out in the modern era, as cultures converged, and transform the entire world. Once again, he outlined a "Buddhism for human life" *(rensheng fojiao),* emphasizing the importance of adopting the ten Buddhist precepts as the disciplinary foundation of a society concerned with achieving true happiness. He spoke of a "scientific Buddhism" that freely acknowledges the insights and gifts of modern science but is able to perfect scientific theories. Taixu also tried to explain what he meant by an "experientially verified Buddhism" (the term in the German text is "Der bewußte Buddhismus," or a "conscious Buddhism") that discerns the ultimate truth in the silent illumination of an expanded consciousness beyond spoken or written words. Finally, he emphasized a "global Buddhism" that would become the indispensable crucible in which the cultural tendencies of East and West, intuition and reason would fuse to form the religio-philosophical foundations of a universal civilization. "This is an outline of our new Buddhist movement," he concluded. "In order to realize these principles, we have developed a project for an institute for Buddhist research. If you see in this an appeal in harmony with your innermost consciousness, then come join with us!"[50]

Taixu was subsequently elected to the executive committee of the German Research Academy for Chinese Culture. The respected sinologist Richard Wilhelm, acknowledging the stature of those scholars listed on the provisional French committee for the World Buddhist Institute, wrote to his German colleagues to solicit participation on a committee there. Noting the significance of the Mahāyāna Buddhist tradition as a religious force past and present, Wilhelm stressed the fact that the international institute being founded by the Venerable Taixu was not "ein religioses Propaganda Institut" but "ein Institut wissenschaftlicher Forschung."[51] In a brief description of Taixu's efforts, soon published in the scholarly journal *Sinica*—which included a fine pen-drawn portrait of the Chinese reformer—Wilhelm praised Taixu for his reform-minded organizational skills, his global vision, his modern humanitarian emphasis on religious instruction, and his impressive knowledge of western philosophy and science, which "Buddhism could both promote and further enlighten."[52]

On January 30, 1929, Taixu left Germany and returned to Paris, where he participated in several meetings before departing for the United States just over a week later. When he arrived in New York on February 22, 1929, Taixu began a busy schedule of meetings with scholars and religious leaders. On March 5, he was a featured speaker, along with the Confucian scholar Chen Huanzhang, at an "East and West" luncheon in New York City.[53] *The New York Times* reported the following day that attending representatives of both oriental and western religio-philosophical traditions "pledged their support to the associations known as the Threefold Movement, the Union of East and West, the League of Neighbors, and the Fellowship of Faiths, in its program to promote world peace and racial, religious, and cultural unity."[54] The Chinese reformer was quoted as speaking of Buddhism as "the tolerant, receptive, universal faith which is essential to the realization of world unity, in itself a great union of broad-spirited people."[55] Taixu also lectured at Yale University, the Hartford Seminary Foundation, Northwestern University, the Berkeley School of Religion, and other places. As Welch indicates, he spoke in the impressive red robes and regalia of a Chinese Dharma master and was generally well received.[56] Taixu appealed to his audiences for help with his efforts, flattering the Americans as "pioneers in the movement for world peace":

> My ambition in life is to increase human fellowship, virtue, and intelligence, and to achieve universal peace and happiness. In order to realize this wish, it is necessary to effect an integration of civilization, both

ancient and modern, Oriental and Occidental, and to create a universal civilization for this progressive development of mankind. For this reason, I have been traveling in various parts of the world, endeavoring to study the civilizations of the various peoples, and to find the elements of unity.

The English, French, and German scholars with whom I have had the pleasure of conferring, all agree that Buddhism is a very essential foundation for the unification of the various civilizations. The tendency in the East to emphasize religious and ethical contemplation, and the tendency in the West to emphasize material achievement, are both one-sided. Buddhism, on the other hand, teaches the harmonious relationship between man and the universe. It removes the barriers between the different civilizations and will hasten the proper development of their peculiar virtues. It will promote mutual understanding of the different peoples and secure a universal peace.

Furthermore, mankind living amidst scientific discoveries and material development needs an ideal and faith to improve its felicity, virtue, and intelligence. The medieval conceptions of faith have come into contradiction with scientific thought and are no longer adequate. Buddhism, on the other hand, is entirely in accord with science and satisfies the need of the present generation.

But during its long history, Buddhism has become a complicated subject of study. An investigation into the doctrines of the various sects and the teachings in the different languages requires international cooperation of all who are interested.

Buddhist scholars in England, France, Germany, Belgium, Switzerland, Holland, Ceylon, Japan, and other places, as well as those in China, have already outlined a plan for the organization of an international Buddhist Institute and have already established a provisional bureau in Paris. The American people are the pioneers in the movement of world peace and will undoubtedly give their strong cooperation toward the early realization of these plans. The location of the projected institute may be in Europe, in America, or in China. The French friends have already offered a suitable location in Paris. I welcome opinions and suggestions regarding this contemplated project.[57]

When in Chicago, Taixu was pleased to receive word of an important meeting that had recently been held at the Buddhist Lodge in London. On March 1, 1929, in response to his earlier visit to England, representatives of various organizations (the Burma Society, the Japanese Students' Association, the Buddhist Lodge, etc.) had formed a "London Buddhist Joint Committee." The committee announced that its principal purpose was to represent in London the World Buddhist Institute founded by Taixu, although it would also be at liberty to represent in that city "any other Buddhist movement which may subsequently be formed."[58] Inspired by the ecumenical and missionary message of the Chinese reformer, the elected chairman of the Joint Committee, the noted jurist and Buddhist scholar Christmas Humphreys, outlined an entirely new and energetic program of cooperative activities in Great Britain and Ireland. A number of resolutions were passed calling for new measures of organization to propagate Buddhism among various immigrant communities, as well as to sponsor new lecture series and small group meetings to "arouse interest in the Buddhist movement among Londoners."[59]

Taixu, then thirty-nine years old, returned to China from the United States in late April 1929, arriving in Shanghai feeling rather optimistic about the future of his program of modernization and reform. He was encouraged by the response that he had received in the West to his plans for a World Buddhist Institute and to his call for greater cooperation among Buddhists around the globe, and obviously pleased that many had recognized him as a religious leader with both a vision for the modern reformation of Buddhism and a realistic plan for carrying it out. A. C. March, of the Buddhist Lodge of London, had concluded, for example, that "Taixu is a very practical man. He is no dreamer.... Now that China has definitely entered the work of establishing Buddhism throughout the world as a universal religion, we may expect great results to follow."[60]

Despite such estimations and expectations, Taixu's plans for an international center for Buddhist studies were never realized, however. Because of continuing rivalries within the Chinese sangha, lack of sufficient funding in difficult economic times both at home and abroad, and the chaos of the bitter Sino-Japanese War that marked the beginning of World War II in East Asia, the research institute for which Taixu had labored never materialized in China, France, Germany, or elsewhere. The Buddhist master did rename the library of his seminary in Wuchang "The Library of the World Buddhist Institute," and he and his disciples often referred to some of the seminaries that he controlled as special units of the envisioned international organization. Yet to Taixu's great disappointment, he was never able to capitalize on the promising foundations that he had begun to build.

BUDDHIST STRIFE AND A CHINESE WAR OF RESISTANCE

Before Taixu found another opportunity for international travel—ten years later, in 1939—two significant developments had further dimmed his initial optimism about modernizing the Buddhist community. First, Taixu lost his bid to shape the work of the Chinese Buddhist Association founded in Shanghai in April 1929, in response to renewed threats to the Buddhist establishment in China that had arisen while he was en route back from the United States. In addition to sporadic appropriations of Buddhist property in central China, there was Professor Tai Shuangqiu of National Central University's influential proposal, in May 1928, for a broad confiscation of Buddhist institutions and properties for educational purposes—an old idea that the Ministry of the Interior was more than happy to reconsider as the Guomindang improved its political and military position. Dongchu notes that the Buddhist response was organized primarily under the leadership of Yuanying, the disciple of Eight Fingers with whom Taixu had been friends since 1906:

> Convened in 1928 in Nanjing was a National Conference on Education (Quanguo jiaoyu huiyi), which proposed the transformation of monasteries and temples everywhere into schools, and the use of all the monasteries' properties as an endowment. Because of this, Yuanying began to organize the Jiangsu-Zhejiang Buddhist Federation (Jiang Zhe fojiao

lianhe hui), of which he was elected president, and on behalf of which he put forward petitions to the capital. Eventually, he was successful.[61]

Although Professor Tai's sweeping proposal was not adopted, in part perhaps because of Yuanying's efforts, the government did soon effect, in January 1929, the "Regulations for the Control of Monasteries and Temples" (Simiao guanli tiaoli). According to Yinshun, in response to the government's action, on April 12, 1929 the Jiangsu-Zhejiang Buddhist Federation convened representatives from seventeen provinces in Shanghai for a National Conference of Buddhist Representatives (Quanguo fojiao daibiao huiyi). The result was the establishment of the Chinese Buddhist Association (Zhongguo fojiao hui).[62] Yuanying was elected president. Taixu was elected to the standing committee of the association after his return to China later that month. Yet although earlier in his career the reformer had formed a special bond with Yuanying for jointly revitalizing Chinese Buddhism, he was never able to work cooperatively with his older and more conservative colleague. Dongchu claims that two of the reasons for this were Yuanying's inability to accept change and his ambiguous and vacillating posture on Buddhist modernization. "Strictly speaking," Dongchu asserts, "the primary reason why Yuanying and Taixu could not cooperate resulted from the fact that sometimes Yuanying displayed a sympathetic attitude with regard to Buddhist reform and sometimes an antagonistic one."[63]

According to the government's revised legislation, passed in December 1929, "Regulations for the Supervision of Monasteries and Temples" (Jiandu simiao tiaoli), the authority of the Chinese Buddhist Association, along with its local affiliated associations, was newly recognized to address questions of property ownership and financial accountability. Nevertheless, Taixu was not pleased with the overall direction of the national organization. Finally resigning from the standing committee, Taixu directly attacked the association's record when its third national conference convened on April 10, 1931:

> Now that the [immediate problem] of confiscating monastery property to support educational ventures has been defused, if one brings up again the idea of reorganizing the sangha and its monasteries in order to estab-

lish new educational ventures, etc., one is considered to be making a nuisance of oneself.... What is called the general office of the Chinese Buddhist Association has on its staff not a single monk or Buddhist layman of correct faith. If this is so, how can it constitute the most important organization of Buddhists in the whole country, and how will it be able to gain the trust of all of our country's Buddhists and to promote Buddhist interests? Now, I would say if the Chinese Buddhist Association wishes to continue: (1) it must carefully select talented and moral monks and Buddhist laymen of right faith for its standing committee and its office staff. Twice each month, it should report the association's business for review by the general administrative committee and each provincial Buddhist association, so that its affairs are based on open examination; (2) at the very least, it ought to collect normal dues of $30,000, so that besides the standing committee and the office staff having stable operating funds, it can also produce not less than 10,000 copies of the association's newsletter and also provide for the urgently needed "All-China Training Class for Monastic Staff Concerning the Business Affairs of all Buddhist Associations."... If we cannot rise to meet the challenge, we ought simply to close up the Chinese Buddhist Association. I wish that we could first become determined about these things, then afterwards hold another election of officers.[64]

When new elections were held for the executive committee of the association, the forty-one-year-old Taixu and his more reformist-minded colleagues—Renshan, Wang Yiting, and Xie Zhuchen—dominated the committee. In light of this development, Yuanying and the more conservative leaders promptly resigned. Taixu and his group immediately chose to move the offices of the association from Shanghai to more friendly territory, the Pilu si in Nanjing. From there, during the months of late spring, the reformer carried on a busy schedule of lectures, including one before the Young Men's Christian Association. However, with the resignations, charges that the April elections were invalid, and, most importantly, a movement by uncooperative conservative leaders and their constituencies to withhold financial support, the executive committee was finally forced to acknowledge that it had no way to proceed.[65] Conceding the hopelessness of the circumstances, Taixu resigned on June 3, 1931, with a bitter denunciation of those who sought to defend the status quo against any serious attempt to reform or modernize the practice of Chinese Buddhism. As he remarked, "There is no call for me to waste any more of my energy on the Chinese Buddhist Association."[66]

When the standing committee met on June 14 to consider these developments, it was Taixu's lay disciple Wang Yiting who tried to mediate the impasse. Wang recommended, first, that those conservative leaders who had resigned be reappointed and politely asked to serve once again. Second, he suggested that the official headquarters be moved back to Shanghai, to be managed by Yuanying with the personal assistance of Wang himself. Taixu would be asked to manage the branch office in Nanjing, with the help of Xie Zhuchen. As Yinshun observes, with the ultimate acceptance of these surprising proposals, "Taixu's efforts with the Chinese Buddhist Association were completely negated. . . . [Moreover,] because Yuanying opposed any Buddhist reform, the relationship between Taixu and Yuanying could never thereafter be restored."[67] Disappointed, Taixu turned his attention in other directions, hoping that, in time, his reformist agenda would receive broader support within the Chinese sangha.

Although politically defeated in his efforts with the Chinese Buddhist Association and frustrated by conservative Buddhist masters who criticized him, Taixu continued his multifaceted work with his own enthusiastic disciples, encouraging evangelistic preaching, teaching, and social service ministries. In a report published in the *China Christian Yearbook, 1932–1933*, Reichelt described only one of a number of what he termed "Buddhist revival meetings" that had been organized by the reformer and his students during the previous year. Providing readers with a sense of how these events were staged, and some idea of their effectiveness, Reichelt wrote:

> I will give my impression of one of the Buddhist revivals as held during the last year. I select the Wuhan centre, more specially the city of Hankou. Taixu spent several weeks there in the summer of 1932. He was accompanied by some of his best disciples, and as he had sent in advance from the Wuhan centre some of his strongest and best followers, the field was well prepared.

The lectures and group meetings were mostly held in the Buddhist Layman's Association Building (Fojiao hui) and the daily attendance was very good: 500–700 every day. The lectures were usually held in the afternoon. It was a remarkable sight to see the type of people who came. The majority were men, from various walks of life, but mostly from the upper classes, merchants, lawyers, doctors and government officials. An astonishing large percent of students and young, well educated people filled the hall. The rooms were prepared and the external arrangements and images were simple. It was pointed out to me that the new Buddhism in China does away with many of the meaningless images.

After a short and impressive act of worship, Taixu ascended the platform and sitting cross-legged on the seat of honour gave his well-thought out address. He spoke apparently with little emotion, but eloquently and logically. With an undercurrent of fervor he brought his ideas home with striking power to the attentively listening audience. After every meeting a new group of inquirers was received into the brotherhood. This solemn act took place upstairs in a specially prepared room. All of the inquirers paid homage to the great master who sat there motionless and received on behalf of the "Sangha" (the communion of saints) an almost divine adoration.

It was a strange sight to see people from the upper classes, many of whom were moulded in the new and democratic ideas of the new China, prostrating themselves and taking refuge in Buddha, Dharma, and Sangha. Most of them were apparently in dead earnest. They came undoubtedly from genuine religious motives. . . .

Already there were several thousands of Taixu's followers in Wuhan. But never before had they had an experience like this. With a haughty air and smiling faces did Taixu's young helpers inform me that the number of lay disciples in Wuhan had increased to 30,000. And they added: "Among them are sixteen doctors, doctors partly educated abroad, and they have promised to conduct a dispensary for the poor, free of charge —because now they have entered the path."

Most interesting were also the evening meetings held in the ground floor hall with the gilded image of Amitābha in the background, flooded with splendour from a multitude of electric bulbs. There was singing of Buddhist songs, playing of the organ, testimonies, etc. In brief, all that they had seen of the external technique of a Christian street-chapel meeting in a big city was utilized.⁶⁸

In addition to Taixu's loss of status and position within the Chinese Buddhist Association, a second major development further dimmed his optimism about his modernization and mission movement within the larger Buddhist community. The devastation and civil disruption wrought by the Japanese invasion of China in 1937, and the desperate war of resistance until 1945, quickly changed the national and international context for religious reforms. Japan had progressively pressured China from its base in Manchuria, where in 1932 it formally established the puppet state of Manchukuo (Manzhouguo), with the last Qing emperor, Puyi, enthroned as emperor. Chiang Kai-shek sought temporarily to avoid a direct confrontation with Japan, while engaged in a bitter struggle for power with the Communists under Mao Zedong, even though Japan continued its efforts to destabilize north China. Finally, however, Japan acted decisively in an assault designed to bring China under Japanese control within three months, providing an additional support base for its expected confrontation with Russia. As Fairbank has noted, "Japan's full-scale aggression in 1937, first near Beijing on July 7, then at Shanghai in August, really opened World War II, which in China lasted a full eight years, longer than the war in Europe."⁶⁹

As soon as the hostilities began, according to W. Y. Chen, "the Chinese Buddhist Association sent an open letter to Japanese Buddhists, appealing for concerted action to stop the Japanese militarists' drive in north China and expressing the hope that they would 'roar like a lion' *(zuo shizi hou),* or 'raise a thundering voice' *(chu dalei yin)* to wake up the Japanese militarists from their continental dream."⁷⁰ Taixu immediately cabled the Japanese Buddhist Association from Lu Shan in Jiangxi province, requesting their assistance in persuading the Japanese government to find a peaceful resolution.⁷¹ Just that spring, in March, alert to the building tensions, the Chinese master had worked with the Japanese Buddhists of the Higashi Honganji temple in Shanghai in the consideration of his plans for an "International Buddhist Peace Society" (Fojiaotu guoji heping hui), plans that these events obviously dashed.[72] Now, not mincing words, he pleaded in the cable with the leaders of the Japanese association:

> All in the whole world who are born from the Buddha's mouth and are bodhisattvas born of the Dharmakāya have one body and mind and certainly cannot be divided by race or nationality. Yet the authorities of your country at this time, giving expression to their unenlightened greed, have ordered your military to forcibly take north China, to engage in acts of provocation in its ports, thus becoming criminals who destroy the peace of East Asia and the world. They have not only damaged the security of Japanese citizens residing in China, they have also repeatedly massacred Chinese military personnel and civilians who were not resisting. They have engaged in killing, stealing, and raping without principle. There is not a crime of which they are not guilty. As a result, all in China and the world look upon your country with animosity as an extreme example of ignorance and inhumanity!... Representing China's three hundred million Buddhists, I ask your association, leaders of Japan's thirty million Buddhists, with your great compassion and wisdom, quickly to stop the unenlightened greedy anger of your government's authorities, so that the military may be withdrawn and returned to Japan, China apologized to, the demonic war's prosecution ceased, and Buddhism's compassion clearly made manifest. I hope your association can do all that it can about this![73]

Taixu also sent a message to the Chinese Buddhist community, offering counsel as to their responsibilities in the crisis:

> Now that our country, East Asia, and perhaps the entire world is on the brink of a great struggle, all of us, based on Buddhist mercy and compassion, must: (1) earnestly and steadfastly maintain the Buddhist Dharma, so as to pray that the invading country may stop its cruelties and the people's peace may be protected; (2) under the government's unified leadership, prepare courageously to protect the country; and (3) practice rear guard work, like providing first aid to wounded soldiers, taking care of refugees, burying the dead, teaching people how to get into air-raid shelters, immunize themselves against epidemics, and do other commonsense things in a time of war. Everyone as he or she chooses must work earnestly at what is needed![74]

In the fall of 1937, Chiang Kai-shek moved his government's offices from Nanjing far to the west, to Chongqing, Sichuan, as Japanese troops outflanked the Chinese forces attempting to defend Shanghai. The Japanese proceeded rapidly inland to occupy the capital, Nanjing, in mid-December, brutally massacring thousands of civilians in the infamous "Rape of Nanjing." In response to Taixu's call for the Chinese Buddhist community to prepare for service, the Right Faith Buddhist Society of Hankou (Hankou fojiao zhengxin hui), which Taixu served as Guiding Master, organized a first-aid corps *(jiuhu jun)*. In fact, Chou Hsiang-kuang reports:

> After the fall of Nanjing, Taixu was supervising the organization of Buddhist first-aid corps by members of the Right Faith Association of Hankou and also instructed the students of the Sino-Tibetan Buddhist College of Chongqing to receive first-aid training to go to the front. Such Buddhist organizations for first-aid work won national recognition for the famous Golden Swastika first-aid corps.[75]

Other Buddhist groups took up similar preparations, in large part, according to W. Y. Chen, because of a government order "that military training be required of Buddhist monks":

> To the National Government a petition was presented in 1936 requesting that they [Buddhist monks] be trained in relief work rather than in taking up arms, as it is against the Buddhist Commandments to injure life. This petition was accepted, and Buddhist monks have been trained in first aid and other relief work in many places. In August 1937, the Chinese Buddhist Association wired to fourteen cities near Shanghai, where training in relief work had been going on, asking that from five to ten of their best trained men from each place be sent to Shanghai for concentrated training. When the war broke out in Shanghai, these men, working closely with the World Red Swastika Association (Shijie hongwanzi hui), went to the front, and through thick and thin have carried on relief work which is worthy of all praise.[76]

The Japanese continued their conquest of the country as the Chinese fought valiantly while withdrawing farther into the interior. Wuhan, which had become Chiang Kai-shek's military headquarters, was finally occupied after a prolonged battle in December 1938, two months after Guangzhou had fallen. As Immanuel Hsü notes, international sanctions against Japan were not immediately forthcoming, both because of the United States's stubborn insistence on neutrality and because of the European countries' own concerns about imminent threats from Nazism and Fascism. Nevertheless, he comments:

> In spite of everything, the Japanese could not quickly win the war. Tokyo finally resigned itself to a stalemate; it adopted the policy of living off the conquered land with the help of puppet governments. On October 1937, a Mongolian Autonomous Government was created in Chahar and Suiyuan, with Inner Mongolian Prince De [De Wang, or Demchukdonggrub, b. 1902] as the figurehead ruler. On December 14, another puppet "provisional government" was established in Beijing, with Wang Kemin as the front man; it governed the five northern provinces of Hebei, Chahar, Suiyuan, Henan, and Shandong. On March 28, 1938, a third puppet government was set up at Nanjing under the formal leadership of Liang Hongzhi, with jurisdiction over the three eastern provinces of Jiangsu, Zhejiang, and Anhui. But none of the three leaders had the national stature necessary to achieve unification.[77]

Although Chiang Kai-shek vowed to continue the desperate war of resistance, at this point much of the Chinese populace and many Guomindang leaders expressed despair and a sense of hopelessness in their national suffering. Taixu was disheartened both by the dire circumstances of the nation as well as by the increasingly dim prospects of any significant change within the Buddhist sangha. Soon after the fall of Nanjing, he wrote a brief essay entitled "Wo de fojiao geming shibai shi" (The History of My Failed Buddhist Revolution), confessing his disappointments both in himself and in the conservative leaders who opposed his reformist goals:

> My failures doubtlessly have resulted from the considerable strength of my opponents and from my own weaknesses. For the most part, my ideas were sufficiently good, but my efforts to put them into practice were not. Even though I could instruct others, when it came to actually leading others, I was unable, so I ran into the situation of putting things in motion but not being able to maintain leadership of them. Still in the

end, though, I have confidence that my theories and my instructions were good. If we had persons who could adequately put things into practice and lead others, then certainly we could establish the Buddhist principles and systems adapted to a modern China.

My past failures and weaknesses came from my own many personal characteristics and from many unique circumstances that I encountered. For example, in the first period [of my efforts,] it was by chance that I ignited the fervor of the Buddhist reformation, and in the second period, it was unexpectedly that I initiated the now common practice of lecturing and starting schools. In the third period, it was unexpectedly that I organized the leadership of the Chinese Buddhist Association. By and large, these things happened by chance. They did not result from extensive planning, consideration, and strenuous effort. Therefore, because frequently these things resulted from my attitude of responding to situations according to the circumstances, it was easy to become disorganized and difficult to remain firm and resolute.

Although I am doing my best with regard to my goals and activities, given my premature decline in body and mind, I can only, according to each situation, try to eliminate my karma; I cannot make any new contributions. The following generations should know my weak points and their causes and correct themselves and do their best. Having had high expectations of me, they should not judge me too harshly. Then perhaps my Buddhist theories and instructions will not lose their usefulness as those who come after me take my failures as the mother of their successes.[78]

A MISSION TO SOUTH ASIA

During the war years, Taixu was fortunate enough to be able to arrange travel abroad one more time. In 1939, in consultation with government officials in Chongqing, he organized a Chinese Buddhist Goodwill Mission (Fojiao fangwen tuan) to South Asia. The Chinese Buddhist master departed in November of that year, via the new Yunnan-Burma highway, and did not return until May 1940. Members of his entourage included Cihang, Weifang, Weihuan, and other monks who had studied Buddhism in countries of Southeast Asia. Also included in the mission were two lay members who served as interpreters: Professor Tan Yunshan, director of the China College in Rabindaranath Tagore's International University, and Professor Chen Dingmo from Guangdong.[79]

In Burma, Ceylon, India, and Malaya, Taixu was warmly and enthusiastically received almost everywhere. At his first major stop, in Rangoon, on December 6, 1939, more than two thousand monks and ten thousand laypeople met him at the train station.[80] Taixu's primary personal agenda was "to worship at Buddhist holy places, to visit with Buddhist leaders in each locale, to help foster the feelings of being joined together in one faith, and to preach transformation through the Buddha's Dharma."[81] Yet Chiang Kai-sheks's government had pledged financial backing for the goodwill mission to South Asia specifically so that Taixu could seek political support for China in its costly war of resistance against the Japanese. Aware that the Japanese had been using Buddhism for propaganda purposes in Southeast Asia for years, Guomindang leaders thought that perhaps the well-known reformist monk could effectively promote its cause in countries with significant Buddhist populations.[82] Therefore, according to Yinshun, during these visits Taixu was supposed to proclaim "that because of the struggle of the Chinese for an independent existence and for fairness and justice, all Buddhists were unanimously in harmony with them in working for it."[83]

How seriously Taixu took this "official" task on behalf of the Republican government has been questioned by a Ceylonese informant interviewed by Welch who did not recall, in the midst of Taixu's widely attended presentations in the country, any attempt to garner support against Japanese aggression.[84] Based on Yinshun's brief account of the trip, it would appear that, in his addresses, Taixu often referred to the perilous situation in the contemporary world, to China's war of resistance, and to rumors of an expanding global war —but without expressly condemning Japan. In India, Taixu seemed once again to blame the world's problems primarily on the nature of western culture, which he described as an aggressive materialistic culture that was infecting and destroying China and India, the two other great cultural spheres in the world.[85] An emphasis on morality, established on the foundation of the Buddhist "cosmological viewpoint," was the only effective antidote to this destructive infection, he maintained.

Taixu's approach to the foreign mission trip was based on his recognition that better Chinese relations with citizens of the countries of South and Southeast Asia was desirable both for a global Buddhist mission and for Chinese national sovereignty. Thus, in his conversations in the region, he emphasized the history of affable intercultural and international relations between China and the countries that he visited. In addition, he highlighted the beneficial relations that existed at the time between the Chinese Buddhist community and the Nationalist government in China, even when that meant stretching the truth for political reasons. Although Taixu was not the outspoken anti-Japanese propagandist that the Guomindang hoped for, his role as an official representative of the Chinese government was obvious. The editors of the journal *China at War*, for example, record in their account of his trip that "at many places, he was addressed as 'His Holiness Taixu, Buddhist Archbishop of the Chinese National Government.'"[86] They also note:

> In India, Abbot Taixu presented a silver pagoda to the historic Mahabodhi temple at Bodhgaya, on behalf of Generalissimo Chiang Kai-shek, as a token of China's deep appreciation of Indian civilization and culture. He told those who welcomed him that though he was in India he did not feel that he was in a foreign country. He realized that although centuries intervened, the spirit with which India in the past received Chinese pilgrims was still there.
>
> In China, Abbot Taixu said on one occasion, Buddhism had its ups and downs but the National Government was making a supreme effort to rehabilitate Buddhism by reforming the monasteries and priests. He also hoped that it would be possible in the future to cultivate the age-old friendly relationship between the two countries more closely. . . .
>
> The day he stepped on Ceylon soil, the Chinese Buddhist leader said: "China and Ceylon have had contact with each other not only in recent times but also for a long period stretching back into the past. The Buddhism that was taken to China was not only from India through the Sanskrit language but also from Ceylon through the Pali language."

To Ceylon Buddhists, Abbot Taixu, also on behalf of Generalissimo Chiang Kai-shek, presented a pagoda-shaped casket as a token of goodwill of the Chinese people toward the Buddhists in Ceylon.

The mission also had a successful trip to the Malay states.[87]

In Taixu's first address upon returning to China in May 1940, delivered at Yunnan University (Yunnan daxue), the first thing he noted was the high respect that his hosts had for the valiant Chinese defense of their country against the ruthless aggression of the Japanese. He remarked that although the leaders of Japan had said publicly that their military could defeat China in three to six months, people in the countries he had visited "knew that not in six months, not in a year, or a year and a half, not even in fifty years would our enemies be able to destroy China. On the contrary," he asserted, "Japan will probably soon destroy itself. While in former days those countries sympathized with, believed, and sided with Japan, now," he concluded, "all of them have turned and believe and side with us."[88]

Whether or not Taixu fully satisfied the Chinese government's expectations, he did apparently accomplish many of his own personal goals in Buddhist ecumenical dialogue. The Chan master favorably impressed many monks and laypeople in his host countries by his vegetarianism and careful observance of Theravāda disciplines. Moreover, he was well received by the many Buddhist leaders with whom he met to discuss strategies for the realization of religious cooperation and unity. This was particularly true in the case of the great Buddhist scholar of Ceylon, G. P. Malalasekera, with whom Taixu visited at length in late February and early March. The two leaders discussed possibilities both for a Chinese-Ceylonese Culture Association (Zhong Xi wenhua xiehui) and for a World Buddhist Federation (Shijie fojiao lianhe hui), since the federation that Taixu had helped to establish in 1923 had long since ceased to function.

When Malalasekera expressed his opinion that a cultural exchange association was the most practical idea for the time being, Taixu responded that he would first have to report to the Chinese government.[89] Nothing further developed. Yet as Xuming indicates, in 1950, three years after Taixu's death, when Malalasekera founded the World

Fellowship of Buddhists (Shijie fojiaotu youyi hui), he specifically credited the Chinese reformer, remarking, "Having been inspired by Taixu's world Buddhist movement, I initiated it."[90] Comments Welch, "Thus the ecumenical impulse that had originated with Dharmapala in 1893 and had been transmitted from Yang Wenhui to Taixu to Dr. Malalasekera, returned to reach its fulfillment in Ceylon a half a century after it began there."[91]

INTERRELIGIOUS COOPERATION AND BUDDHIST REORGANIZATION

During the last seven years of his life, Taixu continued to encourage both national and international Buddhist cooperation and organization, and to promote education and programs of social welfare. In his autobiography, John Blofeld recalled his interesting visit with the reformer in Chongqing, where Taixu based most of his activities during the war years:

> In war-scarred Chongqing, grey and battered city built upon a thousand flights of muddy steps at the confluence of two rivers, where a cloudy sky is so common that "the dogs bark at the sun," and where Japanese planes rained death once each day for months on end, both duty and inclination led me to the war-lapped islands of peace which still survived in that ravaged land. My duty lay in cultivating the acquaintance of Chinese intellectual leaders, in visiting widely scattered universities which had taken refuge far inland, and in arranging for limited help to be given in the form of teachers of English, books and laboratory equipment, and of fellowships and scholarships for Chinese scholars going to Britain. Among the scholars with whom my work brought me in contact was the Venerable Taixu, sometimes called by Westerners "the Chinese Buddhist Pope," on account of his efforts to unite the various temples and laymen's organizations into a single body powerful enough to defend itself against government depredations. The National and Provincial Governments, composed largely of officials who had been nurtured on the anti-religious propaganda forming part of the school

curriculum during the time of the Guomindang Government, were constantly requisitioning temple lands and monastery buildings for other purposes, and sometimes so that individual officials could get further revenues into their own hands. Temples and monasteries had been powerless to resist, as there was no "Church" organization, each of the larger temples and each of the laymen's associations being self-governing communities....

Taixu's dream was to have a well-knit organization like that of the Tibetan or Catholic Churches not, as his enemies averred, in order to throw the weight of religion into the political game, but both as a measure of self-defense and in order to have some means of bringing all temples and all monks up to the high standard already achieved by the best of them. I never came to know him intimately, partly because his Zhejiang dialect was so thick.... In appearance, he was a short, tubby man who shaved his head in the orthodox style but wore a long, drooping "Mandarin" mustache. His eyes were kind and his face mirrored essential goodness of heart, without suggesting either saint or sage. He was, I think, a born administrator of the sort that every organized religion requires to look after those material aspects of its welfare with which contemplatives and recluses cannot be bothered, and for which they seldom have the right capacity.

Once, while we were sitting upon the terrace of a bombed temple in the heart of the city, ... Taixu told me of his plans for establishing modern schools in all the larger monasteries, both for the improvement of Buddhist scholarship and to teach the novices something of modern science, English and other "lay" subjects.

"There is a lot of opposition to my scheme even from among Buddhists," he observed. "People are so prejudiced against innovations. They do not see that, if Buddhism is to hold its own in a modern world, it must be modernized. If not, the Government will do to us what your Henry VIII did to the Catholic missionaries in England."

My surprise at this display of unmonkish erudition caused him to smile gleefully. Then he added, speaking through an interpreter who understood his peculiar dialect and could render it into Mandarin: "The authorities are good to the Christian missionaries. Why? Because China owes them its first modern universities and countless schools at every level from kindergarten to college. Why should we Buddhists continue to lag behind?"[92]

In January 1941, Taixu proposed the establishment of a Committee for the Reorganization of Chinese Buddhism (Zhongguo fojiao zhengli weiyuan hui), probably hoping that his patriotic efforts on behalf of the Nationalist government might contribute to its prompt approval of the plan. Offices were prepared at the Ciyun si on Lion Mountain (Shizi Shan) near Nan'an. Yet according to Yinshun, the Ministry of the Interior (Neizheng bu) refused to cooperate in the matter with the Ministry of Social Affairs (Shehui bu), so the proposal could not be immediately approved and the plan realized.[93] Welch suggests that the primary reason for the refusal was the Ministry of the Interior's desire "to continue taking over monastic property unchallenged," a desire on which a compromise could be reached only after the conclusion of the war.[94] For Taixu, now in his early fifties, reorganization would have to wait.

Taixu's ecumenical concerns, however, were increasingly being extended to interreligious cooperation and dialogue. In January 1943, he participated in the founding of the Association of Chinese Religious Believers (Zhongguo zongjiaotu lianyi hui).[95] Its executive directors were a remarkable group of leaders who included, in addition to the Buddhist master Taixu, the Roman Catholic Bishop of Nanjing Paul Yu Bin (1901–1978), the Protestant Methodist Bishop Chen Wenyuan, the "Muslim General" Bai Chongxi (1893–1966), and the "Christian General" Feng Yuxiang (1882–1948).[96] According to the *China Handbook, 1937–1945,* the interreligious association, which in 1945 had a membership of three hundred, was organized "to advance freedom of religion with special emphasis on spiritual enrichment and social service. [Its] principal activity is to pool together efforts of people embracing various religious faiths for the furtherance of the cause of peace among all nations."[97]

All those associated with the organization's founding had close ties to the Guomindang, and it may have been political interests more than religious sensibilities that actually drew the group together. A few informants in Taiwan have suggested that the "interreligious association" was actually a *bai shoutao* (literally, a "white glove"), meaning that rather than representing a real grassroots organization, it was made up of a select group of religious leaders with connections to the Guomindang who were called together when special needs arose. In fact, not all members of the group were recognized for their exemplary religious tolerance and their interest in interreligious dialogue and cooperation. During the Northern Expedition of the late 1920s, for example, the Muslim General Bai Chongxi was reported to have led his troops in destroying virtually all the Buddhist monasteries in Guangxi province and expelling the monks. The Christian General Feng Yuxiang, who was known for the strict moralistic elements of his military discipline, encouraged similar anti-Buddhist actions in several northern provinces. Welch states that "a resident of Henan in 1931–32 recalls that Feng's troops went about Buddhist temples breaking the heads off stone and bronze images and using wooden ones for fire wood (a policy suggested to him by his Christian advisers)."[98]

Nevertheless, as Joseph Kitagawa notes, the organization continued to function after moving its operations to Taiwan in 1949.[99] It was still in existence in 1988, when it commemorated the death ten years earlier of its last charter member, Paul Yu Bin, who in Taiwan reestablished Fu Jen (Furen) Catholic University, formerly of Beijing, and was made a cardinal. According to Howard Boorman, Yu Bin had once served as a member of the National Assembly and was a member of the ruling party, although Kang Junbi, a staff representative of the interreligious organization, specifically claims that he "was not a member of the Guomindang."[100]

One of the last major efforts undertaken by the organization during Yu Bin's lifetime was a goodwill tour of the United States in the fall of 1977. Concerned that President Jimmy Carter might endanger Taiwan by altering U.S. foreign policy and recognizing the People's Republic of China—which, of course, he did the following year—Cardinal Yu Bin, Presbyterian minister and President of the Taiwan Council of Churches Chen Xizun (C. C. Chen), Executive Director of the Chinese Muslim Association Haji Ahmed S.T. Xie, and Executive Director of the Chinese Buddhist Association the Venerable Wuming, among others, called on Americans to join them in "speaking out for the liberty of belief for all people of the world," something they feared they would lose if Taiwan fell into the hands of the Communists.[101]

Whatever forces and interests led to the organization's establishment in 1943, Taixu believed in its announced purposes and sought to use its forum to advance his own dialogical agenda. In May 1945, upon attending a celebration commemorating the second anniversary of the interreligious association, Taixu wrote, for example:

> With regard to the inability of the human spirit to manage material things, that certainly comes from the fact that the human spirit is not healthy enough. That is to say that religious believers have not really taken responsibility for treating and curing the human spirit. This is truly the duty of believers of every religion! In examining the reasons for this failure to do our duty—whether it results from the fact that we do not do our best to accomplish good, do not make use of things appropriately, or do not seek harmony with one another—I feel that first we must establish friendly relations among the several historic global religions. If the several historic global religions can amicably advance the extent of their mutual understanding, they will be able not only to avoid conflicts caused by misunderstandings—to the point that the religions utilize their energies to fight and destroy one another—but can each benefit from learning from the others' experiences. They can make up for their own deficiencies and expand on their own strengths, so as to do their best skillfully to reach their potential. Subsequently, the brilliant and luminous spirit of each religion will command humanity's admiration and respect, enough so as to be able to restore and advance humanity's health.
>
> The announced responsibilities of the Association of Chinese Religious Believers are five: to support policies that build up the country and defeat the enemy [Japan], to respect religious freedom, to lift up spiritual cultivation, to practice diligently social service, and to promote world peace....
>
> If the Association of Chinese Religious Believers takes on such a great mission as this, how can each member but strive to achieve these goals with great determination? How can the government and society be but compelled to help it?[102]

In a similar way, Taixu served, from 1944 until his death, as an executive director of the Philosophy of Life Institute (Rensheng zhexue yanjiu hui). Founded in Chongqing on October 21, 1944, the institute reported an interreligious membership of three hundred in 1945. Its stated purpose was "to study philosophy of life for a fuller understanding of the ultimate aim in life, realization of an ideal social set-up, and furtherance of the building of a new state."[103] Operating at least one branch institute, its activities included sponsoring lectures, publishing periodicals, compiling a life philosophy series, instituting an awards program for outstanding books on life philosophy, and other cultural projects. Bishop Paul Yu Bin (who in 1969 had become the second Chinese to be designated a cardinal in the Roman Catholic Church) served as the institute's president. In addition to Taixu, the executive directors included well-known Guomindang members and government officials Hu Shuhua and Liang Hancao.[104]

After the end of World War II, Taixu renewed his efforts to gain control of a truly national Buddhist organization. In 1945, his earlier plan for a reorganizing committee to oversee Buddhist affairs (filed with the government in 1941, after his goodwill mission to South Asia) was substantially approved by the Ministry of the Interior and the Ministry of Social Affairs. Therefore, Taixu was able to lead in the establishment of the Committee for the Reorganization of Chinese Buddhism (Zhongguo fojiao zhengli weiyuan hui), which eventually acted to revive the Chinese Buddhist Association (Zhongguo fojiao hui), originally founded in Shanghai in 1929. The nine-member organizing committee consisted of six monks—Taixu, Xuyun, Yuanying, Changyuan, Quanlang, and Zhangjia, the Mongolian Living Buddha Hutukhtu (1889–1957), and three laymen—Li Zikuan (1882–1973), Qu Wenliu (1881–1937), and Huang Qinglan. Chosen for the three-member standing committee were Taixu, Zhangjia, and Li Zikuan, the old revolutionary who was Taixu's lay disciple. The selection, in effect, gave Taixu majority control of the fledging organization for the last two years of his life.[105] As Taixu wrote at the time of the government's action,

> Now fortunately the people's war of resistance has been won, and the reconstruction of the country can begin. The Ministry of Social Affairs

and the Ministry of the Interior have applied for and received permission from the Executive Yuan for the establishment of a "Committee for the Reorganization of Chinese Buddhism." Within six months or a year we will convene a representative assembly of all Buddhists in the country to forge a strong national Buddhist association, with branch organizations in each province, city, and county, in order to adapt rapidly to the necessity of becoming a new China and one of the world's Big Four Powers *(si qiang)* and also of making Buddhism into a new Buddhism for a new China.[106]

However, hopes for a peaceful new China as one of the Big Four Powers were soon shattered in civil strife. In late 1945, after unsuccessful attempts by the United States to mediate the growing postwar struggle between Chiang Kai-shek's Nationalist troops and Mao Zedong's Communist forces, President Truman appointed General George C. Marshall a special presidential ambassador to China. In January 1946, Marshall's negotiations remarkably achieved a cease-fire. Soon a Political Consultative Conference was convened between the Guomindang and Chinese Communist Party to discuss possibilities for a coalition government and a joint national army. Yet with the two sides extremely distrustful of the other, and each confident that it could win a military contest, the negotiated cease-fire was short-lived, and the preliminary plans for a coalition government soon dashed in the bloody eruption of civil warfare. Conceding failure, and frustrated at the total unwillingness of the two parties to compromise, Marshall was recalled to the United States and departed China in January 1947.

Troubled by these tense political developments, Taixu nevertheless began preparatory efforts for a national Buddhist assembly. In addition, he continued administration of his various ministries in south China, working to revitalize Buddhist practice for a new Chinese society and the new world order that he hoped would dawn. Discouraged by the lack of progress toward needed economic and social reforms in the country, in late 1946 Taixu even considered forging more direct means of Buddhist involvement in political affairs. According to Yinshun, "feeling deeply that the sangha ought to coordinate with the revolutionary movements in politics, Taixu entertained the idea of organizing a political party."[107] Yet the Buddhist master ultimately recognized that this would be divisive and counterproductive. Thus, on the one hand, he urged his followers to be knowledgeable about and involved in political efforts for reform, and accordingly, they became active members of diverse political parties: the Guomindang, the Democratic Socialist Party, the Youth Party, and even the Communist Party. On the other hand, in February 1946, Taixu stated explicitly his view that Buddhism should not organize a political party.[108]

In the summer of 1946, Taixu was appointed chairman of the board of trustees of the Buddhist Culture Society (Fojiao wenhua she), which Li Zikuan founded primarily to distribute his master's writings. Work began on a Buddhist dictionary, as well as on the society's most important project, *Taixu dashi quanshu* (The Complete Works of the Venerable Master Taixu). The Chinese reformer also began to serve that summer as chairman of the board for the Chinese Buddhist Hospital (Zhongguo fojiao yiyuan) established in Shanghai's Xizhu si, helped provide guidance for the opening of the Buddhist Youth Association of Shanghai (Shanghaishi fojiao qingnian hui), and went to the capital to preach the Dharma in a prison.

In February 1947, Taixu went to the Yanqing si near Ningpo to deliver what would be his last series of lectures, "The Bodhisattva's Context for Learning" (Pusa xue chu). On March 5, he attended the seventh meeting of the Committee for the Reorganization of Chinese Buddhism, which convened in the Yufo si in Shanghai. The most significant decision from that session was the agreement to hold the first representative national assembly of Chinese Buddhists on May 27 in Nanjing—an assembly over which Taixu would not be able to preside, although his dream of a new Chinese Buddhist Association would be realized there. On March 17, twelve days after the committee's planning conference was convened, Taixu died suddenly at the Yufo si in Shanghai. He was fifty-seven years old.

Taixu's death was reported to be the result of a stroke brought on by high blood pressure, "an illness," Welch quips, "consistent with his temperament."[109] Reichelt adds that the monk's death was hastened by "bomb shock" that Taixu had suffered during a Japanese air attack on the suburbs of Chongqing.[110] Whatever the exact cause of his death, the controversial Buddhist master died with a number of his close disciples, both monastic and lay, chanting the name of Maitreya at his side. Indeed, they "prayed that Taixu might be reborn above in the Tuṣita heaven, so that he might come again among humanity."[111]

After more than three thousand people came to the Shanghai monastery to pay their respects, Taixu's body was transported to the Haichao si in Hangzhou, where, on April 8, Master Shanyin, one of Taixu's closest friends in the sangha *(daoyou)* and an editor for *Haichao yin,* preached the Dharma and presided over the cremation ceremony.[112] Yinshun states that Taixu's devoted followers searched carefully through the ashes and collected more than three hundred sacred relics. He also testifies, with a note of personal piety, that Taixu's "heart was not damaged, but was a whole relic, which sufficiently proves the greatness of the power of Taixu's bodhisattva vow."[113]

On June 6, the Nationalist government issued a statement of commendation that read:

> The monk Taixu made a profound study of philosophy and his goals and conduct were pure and exemplary! All of his life, throughout this country and beyond it, he propagated religious teachings. The power of his vow was great! During the Sino-Japanese War, he organized a first aid corps of Buddhist monks that went with the troops to be of service to them. His patriotism was especially worthy of praise! It is with very deep regret that we now hear of his death. We are responding by issuing this proclamation to recognize his loyalty and scholarship.[114]

Notes the monk Xuming:

> When the Venerable Master Taixu died in Shanghai on March 7, 1947, in China and in all parts of the world, all who had ever met him or heard of him grieved. For although he was a Buddhist master in China, his compassion, great vow, and influence extended far beyond the limits of China. Indeed, he took the peace and happiness of all the peoples of the world as his responsibility, taking up as his great tasks the reformation of Chinese Buddhism and the Buddhist transformation of the entire world.[115]

Taixu was a central figure in the movement to reform and revitalize Chinese Buddhist communities in the Republican period. He was a committed modernist who tried to effect change through a number of controversial initiatives. Many Chinese revered him as one who truly understood the Dharma and lived in harmony with the Dao. Some thought him an exemplary leader whose mission contributed not only to the vitality of the Buddhist community but to the nation's cause in years of crisis. Others, both inside and outside of the Chinese sangha, questioned the purity of his motives and faulted him for pride and self-interest. Many conservative leaders within the monastic community did not like his humanist leanings and distrusted his utopian visions for a reorganized religious community. Thus Welch is correct in stating that the majority of Chinese Buddhists in Taixu's time felt considerable ambivalence about him:

> They were pleased that one of their own had managed to become so famous, and they acknowledged the value of some of his ideas, but he did not correspond to their concept of what a monk ought to be. He seemed to them to talk about Buddhism more than he practiced it. The monks they most respected—Xuyun, Yinguang, Dixian, Hongyi, Laiguo, Tanxu—were persons for whom practice was of the essence, who remained aloof from the world rather than seeking for status in it, who wanted to restore Buddhism to what it had been rather than make it into something new. They feared that, if it were made into something new as Taixu seemed to be proposing, it would no longer be Buddhism.[116]

Making Chinese Buddhism into "something new" was at the heart of Taixu's career. When the reformer spoke of a "new Buddhism," "new monks," and a "new global culture," many naturally wanted to cling to the old and familiar. Yet Taixu believed that the scientific revolution had redefined the context for religious commitment in the modern era. Chinese Buddhists, he argued, could not simply "go back" to revalorize the common practices of the past; preaching the Dharma effectively in the future would require something more. Going boldly forward naturally meant reaching back to recover the courageous and caring spirit of the one who originally discovered the Dharma in our age, but it simultaneously meant change and adaptation to a new and evolving social world.

CHAPTER 4

MAHĀYĀNA AND THE MODERN WORLD

Yu-yue Tsu has asserted that the first phase of the revival of Chinese Buddhism that began during the final years of the Manchu dynasty was primarily political rather than spiritual in nature. That is, the most important attempts to reform and reenliven the Chinese Buddhist community during the waning years of the Qing and the initial years of the Republican period were predominantly organizational in character.[1] Deeply troubled about Buddhism's precarious position within Chinese society, members of the sangha as well as laity pondered how to reorganize their religious community in order to respond more effectively to changing circumstances. They were concerned about both negative external perceptions of their tradition and internal Buddhist problems. Neither, they realized, would be easy to address. Many intellectuals and ordinary citizens alike saw no relationship between the practice of Buddhism and efforts to remake and strengthen the nation. In addition, the sangha seemed helpless to deal with the debilitating issues of regionalism, factionalism, and the erosion of lay support caused by the large numbers of monks seeking personal gain by performing rites for the dead.[2]

The principal reason for the failure of all the efforts in the first organizational phase of the Buddhist revival in the Republican period, Tsu concluded, was the obvious need for a prior spiritual reawakening within the whole Chinese Buddhist community. What was required was the emergence of competent, consistent, and challenging visionary and ethical leadership. Writing in 1921, Tsu commented:

> The failure of the first wave of Buddhist revival to achieve spiritual results was in large measure due to the lack of a truly great spiritual leader. Now such a leader seems to have appeared in the person of Taixu fashi [Dharma Master Taixu], a monk of great learning and saintly character, and with his appearance has commenced the second wave of Buddhist revival. As the first was political in nature, the second is essentially spiritual. A genuine desire to reform monasticism, to reconstruct Buddhist theology according to modern philosophy, and to promote human welfare on the basis of the teachings of Buddha is the dominant note.[3]

Although Tsu's estimation of Taixu's role as the sole catalyst for a "second wave" of the Buddhist revival is overstated, the Chinese reformer did make an incomparable contribution to the revitalization of the Buddhist community in the Republican period. He did so by trying to relate Mahāyāna Buddhism to life in a new China, and by offering an engaging description of the bodhisattva's path in the twentieth century—a modernist, social-activist portrayal that some judged to be, according to traditional standards, a betrayal of Buddhism. Yet it was clearly a portrayal to which many sincere Chinese Buddhists rallied, and one in which many in the People's Republic of China, in Taiwan, and elsewhere continue to find hope.

Taixu conceived of his role as that of an interpreter of the ancient spiritual truths of Buddhism and expositor of their modern application. In that role, he expressed his concerns about the need for safeguarding religious freedom and raising Buddhist standards. Therefore, as Taixu claimed at Eight Fingers' funeral in 1912, he was strategically committed to advancing three "revolutions" within his religious community. With regard to an "organizational revolution," as we have seen, Taixu was a tireless theoretician, if not always an accomplished master at implementation. Concerning the sangha's needed "economic revolution," he sought to ensure the long-term financial stability of institutional Buddhism by calling for productive work by monks and closer ties to the growing number of educated laity.

Through an "intellectual revolution," the reformer hoped that Buddhists could learn to express the Dharma in ways that were inspired by scripture, faithful to the original spirit of Śākyamuni, and appropriate for the time.[4]

What China and the world needed most, Taixu asserted, was a revitalized Buddhist community intent on attaining enlightenment, invigorated by modern educational reforms, and involved in compassionate service in the ways of a true bodhisattva. As Frank Millican commented in 1923:

> At this time of general intellectual awakening and mingling of the social, political, and religious systems of the world, Buddhist thought in China is hidden in classical books, many of which are not easily available to the reading public. It is also truly bound by an ancient and stilted literary style which only expert scholars of Buddhism are able to read understandingly. The situation is even worse than that of Christianity in Europe before the Bible was printed in the vernacular. And, doubtless, history, as well as modern tendencies to discard or neglect anything that is not provided in convenient form, have forced upon Taixu and modern devotees of Buddhism the conviction that, if Buddhism is to survive, it must be restated not only in language which the ordinary scholar can readily understand but also in terms familiar to the modern mind.[5]

Accordingly, Taixu sought to restate Chinese Buddhism by emphasizing a particular form of Buddhist piety that he judged to be especially relevant to the modern world. This was a form of piety with elements that were certainly not without precedent in the history of Chinese Buddhism, but one that was given especially sharp focus in Taixu's life and work. As an ethical pietist, his basic understanding of his spiritual tradition tended to revolve around social responsibility. He was concerned that Mahāyāna Buddhism address the unique ills of the present age and engage in the transformation of this world into a pure land.

A conceptual revolution appeared crucial from Taixu's perspective because human thought patterns were intrinsically related to human actions. Commenting on the consequences of incorrect assumptions and perceptions for moral responsibility, he once observed:

If there is the distinction made between other persons and myself, and one takes that distinction and acts on it, then the opportunity for killing another arises; and when love and hate are distinguished, and one takes that and acts on it, then stealing and coveting arise; and when there is the distinction made between male and female, and one takes that distinction and acts on it, then lust and desire arise. If you take these three basic distinctions and act on them, then the whole world will continue to evolve, and all sentient beings will continue one by one, and the karmic fruits will revolve, and conditional arising will be endless.... But if you can stop making these distinctions and cease from distinguishing between these things, then the deluded can turn toward enlightenment. Those in darkness, misery, shame, and foul vice can turn toward light, comfort, dignity and purity.[6]

For any account of Mahāyāna Buddhism to be meaningful, Taixu argued, it would have to focus on the interrelationship between the tradition's most profound and comprehensive visions of the universe and the ethical paradigms appropriate to the modern world. Buddhist leaders would have to begin to link compelling understandings of the cosmos to constructive images for life within modern societies. If this could be accomplished in creative new ways, he asserted, greed, hatred, and delusion could be diminished, and people everywhere could be drawn toward the unique potentialities for a global community that existed in and through the bodhisattva's path. Yet too many people misunderstood Buddhism to be an otherworldly religion whose monks and nuns were concerned merely with their own spiritual welfare. For the wide currency of this misunderstanding in China, Taixu charged, Buddhist practitioners had only themselves to blame. Nevertheless, at the very heart of Mahāyāna teaching was the dynamic link between wisdom and compassion that defined the true way to buddhahood. Therefore, the task was to show how a transforming vision of emptiness could undergird ethical paradigms, while the attempt to realize such transforming paradigms in one's daily life could lead finally toward a more complete experience of enlightenment.

Thus, for Taixu, the central question was the meaning of Mahāyāna in the modern world. The root problem with which he struggled was how to think and act responsibly as a Buddhist in the twentieth century, in relation to the crises of the time. In restating his tradition, he wanted to direct his community toward a modern form of Buddhism *and beyond*. That is, he dreamed openly not only of his nation's immediate future but of a distant utopian era when Śākyamuni's goals would be accomplished throughout the cosmos. This utopian propensity drew Taixu forward into a radicalization and simplification of his heritage.

In a variety of ways, as noted in Chapter 3, Taixu was actually wrestling with the issue of the portability of Chinese Buddhism. Here the issue was not merely the religion's potential for successful contextualization and indigenization within different national, ethnic, or cultural settings—although this was an important question—but its portability into an enlightened future the full dimensions of which he could not know. Travelers, he seemed to be saying, needed to travel lightly and recognize the fact that they were traveling. Despite erroneous suggestions in word and deed to the contrary, Mahāyāna Buddhism was not a static place in which to remain; rather it was, quite literally, a "great vehicle" *(da sheng)*, a spiritual conveyance.

In terms of strategic goals, Taixu pondered how to capture the imagination of the increasing numbers of educated young Chinese who considered Buddhist modes of thought and action to be antiquated and darkly pessimistic about the human realm. He tried to define essential Buddhism in a way that was compatible with the sense of buoyant optimism, life-affirmation, and scientific progress so characteristic of modern intellectuals in his day. In so doing, Taixu and his colleagues faced the perplexing task of presenting the Dharma in forms not wholly unacceptable to Chinese Buddhist conservatives and yet sufficiently attractive to social and religious progressives. Theirs was the vexing problem of remaining attentive to traditional Buddhist visions and norms while outlining a new agenda in harmony with the secularizing trends of modernity. Their conundrum was how to talk directly and enthusiastically to those who would listen about a "new Buddhism," while claiming that it was not wholly new but the very essence of the authentically old.[7]

The purpose of this and the following chapters is to offer a reasonably succinct summary of Taixu's efforts to restate Buddhism in the Republican period. That aim is complicated by the very size of the written record. The Chinese master was a popular lecturer and prolific writer who wrote an incredible number of books and essays.[8] Although he was clearly not the systematic expositor of doctrine that his most gifted student and biographer Yinshun eventually became, Taixu was certainly more than an activist "pamphleteer," as he has been called.[9] Indeed, his way of presenting both the theoretical and practical dimensions of the bodhisattva path set a pattern that became widely influential. Thus I highlight only some of the major themes in Taixu's reformist mission. My goal is not to offer a comprehensive account of Taixu's writings in relation to the three revolutions in organization, economy, and thought that he called for at Eight Fingers' funeral, but simply to characterize the direction and unique thrust of his teachings as he sought to help his co-religionists answer a persistent question of the day: Will Buddhism wither away in China or "will the religion of the Enlightened One that now flickers behind the walls of lonely cloisters and monkish cells flame forth again as the Light of Asia?"[10]

In view of the familiar appellation for Śākyamuni of "the Great Physician," I focus in this chapter on Taixu's own diagnoses of the primary "diseases" afflicting modern civilization, and on the life-saving first aid that he proposed—namely, "a Buddhism for human life." As Taixu once remarked, "The Buddha is called the Great Lord of Healing *(da yi wang)*. His Dharma heals the sick minds of this world, and the basic meaning of 'to save' *(ji)* is 'to heal' *(yi)*."[11] Like physicians who diagnose physical illnesses, Taixu offered his own assessments of contemporary forms of spiritual suffering that continue to stand in opposition to Buddhist images of the enlightened life. And just as doctors prescribe treatments and lifestyle regimens that can effectively restore the health of patients with serious diseases, so Taixu confidently offered a restated, modern form of Buddhism as the world's only hope for a more just and peaceful future. Indeed, in sharp contrast to the troubled, self-centered, and self-destructive society that he observed around him, the reformer spoke optimistically of a Buddhism for the living, and of a humanitarian utopia that could actually be realized in this world of time and space. On behalf of a suffering world not even fully conscious of the dimensions of its own suffering, the Buddhist master's goal was to shape a practical discipline of spiritual healing for all beings.

THE DILEMMAS OF MODERNITY

In his 1935 book, *Foxue de jianglai* (The Future of Buddhism), Taixu observed that modern science has created a radically new context for human existence, one with both beneficial and harmful consequences for many aspects of communal life. On the one hand, because of numerous technological advances, resources that enhance material standards of living have become extraordinarily plentiful throughout much of the world. The Industrial Revolution has led to a restructuring of economies that has permitted most people and communities to enjoy material advantages undreamed of a century before. On the other hand, Taixu asserted, this "blessing" has also become a terrible curse. Although from a material standpoint modern science may have made life "easier," it has simultaneously served to undermine traditional morality and produced chaos. As Taixu remarked,

> From now on, the lives of human beings will be naturally very rich in material things. This is because through scientific progress we are discovering an unlimited hidden treasury of natural resources for living. At the same time, by using scientific tools and methods we will continue to advance and strive for further progress. With regard to improving people's living standards, the significance and contribution of these tools and methods will be great.
>
> We know that the special gifts that science has bestowed on the lives of human beings can be said to be considerable. However, when the impact of science on human morality is carefully examined, it has not had a beneficial affect. In fact, not only has science not had a positive influence, but in the past few decades moral principles that have been established on a philosophical basis have undergone an increasingly critical attack from science and indeed have lost their foundation. [Furthermore,] moral principles that have been established on a religious basis of divine authority have also been overturned. Because of these

developments, throughout the world the central point of orientation for moral behavior has been completely lost.

With regard to the relation of science to morality, then, does it or does it not have a beneficial affect? From these developments we can fully understand [the correct answer]. As a result of scientific advances, our lives are becoming materially more prosperous each day, while simultaneously our consumer desires also increase. We are utilizing the knowledge and tools of science to the fullest extent in order to exploit the development of natural resources—what may be called the subduing of nature. Therefore while our technological capabilities are rapidly increasing, conflicts sparked by our ever-rising consumer desires and powers are also developing into serious crises unprecedented in history. Ours is becoming an age of intractable problems for which there will be no easy solutions.[12]

In the modern world of science, the failure of religious or theological ethical systems to provide adequate moral guidance, Taixu observed, may be understood by recognizing their weak and obsolete cornerstone. This foundational delusion may be identified as the belief that human beings are "children of the gods." All forms of traditional theistic systems, according to Taixu, transmit behavioral norms that are not established on any humanistic basis. The origins of their behavioral paradigms are clear: they originate from beyond the time and space continuum of human existence within this world. Historically, the Buddhist master admitted, theological ethics of this type have played an important part in the evolution of human society. In many cases in the past—where the belief in deities and their powers of retribution and blessing could be sustained—the attempts of various individuals and groups either to imitate the moral actions of their gods or to obey faithfully their divine commandments have contributed to creative and harmonious social orders. Throughout recorded history, many deeply religious persons, seeking earthly and paradisaical rewards and fearing eternal punishments, have sincerely tried to adhere to their society's sanctioned modes of behavior in both their private and public lives. However, in the contemporary world, Taixu stated, primitive theistic beliefs no longer carry any real force. Modern science has effectively swept away all god-language by correctly identifying it as a form of mere wish-fulfillment, as an ultimately debilitating self-deception. Therefore, Taixu concluded, any ethic for the present or future that is established on the injunctions, prohibitions, or expectations of heavenly deities has been totally undermined by science.

Philosophically derived ethical principles have enjoyed no more success. The primary reason for this, Taixu commented, is that all philosophical systems are based on the elaboration of particular human ideas and ideals that are inevitably in competition with other ideas and ideals. Because their origin lies fully within the realm of time and space, they have not been able to motivate and inspire all people to reach common understandings of the meaning of life and death—or to reach agreement on appropriate modes of action within community. In sum, philosophical principles are intrinsically relative and just as ineffective as theological principles when it comes to providing a viable foundation for a truly universal ethic in an age of modern science. Our basic dilemma, declared Taixu, is simply this: "Humanity has completely lost the centerpoint for morality."[13]

This fact has dangerous implications for the entire human community, claimed the Buddhist master, because scientific technology, however beneficial, is unmistakably related to the increasingly destructive spirit of consumerism that afflicts modern societies. That is to say, as human lives improve materially, human desires are fueled for ever greater pleasurable enhancements. Eventually, Taixu suggested, not only will the unequal distribution of goods become a volatile issue, but the capabilities of modern technology will not be able to keep pace with the perpetually increasing material desires of human beings. The consequence will be an unprecedented explosion of violence between the rich and poor—namely, between the privileged, who have both material goods and the power to control their distribution, and marginalized peoples who have neither goods nor power.

In the first two decades of the twentieth century, averred Taixu, the world witnessed the bloody prelude to that impending struggle. World War I should be seen as the opening drama in a modern social cataclysm. The lives and well-being of our ancient ancestors were largely threatened by things and events in the natural world: poisonous snakes, carnivorous animals, floods, and other natural calamities. Yet these external threats now pale in comparison to those presented by the development of increasingly unrestrained and self-centered minds. Science may have diminished most external threats in nature, but it has also engendered new manifestations of internal threats latent in the human personality. Indeed, because the foundations for all religious and philosophical ethical systems have been eroded while technological advances have increased the desires for material goods, individual people consider only themselves and seek only to satisfy their own instinctive cravings. At times, many are quite willing to employ force to achieve their selfish aims, assaulting and killing one another in the process. "In the confrontation between nations, races, and socioeconomic classes," the reformer observed, "each one exposes to the fullest extent the selfishness of their animal desires."[14] In sum, he concluded, the greatest contemporary threats to human life are "self-generated."

Taixu further charged that the egocentric mentality that leads to social inequalities and violence may be identified as the byproduct of a type of culture that has developed uniquely in the modern West. The reformer argued repeatedly that although western culture has made the greatest progress in improved standards of living in the material sense, it has failed miserably in the development of the moral life. Western culture is essentially "a culture of making and using tools," he asserted, one that has effectively raised expectations and desires for material possessions while suppressing human drives toward realization of the common good.[15]

Taixu was not an unsophisticated opponent of western science and technology. Nevertheless, his descriptions of the human condition in the modern world are reminiscent in many respects of Max Weber's discussion of the contemporary capitalist's "iron cage" of economic compulsion.[16] For example, addressing his Paris audience in 1928, Taixu remarked:

> Scientific discoveries have brought about a certain doubt as to religious evidence. The old gods and religions seem to have been shaken in the

wind of science, and religious doctrines have no longer any defense, and the world at large seems to be handed over to the tyranny of the machine and all those monstrous powers to which science has given birth.[17]

Echoing this same theme in 1940, when visiting India, the reformer delineated three great historic cultures: those of India, China, and the Euro–North American West. Contrasting the three while pointing to the need for a cultural synthesis, he commented:

> You may take the cultures of the world and divide them into three kinds. The first is a culture that cultivates a holy and pure inner mind; the second, one that improves human relations; and the third, one that manages material capabilities. Developing respectively from these three types are Indian culture, Chinese culture, and Western culture. In the past, China and India have made enormous contributions to the world. However, now both are being influenced by the West. On the unfortunate path taken by Western culture, human beings and material things are considered to be of equal worth. Therefore the world's crises deepen every day. I hope that in the future we will not lean to any one extreme. Material resources must be developed while at the same time our spirits are cultivated and ethics emphasized.[18]

As these remarks suggest, according to Taixu, any remedy for this fundamental crisis of the modern world must be based on a careful examination of the relation between religion and culture. It is the development of culture that has distinguished the human species from the rest of the animal kingdom and marked its evolutionary transformation from a primitive to a civilized state. Religion, philosophy, government, economics, science, literature, the fine arts—all are important aspects of culture. However, religion is its most determinative single dimension, Taixu asserted. Religion represents a people's sense of ultimate meaning and value; it produces patterns of relationships and creates community.

In some of his writings, such as *Foxue de jianglai,* Taixu identified not three but four basic types of religio-cultural perspective. First there are cultures in which people seek primarily to alter the external world—that is, to refashion their environment to create a more conducive context for human satisfaction and fulfillment. A second type of culture exhibits the opposite tendency, focusing not on external realities but on each person's inner spiritual nature. In such cultures, Taixu wrote, when people encounter inevitable hardships and perplexities, they characteristically seek to adjust not their external circumstances but, through concentrated introspection, their personal religio-philosophical worldview. The third type of culture is one in which people seek to change neither the external world nor their internal stance, but to remain in a state of utter passivity and nonassertive harmony with all things. Resignation rather than any kind of transformation characterizes this kind of culture.

A fourth type provides a totally different cultural ethos. In this most important type—to which societies shaped by Mahāyāna Buddhism belong—people seek fulfillment and enlightenment both by developing and adjusting the character of their own inner life and, simultaneously, by working to effect beneficial changes in the external world. As Taixu himself put it, "Such cultures plan to transform completely both internal and external realities."[19] If the dilemmas of the twentieth century are to be successfully addressed, he concluded, only such a religio-philosophical perspective will suffice.

Beyond the need for this fourth type of culture, a globalized community in crisis requires a religious faith that enables people to transcend the prejudices of their various local cultures. According to Taixu, such a community needs a truly universal religio-ethical system. Christianity has shaped the highly industrialized culture of Western Europe and the United States. Islam has shaped the Middle Eastern and African cultures, while Hinduism, or Brahmanism, has determined the cultural life of India. Yet of all the religious traditions in the world, he averred, it is Buddhism that has shown the greatest capacity for transcending the powerful ethnocentric particularities of local culture. From its origin on the Indian subcontinent in the sixth century B.C.E., the religion has spread throughout Central, Southeast, and East Asia, and within the last century even to the West. While traditions like Hinduism, Daoism, Confucianism, and Shinto have never escaped in any substantial way the boundaries of their respective homelands, Buddhism has achieved remarkable success in worldwide mission as a truly universal religion.

Moreover, the reformer emphasized, wherever the Dharma has been faithfully practiced, Buddhism's influence has been dramatically positive in every aspect of human life and achievement, demonstrating its great practical value for the establishment of human community. Such a beneficial influence could not be reasonably shown for Christianity, which, Taixu maintained, is in any case intellectually untenable in the modern world. Therefore, he declared, in selecting and synthesizing the best elements of local cultures to form a new "global culture," Buddhism must be a fundamental component. Without the fusion of eastern and western cultures and the adoption of Buddhism's unique spiritual principles, the consumer-oriented, technological civilization toward which the entire world is rapidly moving will have no foundation except that of an egocentric individualism, no future but competitive struggle and the exercise of power. Buddhism, he proposed, can provide the only basis for "a universal civilization and a universal philosophy" because it teaches that all sentient beings are one and that "all human egos are bound together by bonds of sympathy."[20]

In addition to a religio-cultural perspective that seeks to transform both internal and external realities and a religious tradition capable of transcending local cultures, there is a third requirement for addressing the dilemmas of modernity: namely, a religion fundamentally in harmony with science. On the one hand, Taixu asserted, a careful investigation reveals that "Buddhism is the only religion which does not contradict scientific truth."[21] Everything that modern scientific research has discovered about the complexity and interdependent nature of reality by using both telescopes and microscopes has served only to confirm the religio-philosophical insights found in the Mahāyāna scriptures. On the other hand, he claimed, Buddhist truth is also "unscientific" and not limited to the truths discovered through experimental research. While always in consonance with the insights of science, Dharmic truth transcends and perfectly completes them. According to Taixu, scientists have not gone far enough in their research into the mysteries of nature. As they proceed, they will be able to verify, yet never disconfirm, the Dharma that the Buddha revealed. As Taixu once put it,

> The scientist claims that scientific knowledge is the whole truth and stops there. In this he resembles the blind man who, after examining the body of an elephant, declared the ear to be a fan and the tail a broom. If we compare the elephant and all the organs of its body to the universe, then the blind man may be compared to the scientist who has never realized an absolute, universal perception of the universe. Scientific methods can only corroborate the Buddhist doctrine; they can never advance beyond it....
>
> Science, therefore, can never be the main support of Buddhism, although it may act as a valuable auxiliary and much may be expected from uniting the two methods of investigation.... The scientist, however, is constantly trying to improve his instruments rather than to perfect his inner vision. This is like depending on our bodily senses. The main principles of the Buddhist doctrine, therefore, are "unscientific" and sweep away all the false conclusions at which science has arrived. Otherwise, it would be impossible to overcome ignorance and attain enlightenment.
>
> If life, however, were founded on the six pāramitās—the six perfect virtues of the bodhisattvas—and these in turn were realized to be in accordance with scientific research, then we might hope to enter into the pure realms of Buddha and emerge from the chaos of fire and brimstone into which we have fallen.[22]

Summarizing elsewhere this same dialectical perspective on science and scientists, Taixu stated:

> Those who criticize science say that science is responsible for the weapons of warfare and therefore is harmful. Those who praise science point to the great material achievements of modern civilization which benefit mankind. We need not join the controversy, although those who have gone through the World War cannot be blind to some truth underlying this criticism. We should note, however, that the criticism refers to

the fruits of science. Science itself is a method which is beyond criticism. Science is always open-minded, ready to discard what is disproved and to adopt what is verified, in order to reach the truth of reality. However, there is one obstinate superstition among scientists, and that is, they believe this scientific method is the only road for arriving at truth, and fail to realize that the ultimate reality of this universe cannot be penetrated by it.

In general, what is a gain to science is a loss to religion. Those religions with doctrines of gods and souls fundamentally lack the stability of truth and are easily shaken. But Buddhism benefits by the discoveries of science. The more science progresses, the clearer Buddhism becomes, for Buddhism explains the truth concerning the universe. Take an illustration from astronomy. In ancient times, men thought of heaven as above and the earth below; then came Copernicus who taught that the sun was the center of our system. Now we have arrived at the idea that there is no one center anywhere in the astral universe. This supports the Buddhist conception of the great unlimited void, embracing numberless worlds, all interwoven like a spider web. Science helps us to understand Buddhism by offering suitable analogies. But the core of Buddhism science cannot reach, for it has to do with inward illumination, the direct insight into the reality of the universe, an intuitive experience only acquired by oneself, where all logic, analogy, or scientific hypothesis are of no avail. When scientists insist that theirs is the only method of arriving at truth, they remind one of blind men trying to understand an elephant by the sense of touch. They will get partial impressions of the different parts of the animal and what strange impressions as compared with a living elephant as seen by a man with normal eyesight.[23]

Wing-tsit Chan once observed that although Taixu argued vehemently that Buddhism was entirely harmonious with science and that Einstein's theory of relativity confirmed the basic insights of Buddhist idealistic philosophy, actually "Taixu did not know much about science or Einstein."[24] Of course, the extent of the monk's scientific education was limited. Nevertheless, in 1926 Frank Millican commented at length on the reformer's rationale in emphasizing the necessity of developing a "scientific Buddhism":

We shall be prepared to understand why Taixu attempts to associate Buddhism with science rather than with religion. He rejects anything that suggests the supernatural or metaphysical. Science, he observes, sticks close to the facts of experience and thus is in position to have its conclusions constantly checked up by means of further experiments. Buddhism, he claims, has this same scientific approach to the problem of the understanding of the nature of life and of the universe. Yet it is much broader in scope. It goes beyond a study of the physical sciences and includes the science of psychology. Since to Taixu, the Idealist, the universe in its final analysis is of the nature of mind there is no justification for the arbitrary limitation of the field of science to the so-called physical sciences. The scientific method should operate on different levels. There are, first, the so-called physical sciences based on the six senses. Then there is the scientific study of thought processes. Beyond this there is the more profound science of direct intuitive acquaintance or enlightenment known only to a few choice souls who have seen through the nature of existence and have come to a consciousness of reality beyond all the illusions and distractions of life. This experience is attained by means of quiet abstraction and intuitive response to the universe. The Buddhist Hall of Meditation is the laboratory for this more advanced type of scientific research. And the materials for the experiment are none other than one's own bodily senses and his mind. . . .

This more comprehensive view of science includes three stages. The first is a direct conscious experience of the things of our environment *(bianjue)*. The second is an understanding of the law which operates in our environment—the law *(lüfa)* of growth and decay and all the changes that take place in the phenomenal world. The third is the final stage of harmony in which one sees beyond the changing phenomena of existence and becomes conscious of reality—the reality in which there are no distinctions as this and that, good and evil, self and nonself. This final stage—which is salvation—in which the person has come to understand the three above stages of life is Taixu's goal for life. This stage of perfect Buddhahood, he tells us, involves a belief in Buddha, the Law, and the Order; it involves true faith and a belief in the law of cause and effect. It further involves conformity to the ten rules of good conduct and the ability to rise above the things of desire which are the cause of suffering.[25]

A BUDDHISM FOR HUMAN LIFE

Taixu located the convergence of the three religio-cultural elements required for addressing the contemporary crisis—namely, a tradition that transforms both the self and the world, that transcends local culture, and that is in harmony with science—in what he called a "Buddhism for human life," or "Buddhism for the living" *(rensheng fojiao)*. This was a theme that Taixu first began to explore in a 1928 lecture in Shanghai, and it was one that he continued to detail until his final lecture on the subject in Zhenjiang in August 1946.[26] As Hong Jinlian has remarked, this seminal concept is rooted in the various influences of late Qing modernism, Tiantai philosophy, Chan iconoclasm, and western scientific optimism.[27] On the one hand, in propagating a Buddhism for human life, Taixu was influenced by aspects of western humanism that were sweeping Asia and by the radical enthusiasm of the reformers of the New Culture Movement. In this sense he was a Chinese intellectual of his times, urging the nation to embrace the challenge of building a new country with new values within a new world order. In fact, he presented his "Buddhism for human life" as a complement to and perfection of Sun Yat-sen's form of nationalism. Thus, just as political leaders were taking the best of China's five-thousand-year-old culture and blending it with the best of western scientific culture to produce a "three-principles-of-the-people culture" *(sanmin zhuyi de wenhua)*, so Mahāyāna Buddhists were establishing connections between the best results of that process and the virtuous conduct of the first ten grades of bodhisattva faith *(shi xin wei)* in order to establish a practical Buddhism for the living.[28] On occasion, Taixu even referred to his own efforts in terminology that paralleled Sun's *sanmin zhuyi,* advocating a "three-principled Buddhism" *(sanfo zhuyi)* that entailed an ideal sangha of Dharma teachers *(foseng zhuyi)*, an ideal lay Buddhist order of active bodhisattvas *(fohua zhuyi)*, and a national culture infused with the spirit of Mahāyāna Buddhism and reaching out to the entire world *(foguo zhuyi)*.[29]

On the other hand, although external influences must be acknowledged, the sources of Taixu's position were profoundly Buddhist. Taixu wanted to focus attention on classic, if neglected, Mahāyāna themes about the nature of the truly enlightened life. Many interpreters have failed to recognize this fact in explaining Taixu's teachings, as Hong has noted:

> Most people give greater attention to the fact that Taixu was following secular responses [to events of his time] and ignore the ultimately scriptural ideals of his Buddhism for human life. Because of this fact, most people think that the main point of his "Buddhism for human life" was a response to the conflict with the cultural ideals of Confucianism, or was merely blending harmoniously together the new knowledge of the world. That is to say, it represented a secularization [of Buddhism] and that's all. As Yinshun remarks in his article, "On Entering the World and Buddhism," "most people do not see the [true] sources of Taixu's Buddhism and think it reflects only popular trends and merely a kind of secularization, with the result that the meaning of essential Buddhism does not clearly present itself before the student."[30]

Indeed, Taixu did not aim to present a watered-down, secularized version of Buddhism but to defend and renew the religion by recalling the spiritual foundations on which the entire structure was built.

In so doing, Taixu firmly rejected what he considered to be distorted interpretations of the religious tradition by non-Buddhists. While obviously not uncritical of many within his own religious community, the reformer could not permit to go unchallenged the kind of destructively dismissive charges expressed by Confucianist critics such as Liang Shuming (1893–1988). Once a lay devotee himself, Liang asserted that Buddhism's escapist mentality was wholly inappropriate for twentieth-century China and that those who were trying to reform and revive the religion were only taking advantage of difficult times for selfish ends.[31] In his noted 1922 work, *Dong Xi wenhua ji qi zhexue* (Eastern and Western Cultures and Their Philosophies), Liang remarked that he had read some of Taixu's reformist essays in *Haichao yin* and had discussed the matter with the respected classical scholar Zhang Taiyan. Yet Liang's ultimately negative judgment of Buddhism was unequivocal:

> Many Buddhist scholars say that a Buddhist revival can bring relief to present human suffering and can cause China to experience a great peace without disorder. Yet I dare to say to everyone, if there is a revival

of Buddhism, then China's disorders will be without end.... Confucianism and Buddhism are exact opposites. The former talks about life in the present world and does not discuss things outside of it. The latter only talks about things outside the present world and not life within it. Because of this, Buddhism in our time has no possibility of any great activity [within society], and those who want to encourage such activity have no alternative but to alter the religion's original appearance. So we can remember the article in *Haichao yin* in which the monk Taixu takes as his theme the two vehicles [which ensure rebirth in the world] of humans and devas in order to extend the scope of Buddhism to life in the present world.... Yet in summary, Buddhism is basically useless in this world. If in order to make use of it one has to transform Buddhism's basic appearance, then why even waste time on it? I oppose the promotion of Buddhism and I oppose the reformation of Buddhism.[32]

Taixu responded that Liang Shuming, like many others who denounced Buddhism, had simply failed to understand the religion. Moreover, Taixu wrote, although Liang had placed his faith in Confucianism, informed and courageous people actually capable of responding to China's deepening modern crisis "were not being produced through the study of Confucianism but only through the study of Buddhism."[33] What such critics had failed to grasp, he concluded, was the fundamental link in Mahāyāna doctrine between wisdom and compassion—albeit a link not always evident in daily practice. What Liang and others had failed to comprehend was the broad scope of the Dharma and the foundation of moral instruction common to all paths and levels of spiritual attainment.

In formulating his argument, Taixu sought to explain the close relationship between what he termed a "Buddhism for human life" and the meritorious precepts of the Dharma common to the "five vehicles" of Buddhism. These five vehicles *(wu sheng)* can be considered methods, or conveyances, for rebirth among human or divine beings. On the basis of spiritual attainment, one may be reborn in the world of humans, in a pleasurable heavenly realm, among the śrāvakas pursuing arhatship, among the ascetic and self-taught pratyekabuddhas, or among the buddhas and bodhisattvas. According to Taixu, although Buddhism has delineated the Dharma common to the final three vehicles (i.e., the śrāvaka, pratyekabuddha, and bodhisattva vehicles) as well as the Dharma unique to the final vehicle (i.e., that of the bodhisattvas), all advanced, world-transcending disciplines are grounded in norms or rules that all five vehicles have in common—namely, the noble eightfold path, the five precepts, the ten good deeds, and so forth. Thus these fundamental disciplines are not merely a set of preliminary and possibly dispensable exercises, nor is the practice of the moral precepts only an initial step for beginners along the way.

Indeed, although the practices that lead to supreme enlightenment far exceed in number and scope those common to the five vehicles, they do not transcend the Buddha's basic instructions in the sense of rendering them irrelevant. The foundational precepts of the religion are interconnected with all others and remain at the heart of the path for all bodhisattvas, whether they are accomplished or only just beginning to glimpse the meaning of their great vows. As Taixu put it,

> The reason that common people criticize Buddhism as having nothing to do with human life or ethics is because they know only about the ways of escaping the world according to the Dharma of the three vehicles, and they do not understand the significance of the Mahāyāna teachings and the Dharma common to the five vehicles. Actually basic for Buddhism are the [common] teachings of the five vehicles, which explain human morality and instruct humans how to cultivate good thoughts and actions.[34]

Yinshun wrote about Taixu's approach:

> Feeling the narrowness and poverty of the present decline of Chinese Buddhism, Venerable Master Taixu decided to use the "Dharma common to the Five Vehicles," the "Dharma common to the Three Vehicles," and the "distinctive Dharma of the Great Vehicle" to embrace all Buddhist teachings.... [He] gave high praise to the complete Buddhist teachings, namely, that "having merits and virtues, people can be assured of being born as human or heavenly beings; having wisdom, they can become śrāvakas or pratyekabuddhas. All of these people must rely on all the vinayas, sūtras, and śāstras; if only a part of the teachings

are utilized, one cannot attain enlightenment." These complete Buddhist teachings are worthy of being actively proclaimed.

When the Tathāgata explained the Dharma, he always began by teaching the "proper method"—giving, keeping the precepts, and abandoning desire in order to be reborn in heaven (concentration). Then, to those who might be able to renounce the world, he taught a world-transcending doctrine. Because the emphasis of the Buddhist teachings is on transcending the world, those who compiled the sūtras always skipped over the Buddha's "proper method." The ancient Abhidharma texts began with the five precepts, but the later Abhidharma texts eliminated them.... [Yet] with regard to this, Venerable Master Taixu, penetrating deeply into the Buddha Vehicle with exceptional insight, revealed the real purpose of the Tathāgata's appearing in this world—to teach people to enter the Buddha-way from human lives. Thus, the method for beginners emphasizes both practicing the ten good deeds (without abandoning the worldly affairs of daily life) and following the right deeds of the Human Vehicle to enter the Buddha Vehicle, instead of emphasizing practices of renunciation such as mindfulness of death.

Using right deeds to move from the Human Vehicle toward the Buddha-way rests on gathering the merits of the Dharma common to the Five Vehicles and the Three Vehicles.... According to the complete Buddhist teachings as determined and revealed by Venerable Master Taixu, all these teachings are simply methods for becoming a buddha. This approach not only connects the three levels of the Dharma common to the Five Vehicles, the Dharma common to the Three Vehicles, and the distinctive Dharma of the Great Vehicle, it also connects the teachings belonging to the regular way and the skillful way. This approach reveals the entire sequence of the Buddha-way, and leads one to the supreme buddha realm.[35]

Not only is Buddhism's emphasis on right action in the world so fundamental, Taixu pointed out, but the literature of Mahāyāna Buddhism is replete with heroic descriptions of the bodhisattva's selfless actions on behalf of others. In the *Weimojie suoshuo jing* (Vimalakīrti-nirdeśa Sūtra), for example, one who is a true bodhisattva "views things as impermanent, but does not neglect to cultivate the roots of goodness," "views the world as marked with suffering, but does not hate to be born and die in it," "sees that there is no permanent ego, but is tireless in instructing others," "sees that there is no birth, yet takes on the form of birth in order to share the burdens of others," "embraces the view of emptiness and nothingness, yet does not discard one's great pity."[36] Of course, this "pity" or "compassion" *(ci)*, Taixu stressed, does not mean "love" *(ai)* as the term is commonly employed in the western religious traditions. "Love" in this sense, he charged, is defined in relation to the erroneous concepts of "self" and "others." Indeed, it can be shown that "loving" actions are intrinsically directed toward benefiting the self, even when their ostensible goal is to help others. In contrast, Taixu wrote,

> From the Buddhist perspective, love comes from the causal interrelationship of all things. Therefore, in keeping with Buddhist principles, it is not called "love" but is referred to as "great compassion." Seeing the suffering of all living beings, in his great compassion the Buddha made up his mind to relieve this suffering. This cannot be compared to the kind of covetous love that arises from promoting oneself. For this reason it is a great compassion that is pure and good and without a trace of evil. This kind of great love is the mother of all the buddhas and the source of all Buddhist truth.[37]

Not understanding the great compassion of a bodhisattva, averred Taixu, Liang Shuming and others have mistakenly concluded that Buddhism has no beneficial function in the modern world. Yet, quite to the contrary, given the extent of human suffering and the potentially disastrous possibilities for evil in the twentieth century and beyond, ours is "the most appropriate age ever for proclaiming the Buddhist Dharma."[38]

In further explicating his use of the innovative term "a Buddhism for human life," Taixu commented that it is necessary to recognize Buddhism's two basic principles for mission: to state the truth and to respond to the needs of sentient beings. "Without the truth," he stated, "Buddhism loses its substance *(ti)*; without responding to need, it loses its function *(yong)*."[39] Practitioners must comprehend both the essence of Buddhist teaching as well as the variety of doctrinal and ritual expressions that have developed as Buddhists have responded to changing human needs and circumstances. Thus, students of the religion must comprehend the similarities and differences between the kind of anti-Brahmanistic Nikāya Buddhism that developed in India and Southeast Asia and the kind of Mahāyāna Buddhism that flourished in Central and East Asia. In short, Chinese Buddhists must be aware that they are transmitting an ancient and timeless religious message that transcends culture, while simultaneously understanding how their particular culture has affected both various elements of monastic living and the methods and metaphors for communicating the Dharma within schools as different as Tiantai, Chan, Zhenyan, and Pure Land.

According to Taixu, because Buddhists have historically maintained this dual concern for universal truth and human need in different mission contexts, they are uniquely prepared to contribute to the global culture emerging in the twentieth century. The globalization process is creating a synthetic, international culture in which the special characteristics of different peoples are being selectively appropriated according to three interrelated standards: a realistic perspective on human nature, a scientific perspective on truth and falsehood, and a "communitarian" perspective on the social order.[40] A reformed, modern expression of Mahāyāna Buddhism, he declared, stands in a unique relationship to that potential cultural synthesis because it is in fact in harmony with all three.

Moreover, Taixu claimed, a "Buddhism for human life" requires that all religious practices that have to do with gods and ghosts be immediately discontinued. These are superstitious activities incompatible with the highest truths of Mahāyāna. According to popular misconceptions, Buddhism is concerned primarily with death and the travails of souls in hell. Though such a view does recognize that the character of one's life in this world is important—if only because the character of one's afterlife depends on it—in its weighted attention to the dead it disregards the conditions for life in this world and does not penetrate to Mahāyāna's ultimate views about nirvāṇa and saṃsāra. As Taixu explained it,

> So-called death is actually a part of life. Only when we are able to understand life will we be able to understand death. On the contrary, if we

only understand death, not only will we not understand life, we will not really understand death. Therefore, in view of negative interpretations of Buddhism, we can dispense with the previous inferior practices of the religion as we go about improving actual human life.[41]

Therefore, rather than focusing on rites for the dead, all practitioners should energetically enter upon the bodhisattva's ten periods, or stages, of development *(shi zhu)* and the ten activities required for the universal welfare of others *(shi xing)*.

Taixu knew that it would be difficult to overcome popular misunderstandings of Chinese Buddhism and disassociate the religion itself from the worship of deities and spirits. Hence he believed that four distinct elements would have to converge in the lives of those committed to religious reform:

First, on the basis of his own life, he knew that *genuine religious conversion experiences* would shatter all superficial perspectives on reality and lead individuals to take up the disciplines of a religious path. These conversion experiences would destroy the illusion of self and others and establish a true basis for community.

Second, integral to and proceeding from these religious experiences, *great vows to engage in compassionate service within the world* were necessary. If Buddhism involved only extraordinary transcendental experiences and sanctioned a withdrawal from society rather than an engagement with it, then the religion could not long survive in a modern society.

Third, Buddhist reform required those who, beyond extraordinary life-changing experiences, had *practical knowledge of how to accomplish things in the everyday world*. What was needed was a practical sense of how to express spiritual insights in concrete ways that transformed both internal and external realities.

Fourth, *courageous moral actions that were appropriate to the uniquely dangerous circumstances of the age* were essential to reform. Thus a sensitivity to current needs—a sense of "Dharmic timing" as it were—was critical to a revitalized religious community.

Taixu judged that because, historically speaking, successfully adaptive religions had manifested all four of these elements to one degree or another, no effective revival of Buddhism in the modern period would be possible without them.[42]

Rejecting both Confucian humanism and all forms of popular religion that venerated gods or ghosts, Taixu sought to outline a style of moral reasoning appropriate for a modern, socially engaged Buddhist. He realized that many religious people relied on the commandments of deities external to the world, judging actions to be right or wrong because they had been either enjoined or forbidden by a divine power. Others adopted a teleological or utilitarian position, maintaining that moral acts are those that produce the best possible consequences or the greatest happiness in each unique situation. Still others preferred to define moral goodness in terms of one's motivation, intention, or disposition. In this last case, noted Taixu, "all human behavior must be judged by the motives in one's mind. So if that person's mind is good, the person is moral, and if the person's mind is evil, the person is immoral."[43]

Yet all these approaches are clearly inadequate, according to Taixu, so that we need to establish a new standard for judging right and wrong. "One-sided theories" are those that base moral goodness either on simple obedience to one's own set of divine commands (which are often in conflict with other people's divine commands) or on merely human calculations about happy consequences or hidden motivations. Both these types of moral reasoning, he asserted, fail to attend to the great principles of the universe. The great principles of cause and effect, which are the primary subject of Buddhist investigation into the nature of things, provide the only sound and unchanging basis for moral judgment. Grounding his sense of "what ought to be" in the most comprehensive understanding of "what is," Taixu directly related sound moral reasoning to a theory of knowledge. Thus, he claimed,

> Human beings should have two sources for knowledge: scientific and religious. Philosophical knowledge is only an extension of these two and is not independent of them. Scientific knowledge is certainly important,

but religious knowledge is also very important. Knowledge established on the basis of science, philosophy, or inferential reasoning is partial. Sense perception is fragmentary, and inferences are not facts. Therefore they do not provide thorough and certain knowledge. . . . What about attaining complete and certain knowledge? I think that only spiritually perfected persons are able to attain it. The kind of knowledge that is gained through spiritual perfection is complete, whole, unequivocal, and verified through personal experience. Those who have this knowledge can thoroughly understand the truth about human life and the cosmos. . . .

The old morality of the past has now lost its basis, so we need to establish new moral standards. . . . Yet providing humankind with new standards for moral behavior cannot be done with one-sided knowledge. If standards for moral behavior are established on the basis of one-sided knowledge, innumerable immoral practices will arise. How, then, can we not rely on one-sided knowledge? Through an enlightenment which takes the entire universe as its object. In other words, the standards for morality must be established on the basis of great natural principles which can apply to the entire universe and all human life. What is in harmony with these great natural principles is good and moral behavior, and what is not in harmony with them is not good and moral behavior. Only thus we can establish moral standards on an unshakable basis.[44]

Taixu then proceeded to specify his own convictions about the most comprehensive and profound knowledge and how insights into it could provide practical guidance for moral decision-making. He concluded:

According to the Buddhist scriptures, the perfect, great natural principle is the doctrine of cause and effect, the doctrine of the causally produced nature of all things. To explain the truth about human life, we should use the law of causality according to which bitter fruits result from evil actions and pleasing fruits result from good actions. This is profoundly grounded in the nature of the cosmos, as I have explained. All events and things in the universe arise because of the interrelationship between individual and corporate karmic factors and not because of a single factor or a sovereign creator god. Therefore, one-sided theories cannot serve as standards for human moral behavior. This is my conclusion after studying the great principle of causality. Whether as big as the sun and moon or as small as a caterpillar, nothing comes into being except through causality. From this we can see that all things in the world are completely interrelated and nothing exists independently. This is [the meaning of] the universal principle of cause and effect.... So with regard to human behavior, there are two conclusions. First, if a person harms another, both persons are harmed. Second, if a person benefits another, both persons benefit. Thus when we consider doing something within society, and we take benefiting others as our primary concern, then this is good and moral. If we take harming others as our primary concern, then this is evil and immoral. The standard for human moral action should be whether it benefits others or not.[45]

Taixu's basic position may be interpreted as a form of ethical naturalism. That is, although he does not maintain that specific rules about "what ought to be done" can be simplistically deduced from descriptive statements about the nature of "what is," he does agree with other ethical naturalists that "normative principles contain descriptive terms."[46] In addition, his argument parallels in some respects Paul Tillich's call for a "theonomous," as opposed to a "heteronomous" or "autonomous," basis for ethical judgments. Like Tillich, Taixu rejects as an adequate ground for moral action both divine commands imposed externally from above (heteronomy) and common human reasoning from mere sense experience (autonomy). Rather, he opts for an ethic based on a profoundly spiritual and transformative insight into the very nature of the universe. In this sense, as in Tillich's position, the ground for ethical judgments is to be glimpsed in the very nature of the cosmos, although at the same time it is to be found within one's own mind. Tillich refers to this as a divine order (theonomy) that transcends a subject-object dichotomy, which requires that individuals either impose their own autonomous will or have one imposed heteronomously upon them. In a parallel way, for Taixu, moral judgments are grounded in a process of codependent becoming that transcends all inadequate subject-object distinctions.[47]

The ideals of right thought and action are two. The first ideal is that of "improving human life" *(rensheng gaishan)* or "improving the world" *(renjian gaishan)*. The reformer constantly spoke of the fundamental precepts of the bodhisattva's path, which provided a basis for beginning to talk imaginatively about the creation of "a pure land in this world" *(renjian jingtu)*. The second ideal is that of "becoming a buddha" *(cheng fo)*. Taixu frequently declared that despite the weight of one's karmic past, "every person has the possibility of becoming a Buddha."[48] Everyone can turn and follow in the footsteps of Śākyamuni. Every person can realize his or her buddha-nature by engagement with the Enlightened One's four most important tasks: defeating the "demons" that distract us from the right path *(jiang mo)*, attaining the perfect knowledge of a buddha *(chengdeng zhengjue)*, turning the wheel of Dharma by teaching others the truth *(zhuan falun)*, and saving others by ferrying them over from the state of suffering to the state of enlightenment *(du zhongsheng)*.[49] In a 1939 address, Taixu explicitly linked the ideal of becoming a buddha to China's republican revolution and the ongoing war of resistance against Japan:

> Śākyamuni's conquering Māra and all the fundamental illusions and passions was the beginning of his becoming a Buddha, and thus of the world having the precious jewel of a Buddha. By preaching he turned the wheel of the Law, which was the beginning of the world having the precious jewel of the Dharma. His efforts to save others led persons to become bhikṣus, arhats, and bodhisattvas, and thus was the beginning of the world having the precious jewel that is the sangha. Through the establishment of these three jewels, there began to be Buddhism in the world. Having Buddhism, the world then could enjoy the light that illumined the whole cosmos. Therefore his conquering the illusions and passions was the most important stage in becoming a Buddha and saving the world. . . .
>
> The so-called conquering of illusions and passions destroys all the dark things that disturb and obstruct, just like a revolution must first destroy the evil power of all bad systems and customs. From this we can see that the meaning of becoming a Buddha to save the world very much corresponds to that of a revolution to save a country. The origi-

nal goal of a revolution is to establish something new. But first it must start by destroying things. Because formerly China's political power was held either [by emperors] according to the traditional autocratic system or by competing warlords who segmented the country, the government was not able to respond to needs and concentrate its strength to achieve the aims of defending the country and protecting the people. . . . In recent years imperialistic acts of unfair restraint and oppression against our country have reached a most serious stage, a most critical point, just like when the Buddha Śākyamuni vowed under the Bo tree, "If I do not become a Buddha, may I not arise from this seat," because the vow caused Māra to become afraid and jealous. So Māra manifested all kinds of demonic powers in order to disturb and harm the Buddha. Māra took all things dark, unenlightened, and disturbing to be his life. So if the Buddha did not conquer these demons then he could not become a Buddha, but on the contrary would forever remain under Māra's control. Now China is faced with this kind of situation. So if we are not able to engage in a war of resistance [against Japan] in order finally to prevail, then we will not be able to establish the country, but to the contrary become those vanquished by our enemies.[50]

As Taixu had suggested earlier, in his lengthy essay entitled "Ziyou shiguan" (A Historical Perspective on Freedom), the path toward becoming a buddha, toward becoming truly free from all the "demons" that bind and afflict humankind, involves tearing down and rebuilding the faulty mental structures and harmful social structures that frame human experience. These two kinds of structures are interrelated. Liberation requires becoming enlightened to the transformative implications of the doctrine of no-self and, on that basis, becoming engaged in the practical struggle for just and compassionate social, educational, economic, and political structures in society.[51] According to Taixu, Buddhists cannot effectively pursue spiritual wisdom without engaging in the daily quest to establish a pure land in this world. Hence he sought to inspire his followers with an expansive new idealism and utopianism, while simultaneously calling for a new Buddhist realism *(xianshi zhuyi)* and pragmatism in solving the world's problems.

POLITICAL REALISM

As Welch has appropriately commented, "probably the closest thing to a 'political monk' during the Republican era was Taixu."[52] The reformer acknowledged in his autobiography that as a young man his basic sympathies were with the Chinese anarchists. He maintained that anarchism and Buddhism were very close in political perspective, although he came to believe that the country could best make progress toward anarchism through a form of "democratic socialism."[53] He claimed that socialism and Buddhism similarly advocated human equality and social welfare, and he was impressed with the principle that people ought to contribute to society according to their abilities and receive according to their needs.

Early in his career, Taixu embraced the hope that socialists could eliminate monopolies controlled by wealthy capitalists, whose insensitive power and greed continued to cause such hardship for the peasants and urban working class. Yet by the mid-1920s, Taixu began to express a more moderate socio-economic perspective. He moved more toward the political center, distancing himself from those in the Communist Party and developing relationships with important Guomindang officials. As Welch observes:

> Perhaps because he had his fingers burned by encouraging radicalism among his students, or perhaps because he felt that the prestige for Buddhism could best be won by supporting the central government, or perhaps simply because he was getting older, Taixu became politically more conservative. In 1924 he wrote an article entitled "A Warning about the Communist Party," in which he said that the latter ought to be called "the party of killing and destruction, not the party of common property" (which is what its name means in Chinese).[54]

Taixu's moderating political views appear to be related to his evolving judgments about proper strategies for change. It might be said that the monk finally chose to situate himself somewhat right of center on the political spectrum, between the Guomindang on the right and the Communists on the left. The fundamental issues that he had to weigh carefully were the role of social conflict and whether, within the context of his "Buddhism for human life," the most effective strategies for ultimate transformation ought to be designed narrowly, for the individual citizen, or more broadly, to include the socio-political structures in which all persons found themselves.

As Arif Dirlik maintains, the Guomindang's perspective on change was quintessentially expressed in Chiang Kai-shek's New Life Movement (Xin shenghuo yundong). Initiated in 1934, the movement was based on the view that the salvation of the country could be attained most directly through hygienic and behavioral reform of the individual. Chiang's two most important goals for the Chinese populace were personal "cleanliness" *(qingjie)* and "discipline" *(guiju)*, both of which were intended to connote a certain measure of militarization of the citizenry. In response to widespread criticism that the New Life Movement was too conservative and narrowly conceived, leaders of the Guomindang claimed that the program aimed to alter the very basis of social behavior. Chiang himself asserted, for example:

> In order to become a healthy modern *(xiandai)* citizen, it is necessary first to have a strong and robust body; having a strong body, [one] then has a strong spirit; having a strong spirit, [one] can then acquire all the abilities to strengthen the nation; having all kinds of abilities to strengthen the nation, [one] can naturally defend the state and glorify the nation, help our state and nation to forever accord with the world and not again suffer from the aggression and oppression of foreign countries or receive disdain and insults.[55]

According to Dirlik, this conservative political philosophy developed primarily out of an abhorrence of social conflict. Because such conflict was traditionally judged to be the result of moral decline, the Guomindang denied it any important role in social change.

In contrast to this conservative position, the Communist Party took a much broader view. As Dirlik remarks,

> Communist policies were based on the premise that class struggle—or, in a more generalized sense, social conflict—was the motive force of social change, and social transformation the foundation of political change.... The dominant Communist view embodied in Mao Zedong's thought has conceived the relationship between individual improvement and social change as a dialectical one, with changes in one depen-

dent upon—and, in their turn, determinative of—changes in the other, a conception consistent with the Marxist view of man as "the ensemble of social relations.". . . Whatever the conditions of rural mobilization and the occasional changes in Communist tactics, it is evident that it was their sustained ability to improve the people's livelihood, as well as their involvement of the people in social change, that was to a great extent responsible for the hold they came to have over the population. The people, mobilized in the revolutionary transformation of their own lives, were much more responsive to Communist guidance, even in the cause of "cleanliness" and "discipline," than they ever were to the Guomindang.[56]

Taixu's early associations with anarchists and revolutionaries who wanted to overthrow the Manchu dynasty led him, as a young man, to see the importance of institutional and structural change. He spoke freely about the need for racial, governmental, economic, and religious forms of "revolution" *(geming)*. He once remarked, "Even the idea of revolution growing out of love for the people . . . is in harmony with Buddhism. . . . In the process of a revolution there is always a phase of destruction preceding reconstruction."[57] Both his active support of the 1911 anti-Qing revolution and his involvement with the so-called invasion of Jin Shan reveal his implicit understanding that a certain amount of conflict and suffering would be necessary in the transformation of society and sangha.

Yet as he matured and confronted the actual consequences of division and violence, Taixu could not ultimately justify systematic class conflict as a means to an end. As a Buddhist, his understanding of moral intentionality was integrally linked to certain normative modes of action within his tradition that would not comfortably permit him to adopt Mao's communism. In the final analysis, then, without abandoning his basic affirmation that individual development and social progress were dialectically related, as the socialists and communists maintained, he adopted a position much more in consonance with the Guomindang than with the Communist Party.

As a result, Taixu spoke expansively about the harmony between Buddhism and Sun Yat-sen's "three principles of the people" *(sanmin zhuyi)*, even stating in one article that "Buddhism is the ultimate goal of Sanminism and Sanminism is Buddhism put into practice."[58] He wrote favorably about the concern of Chiang Kai-shek's New Life Movement for propriety *(li)*, justice *(yi)*, honesty *(lian)*, and sense of shame *(chi)*.[59] He occasionally quoted Sun and Chiang, stood proudly at the side of the generalissimo for a photograph in 1928, traveled abroad twice as a goodwill ambassador of the Nationalist government, and accepted state subsidies for the operation of his seminary near Chongqing.[60] Some people even came to think that he was secretly a member of the Guomindang, although the suggestion was always denied by those closest to him.

Taixu wanted all his followers, monastic and lay, to be knowledgeable about current political issues and events and active in addressing social problems, despite the fact that most monks during the Republican period remained totally uninvolved in such "worldly" affairs. In fact, as Prip-Møller's research in Republican China has documented, a number of Buddhist monasteries at the time even prohibited monks from discussing politics, posting signs that read, "Whoever delights in talking politics and whose heart is bent on secular matters will not be allowed to live in the monastery."[61] Nevertheless, Taixu urged his followers to adopt a realistic perspective on politics, aware that one of the most critical general concerns of humankind was finding "the most reasonable and perfect form of politics."[62]

Taixu maintained that the traditional Buddhist ideal of an enlightened ruler *(cakravartin)* provided a parallel both to the ancient western concept of a philosopher-king, as recommended by Plato, and the ancient Chinese concept of a sage-king. Thus those rulers who gained insight into the absolute emptiness and interdependence of all things would doubtless exceed all others in governing with wisdom and compassion. Accordingly, they could advance human rights and freedoms like those enjoyed in Europe and America while preventing what had resulted from such freedoms within the western context— namely, an unceasing competition between individuals that appeared to promote equality but that actually encouraged inequality, economic classism, and imperialistic colonialism. Explaining the origins of socialism, Taixu argued that it had developed in reaction to the excesses of western individualism:

> Socialism opposed democracies because, although democracies claimed that all persons were free and equal, all were by no means free and equal. Only a minority of persons was free; the majority was not free. It reacted against the fact that [in democracies] all economic resources were enjoyed by and controlled by only a few people, as it also reacted against the politics of traditional nationalism. Thus socialism was formed. This kind of socialism is something that many individuals organize as a group, so that in such groups all kinds of benefits can be shared and help the majority of the people.[63]

Although Taixu was greatly influenced by socialist perspectives in formulating his judgments about forms of western democratic capitalism, and believed that socialist analyses of the reasons for conflict between the bourgeoisie and proletariat were largely correct, he was not a naive promoter of socialism but was alert to different expressions of socialism and to the contrasts between collectivism *(jichan zhuyi)* and communism *(gongchan zhuyi)*. Thus he recognized the positive religio-philosophical impulses that contributed to the rise of socialism while rejecting both Marx's economic determinism and its reductionistic views of religion. He also acknowledged the lively debate between those who believed in the activist role of the central government and those anarchists who wanted to get rid of it. Above all, Taixu wanted to distinguish between socialists who were advocates of gradual, peaceful reform and those who were proponents of rapid change through violent revolution. Although he appreciated the socialists' aims and thought them to have much in common with those of Buddhist modernists, eventually he judged them to be seriously flawed. He wrote in 1935:

> With regard to the errors of socialist means, we can enumerate four: (1) socialists consider the external environment and forget about individual persons. What they emphasize is entirely the reconstruction of the environment, the restructuring of society, but not the reforming of the mind and body through personal moral cultivation. There is an ancient saying, "From the Son of Heaven to the commoner, all must take the

cultivation of the self as the essential task." If the self is not cultivated, then the family will not be orderly, the country will not be [properly] governed, and the society will not be just. (2) They focus strictly on property and neglect morality. They think that bad environments result from property inequities, so they only try to alter the property system without realizing that economic classes also result from changes and developments in psychological states and desires. (3) They seek to correct the present consequences of previous actions while ignoring the root causes. The various classes that humans have created are also all the consequences of previous deeds. Because the original actions were different, the karmic consequences are different. So if they think that they can merely remove the consequences, such as despots and capitalists, without realizing the need to improve the root causes, then while their aim is certainly a good one, they can only get rid of evil results but they cannot sow good seeds. Thus in the twinkling of an eye the warlords become dictators and the criminals, tyrants. This is tantamount to changing merely the form but not the substance. This doesn't help anything! (4) They try to eliminate individual property but allow a person's grasping for such to continue. They eliminate all classes and nationalize all property, so that people forget the boundaries that delineate the things that belong to the self. The intention of communism is for everyone to attain what they each privately desire, but their grasping desires only become more intense. Since individual property comes from grasping for things, how can the possessing of things be forgotten if the self's grasping is not eliminated? And as a result, people become lazy and do not like to work hard. They only want to obtain things without making an effort. Many kinds of industries, therefore, will not be productive, and the whole situation will ultimately return to its previous state.[64]

In the 1920s, Taixu had expressed the fear that the most pressing danger in the twentieth century was the possible conflagration of societies in class warfare. The danger was not so much that the rich and powerful would continue to dominate and oppress the poor, but that the poor would rise up violently to overthrow the rich. Hence he urged the poor not to follow the incitement of revolutionaries who could possibly destroy evil but who could not establish the good, who could kill but not thereby give life to a more perfect way. In a parallel manner, he sharply warned the privileged classes in China and around the globe:

> From now on, the world's most dangerous issue will not be the tyranny and struggle for hegemony by those who constitute the powerful class internationally. It will be the fact that those who are weak will unite to seek revenge on those who are powerful. The danger will not lie in the monopolies and competitions of the capitalist class, but in the united struggle of resistance by the poor against the capitalist class. In fact, this kind of situation is already happening! Throughout the world the weak and the poor already are becoming out of control like a raging fire or blaze on the prairie, or like a tiger or rhinoceros breaking free from its cage. The powerful class and the capitalist class are already facing their total collapse, being surrounded on all four sides [by the weak and the poor]. So as I have said before, only Buddhism can save us in this dangerous crisis.[65]

The reformer argued that if Buddhists were to help heal the wounds of a divided global society and prevent the uncontrolled violence that was certain to erupt, then even members of the sangha had to become active in political affairs. After World War II, some of his monastic and lay supporters hoped that Taixu would go even farther and endorse the formation of a Buddhist political party to increase the religion's influence on public policy. The monk acknowledged that he had seriously considered the possibility and was "slow to decide."[66] He knew that in Burma many monks had participated in political activities and had even joined in the military resistance against the invading Japanese. He recognized that in Sri Lanka the sangha was split over the decision by some of its members to form a Buddhist political party, while in Tibet certain lamas even served as local government officials.

Taixu realized that there were real advantages as well as disadvantages to political participation and organization in China, especially for the monastic community. One the one hand, if monks and nuns considered their life and work to be completely beyond politics, they could easily find themselves ignored or, even worse, persecuted, and their institutional properties appropriated by unfriendly governments.

On the other hand, if they became too directly involved in politics, they could quickly find their independence compromised by such associations and, as a result, public respect for their religious leadership diminished.

The best course, Taixu judged, was to encourage participation in political activities for both lay and monastic followers while simultaneously discouraging monks and nuns from serving in any elective office or in the formation of any specifically Buddhist political party. He thus affirmed not only the constitutional right but the responsibility of every Buddhist, including members of the sangha, to listen to the concerns of the people, study public policy issues, and seek practical solutions for the benefit of all sentient beings. Yet he also dissuaded monks and nuns from pursuing political careers in which they could be called upon to exercise power over others, be feared or envied because of the authority of their office, and lose time and opportunity for important religious duties. By rejecting the idea of a specifically Buddhist political party, he also avoided making party affiliation a divisive religious issue. As he wrote,

> Lay Buddhists can participate as much as they wish in various political parties and associations, or they can organize political parties using other names, but they must not use the name of Buddhism in order to organize a political party.
>
> Again, some Buddhists are members of the Guomindang, the Youth Party, the Democratic Socialist Party, the Democratic League, or even of the Communist Party. Even more Buddhists are not members of any political party or association. Since they have already decided to join certain parties or associations, or not to join one, were we to organize a Buddhist Party we could not ask them to change their affiliation and join the Buddhist Party. And if the Buddhist Party were to become yet another independent party, then we would alienate ourselves from them. My friends who study Buddhism and lay Buddhists are members of different parties and associations, or they have chosen not to join such groups. Through philosophical, literary, cultural, educational, charitable, and other activities, I have friendly relations with members of every religion, and with nonreligious people as well. If I were to lead a

Buddhist political party, then on the contrary all these ties would be reduced. Therefore Buddhism does not want to organize a political party.[67]

ENVISIONING A LASTING PEACE

Although Taixu had always been known within the Buddhist community for his modernist perspectives on social activism, after the 1937 Japanese invasion that initiated the long Chinese nightmare of World War II, he was increasingly outspoken on specific social and political issues. From the vantage point of the Dharma, he sought both to critique the destructive forces that he saw at work in the world and to envision a more equitable and peaceful world. In a significant 1943 essay entitled "Lianheguo zhansheng hou zhi pinghe shijie" (A Peaceful World After the Allied Victory), the Buddhist master outlined a number of his assessments of the world's situation and concrete proposals for the post-war era. It was his position that no expedient compromises could be forged with the Axis powers in order to end the war. All people should realize, he asserted, that the Axis countries' aggression was based on three wholly unacceptable principles: "first, militarism; second, racism; and third, a cruelly autocratic and superstitious form of heroism."[68] Therefore, anything less than total surrender on their part would be nothing but a temporary armistice that would be followed by further fighting as the struggle for true freedom from their tyranny continued. Confident in the ultimate victory of the Allied forces, he thought it important to describe the conditions necessary for a lasting peace marked by the "absolute equality" of all nations and the universal will of all peoples to live in harmony.

The key to that future, he asserted, will always reside within human minds—that is, within peaceful minds that generate peaceful lives. According to Taixu, the human mind can, in fact, be linked to four basic kinds of ambition *(xinzhi)* that determine moral behavior. The first and most prevalent kind of ambition is to benefit oneself and one's family; the second most prevalent is to serve one's national or ethnic group; the third is to benefit all humankind; and the fourth is to save all sentient beings in the universe. Given the complexity of human personality, most people's thoughts and actions at any given moment are expressive of more than a single ambition. However, the far-reaching fourth ambition, Taixu asserted, is distinctly that of the bodhisattva of Mahāyāna scripture and tradition. As a spiritual ideal, it motivates far too few in this world and should be considered the supreme ambition that remains for virtually all human beings a future goal.

More immediately or pragmatically, however, the first three kinds of ambition must be reprioritized in reverse order. The benefits of all humankind must come before nation, family, and self. Only when individuals, families, and nations are willing to sacrifice their own interests for those of the whole human community will the cornerstones for a lasting peace be put into place. Thus the new mandate for every Buddhist must become, in a real sense, "to break his relations with not only his family but also with his country . . . [in order to] look upon the people of the world in the same brotherly spirit."[69] The reformer remarked:

> Some will ask: Since you de-emphasize the benefits of national and ethnic groups, is not your position close to the internationalism of the Communist Party? This is definitely not the case. We should realize that the Communist Party's proletarian class internationalism is based on division and struggle, but the good of all humankind is based on peace and harmony. The good of all humankind includes the good of all nations and ethnic groups. So certainly we can accommodate the full development of that which benefits national and ethnic groups while not undermining the establishment of a long-lasting peaceful world in which all persons benefit.[70]

Taixu thought that the global society of the post-war era would require appropriate educational, economic, and governmental structures to maintain a lasting peace. With regard to education, the Buddhist master argued that its scope was universally too narrow. In every country the primary aim of educators was merely to prepare individuals for productive work within the economic, political, and military organizations of their state. A new perspective on education had to be developed to encompass the more expansive goal of preparing people to become global citizens and contribute to a harmonious global culture. For this, a holistic form of education was needed that would lead both children and adults toward a richer, modern vision of the complementarity and interdependence of all peoples.

Though present-day colleges and universities might claim to provide "higher" education, Taixu observed, it is clearly not the "highest" education concerned with moral culture. Hence what is needed at the post-secondary level is a new "international" or "global" university, established jointly by leaders from all nations and with branch campuses throughout the world. "What we need," Taixu remarked, "is an institution where great souls are trained":

> The mission of this university and its branches will be to form a new world culture out of the different cultures, to eliminate all differences and prejudices, to bring about the free flow and assimilation of cultures and to lay a cultural foundation for peace.... Universal equality, freedom, justice and love must be taught to the future generations. Furthermore, the field of human activities must be expanded to reach out to the entire universe, to all spheres of nature. Through such broadened education a healthy body and healthy soul will be established in every individual. Man will become a harmonious part of nature. Instead of limiting his sphere of activities to his immediate surroundings his outlook will be the universe and heaven and become truly a part of the trinity of heaven, earth and man.[71]

With regard to economics, Taixu advocated free trade and economic cooperation. "Free trading and equal access to raw materials and markets," he wrote, "must exist in the peaceful world to come."[72] Large countries and small must respect one another as equals and work together for economic progress and improved living standards for all peoples. Unbridled capitalism must be recognized as the destructive force that it is, he asserted, as most world leaders, including the U.S. President Roosevelt, had already come to admit. Large companies that irresponsibly manipulate national and international markets for their own gain must be regulated in order to encourage economic forces that benefit all levels of society. "Capitalism and the profit system must go," Taixu flatly asserted. "All economic activities must be undertaken with national and universal welfare in mind. Production and consumption must be planned and controlled. There should be no deficiency and no waste."[73]

Four additional economic principles were important for the postwar era. First, said the Buddhist reformer, rich countries should help poor countries; developed nations should grant assistance to underdeveloped nations. Taixu realized that there were significant differences in economic status between the industrialized and the nonindustrialized world. Therefore he commended especially the United States for taking the lead in offering financial assistance for developing nations.

Second, after the defeat of Germany and Japan, along with their allies, economic aid should be granted to them for reconstruction and rehabilitation and no war reparations demanded.

Third, immigration policies should be liberalized. To promote economic efficiency and productivity, both immigration within the national borders of large countries like China, as well as international immigration, should be encouraged, especially to undeveloped countries in Africa and South America. Likewise, all forms of discrimination against immigrants should be ended.

Fourth, monetary policies should be strictly monitored. Government restraints should seek to stabilize prices and prevent the chaos often caused by rapid inflation.

With regard to global politics, Taixu was optimistic that the world was moving toward a universal democracy. Nevertheless, he declared, "With regard to each nation's internal political system, of course it remains a principle that the people should decide the issue by themselves. There is no need to force democracy on people, for sooner or later gradual progress can be made in enlightening them."[74] This modernizing process of political "enlightenment," as Taixu described it, involves the awakening of all nations to the desirability of both democratic freedoms and a centralized form of "global government."

With regard to a democratic form of government, the nations who had less experience with democracy, including China and the Soviet Union, would learn from those who had more experience. Thereby rapid progress could be made toward defining universal rights and obligations. Colonies would necessarily be given their independence, because all forms of colonial oppression and imperialism were obvious impediments to lasting peace. Taixu called on Great Britain in particular to set an example in this.

With respect to an international form of government, the Buddhist master believed that an impetus for political unification in the post-war period would surely emerge from the close cooperation between China, the United States, Great Britain, and the Soviet Union. The signs of movement toward political unification would be a viable "world court," a respected "world congress," and a unified military force. The Permanent Court of International Justice (also popularly called the "World Court"), which sat at The Hague, had ceased to function, for all intents and purposes, after the German occupation of the Netherlands in 1940. Moreover, the operations of the ineffectual League of Nations in Geneva were virtually dead. Nevertheless, Taixu saw in both institutions foundational steps to the future. He envisioned a new court with real powers to settle disputes and protect the rights of the poor and the weak. And he called for a new international organization with proportional representation to foster cooperation and peace among all peoples. "Within three to six months after the end of the war," he stated, "a 'World Congress' (Shijie daibiao dahui) must be formed. Germany, Italy, and the other Axis powers must join this representative organization within one to three years."[75]

With regard to a military, he called for strict arms controls and the creation of a single international force, stating:

> It [the World Congress] should control the military forces of all the nations and have the power of military sanction against aggressor states and those who should refuse to submit to the justice of the Congress. Its military strength should be formed by taking over arms belonging to the defeated Axis nations and those of the Allies. In addition, no nation should be allowed to manufacture arms for its own use in the future. The Commander-in-Chief of the Congress Armed Forces should be appointed by rotation from China, the United States, Great Britain, the U.S.S.R., and five other neutrals to avoid the abusive power by any nation or individual.[76]

Beyond all his specific educational, economic, and political proposals for the creation of new international programs and institutions in the post-war era was Taixu's overarching call for the nurturing of a truly "moral culture" *(daode wenhua)*. To achieve a lasting peace, what the world needed most fundamentally was a sweeping spiritual transformation, a universal change within the human heart that would alter the very fabric of social interaction and political engagement. In the present world, Taixu observed, "parties are formed for the defense of common interests, so that the whole world may be said to be composed of coalitions of all sorts, which are always on the alert, and whose object it is to use every possible means to suppress their rivals."[77]

However, according to Taixu, democracy must finally yield more than the protected right of individuals and coalitions to participate in power struggles for their own benefit. From the Buddhist perspective, such a limited understanding of democratic goals would guarantee only the continuation of a destructive individualism while ignoring "the link that unites our lives with that of every living being."[78] Ultimately, he claimed, each person has to see clearly that "all human egos are bound together by bonds of sympathy, and each of them radiates a subtle influence which reaches all those who can respond to it."[79] Accordingly, as C. Yates McDaniel observed in 1935, Taixu and other Chinese Buddhist modernists argued, in essence, that because all sentient beings manifest buddha-nature, "democracy is government based upon compassion and love, and the recognition that one is the servant of all."[80] For Taixu, the acceptance of servanthood was the defining task of the bodhisattva's way.

CHAPTER 5

A CREATIVE RECOVERY OF TRADITION

The central spiritual paradigms of any religious tradition can be understood to address the existential situation of the majority of individual people who are perceived to form its holy community. The Confucian scholars of classical China, for example, understood their community, in the midst of disorder, to be on the way—via the rectification of names and the extension of virtue—to an all-embracing experience of the unity of heaven, earth, and humankind. This was the attainment of the rare yet paradigmatic *junzi*—the "superior man" (James Legge), the "gentleman" (Arthur Waley), or the "profound person" (Tu Wei-ming).[1] According to the metaphysics of the early Confucians, the universe was a thoroughly moral one. Each person possessed both an "evaluating mind" capable of discovering the inherent order of the cosmos and an ability to emulate exemplary behavioral models.[2] Indeed, argues Hu Shi, the basic logic of Confucianism began with the attempt to discover, through the study of names, what things ought to be and do.[3] Discovery was the key to the regulation of the social and political order by means of an elaborate system of relational ideals *(li)* attributed to an absolute and a priori origin.[4]

Mahāyāna Buddhism, in contrast, presented the Chinese with a spiritual path toward a wordless wisdom that was beyond all names and forms and the suffering associated with them. Such was the attainment of the paradigmatic bodhisattva. In view of Buddhism's radically different understanding of reality and philosophy of language, early Chinese masters such as Daoan (312–385) and Sengzhao (374–414) saw the necessity of directly attacking the Confucian claim that "names correspond to things." Accordingly, moral development was presented not as progressive discrimination but as progressive forgetting *(jian wang)*. Bodhisattvas were worthy of praise precisely because, having "forgotten" all names and forms as sources of binding attachment, they were freed to act compassionately within the world. Having defeated the temptations of the great deceiver, Māra, to grasp for names and forms, and having been shaken by the transformative truth that "form is emptiness and emptiness form," bodhisattvas were freed to become friends of all sentient beings, refuges for all those who suffer.[5]

The Confucian *junzi,* therefore, was one who practiced a comprehensive discrimination based on a linguistic coding of cosmic order. A classical emphasis within the tradition was on ethico-religious cartography via lexicography. To employ Jonathan Smith's terminology, the typical Confucianist was engaged in a "locative" project, locating and attuning all aspects of the human microcosm in relation to the heavenly macrocosm—a project that the *junzi* had successfully completed.[6] The career of a bodhisattva presented the Chinese with a sharply contrasting spiritual trajectory, for in Buddhism it was the evil Māra who enticingly offered the linguistic code as an actual map of reality. Therefore, the Buddhist masters sought to recontextualize human existence by reference to a nondual realm, or dimension of experience, that was beyond language and ordinary categories of understanding but that, once discovered by the bodhisattva, provided both release from and meaning for life within this world of time and space.

Moreover, because Chinese Buddhists generally believed that all beings were endowed with "intrinsic enlightenment" or an original "buddha-nature," the arousal of the thought of enlightenment *(bodhicitta)*—the decisive conversion experience that was held to initiate the bodhisattva's spiritual journey—was understood to be, potentially, only a breath away. Most Buddhists in China assumed that in the karmic past of any new bodhisattva, there was a point at which some enlightened figure had planted a seed of truth that took root in a virtuous disposition *(gotra)*. Subsequently, "after many lifetimes, thanks to the infused grace of the various teacher-saviors and the merit earned by responding to them, a person becomes able to put forth the *bodhicitta*."[7] Surprisingly "graced" in this manner, new bodhisattvas proceed to consolidate their *bodhicitta,* take their public vows of compassionate service, and advance along the path of enlightenment while working for the welfare of all living beings.

Taixu's own portraits of the bodhisattva path were not strikingly original or controversial. Nevertheless, they may be said to constitute a creative recovery of tradition that reveals his particular form of piety, for in defining the bodhisattva's path of action, the reformer sought to recover and underscore the elements of his tradition that were especially relevant for a socially engaged "Buddhism for human life"—elements that were often neglected in contemporary China. He aimed thereby to inspire self-confidence in common bodhisattvas, urging them to dream great dreams about what they could accomplish in the world. He wanted to remind them of the precepts and perfections, and to encourage them to think creatively about establishing a pure land on earth. He hoped to reshape the community of monastic bodhisattvas to teach and model the Dharma more effectively. And he sought to offer a compelling apologetic for his understanding of a modern form of Buddhism, in light of sharp criticism from both inside and outside of the Chinese sangha.

ILLUMINATING THE TRUE WAY

Jan Yün-hua has observed not only that the idea of the bodhisattva was one of the most important and popular themes in Chinese Buddhist literature, but also that these great beings were presented through a threefold typology that "introduced a new image of the religious founder through past lives of the Buddha; it provided a spiritual map to man, and indicated that the religious goal was attainable through cultivation; [and] it brought to the Chinese masses a warm, compassionate and powerful personal deity."[8] Thus, (1) through the Jātaka tales of Gautama's previous lives, Buddhism presented an image of religious and moral leadership far more expansive and imaginative than that of the ancient sage-kings of China; (2) it introduced the striking idea of the achievability of the religious goal through individual cultivation; and (3) it offered the hope of salvation through the skill and power of compassionate deities—namely, the celestial or "phantasma bodhisattvas," as Lancaster has referred to them.[9]

Two controversial issues about this threefold typology are significant for understanding Taixu's presentation of the bodhisattva path. First, although all Buddhists acknowledged that the bodhisattva's career is a long one of practicing the perfections *(pāramitā)* through numerous stages *(bhūmi)* of prescribed spiritual development, questions arose about how applicable this path was to normal human beings.[10] The historic debate concerned the extent to which a typical follower should interpret the *inspirational* bodhisattva career of the Enlightened One as an *aspirational* model. On the one hand, there is little in the Jātaka tales to suggest that Gautama's unique path of spiritual virtuosity constitutes a practical ideal to be embraced by the entire community, little encouragement to imagine that everyone should aspire to such an illustrious and noble religious career. Accordingly, most teachers of the Theravāda tradition have continued to interpret the Jātaka tales as inspirational reading—that is, as literature that reminds adherents of the extraordinary wisdom and compassion displayed through many lifetimes by the solitary buddha of this age.

In the Mahāyāna tradition, on the other hand, the bodhisattva path that Gautama trod so tirelessly is portrayed as a universal ideal. Members of the Mahāyāna community are meant not only to be inspired by the Buddha's glorious career, but to aspire to become like him in the realization of their own buddha-nature as well. This is directly related, of course, to the community's self-definition; the "Great Vehicle" (Skt. Mahāyāna) is synonymous with the careers of bodhisattvas. As Peter Gregory has noted, Chinese Buddhists generally followed the presentation in *The Lotus Sūtra* that defines śrāvakas as those disciples who attained liberation through contemplation of the Four Noble Truths, and pratyekabuddhas as those who achieved release by penetrating the truth of conditioned origination (Skt. *pratītya-samutpāda;* Ch. *yuanqi*). Yet these two vehicles lead to an arhatship that is markedly inferior to the goal of the bodhisattva path. That goal, which the *Lotus* assures disciples that they will ultimately attain, is nothing less than supreme buddhahood.[11]

The presentation of the religious community's central paradigm, therefore, primarily addresses those new bodhisattvas struggling to remain faithful to the enlightened life that they have only recently understood to be a real possibility for them personally. Thus the bodhisattva ideal appeals to those persons who, inspired by the buddhas and bodhisattvas of the ten directions, aspire to attain the selfless, transcendental path on which those great beings course.

In affirming the applicability of the bodhisattva path for all people, Taixu distinguished sharply between the perspective of the Nikāya schools and that of Mahāyāna tradition. The Chinese reformer observed that the paths of the śrāvakas and pratyekabuddhas are full of pitfalls and not fully in consonance with the absolute selflessness that Śākyamuni realized. Their limited goal of self-enlightenment is not the highest goal to which all Buddhists should aspire. He remarked:

> Mahāyāna followers seek self-enlightenment in order to awaken others, so that all might together realize eternal truth. Nikāya Buddhism is like a single wheeled cart; Mahāyāna is like a train or a steamship in which everyone can sit together. Nikāya Buddhism lacks vows of compassion, whereas Mahāyāna's compassionate vows are profound. In other words, the difference between Mahāyāna and Nikāya Buddhism is essentially that between manifesting the bodhi-mind and an unwillingness to manifest it.[12]

Second, in addition to this basic distinction between Nikāya and Mahāyāna Buddhism, Taixu emphasized one particular response to the bodhisattva ideal within the Mahāyāna community itself. As Luis Gómez has remarked, in Mahāyāna there is a natural tension "between the notion of Bodhisattvas as supernatural beings on the one hand, and on the other hand Bodhisattvas as human ideals: 'Bodhisattva' as a state of perfection attainable by real human beings, and 'Bodhisattvas' as a name for immanent or potential enlightenment inherent to conscious life. This tension is part of the dynamics of the myth, and does not imply that only one of the alternatives must be the orthodox or 'true' definition of 'Bodhisattva.'"[13] Accordingly, Sangharakshita has stated, Mahāyāna masters have historically differentiated two basic religious responses of the heart:

> The first, which may be termed the active or masculine response, consists in determining to become a Bodhisattva oneself and to take part in the great work of universal emancipation. The second, the passive or feminine response, consists in resolving to have complete faith in the power of the Bodhisattva's vow and to allow oneself to be saved by him. These two responses or reactions of the devotee when confronted by the Bodhisattva Ideal form the psychological basis of what Nāgārjuna terms the "difficult path" and the "easy path.". . . In the Mahāyāna the distinction is between the Bodhisattva (or Bodhisattvas: the Ideal is singular only in the abstract) who out of compassion vows to establish a Pure Land and liberate all beings, and those who by virtue of their faith in him are reborn into that Pure Land.[14]

The *Mūlamadhyamaka-kārikās* (Fundamentals of the Middle Way) and other important works of the renowned Buddhist philosopher Nāgārjuna (c. 150–250) were rooted in the analytic concerns of the Abhidharma literature and the wisdom perspectives of the Prajñā-pāramitā texts. However, through a dialectic of oppositions intended to highlight the absolute emptiness of all things *(śūnyatā)*, they provided legitimacy for both these religious responses: the "difficult" path of self-reliance, and the "easy" path of dependence. In the late Qing and Republican periods in China, most monks and nuns became familiar with both paths and examined their own personalities and capabilities in relation to these two forms, or expressions, of piety. Moreover, most masters were supportive of the dual practice of Chan and Pure Land and judged the two to be complementary.[15] According to Chün-fang Yü, this was even true of the Pure Land master Yinguang, who was largely responsible for the revival of Buddhist devotionalism in the period.[16]

Despite the fact that Taixu occasionally sanctioned such dual practice to attract the masses, as has been noted, the growing popularity of Pure Land devotionalism concerned him. Kenneth Ch'en has stated that "of the four million or so lay devotees of Buddhism in China during the 1930's, it is estimated that sixty to seventy percent considered themselves to be followers of the Pure Land School."[17] No source for the estimate is cited, and the figure may be merely Ch'en's own guess, but by all accounts of Buddhism in the early twentieth century, Pure Land piety was dominant within the lay community and growing within the sangha. The monk Zhenhua confesses that he was often moved to tears when reading some of Yinguang's *gāthās,* which proclaimed in sum: "With Chan there's no one but yourself, while Pure Land borrows Buddha's strength; when these are on a balance weighed, Pure Land seems best suited to our need. . . . For men in times of Law's decay, this way alone can meet the test."[18] Taixu emphatically disagreed with such teaching and asserted that too many lay devotees and too many monks were satisfied with the passive way of dependence without understanding its profound doctrinal basis or the value of the active way.

In accord with his emphasis on a "Buddhism for human life," Taixu attempted to redress what he considered to be an unfortunate imbalance within the Chinese Buddhist community between these two possible forms of Mahāyāna piety. This effort was grounded in his belief that the active way, the way of self-reliance, was the most appropriate and responsible form of Buddhist practice in the modern world, and that the dominance of the passive way, the way of dependence, had led to deleterious misunderstandings of the religion both inside and outside of the Sangha. In other words, as an ethical pietist for whom religion primarily meant doing things—above all, engaging in compassionate forms of social interaction—the visionary and otherworldly emphasis of Pure Land devotionalism was counterproductive.

Thus Taixu was convinced that, rather than encouraging members of the Mahāyāna community to proceed energetically in their own practice of selfless service in the world, such devotionalism had led them to postpone action in favor of reliance on visualization of the pure lands, the worship of images, and the recitation of the name of

Amitābha Buddha *(nian fo)* in hopes of rebirth in another cosmic realm. In fact, as Taixu emphasized in his last series of lectures, many people were confused about the true nature of a bodhisattva:

> Everyone knows the name "bodhisattva," but most people really do not understand its true meaning. Usually people take images to represent bodhisattvas. If they see an image made of mud or carved of wood, or sculptured in relief, or made of metal, or painted, or made of paper, then they all call these images "bodhisattvas." They even refer to imported toy dolls as "foreign bodhisattvas." This is mistaken. This latter habit has especially become a most serious error. We ought to realize that among such images are images of bodhisattvas. However, there are also images of buddhas that have a higher status than bodhisattvas, and there are images of ancient sages and worthies that have a lower status, and even images of demons with the head of an ox and other evil spiritual beings. So we cannot ignorantly call all of them "bodhisattvas." At the same time, we certainly cannot refer to bodhisattvas and images of bodhisattvas as if they were one and the same. If one of us who is living has the heart of a bodhisattva and does the good deeds of a bodhisattva, then that person is a bodhisattva.
>
> *"Pusa"* [bodhisattva] is a rough transliteration of the original term, which in the Indian language sounds like *"puti saduo."* The meaning of *"puti"* [bodhi] is awareness or wisdom; *"saduo"* refers to sentient beings. So together they mean "beings whose essence is wisdom."
>
> The original meaning of "bodhisattva" is one who can manifest a bodhi-mind, who with great wisdom seeks for enlightenment and with a great compassionate heart helps all those who suffer. This is a bodhisattva. Therefore we can take this bodhi-mind as our starting point in order to seek this [enlightenment] and to transform things. If we not only entertain the ideal but are actually able to practice it, we may be called true bodhisattvas. So bodhisattvas are those who are awakened to the truth. They are able to become enlightened themselves and then to awaken others so that all make progress in cultivating supreme enlightenment. These are enlightenment beings. Therefore bodhisattvas are obviously not lifeless images but those who have a bodhi-mind.[19]

According to Taixu, the most efficacious path for those pursuing bodhisattvahood is not through some celestial realm or distant pure land. Rather, it takes our common, ordinary human experience on this plane as its starting point and "proceeds step by step toward sacrality and creates a pure land, progressing from shallow to deep, changing the inferior to the superior."[20] Yet Taixu was not oblivious to the "dynamic" of the bodhisattva myth and its "extraordinary" dimension. In fact, his student Yinshun was later to criticize him for not sufficiently attacking the worship of celestial buddhas and bodhisattvas.

It might be said that Taixu was trying to recover this very dynamic in his tradition by highlighting the "ordinary" and looking for the miraculous not so much in the heavens as in the human heart. As he put it elsewhere, "In Buddhism, the bodhisattva is certainly not an idol shaped from clay or carved from wood, but is a kind of person who has great thoughts about transforming the cosmos and improving human life."[21] For Taixu, because all human beings are capable of manifesting this great bodhi-mind, all are by nature bodhisattvas, even if they do not recognize it; they need only awaken to this fact and take up the path toward a full and complete enlightenment. "Buddhism puts the emphasis on actual conduct in life, on living the truth," he wrote. "It does not end in talk."[22]

A PRELUDE TO THE PATH

The traditional prescriptions for learning the path step by step are detailed in the Mahāyāna tradition for the typical bodhisattva (that is, for the bodhisattva who still has far to go in his study). Accordingly, Taixu commented, "The study course that I am advocating is especially for encouraging bodhisattvas who have only just begun to aspire to a bodhi-mind. The intent is to help people to become great-hearted common bodhisattvas, not those bodhisattvas who are instantly able to transcend the two vehicles [of the śrāvakas and pratyekabuddhas]."[23]

The course of study involves progression through a series of ten stages *(shi di)* involving both visionary and ethical attainment. The course, Taixu said, is much like one's progression from kindergarten to advanced doctoral studies. It proceeds through three basic movements: (1) preliminary expressions of "right faith" *(zheng xin)* and taking refuge in the Three Jewels *(san bao)*; (2) conversion experiences, which constitute the production of the thought of enlightenment that issues forth in great vows of compassion *(bei yuan)*; and (3) practice of the Six Perfections *(liu du)*.

For Taixu, preparation for the long course begins by a simple opening of the heart that is more profound than mere intellectual assent. "According to the *Huayan jing*," observed the Chinese master, "'faith is the origin of the way and the mother of merit that nurtures the roots of all goodness.'. . . Therefore even if practitioners perform every kind of good deed, if they do not have faith, their deeds are polluted and unclean and insufficient to attain the highest path."[24] As he commented elsewhere, "It is difficult to discover the truth of Buddhism in the theories and innumerable works that have been written on the subject. To grasp it we must first of all open our hearts after the manner of the Buddha; it is enough if we have glimpsed the truth for an instant, and although we cannot expect to attain to perfect enlightenment immediately, nevertheless, we shall have the consolation of never again falling into an inferno of darkness."[25]

People give witness to the opening of their hearts in faith, he explained, most importantly by taking refuge in the Three Jewels of Buddhism. In a spirit of self-sacrifice, they should joyfully declare in the presence of others, "I take refuge in the Buddha, the Dharma, and the Sangha." With excited anticipation but a calm mind, they should prostrate themselves and dedicate their lives to making this statement actually meaningful day by day. According to Taixu, the feelings commonly associated with taking refuge in the Three Jewels are much like those of a person who, after having encountered terrible difficulties in the world, returns home to the security and understanding of compassionate parents.

As one way of distancing himself from those who emphasized dependence on celestial buddhas and bodhisattvas, Taixu maintained that, among the three refuges, taking refuge in the Dharma always has precedence. "The Three Jewels are the Buddha, Dharma, and Sangha," he stated, "but in the order of their importance for awakening faith, it begins with the Dharma."²⁶ According to Taixu, the Dharma in which Buddhists take refuge has two meanings. The narrow or more common meaning of "Dharma" refers to those things specifically taught by Gautama. Yet the term refers more broadly to truth in its all-encompassing sense. This universal truth is discerned through a wisdom that lays bare the nature of reality as it really is. Therefore, Taixu maintained, those who wish to enter the bodhisattva path fundamentally take refuge in this holistic Dharma and not in any particular buddha or celestial bodhisattva.

Nevertheless, while those who wish to become bodhisattvas ought to consider the Dharma as their principal refuge, their secondary refuge is, of course, Śākyamuni. He is not only their master and model, according to Taixu, but their "good friend"as well. "The Buddha is not a creator of the cosmos and human life," he remarked, "nor is he a lord of the universe who causes misfortunes and grants blessings. He is one who has completely awakened to the truth about the cosmos and human life and at the same time has expounded numerous enlightened principles to instruct people. . . . Before he awoke to the truth, he was the same as all other sentient beings. However, through his teachings about enlightenment, he has become a good friend of all beings."²⁷

Taixu believed that all those taking up the bodhisattva path should recognize that taking refuge in Śākyamuni means taking refuge in all the buddhas of the ten directions and three realms "because the wisdom and virtue of the buddhas is perfectly complete and all buddhas are absolutely equal. So while we only take refuge in our root teacher Śākyamuni, in principle we also take refuge in all of the buddhas."²⁸ The ultimate goal is to realize what these great beings have already realized—that is, to achieve buddhahood *(cheng fo)*. Taixu wrote:

> The doctrines of Buddhism concern transforming this world of physical and mental phenomena from one in which there are a myriad of living beings into one in which there are buddhas. This world and a buddha-realm are not separate because all living beings are in fact already buddhas. If this is so, what is the distinction between buddhas and all living beings? Although both reside in this world of physical and men-

tal phenomena, the myriad of living beings are confused and deluded. For this reason their activities in the world, which stem from their physical and mental states, are disorderly and harmful. As a result, the world has become one of hardship and suffering.... Yet if their minds become like mirrors, then what is reflected in the clear brightness of the mirrors will also become clear and bright. Then a buddha-realm will consist of all living beings. We need only an opportunity for cultivation and we can straighten out and transform the world of physical and mental phenomena. Then every person will have the possibility of becoming a buddha. It is for this reason that the Buddhist scriptures say that every living being can become a buddha.[29]

Finally, those hopeful of realizing their buddhahood must take refuge in the Sangha, the community of people who both believe the Dharma and seek to abide in it while supporting one another. "The meaning of 'Sangha,'" explained Taixu, "is 'a unified community.'"[30] In India, he remarked, the term originally applied to any group of at least four monks who lived together according to Buddhist monastic disciplines. Subsequently, it came to be used more broadly for the entire community of monastic and lay followers. Accordingly, Mahāyāna broadened its understanding of the third refuge. In Mahāyāna, as Sangharakshita has observed, refuge in the Sangha means "not refuge in the Stream-Entrant, the Once-Returner, the Non-Returner, and the Arhant, who for the Mahāyāna typify spiritual individualism, but in the Assembly of the Bodhisattvas."[31]

Scholars have differed in their interpretations of a fundamental ambiguity about the monastic sangha that is reflected in Taixu's writings. For example, acknowledging the difficulties in characterizing the reformer's position, Gotelind Müller emphasized the aspects of his work that highlight the significance and unique efficacy of the monastic career.[32] Holmes Welch, however, accenting Taixu's negativism toward the monastic system of his day, argued that the Chinese master "had grave doubts about monkhood" and "seriously contemplated returning to lay life himself several times."[33] These two interpretations are finally grounded in Taixu's functional evaluation of both the monastic and the lay career. According to Taixu, if persons can best deepen their bodhisattvahood and advance the Buddhist mission as monks or nuns, they should adhere to the monastic life, whereas if they can best make progress toward these ends as members of the laity, then they need not view the lay life as a fundamentally less worthy career.

On the one hand, Taixu specifically recommended the stricter regimens of the monastic life, especially for those bodhisattvas who had only recently taken up the path. He never abandoned the monastic order himself and recruited other gifted lay followers to join it.[34] Despite his own sharp criticism of most of the Chinese monasteries of his day, and of the practices of the majority of the monks and nuns who lived in them, Taixu resented the sweeping denigration of the monastic order by lay critics, such as Ouyang Jingwu, and by former Buddhists who had renounced the religion, such as Liang Shuming. On the other hand, by asserting that monasticism was not necessarily the right choice for everyone, and by readily accepting the practice of moving back and forth between monastic and lay careers, he confused and dismayed many Buddhist leaders.[35]

In sum, Taixu held that the deeply personal decision about the two careers was essentially a vocational one—and one that, in accord with the implications of Mahāyāna doctrine, was of no ultimate consequence vis-à-vis a person's potential for attaining full enlightenment. Historically, Śākyamuni's monastic way of life had been shown to be more advantageous for realizing selflessness for most people.[36] For Taixu personally, it remained the more highly regarded choice, and one without which the transmission of the Dharma would be immediately jeopardized. Yet the monastery could not be regarded as an absolute religious end. Ultimately, he averred, if a person was not willing to manifest a bodhi-mind, it did not matter whether he or she practiced the religion as a monastic or as a householder. "In Mahāyāna Buddhism, the bodhisattva's course of study considers the manifestation of bodhi-mind as its greatest aim," he emphasized, "... the bodhisattva's preparation lies most importantly in spiritual and practical actions; it has never been restricted to a fixed form."[37]

Indeed, Buddhism was established on the interdependence of the monastic and householder forms. To validate only one form would not only contradict Śākyamuni's intentions but result in "a dead rather than living Buddhism."[38] Accordingly, as Reichelt observed in 1934, Taixu remained intimately related to the educated Buddhist literati and granted them an influential role in both administration and worship, "a concession formerly quite unthinkable in Buddhist circles." Reichelt stated:

> In former days it was recognized that a "jushi" could never take the place of an ordained monk. In the taking of all the great vows, an ordained monk was supposed to have been initiated in a special way through the *biqiu* ordination, so that he could influence all the different spheres in the wheel of Karma. A fierce controversy arose some years ago in connection with the question of whether a highly devoted and learned lay Buddhist who greatly overshadows the average monk, both in regard to a pious life and a deep understanding, might officiate during worship. The conservative monks most energetically opposed their right to do this. Not so with Taixu. Without compromising himself he found a *modus vivendi,* whereby the leading lay devotees could officiate *together* with a group of monks. Some of these prominent lay devotees and higher type monks will, from time to time, follow their esteemed leader Taixu on his journeys, when he conducts lecture series and modern "revival meetings" in different centres of China.[39]

One of Taixu's most significant contributions in this area, according to his student Dongchu, was the understanding counsel that he consistently offered to young monks who chose to return to lay life.[40] Taixu observed that, although during the early Republican years there seemed to be a slight increase in people joining the order, the total number of monks and nuns remained essentially unchanged because of the many monastics who chose to leave the monastery for secular life. He recognized that in most cases these people subsequently suffered from a tremendous sense of failure, shame, and guilt. Most of them, in fact, hid their monastic past from others and cut themselves off from the Buddhist community altogether.

Taixu wanted to encourage such persons to remain active as laypeople within the Sangha rather than become thoroughly secularized citizens without any commitment to advancing the Buddhist mission.

He even recommended that they organize, with a real sense of pride, an "Association of Former Buddhist Monastics Who Returned to the Lay Life" (Sengqie huansu fotu hui) to promote and defend the religion and serve the public.[41]

Nevertheless, Taixu thought that some regulations were necessary to protect the integrity of the cloistered community. First, he suggested, while it ought to be fairly easy for believers to go back and forth between the two forms of Buddhist communal life, after someone had left the order to return to lay life a third time, that person should not be permitted to return to the sangha. Second, to avoid any possibility of misrepresentation, former monks and nuns living as lay Buddhists should always wear secular clothes and use their secular names. Third, until such time as they returned to the monastery, they should keep the minimal Dharmic requirements for a householder bodhisattva and not live as ordinary non-Buddhists. Fourth, when returning to the monastic life, they must completely start over with the tonsure rite and the taking of monastic precepts.[42] His concern was with the purity of the monastic sangha. As he once wrote,

> The laws of Buddhism permit individuals to renounce their precepts and return to lay life. This return is not necessarily because they are unable to keep the precepts. It may be because they want to engage in activities related to saving the country and protecting the religion. But those who cannot keep the basic four precepts of the monastic path—against sexual misconduct, stealing, killing, and lying (especially against illicit sexual relations)—must return to the laity.... Thus the monastic community will be able to remain pure. If the monastic community remains pure, then the Buddha, Dharma, and Sangha all will continue to receive the people's respect and reverence. To renounce the monastic precepts is not the same as abandoning one's faith in the Buddhist Dharma. One should still keep the three refuges and five precepts—at least the three refuges—and advocate and sing the praises of the Buddha, Dharma, and Sangha, support the Three Jewels, and become an example for lay householders. By such actions a person is still able to help Buddhism flourish.[43]

THE TURN TOWARD ENLIGHTENMENT

Taking the three refuges as a way of being in the world, those of right faith who would become bodhisattvas commit themselves to the study and practice of the Dharma in the hope that the thought of enlightenment might actually arise within them. In this regard, Taixu reminded his students that life on this earthly human plane is extremely significant and precious. This is so, he stated, precisely because, in the Buddhist scheme of salvation, the human plane is the most crucial stage within the three great realms of desire, form, and formlessness.

From a Buddhist perspective, the definition of those who are subject to instruction is a somewhat complicated issue, Taixu remarked: "There are beings whose intelligence and knowledge is lower than humans, and there are beings whose knowledge is higher. Despite this fact, all consider the human plane to be the pivotal point for the rise or fall of all sentient beings [in levels of spiritual awareness and levels of existence]."[44]

Those human beings who are not diligent in good actions, he continued, will fall in subsequent rebirths in the direction of levels characterized by increased suffering, while those who make concerted efforts to cultivate themselves according to Dharmic principles will rise in the direction of levels of increased equanimity. Thus the human plane is the turning point—the fundamental pivot, or axis—in the process of spiritual transformation on which the future of all depends.

Moreover, wishing to counter overly deterministic interpretations of karma, Taixu frequently asserted that human beings have sufficient freedom for such decisive turning. As Hong Jinlian has observed, while acknowledging that every person's freedom is limited by biological and social factors, the Chinese master claimed not only that humans were those sentient beings most able to rise above their given circumstances, but also that "by relying on the Four Noble Truths and the Eightfold Path, they could truly make evolutionary progress to attain in the end complete and perfect freedom."[45]

Karmic histories may serve to predispose people toward certain thoughts and behavior, but they never fully determine human choice. Indeed, Taixu stated,

> Although human beings are only one form of sentient life, their wisdom and compassion are greater than those of other beings. Therefore, they are able to use their intelligence to investigate the myriad things in existence. Furthermore, with accumulated human knowledge, they are able to engage in different kinds of interchange and assistance, and through this activity to perfect a creative advance.[46]

In consonance with the impatient yet optimistic spirit of modernity, Taixu chose to emphasize that right faith in the Three Jewels and the production of a bodhi-mind were not of necessity the product of arduously accumulating karmic merit over the course of many lifetimes. Although for many bodhisattvas this might indeed be the case, the Chinese master wanted his students to hear his message about a "creative advance" as one of immediacy and hope. Thus Taixu maintained that if practitioners have a reasonably good karmic background, have received a fair amount of education, are devoted to further study, and can believe joyfully in the bodhisattva's way, they can directly receive the right faith that leads to enlightenment.[47] Bodhisattvas can in this very lifetime become awakened to their bodhisattvahood. Moreover, this is true for women as well as for men.[48]

With regard to producing the thought of enlightenment in Mahāyāna, D. T. Suzuki once asserted that *bodhicitta*, or the "intelligence-heart," is awakened in us "either when love for suffering creatures (which is innate in us) is called forth, or when our intellect aspires after the highest enlightenment, or when these two psychical activities are set astir under some favorable circumstances."[49] Although the fortuitous convergence of favorable karmic background, emotions, and aspirations can never be predicted for any given person, the transforming religious experiences that mark the real turning point in the bodhisattva career are, according to Taixu, both life-shattering and life-renewing. They are like the crumbling of a huge mountain that has obstructed one's view, thus creating new vistas of the distant horizon. In fact, Taixu asserted, all religions are grounded in functionally similar types of decentering and reorienting spiritual experiences. As he commented in 1933,

> What today is called "religion" *(zongjiao)* in ancient times was called "education" *(jiaohua)*. If you examine the structural elements of religion, there are reasons for it to be called education. It certainly results from one special characteristic. The founders of all religions and all new religious sects or denominations must have had at the very heart of their spiritual life experiences that surpass conventional understanding. These kinds of experiences are extraordinary spiritual experiences. What we ordinarily know, for example, through hearing, seeing, smelling, touching, and tasting all comes from sense contact. These kinds of sensations can form knowledge through intellectual activities and inferences of thought. However, religions are established not merely on this kind of knowledge, but even more on extraordinary experiences. . . . Christianity, Islam, and Buddhism all have this element. In China, Confucianism, Daoism, and other religions without exception also have it.[50]

In a 1940 article entitled "Wo de zongjiao jingyan" (My Religious Experiences), Taixu acknowledged three separate religious experiences that were pivotally important in his early life, each drawing him ever more profoundly into the Buddhist world.[51] As noted earlier, the first and most significant event took place in 1907 at the Xifang si, where the young novice had just begun his first studies of Mahāyāna scripture. It was, he remarked, the real beginning of his "new life" in Buddhism. As he later recalled in his autobiography,

> One day when reading scripture, suddenly I lost a sense of the world of physical and mental phenomena. In a state of emptiness, I experienced a spiritual brightness. The innumerable worldly defilements became completely luminous, like pure images floating in the air. Although I sat there with the scriptures for several hours, it seemed to be only an instant. Several days later, my body and mind were still light-hearted and contented. Within the next several days, I read the rest of the Prajñāpāramitā scriptures, as well as the *Avataṃsaka Sūtra,* and immediately I had insight into the nature of all things. . . . This was for me the slough-

ing off of all the defilements of the world and achieving the beginning of my new life in Buddhism.[52]

Subsequent memorable religious experiences occurred in 1914 and 1916, deepening Taixu's commitment to the bodhisattva path. "Through each of these three meditative experiences," he remarked, "my psychological as well as physiological conditions were changed."[53] The "new life" that the path represented, according to the monk, involved an unchangeable and unshakable faith in Mahāyāna. Attaining that kind of enlightened faith, he said, "is like eating a small diamond that can never be digested."[54] Yet meditative trance can quickly become a dangerous attachment if it is unrelated to compassionate activity. Thus while testifying to the significance of his own three religious experiences, Taixu concluded, "Because a compassionate vow of the heart is so important, I did not continue deeper into meditative trance *(chanding)*. Therefore I had no further experiences [of this kind]."[55]

Taixu emphasized that in Mahāyāna the production of a bodhi-mind and the four great universal vows of a bodhisattva *(si hong shi-yuan)* are integrally interrelated. While the thought of enlightenment is a private experience inaccessible to others, the vows are public declarations. For the true bodhisattva, however, they are inseparable. As Har Dayal has explained, "*praṇidhāna* [a bodhisattva's vow of compassion] is both the cause and the result of the Thought of Enlightenment."[56]

Similarly, according to Taixu, the four universal vows are completely interrelated. Yet in contrast to their traditional order, the fourth resolve is the most fundamental: "I vow to become perfect in the supreme Buddhist law." The effort to attain the highest level of understanding—the wisdom of a buddha—he argued, must always remain the bodhisattva's greatest hope and desire. This is achieved, however, only through the complementary and simultaneous fulfillment of the other three universal vows. Becoming a buddha, therefore, means manifesting the unsurpassable Dharma for the sake of all other beings. "To become a buddha," asserted Taixu, "means taking as one's goal the preaching of the Dharma in order to save all living beings. If one does not act to save them, then there is absolutely no way to attain Buddhahood. Therefore one makes the first resolve, 'I vow to save all sentient beings.'"[57]

This entails, he noted, the elimination not only of one's own passions and delusions but of other people's as well. The two are not sequential in Taixu's mind; rather, they are fully coordinated and interdependent activities. "True bodhisattvas," he remarked, "take the heart of all beings as their own hearts, so that only when the passions and delusions of all other beings are destroyed are their own passions and delusions finally silenced."[58] Therefore true bodhisattvas take the second universal resolve, "I vow to put an end to all passions and delusions."

Of course, the cultivation of wisdom is required in order to understand fully the hearts of others, comprehend Buddhism's ways of healing, and hence be equipped to save all beings from error. To become a bodhisattva thus means to become a student. As Taixu put it, "How is this wisdom to be engendered? It comes from study. For this reason, the Buddha said, 'Within the three worlds, all the buddhas have arisen from a foundation of learning.' So if people are not willing to study, they will always be situated among the foolish. How, then, can they take part in becoming a buddha?"[59]

For the bodhisattva, study involves reflection both on internal and external realities and on the multiple doors to enlightenment *(fa men)* within the Mahāyāna tradition. According to the reformer, "The illnesses of sentient beings are innumerable and limitless. Yet the Buddha said that the medicines of the Dharma which cure illnesses are also innumerable and limitless. Therefore those who want to become buddhas and save beings must study all doors to enlightenment and make the third resolve, 'I vow to study and learn all methods and means.'"[60]

These are the four universal resolves of all bodhisattvas, and to contradict them in thought and action is a great sin. In fact, Taixu explained, within the traditions of the monastic community there are four great *pārājika dharmas (ta sheng chu fa),* or serious offenses, that result in permanent expulsion from the order (namely, sexual intercourse, theft, killing, and false proclamation of superhuman faculties). These four monastic sins have parallels that are more broadly applicable to all bodhisattvas. The first unpardonable sin for a bodhisattva, Taixu says, is "to lose one's beneficent heart" *(shi lirenxin),* so that one is unwilling to sacrifice anything for the sake of another. The second is "to lose one's great compassionate heart" *(shi beixin),* so that when asked for material assistance by poor and suffering people, the bodhisattva gives no aid, or when asked for instruction in accord with the Dharma, the bodhisattva offers no guidance.

The third sin is "to lose one's great heart of sympathy" *(shi cixin),* so that when people come to the bodhisattva to confess their transgressions against the Dharma, the bodhisattva rejects them and is unwilling to accept their confessions. The fourth unpardonable sin is "to lose one's great wisdom heart" *(shi zhihuixin),* so that "one slanders the teachings of Mahāyāna and with perverse views establishes a false Dharma to entice and deceive others."[61] Committing any one of these four sins results from a failure to protect and promote the bodhi-mind and is clear evidence that the person has lost the qualifications necessary for the true bodhisattva path.

PRECEPTS AND PERFECTIONS

The essence of the true path is the practice of the precepts and perfections. The initial practice of both monastic and householder bodhisattvas actually consists of the five precepts *(wu jie)* and their fuller elaboration in the ten meritorious actions *(shi shan).* Asserting that the active doing of good fulfills and completes the passive avoidance of evil, Taixu typically listed the traditional five precepts in a way that included both a negative and positive component. Thus he enumerated the five basic precepts as: (1) not to kill, but to express love; (2) not to steal, but to benefit others; (3) not to act in a lewd or lustful way, but to act with decorum; (4) not to lie, but to speak with sincerity; and (5) not to drink intoxicating beverages that affect the body and cloud the mind, but rather, with wisdom, to regulate the body and mind. The first four of these, Taixu stated, are called the "precepts of natural law" *(xing jie)* because they prohibit acts that harm other beings. The fifth is referred to as a "precautionary precept" *(zhe jie)* because it is intended to prevent careless and intoxication-related moral lapses of the first four kinds.[62]

The Chinese monk acknowledged that, by citing the precepts in this way, he was linking the five negatively formulated Buddhist precepts with the five positively stated constant virtues of the Confucian tradition—benevolence *(ren)*, righteousness *(yi)*, propriety *(li)*, sincerity *(xin)*, and knowledge *(zhi)*—as others had done before him. Elaboration of the precepts yields the ten meritorious actions: abstention from taking life, stealing, and sexual misconduct; from false, malicious, harsh, and senseless language; and from covetousness, ill will, and wrong views. While the five precepts and ten meritorious actions are required of all bodhisattvas, monks, and nuns must keep an additional five precepts: abstention from (a) adorning one's body with flowers or perfumes, (b) engaging in or being entertained by singing and dancing, (c) sleeping on a high or broad bed, (d) eating at prohibited times, and (e) accumulating money or material goods. Although these additional five precepts are not required of householder bodhisattvas, Taixu encouraged his lay followers to practice the first four of them occasionally for specific periods of time, as beneficial religious disciplines.

By attending to the substance and spirit of all the precepts, monastic and householder bodhisattvas guard their *bodhicitta* and lay the foundation for the most difficult phase of the path, the practice of the Six Perfections *(pāramitās)*: giving, morality, patience, zeal, concentration, and insight. According to Taixu, the practice of the perfections has a profoundly transformative effect on new bodhisattvas. Making the four universal vows, he remarked, is like creating a great sea basin so large that filling it would require immense mountains of soil. In effect, the perfections fill the basin of the sea with the mountains—the promise with the practice. "If this does not occur," wrote the Chinese master, "then the vows amount to nothing and one is a false bodhisattva and not a true bodhisattva, for the way *(dao)* of a bodhisattva consists in practicing the Six Perfections."[63]

Unfortunately, bodhisattvas new to the path never fully grasp the practical scope of the perfections' true meaning. For example, the first perfection, giving *(bushi)*, is often misinterpreted as charity or the simple sharing of surplus financial resources. Yet in Mahāyāna, Taixu claimed, its meaning is far more profound. To begin with, he said, a bodhisattva can distinguish between "internal gifts" and "external gifts." The former involve sharing one's physical body, or parts thereof, even to the point of giving one's life for sentient beings in need. Buddhist literature about bodhisattva activity is replete with stories of blood, eyes, arms, and the like being selflessly offered. External gifts, in contrast, refer to personal property or other material goods that are freely directed to those who require them or can benefit from them. In fact, giving may include a variety of actions, from offering instruction in the Dharma to acts of heroic rescue when the lives or liberties of others are threatened. Yet each act of giving, according to Taixu, is perfected by bodhisattvas as they identify with other persons and willingly sacrifice themselves for the benefit of others, knowing that, ultimately, no "others" exist apart from "self."

The second perfection, morality *(chijie),* is often thought to mean the simple observance of specified behavioral prohibitions. On the contrary, the Chinese monk remarked, perfect morality is far more encompassing. The negative or passive *(xiaoji)* dimension requires cessation of evil acts, while the positive or active *(jiji)* dimension involves performance of morally meritorious acts. For monastic and householder bodhisattvas, morality means "not lip service but real practice."[64] Moreover, morality is not merely preparation for the path: it is path activity. As it is gradually perfected, it transcends mundane moral observance by moving beyond the perception of distorting dualities involved with separate moral actors, although the practice remains. Responding to critics who judged Buddhism to be a strictly otherworldly religion, removed from the concerns of daily life, Taixu asserted:

> In China, many scholars as well as common people, because they have not understood Buddhism, have made all kinds of mistaken criticisms of the Dharma. They have often thought that Buddhism is not concerned with social morality or human life. Especially with respect to those scholars who have discussed Chinese philosophy or philosophies of human life, this kind of misunderstanding is increasingly problematic. Actually, with regard to the reason for Śākyamuni preaching the

Dharma, although his motive was broadly [to aid] all sentient beings, his central concern in preaching the Dharma was human beings. Therefore, Buddhism is truly a religion concerning humans, and all the theories and principles of morality set forth by the Buddha are not unrelated to the human realm. Therefore, when it is said that Buddhism is not concerned with social morality and human life, those who have studied the Dharma even just a little bit know instantly that such a statement is wrong.[65]

The scope of patience *(renru)*, the third perfection, has also been insufficiently understood. Although for some it may mean simply not being hasty or impetuous, for Taixu it represents, far more profoundly, the perfection of forbearance and forgiveness in the face of insult and persecution. As conscientious bodhisattvas strive to live up to their great vows of compassion, he observed, many people in this wicked age will try to obstruct and willfully destroy whatever good bodhisattvas are able to accomplish, seeking to discredit those on the path and sway them from their resolve. Yet despite these attacks, according to Taixu, true bodhisattvas "not only endure the insults but, repaying hatred with kindness, refuse to abandon such people."[66]

The fourth perfection, zeal or vigor *(jingjin)*, is often understood to mean mere diligence in accomplishing a task. Yet one can be diligent, noted the reformer, in pursuing unworthy goals as well as worthy ones. Thus, for bodhisattvas, "zeal" specifically means an unflagging spiritual and physical energy for the requirements of their self-sacrificing career. The Chinese character *"jing"* in the compound denotes both purity *(jing chun)* and simplicity *(wu za)* of spirit, while the character *"jin"* means "to advance." Thus, with an uncomplicated spirit of service, bodhisattvas course in an enlightened path, never allowing their individual concerns to determine the most appropriate action, resisting laziness, and taking upon themselves the most important responsibility on earth: awakening all sentient beings to the truth.

Concentration *(chanding)*, the fifth perfection, is widely misunderstood both inside and outside of the Buddhist community, according to Taixu. It is a great mistake, he argued, to assume that meditative concentration requires achieving, through physical austerities and mental disengagement, a state in which one becomes like wood or stone. Such a state might be said to characterize the negative or passive dimension of sitting in meditation to control a scattered and confused mind. However, such a popularly held view is incomplete. "The comprehensive view of concentration," stated Taixu, "means in every circumstance holding on to one's vitality *(huo li)* so as to be able to accomplish everything. Thus concentration certainly does not refer merely to the negative or passive dimension in which one cannot do anything, but rather more correctly to the source of the vitality for undertaking all things."[67]

In essence, concentration is related far more significantly to action than to non-action. As Callahan once commented, "Taixu seems to regard meditation primarily as a means for improving conduct, not as an end in itself. These beliefs afford a religious basis for Taixu's emphasis upon social service and philanthropy."[68] Some Buddhists, declared Taixu, "feel that their own existence is extremely painful. Therefore they hold to the empty side of Buddhist emptiness *(kong)* in order merely to seek an escape from the realm of birth and death and attain absolute spiritual equanimity and non-action. . . . Because they lie around in a drunken stupor in a state of samādhi focusing on emptiness *(kongsanmei)*, naturally they are never able to reach the complete and perfect spirit of Buddhism."[69]

The sixth perfection, insight or wisdom *(zhihui)*, means, in the simplest terms, learned knowledge. Yet contrary to the opinions of some, this wisdom is neither fully continuous nor discontinuous with knowledge derived from the senses, according to Taixu. On the one hand, Dharmic wisdom and worldly knowledge are closely related because both are finally concerned with investigating the true nature of things. Therefore bodhisattvas need to pursue learning through the normal disciplines of the arts and sciences, becoming adept at thinking carefully and clearly and at understanding all aspects of the world around them.

On the other hand, the experiential insight that is at the heart of the enlightened life, that was realized by Śākyamuni, and that is reflected in Buddhist scripture and tradition transcends and completes all worldly knowledge, Taixu maintained. Thus bodhisattvas must seek, beyond all conventional bits of knowledge, that superior and comprehensive wisdom which is available only through an awakened bodhi-mind. In essence, true bodhisattvas integrate insights from both sources. Indeed, as Taixu pointed out, "*The Vimalakīrti Sūtra* says, 'There are no places that are not places for bodhisattvas to teach.' Now I say that with regard to places for bodhisattvas to learn, it is the same."[70]

ESTABLISHING A PURE LAND ON EARTH

Bodhisattvas course in the unified practice of the Six Perfections, with the practice of one perfection simultaneously entailing practice of the other five. Moreover, especially in their teaching of all other beings *(huadao dazhong)*, as they seek to draw all sentient beings to Buddhism, bodhisattvas manifest "the four all-embracing virtues" *(si shefa)*—namely, generosity in giving to any being in need *(bushi)*, affability in speaking with people *(aiyu)*, altruism in relating to others *(lixing)*, and cooperation in pursuing worthy common aims *(tongshi)*. In the Mahāyāna tradition, the object of the four all-embracing virtues is the conversion of all sentient beings. Taixu asserted that bodhisattvas convert others most readily when they embody with integrity the truths that they proclaim verbally, when they identify and associate with common people in all walks of life and in all circumstances, and when they devote themselves to compassionate service, whatever the cost. Wrote the monk,

> If those on the bodhisattva path, in accord with the depth of their own intelligence and ability, adopt the practice of the Six Perfections and the four all-embracing virtues, then they will complete their bodhisattva personality. In whatever walk of life, whether their service is in the cultural sphere, education, benevolent work, the government, the military, or as a student, a merchant, or a farmer, . . . they will establish a practical Buddhism for human life and build a paradisaical pure land of peace and happiness.[71]

According to Mahāyāna doctrine, a pure land *(jingtu)* is one of two kinds of world systems, or buddha-fields *(focha, fotu,* or *foguo),* over which a buddha has special spiritual authority. An impure buddha-field, like the one suffering under "the five dreaded calamities of degeneracy" *(wu zhuo)* into which Śākyamuni chose to be born, is far different from a pure buddha-field, the most famous of which is Sukhāvatī, the abode of Amitābha. In an impure land, sentient beings of all kinds (superhuman, human, and subhuman) suffer miserably under the influence of the three defilements (greed, hatred, and delusion) and face near impossible odds in producing the thought of enlightenment.

In a pure land, in contrast, the gods and human beings who dwell therein enjoy extremely favorable conditions for cultivating a bodhi-mind. Indeed, that is why such realms exist: certain great bodhisattvas once vowed that, after they had attained final enlightenment, they would establish such advantageous settings in which others could practice the path. When, by virtue of whatever spiritual discipline, Buddhist practitioners are reborn in these pure lands, they can rest assured that they will never regress and be born again in an impure land. Thus they can rejoice in the knowledge that they, too, will eventually attain supreme enlightenment, regardless of how long must be spent in its cultivation.

Like most Chinese Buddhists of his day, Taixu was captivated by the compelling ideal of pursuing enlightenment in the wonderfully conducive surroundings of a paradisaical pure land. Yet his views on the realization of that ideal were far from those of the mainstream of the contemporary Sangha. Rather than focusing on the glories of distant pure lands, which were accessible through reliance on the spiritual merit and power of other great bodhisattvas and buddhas, Taixu visualized this earthly world transformed into a pure land by the dedication and sacrificial hard work of thousands of average bodhisattvas who were mindful of what their concerted witness could mean. Most Chinese Buddhists were content to prayerfully await their rebirth in a celestial pure land; Taixu was impatient about establishing a pure land on earth.

The reformer acknowledged the universal appeal of utopian dreams in an important 1930 lecture entitled "Jianshe renjian jingtu lun" (On Establishing a Pure Land on Earth). From the community's earliest days, he noted, Buddhists have talked enthusiastically of Uttarakuru (Yudanyue zhou), the northern of the four continents that surround Mount Meru in all Indic world systems; Uttarakuru is believed to be a beautiful and superior land in which food is produced without effort and humans live for a thousand years. Similarly, Daoists described ideal states in which the guiding principles of government would be spontaneity *(ziran)* and nonpurposeful activity *(wu wei)*, while Confucians trumpeted the ideal world of a "great community" *(datong zhi shi)*. In the West, Socrates, Plato, and other philosophers envisioned forms of utopias *(wutuobang)*, and the earliest Christians actually embraced (for a period under Peter's leadership) an idealistic form of communism, with the church accepting goods from each believer according to his or her means and distributing them according to people's needs.

Despite the ubiquity of utopian ideals in different times and places, they have usually been rejected out of hand by most "reasonable" people. Indeed, according to Taixu, before enlightened bodhisattvas can make progress toward the goal of establishing a pure land on earth, two unhealthy attitudes must be corrected. The first is the attitude of self-centered optimists who believe that the world is already a marvelous, "pure" land, at least for them. Infatuated with the world, such people have no interest in detaching themselves from it or making any fundamental changes in it. In modern China, Taixu argued, the thoughtlessness and aggressiveness of such people have polarized and impoverished the country.

The second is the attitude of self-centered pessimists who are convinced that no significant changes are truly possible in this impure and sorrowful world of time and space. Lost in dejection and self-pity, a few such people end their lives through suicide; in one way or another, the others also waste their lives, devoid of a sense of meaning and purpose. In China, some seek to escape the social, economic, and political chaos by emigrating to the United States, mistakenly believing that its relative prosperity and stability make it a "pure land." Most seek, through devotional practice, to escape to Sukhāvatī. In either case, according to Taixu, by aiming merely to escape their unhappy situations and by thinking only of themselves, they fail to fulfill what it really means to be a Chinese patriot or a Chinese Buddhist.

Both these self-absorbed attitudes, Taixu asserted, result from a failure to comprehend the true basis of pure lands and from a profound weakness of will. Yet if people could be led to understand how such utopias actually come into existence, perhaps they could be encouraged to participate in the actual creation of a pure land themselves. "The building of pure lands," he remarked, "is not accomplished by Nature; neither are these lands created by gods. Pure lands have come into being from minds of goodness which have arisen in human and other sentient beings."[72] From such minds of goodness come both the search for certain knowledge and appropriate moral behavior. Such knowledge and behavior yield good societies and wonderfully auspicious worlds. The root cause of pure lands, and in fact of all things, may be so explained. Everything from a small blade of grass to a great celestial body has come into being because of the interaction of innumerable causal elements, all of which originate in the minds of sentient beings. Therefore, Taixu wondered,

> If today, based on good knowledge of our minds, we can produce pure thoughts and work hard to accomplish good deeds, how hard can it be to transform an impure China into a Chinese pure land? . . . All persons have this force of mind, and since they already have the faculty *(benneng)* to create a pure land, they can all make the glorious vow to make this world into a pure land and work hard to achieve it.[73]

Minds that are not tranquil and pure, minds that are confused about the true nature of things, cannot create pure lands. Therefore one must understand through mindful activity the process of becoming that lies at the heart of the Buddhist message. Significantly, in Taixu's view, this ancient insight of the supremely enlightened buddhas now finds confirmation in the modern science of the twentieth century:

The most recent discoveries of modern science are constantly able to prove the truths of Buddhism. Formerly, according to nineteenth-century science, all the myriad things of the world resulted from the coming together of material atoms. So material atoms were recognized as the building blocks of all things. However, when we come to twentieth-century science, the fact is recognized that there are ultimately no simple building blocks for all the myriad things of the world. Rather, absolutely every single thing comes into being as the result of the convergence of many different conditions of causal relations. This theory is rather close to the Buddhist concept of the constituent nature of all things. Thus because the truth in Buddhism about creating a pure land on earth has already gradually come to be accepted, we can directly lift it up for discussion. In sum, the present world in which humans live is certainly not perfect. However, if humans and other sentient beings vow to make it into a pure land, then there is absolutely no way that it cannot happen. We only have to dispense with our preconceptions and use a reasonable amount of labor to create it![74]

According to Taixu, average bodhisattvas new to the path need to be reminded of the powerful and far-reaching consequences of their vows. Due to causal interactions, a bodhisattva's vows—and the wise and compassionate activities that fulfill those vows—change everything. The very fabric of reality is thus altered. Therefore, although no one can deny the enormity of the task of saving all sentient beings, there is no legitimate reason to despair about what will be required—or about the time required to accomplish it. Bodhisattvas need only begin to practice the precepts and perfections, while seeking practical ways to work toward the ultimate goal of buddhahood.

Practicality was not an unimportant concern in China. Taixu realized that even if bodhisattvas understood the theoretical basis for creating a utopia on earth, there would still be considerable debate about the most practical and realistic methods for accomplishing that mission. For this, the reformer argued, two powerful forces would have to be coordinated: an enlightened government, and a community of bodhisattvas inspired by Mahāyāna Buddhism's true spirit. A stable government would be needed to protect the political rights of the people, enact and enforce just laws through punishments and rewards, and systematize the reconstructive work. Indeed, the government would have to supervise a fourfold division of labor. Business and industry would have to be developed to address problems related to the four essential needs of the people: food, clothing, housing, and transportation. Education would have to be promoted to reform ways of thinking and to develop people's abilities. The arts would have to flourish to bring enjoyment to the people, elevating their minds and strengthening their bodies. And morality, which was at the heart of education, would have to be advanced so that the new society would be grounded in values such as integrity, tolerance, and sincerity.

A Chinese Sangha inspired by the true spirit of Mahāyāna, the second reshaping force for an earthly utopia, would necessarily illuminate the healing and transforming way of bodhisattvas while locating all worldly activity within a cosmic framework. Such a Sangha would raise the pursuit of truth and goodness beyond the limited parameters of governmental insight and authority to the most profoundly spiritual bases for an enlightened existence. According to Taixu, bodhisattvas on the true path would propagate a "worldly Buddhism" or a "humanistic Buddhism" *(renjian fojiao)*, a form of the religion that was neither monastically nor devotionally centered but energetically concerned with perfecting human life and advancing the social order.[75] In their socially engaged practice of Mahāyāna, such bodhisattvas would compassionately attend to all three dimensions of human need—spiritual, physical, and social—while, as missionaries of an unsurpassable wisdom, they would recontextualize all family, community, national, and international issues by explicit reference to the Three Jewels of Buddhism.[76] Bodhisattvas would not only develop methods for "curing symptoms" *(zhi biao)* but, more radically than mere governmental representatives ever could, they would cure the root causes *(zhi ben)* of human suffering.

Beyond merely offering an abstract religious rationale for creating a pure land, Taixu was eager to detail plans for concretely establishing a modern pure land in China. Chinese Buddhists, he argued, would need to begin by setting up a special administrative area in which the two forces of enlightened government and true religion could cooperate in an ideal fashion, not unlike the systems that had traditionally existed in Thailand and Tibet. Of all the possible locations within China, he judged that the holy grounds of Putuo Shan in Zhejiang province would be the most suitable location. If that were not feasible, he said, the selected site should at least have similarly ample natural resources: luxuriant forests of bamboo and trees, fertile soil, abundant spring water, and a mountain with a circumference of at least several tens of *li*. Appropriate plots of land within the chosen area should be sown with rice, hemp, and other crops so that basic food and clothing could be provided for ten to twenty thousand people. Because of its special use by the Sangha, all of the designated pure land should be declared tax-exempt by the government.

On a high mountain plateau within the pure land, a great central monastery should be built. According to Taixu's plan, at the very heart of the monastery should stand a large shrine hall dedicated to the Buddha Śākyamuni. This central hall for general use should be flanked on the left by lecture and assembly halls for those studying the special texts of the Prajñāpāramitā (Wisdom Literature) school, on the right by those concentrating on *The Lotus Sūtra,* and to the rear by a Buddhist library. Surrounding these core structures would be adjoining facilities for the study of other significant Buddhist scriptures and practices (including those of well-known schools such as Huayan, Chan, and Zhenyan, as well as less popular schools like those dedicated to Vairocana or Maitreya).[77] Altogether, the great monastery should accommodate between five hundred and a thousand monks. These devotees would study, pray, and work together daily, while expressing the unique aspects of their own schools' special heritages and each year undertaking at least one major project jointly.

Near the great monastery, according to the master's plan, would be a hall for male novices *(shami),* of whom there ought to be about a hundred, where they would take their first vows and be tonsured during an initial period of Buddhist studies. There should be similar halls for ordained nuns *(biqiuni)* and for female novices *(shamini),* who would number between four and eight hundred. Altogether, the facilities for the monastic order should occupy at least 4 square *li*.[78]

The lay Buddhist community should be comprised of about eight thousand people in a thousand different families. These should reside in three grades of villages called, in order of rank, "Ten Meritorious

Actions" villages, "Five Precepts" villages, and "Three Refuges" villages. There should be about ten villages of each grade, and each village should have more than thirty families, or about 270 members. Families in the "Ten Meritorious Actions" villages, nearest the monastic compound, would each be given approximately 120 *mu* of mountainous and agricultural land.[79] Families in the "Five Precepts" villages would each receive 100 *mu,* and those in the "Three Refuges" villages, 75 *mu*.

Village mayors would ensure that their communities had at least two elementary schools for children, a preaching hall, a hall for reading scriptures, and a general gathering or Lotus Society *(lianshe)* hall. Each of the three grades of village would elect a village head, operating under the highest civic leader, the mayor of the holy mountain *(shanzhang)*. These persons would make certain that a high school was established for each grade, along with further specialized educational opportunities for farming and forestry.

Within the designated pure land, individuals would not be permitted to marry or join the monastic community until age twenty. Men who wished to enter the order would be required to study as novices for one to three years prior to ordination, while women would serve as novices for two to five years. All would begin by studying the texts and disciplines of one particular school for at least four years, and then, if successful, proceed to the study of other schools. Those who were successful would be eligible to serve as teachers and various officers within the monastic community. After five years of such service, they would be permitted to travel outside the pure land on mission work. After twenty years on the mountain (or fifteen years on the mountain plus five in service outside it), individuals would be eligible to be selected to serve in the important position of rector *(shouzuo)* of one of the Buddhist schools.

According to Taixu, those who live within the precincts of the pure land ought to pray for the welfare of people in all countries who suffer from calamities and natural disasters. Furthermore, they should send out teams of lay Buddhists under the guidance of senior monastic bodhisattvas to accomplish good works. To explain the purposes of the pure land, they should welcome interested individuals and representatives of all countries and governments who wanted to visit. In an ecumenical spirit, they should periodically welcome Buddhists from all over the world for conferences on the Sangha's global mission. And they should encourage all peoples to set aside some of their money for the establishment of similar pure lands on earth.

RESHAPING THE SANGHA

From early in his career, Taixu was given to this type of utopian planning. By bringing forth quite detailed organizational configurations, he hoped to draw people into a collective dream for a restructured and reconstituted reality of the future. Many Buddhists appreciated his attempts to think through difficult and complex problems and to present concrete solutions. Yet the specificity of his idealistic plans for reform also provided fuel for incendiary negative reactions, particularly to his frequently revised plans for reorganizing the monastic establishment.

Taixu believed that a radical reorganization of the Chinese sangha was an urgent necessity because the poor quality of Buddhist monks in the Republican period was not merely a challenge to the sangha's respected place within society but a grave threat to the very future of the religion in China. Although his harsh critical refrains about his fellow monks won him few friends in the monastic community, the renewal and reorganization of the sangha remained a key element of his message throughout his career. On the majority of the Chinese sangha, Taixu stated sharply:

> First, they are seldom interested in social service or the work of educating the society. The priests or rather monks are generally ignorant, and their services to society are confined to singing of masses or prayers in the funeral services. Secondly, although the monks divide themselves into sects or schools, each pursuing a special object, yet they always fail to accomplish that object. Thirdly, the monks are always religious recluses, taking no interest in the affairs of the community or the country and they are in turn slighted by the Government or the ruling classes.

Fourthly, most of the Chinese Buddhist monks lack the necessary modern scientific knowledge and are also ignorant of the current thoughts and ideas of the world. In view of such disabilities, they are unable to preach the doctrines of the Buddha in such a way as to appeal to the minds of the modern people.[80]

Taixu's controversial plan for addressing this deplorable situation, the *Zhengli sengqie zhidu lun* (Reorganization of the Sangha System), was composed in 1915, during his period of sealed confinement at Putuo Shan, and published in part in 1920, in the first issue of *Haichao yin*. As already noted, Taixu's plan included recommendations for markedly increasing the educational requirements for ordination, for requiring most monks to engage in physical labor to ensure the economic self-sufficiency of the monasteries, for terminating the vulgar commercialization of ritual practice, and for establishing various social-service and educational ventures. In 1921, Yu-yue Tsu observed that the reformer's proposal included a number of ambitious ideas:

> He proposes to have a national system embracing preaching chapels and parishes in every city, a certain number of monasteries and charitable institutions in each province, and a national monastery and university in the capital city of the country. As a part of the national institution he would have a library containing an extensive collection of Buddhist literature and a museum for Buddhist art. Into the museum he would have all images moved, so that other buildings could be free of them. Belonging as he does to the Dhyāna or Meditation School, founded by Bodhidharma in the sixth century, Taixu is opposed to all idolatry, and tolerates it only as an accommodation to the weakness of the masses. As to the monks, he would encourage manual labor as an antidote to laziness and would encourage more time being spent for meditation and study for spiritual development. In his account of his travels in Japan and Taiwan he had a brief reference to his daily life to the effect that it has been his practice to spend at least three or four hours every day in meditation, and he has never allowed a day to pass without it, even the busiest day, during the past ten years. How far he will be able to carry out the reforms he has conceived in his mind only time will show.

Meanwhile he has been influential in winning many serious-minded men and women to the pursuit of the religious (monastic) life.[81]

In his original proposal of 1915, Taixu estimated that the Buddhist monastic community in Republican China consisted of approximately eight hundred thousand men and women. Though in later writings Taixu was to recommend significant reductions, in his first plan he specifically stated that the number of monks and nuns was about right in relation to China's total population.[82] His main interest lay in developing a thorough scheme for systematizing and regulating monastic practice. Therefore he considered a wide range of relevant topics. For example, although he was later to abandon the idea, he initially recommended that the monastic community be tightly restructured around eight central Buddhist "schools" *(zong)*. Four were named after mountains: the Qingliang (Huayan or Xianshou), the Tiantai (Fahua), the Lushan (Jingtu or Lian), and the Nanshan (Lü). Three schools were named after particular monasteries: the Jiaxiang (Sanlun or Faxing), the Cien (Weishi or Faxiang), and the Shaoshi (Chan). One school was named after a period in the Tang dynasty: the Kaiyuan (Zhenyan or Mi) sect.[83]

In addition, as Tsu indicated, Taixu carefully charted the Buddhist institutions that would be required at the county *(xian)*, district *(dao)*, provincial *(sheng)*, and national *(guo)* levels. For example, he felt that every county ought to have one Vinaya hall *(xingjiao yuan)* for teaching Buddhist discipline, one Dharma center *(fa yuan)* for the study of scripture, one Lotus Society *(lianshe)* hall for recitation and meditation, four preaching halls *(xuanjiao yuan)* for the propagation of the faith, and one nunnery. Every district should have ten additional institutions: eight monasteries, each representing one of the eight schools, plus one Buddhist hospital and an orphanage for infants. Every province should also have an "Institute for Religious Adherence" *(chijiao yuan)* to coordinate mission work, plus an orphanage for children. In the country's capital, there should be a central Buddhist Vihāra *(fofa sengyuan)* for research and sangha representation. Moreover, there should be a central Buddhist Bank *(fojiao yinhang)* that would manage all monastic financial concerns, preventing private property claims within the sangha and providing a fair and democratic appropriation of funding for the multifaceted Buddhist mission in China.[84]

Taixu especially liked to create charts, application forms, and certificates, all of which he thought could help regularize monastic procedures and clarify responsibilities. He designed registration forms for infants and children being received by Buddhist orphanages, application forms for men and women wishing to enter the sangha, monastic certificates for bhikṣus and bhikṣuṇīs officially entering the religious life, and so forth. He also summarized in chart form the rules governing a person's decision to enter or leave the monastic order, as well as those for returning to the order after renouncing it for life as a layperson. He set age limits on entering the order (not under fifteen and not over forty) and on various monastic positions.[85]

Finally, Taixu offered guidelines for the education and the professional responsibilities of monastic leaders at every level and in every type of Buddhist organization. Broad educational requirements could be charted, and standardized monastic ranks for teachers delineated, from Venerable Master *(dashi)* to Tantric Master *(yuqieshi)*, Dharma Master *(fashi)*, Meditation Master *(chanshi)*, and Vinaya Master *(lüshi)*.[86] The reformer even offered suggestions for regulating monastic vestments and designed his own system of modern garb, which ranged from a simple, unadorned robe to robes with a secular cut and multiple stripes (five, seven, nine, etc., up to a maximum of twenty-five stripes).[87] Taixu obviously took some delight in attending to such details in his schemes for the future. His big picture of a modern form of Buddhism required applying to the religious canvas innumerable small yet bold strokes of pigment.

By 1927, Taixu had sharply reduced his original estimate of the number of monks and nuns in China. He acknowledged that in 1915, optimistic about the number of novices entering the order, he had used the figure of eight hundred thousand. Yet he had come to think that the overall numerical decline that had begun with the Taiping attacks on Buddhist monasteries in the nineteenth century was continuing, especially as a result of recent anti-Buddhist actions of the Republican government. Thus he concluded that the total number of people active in the sangha could no longer be more than two hundred thousand, not counting those associated with Lamaism in Mongolia and Tibet. Most of this number, Taixu claimed, should be engaged in some form of productive labor to ensure the self-sufficiency of the monasteries.[88]

By 1930, Taixu had given up his idea of using the eight Buddhist schools to reorganize the sangha because, he said, unlike Buddhism in Japan, the schools had no distinct bases within the contemporary Chinese monastic community. By this time he was also prepared to estimate that the sangha had been reduced to about 160,000 monks and nuns.[89] More significantly, he charged that most of that number were not truly qualified to be members of the sangha and should not be called monastics. Rather, they should work at farming or some other type of productive labor to support the much smaller number who actually had the abilities to study scripture and spread the Dharma. As Taixu wrote unabashedly,

> Most monks *(seng)* who do not have the qualifications to be monastics should be working monks, farming and performing labor, so that the elite minority may conduct research and study scripture.... Through the productive work of the great majority of monastics, the minority may be provided for so that they can focus all of their attention on advanced studies. Thus will monastic living be made independent rather than dependent on the people. This is a way to relieve many concerns of our day. Strictly speaking, these individuals who serve as farmers and laborers should not really be called "monks." Because they farm and perform labor and are neither able to cultivate the above mentioned qualifications for monastics nor perform the responsibilities of monastics, they cannot really be called "monks."[90]

The "elite minority" who were truly qualified to be called monastics numbered a mere twenty to forty thousand, according to different texts that Taixu wrote on the subject. These he divided into three classifications: student monastics *(xue seng)*; "normal duty" monastics *(zhi seng)*, also called bodhisattva monastics *(pusa seng);* and emeritus monastics *(de seng)*, or elders *(zhanglao seng)*, who had retired from normal duties. In 1930, Taixu specified that there should be approximately ten thousand monastics engaged in studies in four grades, from basic education to advanced Buddhist research. In addition, twenty-five thousand monastics should engage in teaching and social-service careers, along with a smaller but unspecified number of elders supervising sixty centers for religious cultivation *(xiu lin)* in practices especially related to the Pure Land and Esoteric traditions. The sangha would therefore total thirty-five to forty thousand individuals.[91]

Later in 1930, Taixu again revised these numbers downward, to include only twenty thousand monastics: five thousand students, twelve thousand bodhisattva monastics, and three thousand elders.[92] Of the twelve thousand bodhisattva monastics, five thousand should be spreading the Dharma through public preaching and teaching, three thousand serving as administrators in Buddhist educational institutions, fifteen hundred engaging in Buddhist charitable and relief work, fifteen hundred serving as instructors in the monastic educational system, and one thousand participating in various cultural affairs.[93]

Although Taixu devoted far more attention to addressing the quality of monastics than their quantity, he did think that the two questions were interrelated.[94] Still, it was his fluctuations in actual and ideal numbers that made it difficult for many Buddhists to take his various schemes seriously. Five years later, in 1935, surely in response to criticism, Taixu raised the ideal number of monastics back to forty thousand.[95] As Welch has asserted, it was in large measure "as if he were a child deploying regiments of toy soldiers."[96]

Taixu's ideas about educational reforms were more widely accepted, though in some cases only slowly and grudgingly. To begin with, he was highly critical of secular education in China, believing that the public educational system had utterly failed to prepare a literate and informed citizenry to respond appropriately to the problems and opportunities of the contemporary world. Modernization in public education had come to mean eclectically imitating certain Japanese or western practices without adopting any comprehensive model of educational aims or learning processes. Therefore Taixu proposed that the sangha operate its own nationwide system of Buddhist parochial schools in four grades. Ideally, every county should have a primary school; every few counties, an elementary school; every ten counties, a middle school; and every province, a Buddhist high school. In addition to offering an excellent secular program of education, these schools would provide Buddhist studies—two hours a week for primary students, three hours for elementary students, four hours for middle school students, and six hours for high school students.[97]

Taixu felt that monastic education had improved only slightly during the early Republican period, with the impetus for reform in most cases coming only from the need to resist government confiscation of monastic property. The traditional system of monastic education in China enabled most monks to become familiar with just a few basic scriptures. A limited number of monks had the opportunity to study monastic rules in a Vinaya school or Buddhist doctrine under the tutelage of a Dharma master, who typically specialized in certain sacred texts. This latter system of apprenticeship to an instructor, as Welch notes, "produced a very small number of monks who knew the traditional interpretation of a few texts very well indeed, but it did not encourage originality or adaptation to changing times."[98] Taixu commented,

> In the past, the way of studying the religion has been exclusively to listen to scripture. If persons listened for ten years, then they could also become preaching Dharma masters. This is not a complete monastic education! My idea is that the monastic education which is needed today must include, as sequential elements of a complete system, the study of rules and ceremonies, the study of religious doctrine, and the cultivation of experiential knowledge.[99]

According to Taixu, the beginning curriculum for the study of rules and ceremonies *(lü yi)* should assume that the student is a high school graduate and consist of a two-year course of study for members of the monastic community only. The first six months should be devoted to rules and rites for novices, while the final year and a half should focus on those appropriate for ordained monks. In every province, one special sangha school should offer this basic program of studies.

Taixu divided the second phase of monastic education, the study of religious doctrine, into two levels. The first should correspond to a university level of education and emphasize general doctrinal studies *(putong jiaoli)*. Its four-year curriculum, which should also be open to laypeople as auditors, should lead to a baccalaureate degree. There should be one institution for every three provinces that would offer this university level of Buddhist education. At the second level of doctrinal studies, several hundred especially gifted monks ought to be engaged in a three-year program of advanced doctrinal studies *(gaodeng jiaoli)* leading to the Ph.D. degree *(boshi xuewei)*. A national institute for Buddhist research would need to be established for this purpose.

Beyond these programs, a very small number of monks ought to proceed to an additional three-year curriculum pursuing the cultivation of "experiential knowledge" *(xiu zheng)* at a center for religious cultivation *(xiu lin)*. For their achievements in the specialized skills of reflection and action *(guan xing)* in accord with recognized meditative and devotional practices, such advanced students might receive the Venerable Scholar degree *(dashi xuewei)*. Thus Taixu envisioned a total of twelve years of post-secondary monastic education as the ideal comprehensive program. As the ever-frustrated dreamer concluded in 1938,

> It will be best if we can do things according to this plan! However, if we look at it from the perspective of present facts, the types of religious facilities and funds with which we can accomplish such things do not exist. And even more scarce are the essential persons of talent who can resolve to achieve such a long-term goal, having endured the hardships of the last twenty years. Therefore, everything I have proposed remains merely an unrealized ideal, and that is all.[100]

CRITICISM AND RESPONSE

Taixu projected that unless the country's Buddhists cooperated to reorganize their institutions along these lines, to restate their message in ways responsive to the unique dilemmas of the modern world, and to redirect their energies toward a socially engaged form of Buddhism and the construction of a pure land on earth, the religion would simply continue its present trajectory of decline, so that they "need not wait until it was destroyed by a nonreligious government or foreign religion."[101] The key to survival, he knew, would be to find effective ways to link the best traditions of the past with new understandings appropriate to the future.[102] However, the monk also recognized that those bodhisattvas committed to such reformist efforts would encounter on virtually every front at least three powerful opposing forces: conservative Buddhists, radical anti-religionists, and evangelical Christians.

With regard to conservative opposition within the Buddhist community, it was clear to all practitioners that the style and content of Taixu's message contrasted significantly with popular forms of Pure Land piety in China. As a result, the Dharma master Yinguang, who was spearheading the growing Pure Land movement in the Republican period, charged that Taixu, although intellectually gifted, was a "misguided and dangerous" influence within the sangha. Summarizing a personal interview with Yinguang in 1928, Millican reported that the Pure Land master "did not hesitate to express his disapproval of the efforts to reform Buddhism along the lines advocated by Taixu."[103] In fact, after Millican's wife pressed Yinguang for a response to Taixu's criticisms of him, the Pure Land master's eyes reportedly "lit with some sort of fire" as he observed that with Taixu's "rushing here and there," he "knows nothing of what Buddhism means."[104] Yu-yue Tsu wrote of Yinguang:

> He has embraced the Buddhist monastic life as a protest against and refuge from the wickedness of the world. He decries the social gospel of the liberals as untrue to the Buddhist religion and Taixu as a danger to their faith, for, according to him, Buddhism is fundamentally otherworldly, interested in saving souls out of this world, which is hopelessly lost. Any attempt to compromise with it as the liberals are trying to do in building for a better world, as they say, leads men away from real religion, which is implicit reliance upon the saving power of the All-Merciful Amitābha for passage into his Pure Land Paradise.[105]

Although Yinguang was himself reasonably well versed in the Buddhist sūtras, he nevertheless taught that advanced scriptural studies and meditational disciplines were essentially useless for ordinary believers. In an age of great social disorder and spiritual degeneration, reliance on such difficult methods in the hope of enlightenment was simply foolish. As Reichelt observed, Yinguang's position was unambiguous: "There is a much safer and much quicker way, . . . and that is with a believing heart to ponder and call upon the precious name of the all-embracing Buddha, the Amitābha, boundless in life, in light and in mercy."[106] As Yinguang once wrote to a lay follower, "If you rely on the Pure Land way, faithfully and willingly recite the Buddha's name, and seek rebirth in the West[ern Pure Land], then you can be released from life and death. If you do not rely on the way of reciting the Buddha's name, even those who receive the true transmission of Buddhism cannot find release, not to mention those who do not receive it."[107] Commenting on his own discussions with Yinguang, Millican reported:

> He is a true conservative in both his social and religious convictions. In a personal conversation he stated that China must hold on to the agelong Five Human Relationships of Confucian, that is, Chinese society. And he waxed warm in pointing out that Taixu's efforts to modernize and universalize Buddhism were undermining rather than building up true Buddhism. He feels that Taixu and his group, in trying to give Buddhism a social application in the effort to regenerate society, have missed the true spirit of Buddhism which is essentially otherworldly. And furthermore, since Buddhism has the highest truth it is not necessary to try to harmonize or correlate it with other religions or with modern science. The whole effort of Yinguang is to bolster up the present system and practices of Buddhism as found in its temple life, and to propagate the teachings of the Pure Land. . . . He believes that nine out of ten persons would fail in the exacting task of self-enlightenment and self-deliverance by the Difficult Way of Meditation, so he preaches the way of salvation by faith with an evangelical fervor. His writings abound in accounts of those who have been benefited either physically or spiritually as a result of prayer to Amitābha, the Goddess of Mercy, and others. One of the most striking sections is a letter to the aged and famous Ningbo monk Dixian, in which he urges him to call upon the Goddess of Mercy to heal him of his infirmity. He quotes instances of

her miraculous healing power, and reminds him that if such an honored Buddhist leader is not healed it will bring great discredit upon the cause of Buddhism. He adds, "Since the Goddess of Mercy has this great saving power why not in your extremity throw yourself unreservedly and with all your will upon her mercy and thus obtain physical as well as spiritual comfort?"[108]

On the one hand, Taixu displayed a certain respect for this form of devotional piety. He recognized both its popular appeal and its doctrinal legitimacy within the comprehensive framework of Mahāyāna. Moreover, as Pratt points out, quite unlike the layman Ouyang Jingwu, whose interest in Buddhism was purely intellectual, Taixu was a unique combination of "scholar, thinker, *and mystic.*" Highlighting the reformer's own religious practice, Pratt reported in 1924 that at the Wuchang Buddhist Institute, "in marked contrast to Mr. Ouyang's college, daily worship at the very attractive little temple is a part of the training, and in this Taixu regularly takes part with all his students."[109] Such cultic participation by the reformer, however limited, contrasted with the more radical position of those modernists who stridently opposed all forms of worship and ritual as not merely unnecessary but counterproductive.[110]

On the other hand, Taixu firmly argued that any method of spiritual cultivation that did not effectively serve to eliminate a devotee's sense of individuality and selfhood could not lead to ultimate enlightenment. In commenting on one of the most important canonical Pure Land texts, Vasubandhu's *Wuliangshou jing youbotishe yuansheng jie* (Rebirth Treatise), Taixu emphasized that if any recognized Buddhist method "does not oppose a mind that distinguishes a self, then it cannot [lead to] the attainment of wisdom *(bodhi)."*[111] True bodhisattvas, he asserted, could never seek their own rebirth without simultaneously seeking the rebirth of all sentient beings.[112]

Taixu thus sought to distance himself from Pure Land devotionalism because he judged that, in actual practice, it was both ineffective in eliminating the deluded sense of "self" and inconsistent in linking the future of any one bodhisattva to the future of all other sentient beings. While Taixu taught that it was not inappropriate to show reverence to Gautama as one's spiritual forerunner and teacher, he invariably chose to emphasize the way of self-reliance over the way of reliance on others. Because he considered Pure Land techniques to be expedient primarily for uneducated believers, Taixu was sure that the school's influence would wane as the number of such persons steadily declined in China through educational reforms, both secular and religious. Mistaken in such a conclusion about Buddhist spirituality, Taixu was fortunate that the conservative forces within the sangha did not actively organize to oppose him. Of course, as Callahan quite perceptively points out, in part their opposition "was to the idea of organization itself."[113]

Besides widespread criticism of Taixu's work by conservatives within the Buddhist sangha, there was opposition to it by secular humanists in China. Taixu's efforts to propagate a modern form of Buddhism capable of both benefiting China and becoming the dominant global religion were challenged by intellectuals committed to the view that all religious beliefs and practices were worthless relics of the human past. Such anti-religionists urged officials of government and other institutions to limit the influence of religion throughout Chinese society. They condemned religious commitment for encouraging irrational trust in the power of spiritual beings and in the efficacy of superstitious rituals. In sum, they excoriated all who retarded cultural progress by upholding the value of traditional religion. The respected scholar Hu Shi, for example, charged that all forms of religion had utterly failed to create morally better and wiser human beings. Taking special aim at Buddhism as the principal expression of an outmoded "medievalism" in China, he wrote acerbically:

> What spirituality is there, let us say, in the old beggar-woman who dies in the direst destitution, but who dies while still mumbling, "Namu Amita Buddha!" and in the clear conviction that she will surely enter that blissful paradise presided over by the Amita Buddha? Do we earnestly think it moral or spiritual to inculcate in that beggar-woman a false belief which shall so hypnotize her as to make her willingly live and die in such dire conditions where she ought not to have been had she been born in a different civilization?
>
> No! A thousand times No! All those hypnotic religions belong to an age when man had reached senility and felt himself impotent in coping

with the forces of nature. Therefore he gave up the fight in despair and, like the disappointed fox in the ancient fable who declared the grapes sour because he could not reach them, began to console himself and teach the world that wealth and comfort are contemptible and that poverty and misery are something to be proud of. From this it was only a step to the idea that life itself was not worth living and that the only desirable thing was the blissful existence in the world beyond. And when wise men calmly taught these ideas, fanatics went further and practiced self-denial, self-torture, and even suicide. In the West, saints prayed, fasted, lived on pillars, and whipped themselves at regular intervals. In medieval China, monks prayed, fasted, and, feeding themselves daily with fragrant oil and tying their bodies with oiled cloth, gladly burned themselves to death as offerings to some deity of Mahāyāna Buddhism.

It was those religions of defeatism that sank the whole civilized world underneath the universal deluge of Medievalism. It took over a thousand years for a portion of mankind to emerge from the civilization which glorifies poverty and sanctifies disease, and slowly build up a new civilization which glorifies life and combats poverty as a crime. ...The new civilization of the new age has given to men a new religion, the religion of self-reliance as contrasted with the religion of defeatism of the Middle Ages.[114]

In addition to denouncing Mahāyāna Buddhism and other religions for their otherworldliness, secular humanists charged that the vicious competitiveness of exclusivistic religious sects only further demonstrated their harmful influence on societies everywhere. Hu Shi directly attacked Taixu for copying "Christian denominationalism" and for advocating—in a manner uncharacteristic of the Chinese—exclusive loyalty to Buddhism as an institutional religion. Thus he condemned Taixu's attempt to revitalize the Mahāyāna community as a "stubborn effort to outlive historical usefulness."[115] Identifying the essential spirit of all religious practice as "to live for the good of all humanity,"[116] Hu Shi asked, "Why not frankly transfer all our old loyalty to the new instrumentalities of education which are taking the place of the older religions as sources of instruction, inspiration, and consolation?"[117]

Appreciatively recalling his father's strong rationalist opposition to Buddhism and the weathered signpost on his uncle's home that read "No Alms for Buddhist Monks or Daoist Priests,"[118] Hu Shi at least gave Taixu the satisfaction of being explicitly named as an opponent. Most other anti-religious intellectual leaders did not think the Buddhist reformer worthy of mention; from their point of view, Buddhists and their reforms were irrelevant to China's cultural progress.

THE CHRISTIAN CHALLENGE

Besides being sensitive to conservative critics within the Buddhist sangha and to secular-humanist critics within intellectual circles, Taixu was acutely aware of the powerful and growing influence of Christianity, Buddhism's new religious challenger in East Asia. He realized that many of China's young people who were attracted to the cultural ethos and technological achievements of the West were also curious about its dominant religious heritage. Recognizing Christianity and Buddhism as the two most important religious forces in the modern world, Taixu studied Christian doctrine and invited western scholars to give lectures on the subject to his students and followers. Reichelt, in fact, recalled Taixu's graciousness in inviting him to a Buddhist conference on Lu Shan in 1923:

> Taixu sent me a hearty invitation to attend the conference and to lecture on "The Relation between Christianity and Buddhism."
> I visited Taixu at the Buddhist Academy in Wuchang where so many of the idealistic and higher type of Buddhist monks gather round the pulpit of their beloved and esteemed Master, "Explainer of the Law" *(fashi)*. He therefore knew my viewpoint fairly well, and that I would preach Jesus Christ as the perfect revealer of God and the great Savior of the world. Nevertheless he gave me unlimited liberty to speak as a Christian missionary, and introduced me to the audience with most friendly words, saying that he felt it was the duty at this time of every Buddhist to know the inner truths of Christianity just as well as it was the duty of the Christians to know what Buddhism really means.... I

also had opportunity to talk privately with Taixu. The hours spent with this rare Buddhist mystic in holy pondering over deep questions I shall never forget.[119]

Christian missionaries had become especially known in China for their social welfare work on behalf of the masses—through Christian hospitals, orphanages, schools, and the like. As Philip West has pointed out, most of the missionaries in China were advocates of the liberal Christian Social Gospel, which stressed the immanence of God, the humanity of Jesus, and the fundamental goodness of human nature.[120] Indeed, it could be said that the motive behind Taixu's thorough critique of Christianity was his desire to wrest from the Christians their assumed role as the primary advocates of religiously informed social action for the reform of Chinese society.

As Millican has pointed out, Taixu claimed that Christianity was a dying faith tradition that had run its course in human history. His judgment was based on an analysis of what he considered to be the three fundamental and outmoded ideas on which Christianity was grounded: first, that there is a Creator God who is sovereign over all his creation; second, that there is an eternal soul created by God that is the essence of each human spirit; and third, that there is a redeeming savior, Jesus of Nazareth, who is the only Son of God. According to Millican, in opposition to all three ideas, the Chinese master summarily reasoned, "Now, then, if Cause and Effect are understood the idea of God is exploded. If the unity and succession of all things is understood the idea of a soul is done away with. If human life is understood then the need of a savior is done away with."[121]

Taixu outlined his basic difficulties with the three cornerstones of Christian doctrine in his essay "Wushen lun" (On Atheism).[122] In the modern world of science, the monk began, most intellectuals are advocates of atheistic worldviews, although a few, influenced by western religion and philosophy, still cling to old-fashioned theistic ideas. These, he suggested, generally espouse popular-sounding ideals of individual freedom and equality, based on the belief that each human being is an equally loved "child of God." From this perspective, they encourage all people to relate kindly to one another, under the authority of the one Creator God, and to eliminate any barriers among them. This is a simple and appealing view, remarked Taixu, but unfortunately, in the case of Christianity, one based on a complex of fundamentally erroneous religious conceptions of a sovereign, soul, and savior.

First, Taixu attacked Christian understandings of God by reiterating criticisms articulated earlier by Zhang Taiyan and others.[123] For example, he argued, Christian theism consistently places humankind in an extremely subservient and dependent status vis-à-vis the divine. God is viewed as having unlimited powers, and all persons are forced to submit to God's commands. Furthermore, they must do so happily, noted Taixu, lest their attitudes and actions constitute a rebellion for which they will be cast into a tortuous hell and separated from God for all eternity. Yet despite their disturbingly vulnerable situation, Christians are instructed that they must always address God not only with respect but with affection, as their "Loving Father." Moreover, according to Christian theology, God is supremely wise and good. However, rather than allowing his beloved children to reside with him in his heavenly kingdom and walk with him in his lush garden, God inexplicably causes them to live in a world of injustice, inequality, and terrible suffering.

Further critiquing the Christian affirmation of God's omnipotence and sovereignty, Taixu raised provocative questions about the status of the Devil. Was this "Satan," who supposedly opposes God, created by God? On the one hand, said the reformer, if Christians were to respond that he was not, then obviously there is that which the Creator God did not create, and his creation has its limits. God's creative skills would then be similar to those of any human artisan who creates only what he or she can. Furthermore, if the Devil is not a creation of God, then there must be another who creates devils and whose powers are comparable to, if not greater than, God's. Indeed, how does any Christian know, Taixu asked, that human beings are creations of God and not of the Devil?

On the other hand, Taixu reasoned, if Christians were to respond that the Devil does belong to God's creation, why can't God control him? And since God punishes those who trust and follow the Devil by casting them into hell, why doesn't he also punish Satan by casting him into hell? Moreover, if God, as the creator, was originally able to control the Devil, why would the same good and loving God not continue to do so but let him endanger the lives and well-being of all humankind? Taixu concluded that these questions are insoluble, and that, when pressed, Christians "do not know adequately how to reply and can only laugh dumbly in embarrassment."[124] A supreme self-existent God, he wrote, is like "something caught in the hairs of a ghost or on the horns of a hare—both nonentities."[125]

Second, the Buddhist reformer objected to the Christian idea of an eternal human soul. If one accepts such a mistaken idea, then one is also led to say that all animals and plants have eternal souls, he maintained. This is the perspective of one who fails to recognize the truth of conditioned origination *(yuanqi)*. As an expedient, Taixu acknowledged, the idea of an eternal soul may help some people move beyond the simple identification of the self with the body. Yet such a doctrine permanently separates and alienates all things from one another. It fails to comprehend the true interdependence and interpenetration of all dharmas (phenomena) and, correspondingly, the bonds of sympathy that properly link humans with all forms of life. In so doing, it actually undermines the most profound basis for social responsibility.

The notion of an eternal soul is effectively refuted in Buddhism, according to Taixu, by two central teachings. The first is that of conditioned origination, which is summarized in the statement that "all things are constituted (evolve) by the conjunction of inherent and affinitative elements." The second is that of consciousness-only *(weishi)*, which is succinctly captured in the assertion that "all things are idealistic phenomenal manifestations." "If we combine these two phrases, . . ." argued Taixu, "we have the dominant thread running through all the Buddha's illuminating teachings regarding the nature of the universe." Explicating the two phrases, the monk argued as follows:

> Of all the things in the universe, whether it be the world as a whole, the smallest particle or even the universe itself, it may be said that there

is nothing that exists independently of relations and that is not involved in the temporal succession or continuity of events. All have a history and a social nature. Things appear in this continuity of successive events in mutual relationship, playing the alternate role of inherent and then of affinitative elements in the process of bringing into existence the individual organizations. We may go farther and say that present causes themselves arise from previous causes. So when we think of things we must realize that in their basic natures they are only temporary aggregates appearing in the cosmic process and having no independent existence in themselves. This is what Buddhists mean when they say "all things are constituted by inherent and affinitative elements."

Now what is meant by the phrase, "all things are idealistic phenomenal manifestations"? The word "manifestation" *(xian)* has two meanings. First, it means being manifest and second it means manifesting. "Being manifest" refers to the principles or objects which are made manifest and recognized by means of the five senses, by thought, etc. "Manifesting" refers to the active knowing mind which has power to cause change in the things which become objects of knowledge and thus become manifest. In brief, all things in the moment of becoming objects of mind are changed by the power of the mind. This is what is meant by the phrase "all things are idealistic phenomenal manifestations."[126]

These two fundamental ideas of the Buddha effectively defined a religio-philosophical middle position that avoided the two extremes of substantialism and nihilism. According to Taixu, Buddhist idealism provided an extremely helpful framework for interpreting this mediation. In fact, as Wing-tsit Chan has claimed, Taixu contributed to the interest in idealism by trying to "harmonize the philosophy of Weishi, Huayan, and Tiantai, combining their essential features and removing their contradictions."[127] Lai aptly points out that Taixu's interest in Weishi philosophy paralleled that of many other Buddhist modernists who rejected both Pure Land for its faith stance and Chan for its anti-intellectualism.[128] Taixu believed that idealism was not only Mahāyāna's most sophisticated system of thought but the one that would most easily capture the imagination of the growing numbers of educated people in China, both inside and outside of the Sangha.

In addition, as Hamilton confirms, in Taixu's opinion idealism was also "the system most worth the attention of the Western student of philosophy."[129]

Taixu's interpretation of "Dharma-character idealistic philosophy" *(faxiang weishi xue)*, says Chan, should not be identified with a western subjective idealism that denies an "original substance" while reducing reality to individual consciousness, nor with a western objective idealism that recognizes a "Universal Mind." Rather, writes Chan, Taixu "attempts to combine them both by holding that in the transformations of the eight consciousnesses, they transform both individually and collectively."[130] Moreover, in clear opposition to Ouyang Jingwu's interpretation of Thusness *(zhenru)* as being absolutely transcendental and radically separated from phenomena, Taixu's more synthetic intuitions led him to view Thusness as both transcendent and immanent. These abstract philosophical arguments—on which his rejections of both the idea of an eternal soul and that of an eternal Creator were based—were not simply academic metaphysical speculations but were aimed directly at establishing an adequate foundation for morality. As Taixu himself explained,

> The Buddhist teaching regarding the nature of the universe has nothing of the mystical or mysterious in it. . . . It asserts positively that there is in the universe no such thing as an independently existing individual thing. Everything great or small is made up of a union of many units or elements in a successive continuity of moments of time. . . . Now when this cosmic view of Buddhism is applied to morality it means that there is an inescapable mutuality in life. In working good or ill to another, one is bringing good or ill to himself. . . . The whole cannot separate itself from the individual and the individual cannot exist apart from the whole.[131]

Third, on the basis of Buddhism's cosmology *(yuzhou guan)*, Taixu asserted that humans beings need no divine savior. The monk firmly rejected as fantastic the Christian idea of a supernatural being who breaks in on the natural order to effect an irresistible salvation. To begin with, he could not accept the concept of the absolute divine forgiveness of sin, which he judged to be in conflict with the Buddhist law of cause and effect. On this point Millican once commented:

> Taixu following this philosophical atheistic school puts great emphasis on Buddhist Law or Dharma *(fofa)*. This law of cause and effect runs through all existence. This applied to human life and conduct means that our future is determined according to unchangeable laws by our conduct in this life. According to this law the necessary outcome of a good life is a better future. Thus we may save ourselves, or determine our own destiny. To one of this school, the idea, for instance, that a murderer or other flagrant sinner can escape by any means from suffering the result of his own sins, is repugnant. Since the culprit could escape from punishment by merely repenting and requesting forgiveness from God, would not evil be encouraged? On the other hand, would not the knowledge that a sure retribution is bound to follow deter evil doers?[132]

In addition, Taixu dismissed the traditional Christian view of Jesus Christ as an incarnate Creator God who had descended to earth to offer salvation. In contrast, according to the monk, Gautama can be considered a "savior" only in the highly qualified sense that he is the prime example of one who earnestly pursued the salvific path that leads to perfect enlightenment and buddhahood. As Taixu himself remarked, "Buddha is not a supernatural but a superhuman being who has realized the truth of all existence, and having conformed his life to it, incites us by his compassion to do likewise."[133] Thus, seeking clarification of Christian doctrine, Taixu once asked Millican if every Christian could become a Christ, as Jesus did, and just as any bodhisattva in the Mahāyāna Buddhist tradition could realize his or her own buddha-nature.[134] Reichelt remembers that, following his lectures on Christianity at the 1923 Buddhist conference at Lu Shan's Dalin si, Taixu graciously responded, "Jesus Christ is the incarnated Dao. This I now understand. But for us the chief thing is that *the Dao can also be incarnated in us.*"[135]

Although Christianity was fatally flawed by these three mistaken notions of God, soul, and savior, according to Taixu, it nevertheless had one special contribution to make to the modern history of religion: aiding Buddhism in its development. In an important 1938 lecture entitled "Zhongguo xu yejiao yu Ou Mei xu fojiao" (China Needs Christianity and Europe and America Need Buddhism), Taixu argued that the Chinese Buddhist community ought to reflect on the unique energy and spirit exhibited within the Christian church. Such a spirit could help revive Buddhism in China, thus benefiting the nation and the world. From his perspective, Buddhist practitioners had to recognize that the great scientific and technological accomplishments of the West were intrinsically related to central elements of the Christian tradition, elements that had developed since the Middle Ages and that unfortunately were not present to the same degree within the Buddhist heritage.

The primary aspect of Christianity that Taixu wished to lift up for emulation was its ability to organize and motivate individual adherents in normative modes of religious belief and practice. Christians, he noted, were led to experience their faith as a universal one, leading to a sense of order, harmony, and community with others. The church, he concluded after visiting Europe and the United States, had been able through ritual acts and opportunities for fellowship to instill in individual believers, despite their differences, a remarkable oneness of mind and spirit that shaped their everyday lives and energized them for mission. Chinese Buddhism had once displayed that spirit, he suggested, but in the modern world there was no common spirit or discipline within the religious community. The Sangha appeared dispirited and disorganized. Therefore, he asserted, "we must now learn a lesson from Christianity in order to improve Buddhism, enliven its spirit, and influence the people."[136]

In accord with this judgment, and lamenting the fact that Buddhist monks in China officiated only at funeral services, the reformer encouraged the design of new Buddhist services for celebrating all the important events in a person's life, such as the birth of an infant, the beginning of a child's education, a wedding, a birthday, the birth anniversary of a deceased family member, and so on.[137] When Taixu conducted a modern Buddhist wedding ceremony in Shanghai in 1927, he drew an immediate outburst of criticism from traditionalists within the sangha. He noted that some monastic leaders even believed that such new rites were Communist-influenced.[138]

From Taixu's perspective, Christianity's most compelling aspect was its ability to engender in diverse adherents a singleness of purpose and unified commitment to mission, while its weakest point was its utter inability to permit rational inquiry into the nature of faith. As a result, he observed, within Christian communities there existed an unfortunate and irreconcilable bifurcation between faith and reason, religious and scientific discourse:

> The life of Europeans and Americans is scientific, but their faith is unscientific. While contemporary Europeans and Americans need religion, their religion is divorced from and contradictory to a practical, scientific life. Theirs has become a type of divided and inconsistent life. Thus in order to practice religion, they must cast aside reason; but in order to pursue a practical life, they must cast aside faith. This is the sad situation now in Europe and the United States.[139]

Christians are forced to compartmentalize religion, Taixu argued, because its logic is wholly incompatible with the practical, scientific logic of everyday discourse and endeavor. And just as Christianity can supply what Chinese Buddhism needs, so Chinese Buddhism can supply what Christianity needs: a religious heritage that is not in direct conflict with scientific reasoning but that has the potential to produce a high degree of trust, commitment, and community.

TOWARD A RELIGIONLESS FUTURE

Taixu was convinced that religious believers of all traditions could learn from one another and benefit from one another's experiences. As he once stated, "It is my belief that Buddhism has enough variety in its many aspects to meet the needs of all temperaments and classes of people. Nevertheless it is possible to think that all religions share in some central core of truth to which each forms in its own way a separate gateway."[140] Thus his active ecumenical work within the global Buddhist community—which inspired the creation in 1950 of the World Fellowship of Buddhists—was complemented by his efforts toward greater interreligious cooperation and dialogue. As noted in Chapter 3, in 1943 he participated in the founding of the Association of Chinese Religious Believers, the executive committee of which included, in addition to Taixu, leaders in the Roman Catholic, Protestant, and Islamic communities. Taixu was also serving, at the time of his death, as an executive director of the Philosophy of Life Institute, founded by the Roman Catholic bishop Paul Yu Bin. In the *China Christian Year Book, 1932–1933,* Reichelt wrote of the monk's open and congenial spirit toward members of the Christian church:

> He is always friendly and noble in his attitude towards Christians. Was it not for the—according to his opinion—limited and meaningless Christian idea of God as a personality and a creator, and the equally meaningless idea of Christ as the only perfect revealer of the divine and the only savior of the world—were it not for these things—Taixu would most willingly proclaim Christianity as a special and in many respects a very strong form of Mahāyāna Buddhism, given and adapted to western races.[141]

Although Taixu was an inclusivist who was open to what might be learned in dialogue with adherents of other religions, he nevertheless remained firmly convinced of the absolute truth of the Buddha's Dharma. Yet he clearly emphasized that institutional religion, including the institutional form of religion known as Mahāyāna Buddhism, should be understood as a conveyance (a "yāna," or *sheng*) to the realization of truth—that is, as a means to an end, not an end in itself. Thus he concluded his essay "On Atheism" with an intriguing description of the historical evolution of religion. His primary tenet was that true religion is always preparing people for a religionless future. His arguments reflect a blend of Marxist ideology, with which he had been familiar since his youth, and the religio-philosophical perspectives of the wisdom schools of Buddhism.

In essence, Taixu asserted that when people venerate sages or buddhas, this is not only their own misfortune but, in a significant sense, the misfortune of the one who is declared to be a sage or a buddha. The true sage, he observed, surely hopes that the people will not designate anyone as a sage. In the same way, "true religion must daily take as its ultimate hope that the world will not use religion." How is it possible for sages not to be venerated, he asked rhetorically, and how can the world ultimately dispense with religious practice? Taixu's answer was: by all people becoming sages and all becoming buddhas, "yet because all sentient beings have not yet become buddhas, and all people have not yet become sages, humankind has sages and worthies and the world has religions."[142]

Like the ninth-century Chan iconoclast Linji (d. 867), Taixu considered the reverencing of sages and buddhas to be unfortunate precisely because it turns people's minds from their own responsibilities and potentialities. As long as people depend on the powers of other "great beings," he argued, they fail to develop their own hidden powers for self-transformation. As long as they worship other beings as sacred, they fail to perceive their own sacrality. For these reasons, Taixu considered all forms of devotionalism, whether Christian, Buddhist, or any other, to be expedient expressions that would ultimately give way to a more perfect view. "After the world honors the Dharma for a long time," he declared, "the truth will be spoken, the gates of all expediencies open, the true nature of reality manifest, and atheism will still be considered the final teaching."[143]

To illustrate this point, Taixu recommended comparison with the political realm. Again articulating a Mahāyāna Buddhist argument with Marxist overtones, he wrote, "Progress in the realm of government is from the authority of tribal chieftains to a monarchy, and from a monarchy to a republic, and from a republic to [the ideal of] no government at all. In religion, progress is from [the belief in] many gods to one god, from one god to sages and worthies, and from sages and worthies to no religion at all."[144]

According to Taixu, Mahāyāna Buddhism, which is ultimately atheistic and combines morality with scientific principles, is the most advanced and perfect form of institutional religion. The time will come when the Buddhist Dharma will inform the daily lives of all persons, but "Buddhism" as a formally structured religious tradition will be forgotten, much as "when one catches a hare, the snare is forgotten, or when one catches a fish, the fish trap is forgotten."[145] Thus the essence of the Buddhist tradition will remain, Taixu asserted, and its impact on human life will expand beyond measure. However, it will not be consciously labeled or thought of as "Buddhism." Whatever its merits, Christian theism, because of its place in the evolutionary religious chain and the attachments that it engenders, is obviously not in a similar position to help people move beyond to an ultimate vision of codependent reality.

During this final age of transition toward the religionless future, argued Taixu, the Chinese Buddhist community is called upon to reform and reenergize itself for its mission of teaching and service to all sentient beings. The required reformation of Buddhism, the necessary redefinition of the essential bodhisattva path, is, he recognized, iconoclastic by its very nature because no attachments can be allowed to prevent the attainment of complete enlightenment. Yet the process should not be destructive. Rather, those committed to it should carefully analyze, select, adapt, and utilize within human culture—and within Christianity, as Buddhism's most important competitor and dialogue partner—that which is in consonance with the highest levels of wisdom and compassion as exhibited by the Enlightened One.

As Taixu pointed out in his essay, "Xin jiu wenti de genben jiejue" (The Fundamental Solution to the Issue of the New and the Old), in the twentieth century many are caught up in a bitter clash between extreme conservatism and radical iconoclasm. Their distress, he observed, is largely the result of a failure to follow a middle way and to avoid rigid polarizations within society:

> One perspective considers anything new as comparatively better and anything old as bad. Therefore, one ought to select only that which is new and use it, while merely discarding that which is old. Another perspective considers anything old as comparatively better and anything new as dangerous. Therefore, one ought to rely on the old and stay with it, while blocking the new and shunning its use.[146]

A much wiser perspective, averred Taixu, acknowledges that both the old and the new are complex matters and that neither is wholly good or bad. Therefore Buddhists in the contemporary, pluralistic world should seriously attend to their religious and cultural heritage while learning from others, realizing that their tradition is dynamic, evolving, and finally to be transcended. In an age marked by utopian dreaming, Taixu was intentionally calling his "new monks" to a uniquely modern form of Buddhism and beyond.

Lai has correctly pointed out that the criticisms of Christian theism articulated by Taixu and most of his contemporaries were inadequate and unsophisticated.[147] Taixu tended to caricature Christianity, failing to recognize its diversities and complexities, even as he represented a rather limited and overly rationalistic view of Buddhism as a living tradition. Much more comprehensive and sensitive reflections by Chinese Buddhists and Christians alike on the foundational truths and the elasticity of these two traditions would be required to advance the dialogue. Yet Taixu's unusual intention to listen, if not his often simplistic rhetoric, should be recognized as a significant contribution to Buddhist-Christian dialogue in his day. Although he did not adequately model the spiritual adventure of "passing over and coming back"[148] that most would now assume to be critical to the continuing maturation of such dialogue, Taixu did provide a far more engaging paradigm for interreligious dialogue as a style of life than did most Chinese Buddhist masters in the Republican period.

CHAPTER 6

TAIXU'S LEGACY

None of Taixu's twenty-four tonsure disciples and grandson-disciples proved capable enough in the continuation of his master's work to be widely recognized. In fact, six of them left the order to return to lay life, and two renounced Buddhism altogether.[1] Yet after the reformer's death in 1947, there were prominent members of the sangha in China, Hong Kong, and Taiwan who were appreciative of his legacy and sought to advance his progressive agenda. That was not, however, always an easy or popular endeavor.

REFORM AND REVOLUTION IN THE PEOPLE'S REPUBLIC OF CHINA AND HONG KONG

Classic Marxist theories about the origin, value, and end of religion provided the basic rubric for the state's dealing with Buddhism in the People's Republic of China after 1949. Although Mao Zedong promised protection for religious believers—as long as they were not engaged in counterrevolutionary activities—most local cadres were quick to include Buddhist monks and nuns among those undesirable elements of society to whom the freedoms promised in the "Common Program" (approved by the Chinese People's Political Consultative Conference in September 1949) were not extended. Indeed, stringent new protective control measures enacted by the government, random acts of violence against members of the sangha, and incidents of zealous cadres destroying scriptures and monastic property combined to produce widespread chaos within the Buddhist community. As Welch comments in his *Buddhism Under Mao,*

> Until the Cultural Revolution began in 1966, it was the policy of the Chinese Communist Party to protect Buddhism, while at the same time keeping it under control and utilizing it in foreign policy. Yet in the first years after Liberation there were places in China where monasteries were destroyed, monks were beaten or killed, copies of the Buddhist canon were burned, and sacred images were melted down for their metal. In these places the sangha or Buddhist clergy, already worried about the effects of land reform, was reduced to "a state of terror."[2]

As Richard Bush observes, the radical land reform policies of the Communists caused general disorientation and disorder within the monastic community. Not only were the economies of Buddhist monasteries dramatically affected, but monks and nuns were suddenly cast into a very different life situation for which they were largely unprepared:

> Buddhist properties, especially landholdings, were largely broken up through the Land Reform Law of 1950. Land was confiscated from the monasteries (the abbots of monasteries were classed as landlords) and redistributed to the people, which could mean that monks and nuns might also qualify for a small plot of land just as an ordinary farmer would. For example, the monks in a particular monastery, greatly reduced in number during the first year of the new regime, each received a *mu* (about a sixth of a U.S. acre). Some chose to cultivate that small plot alone; most of them who continued in the monasteries formed mutual aid teams in 1954, were drawn into cooperatives in 1956, and into communes in 1958. Very few monks had previously worked in the fields; in one group of 103 monks only one had any agricultural experience.[3]

The vast majority of the sangha was alarmed and deeply saddened by these unexpected developments. Yet some of Taixu's followers interpreted them as the keys to a new religious future and as a fortuitous destruction of the old, outmoded forms of Buddhism that would prepare the way for the great "creative advance" for which the reformer had labored. As Taixu himself had once said, "In the process of revolution there is always a phase of destruction preceding reconstruction. The bad must be done away with before the good can be brought into existence."[4] Some were persuaded that the radical changes being wrought in the People's Republic of China would effectively eliminate the restraints of a corrupt and moribund Buddhist tradition and provide the freedom for a complete and efficacious rechanneling of its spiritual essence.

Among those who were encouraged that Taixu's "Buddhist revolution" was now truly underway was the monk Juzan, who exercised considerable authority in Buddhist circles on behalf of the government in the period before the Cultural Revolution. Ordained in 1931, after studying under Taixu at the South Fujian Seminary, Juzan was first recognized by the government in 1950 after drafting a letter to Mao that (1) celebrated the heroic struggle of the Communist Party for freedom and equality against the last fortresses of feudalism in China; (2) gave "ten thousand thanks" to the Party for helping to eliminate all decadent forms of Buddhism and all other types of heterodox sects so that "Buddhism would emerge to build a vigorous new life for itself"; (3) urged the government to support "a new form of Buddhism" that might well "facilitate the liberation of the whole country and the promotion of world revolution"; (4) recommended an enforced Buddhist "shift to production" that would smash the old feudal economies of the monasteries; and (5) proposed a "shift to scholarship" for monastics that would eradicate all the superstitious accretions that had become attached to Buddhism, cleansing it of "pessimism and escapism."[5]

Juzan forged ties with Buddhist laymen who advocated similar views, such as Zhao Puchu, and with China's most important Tibetan lama at the time, Shirob Jaltso, while also competing with them for recognition by Party leaders. He was eventually appointed editor of

Xiandai foxue (Modern Buddhism), the journal established to transmit the central government's policies toward Buddhism, to promote Buddhist reforms, and to maintain contacts with Buddhist organizations in countries that recognized Beijing. Welch notes that the publication attempted to popularize ideas such as "(1) productive labor best fulfilled the Bodhisattva vows; (2) the collective life envisioned by the Communists would reduce ego and increase the chances for escaping the cycle of rebirth; (3) the Western paradise was therefore being created here on earth by the Communist party; [and] (4) Buddhist compassion really meant killing bad people in order to save good people."[6] The journal was an instrument of a new Chinese Buddhist Association (Zhongguo fojiao xiehui) founded in 1953, the old association that Taixu helped to reestablish in 1947 having relocated its headquarters to Taiwan.

Shirob Jaltso became the new association's first functioning president after the death of the elderly Yuanying immediately after its founding. Zhao Puchu served as its first secretary-general, and later as its president. They joined Juzan and other reformist colleagues in thinking that they were in an ideal position to press forward with Taixu's ideas that "salvation was to be sought not by withdrawing from the world but by contributing to it" and that "the highest conduct for a bodhisattva is to benefit living creatures."[7] According to Juzan's report, when the new Chinese Buddhist Association convened for the first time, central to the discussion was "how to help the People's Government get rid of charlatans who practice exorcism, sorcery, and other harmful superstitions under the guise of religion."[8] Indeed, Juzan was soon to proffer the view that all religious rituals "hinder production and hold up the execution of governmental orders." To permit them, he suggested, "might stiffen this backward attitude in the religious world and increase the separation of religious believers from the masses."[9]

At the same time, a number of radical Buddhist monks were beginning to advance an even more revolutionary agenda than Juzan. They were not only attacking Pure Land devotionalism and a lack of social and political activism within the sangha, but were demanding that monks and nuns be able to marry and have children, eat meat, drink alcoholic beverages, wear lay dress, and let their hair grow fashionably long as well. In response, leaders of the monastic community reiterated the significance of upholding the Vinaya regulations even in the country's changed socio-political circumstances. The ensuing debate about the shape of the "new Buddhism" continued until the ominous clouds that were gathering just prior to the Cultural Revolution brought on a torrent of religious suppression that, by 1966, had swept away both the Chinese Buddhist Association and its journal. Reflecting on these untoward events in relation to Taixu's reforms, Welch thoughtfully observes:

> In 1928 when Juzan first met Taixu, he submitted a thousand-word statement on his four purposes in becoming a monk, one of which was "the reform of Buddhism." Taixu commented on it: "Here is a scholar who has set himself on the way, and, if well taught and guided by a teacher, he will go far." Later, Juzan studied under him at the South Fujian Seminary and was introduced by him to the master under whom he became a monk.... Other leaders of the new CBA [Chinese Buddhist Association] in Beijing had also been Taixu's followers—men like Fazun, Shi Mingke, Li Rongxi. Yet he cannot be considered responsible for what happened to monastic life under Mao. A cadre formerly in charge of Buddhism in the Religious Affairs Division in Guangzhou had never even heard of his seminal work on reform, *The Reorganization of the Sangha System*. Although much of what he advocated was realized after 1949 (productive labor, public service, political activism, the elimination of commercialized and superstitious rites), it was not realized in his name or because he had advocated it, but rather because it suited the needs of the regime. Nor, I think, would Taixu have been pleased by the way it was realized. He had not wanted to see the sangha turned into a servant of the government in power or to see monasteries turned into museums. He would probably have judged much of the reform of Buddhism after 1949 to be contrary to the Vinaya and to the ethic of compassion.... This is not to say that, if he had still been alive, he would have been able to resist the pressure to follow the leadership of the Party. Perhaps, however, he would have looked back ruefully on his former enthusiasm for bringing the sangha into the world and would have felt

inexpressibly uncomfortable reading, for example, what [the Tibetan lama] Shirob Jaltso wrote in 1960: "Monks have discarded their tolerant, transcendental, 'negative attitude of rejecting the world,' which has been handed down from the past, and they have been stirred into a 'positive attitude of entering the world,' so that they have a completely new mentality."[10]

Julian Pas has pointed out that following the "Ten Years' Chaos" that ended with Mao's death in 1976, Chinese Buddhism began a modest "ascent" as anti-religious rhetoric and overt persecution were brought to an end.[11] Believing that international relations and tourism could be enhanced by preserving Buddhist monuments and artifacts as a part of the nation's cultural heritage, the government even began to help rebuild temples and monasteries that had been damaged or destroyed. Government funds have been supplemented by donations from members of the Chinese Buddhist diaspora and other friends overseas. For example, Kenneth Dean has reported that in Fujian "tremendous amounts of money have been donated by Buddhist organizations in Japan, Hong Kong, and Southeast Asia to the reconstruction of temples and the restoration of Buddhist libraries."[12] Although this slow ascent continues into the present and various institutes for the study of Buddhism have been established, the religion continues to struggle in China, where it has a relatively small number of monks and limited facilities and programs for their education.[13]

Just as Taixu's name was not directly associated with what happened to Buddhism under Mao's leadership, so it does not appear to be closely linked with Buddhism's future in China. As one informant at Fudan University in Shanghai reported to me in 1989, both monks and scholars of religion know of Taixu's place in modern Chinese Buddhist history, but because of his close connections to the Guomindang government, the study of his work has not been encouraged. Nevertheless, during the 1990s new editions of Taixu's writings, as well as scholarly studies of his thought, have been published in simplified characters by the Chinese Social Science Press, and at least one recent doctoral dissertation on Taixu has been written for the faculty of the University of Beijing.[14]

In Hong Kong, of course, the story has been quite different. Although, as Bartholomew Tsui has remarked, Buddhism in post–World War II Hong Kong has yet to be thoroughly studied, three facts seem fairly well established.[15] First, the size of the sangha has fluctuated significantly, rising sharply when refugees flooded into Hong Kong in 1949–1950 and declining almost as dramatically when most of these monastics, like Taixu's student Yinshun, eventually emigrated to Taiwan or other locations. Some, such as Juzan, who fled to the British colony for only a brief period after Mao's conquering forces crossed the Yangzi, soon returned to China. As a result of emigration and only a few new entrants to the order each year, by 1989 the number of monks in Hong Kong, including the New Territories, was reported to be no more than two hundred.[16]

Second, because of the small number of monks in any one temple, the sangha has been fragmented. There has been a proliferation of small temples *(daochang)*, but in general it has not been possible to maintain the communal aspects of the traditional monastic system of China. The largest monastery, Baolian si, on Dayu Shan (on Lantau Island), which was built in 1921, continues to attract pilgrims and tourists because of its gigantic statute of the Buddha, but other historic monasteries, such as the Lindu si and Lingdu si, have fallen into ruin.

Third, despite the fragmentation of the sangha, the Hong Kong Buddhist Association (Xianggang fojiao lianhe hui), first established in 1931, has sponsored a broad range of educational and social service work since the end of the war in 1945. The association has thus embraced the challenge presented by its unique context—as Taixu specifically encouraged its members to do during visits to Hong Kong —of blending the best of eastern and western religion and culture.[17] In fact, writes Tsui,

> It has appropriated to itself all sorts of functions, from being a member of the World Fellowship of Buddhists [since 1952] to running a Buddhist cemetery. This organization had the vision of venturing into education and social work on a very large scale. Today it has about twenty-five schools on various levels under its care, with students numbering about thirty thousand. These make up about half the number of about

fifty Buddhist schools in the Territory. It runs the only Buddhist hospital, seven homes for the aged and the sick, and three youth organizations. All these show that Buddhism has received generous financial support from the general population.[18]

In a brief report on the history and status of Buddhism in Hong Kong prepared for the Sixteenth General Conference of the World Fellowship of Buddhists in 1988, four distinct developments of the last several decades are enumerated, all of which are in accord with Taixu's own inclinations and those of other progressives within the Chinese sangha. Explicitly acknowledging the depth of Taixu's influence on Buddhists in the territory after his lecture series there in 1920, the authors state, first, that in the last thirty years there has been an obvious change from "monastic to urban Buddhism," with a shift from rural temples to inner city temples. Second, there has been a transition in monastic and lay Buddhist education from a "general standard to intellectual standard," with a new focus on higher scholarship and a "faith based on wisdom" rather than on superstition. Third, there has been a change of emphasis from "reclusive practices to serving society." Less attention is now paid to "self-cultivation," it is said, and more to social service "through cultural, educational, [and] charitable work." Fourth, there has been a significant shift from "localized to internationalized Buddhism," with the development of stronger ecumenical ties to other Buddhist fellowships around the world.[19]

ADVOCATES OF REFORM IN TAIWAN

Taixu's legacy is most clearly visible in Taiwan. The reformer's monthly journal, *Haichao yin,* is still being published, his writings are widely available in bookstores, and his life and teachings have been recounted to the general public by touring drama troops.[20] In 1963, Zhu Baotang reported that while the Chinese Buddhist Association in Taiwan had published eight hundred sets of the *Taishō shinshū daizōkyō* (the Buddhist canon) as of that date, it had published a thousand sets of the *Taixu dashi quanshu* (Complete Works of the Venerable Master Taixu).[21] However, as Charles Brewer Jones has indicated, after the Japanese were forced off the island in 1946 and the Chinese Buddhist Association (which was reconstituted in Nanjing in May 1947) relocated to Taipei in 1949, a renewed struggle ensued between conservatives and progressives within the sangha for control of the organization. The Chinese Buddhist Association of the Republic of China, he writes, "had been subject to years of internecine power struggles between a traditionalist faction led by Yuanying, and a reformist faction led by Taixu. After 1949, the disciples of these two figures carried on this struggle, which seemed to go to the reformers at first but ultimately resolved in favor of the traditionalists. The result has been that Taiwan Buddhism has tended toward conservatism, especially in the retention of very traditional Pure Land practices."[22]

Nevertheless, several prominent masters in Taiwan have remained identified with the progressive faction within the sangha, which traces its roots back to Taixu's modernization efforts. Influenced by his interpretation of the Dharma, they have carried on particular aspects of Taixu's "Buddhism for human life" *(rensheng fojiao)* in their own teaching. Advocating a "humanistic Buddhism" *(renjian fojiao)*, their works are some of the most dynamic expressions of contemporary Taiwanese Buddhism. My aim here is only to introduce briefly four of the most important masters—Yinshun, Xingyun, Shengyan, and Zhengyan. Although sometimes at odds with the sangha's conservative mainstream in Taiwan, they have gained a considerable following for a socially engaged form of Mahāyāna Buddhism both at home and abroad.

Yinshun (original name: Zhang Luqin)

Yinshun, Taixu's student and biographer, was born in the spring of 1906 to a farming family in Haining county of Zhejiang province, not far from where Taixu had been born sixteen years earlier. Born prematurely, with health problems, he suffered numerous illnesses as a child. In 1911, the year the Qing dynasty fell in the Republican rev-

VENERABLE MASTER YINSHUN

Source: Yinshun Cultural and Educational Foundation (Yinshun wenjiao jijin hui), Xinzhu County, Taiwan.

olution, Yinshun left the supervision of his mother to begin primary school in the township where his father worked. He proved to be an exceptional student especially skillful in writing. At the age of fourteen, his father sent him to study traditional Chinese medicine for three years. Dissatisfied with the instruction and disinterested in learning about herbal medicines, Yinshun returned to the primary school from which he had graduated to take up a teaching position, which he held for the next eight years.

Although unable to pursue a university education, Yinshun began an extensive self-directed reading program with a particular focus on philosophy and religion. He found that Confucianism provided an inadequate foundation for modern culture because it lacked an appropriate appreciation of spirituality. Although interested in the texts of philosophical and religious Daoism, Yinshun finally rejected Daoism because so much in popular practice seemed to him to be mere superstition. Christianity was of considerable interest to him, as it was to many young intellectuals in the new China. After studying both the Old and New Testaments of the Christian Bible, he stated that he found in the religion's emphasis on faith, hope, and love a spirit that was clearly missing in Confucianism and Daoism. Yet he could not accept several doctrines that he understood to be central to the Christian faith. Recalling his earliest objections, Yinshun later wrote:

> For example, believers live eternally but unbelievers are punished eternally in the fires of hell. So the matter [of one's eternal destiny] is not decided according to human behavior (acts of the inner heart and external actions). The standard is merely whether one believes in God or not. The teaching "follow me and live or reject me and perish," has a strong exclusiveness about it; outside of those persons who belong, all will be destroyed.... Thus according to Christian doctrine (and the idea that you must be born again to be saved), the great majority of people are going to hell. And the omniscient and omnipotent God rejoices that this happens to those who are called his sons and daughters. One can say this is unfathomable, or one can say this is totally unreasonable! I cannot trust that this is a compassionate God, therefore I also cannot believe that Jesus can be my savior.[23]

Turning to Buddhism at the age of twenty, Yinshun found the reasonable, comprehensive, and hopeful religious message for which he had been looking, despite the fact that he could neither understand a great deal of what he read in the Buddhist scriptures nor find in his town educated monks knowledgeable enough to help. In 1928, after the sudden death of his parents, Yinshun began to think about becoming a monk, a decision he made in 1930. Having traveled to Putuo Shan, he was tonsured and given the Dharma name Yinshun by the monk Qingnian (also known as Yushan, 1875–1957), one of Taixu's ordination brothers.[24] Shortly thereafter he received the monastic precepts at the Tiantong si, in nearby Ningbo, under the respected master Yuanying.

Yinshun began his systematic study of Buddhist scripture at Taixu's South Fujian Seminary in Xiamen. His unusual academic abilities immediately brought him to Taixu's attention, although because of Taixu's work elsewhere the two did not formally meet until the following year. Upon learning that Yinshun had health problems, Taixu urged the seminary's head master, Daxing (1900–1952), to give him special care. Yinshun focused his early studies on the literature of the Mādhyamika (Sanlun) and Consciousness-Only (Weishi) schools, while also becoming familiar with Taixu's writings. An extraordinarily gifted student, Yinshun was lecturing at the seminary and occasionally speaking at other schools around the country only a year later. With additional studies at Taixu's Wuchang Buddhist Institute and the publication of a number of his scholarly works, Yinshun began to be recognized as one of the sangha's brightest young monks.

After the Communists' victory in 1949, Yinshun moved to Hong Kong—along with Xuming, Changjue (b. 1927), and other monks—at the urging of Fafang (1904–1951), who promised to make the local arrangements. It was in Hong Kong the following year that Yinshun produced the *Taixu dashi nianpu* (Chronological Biography of Taixu) and subsequently completed his assignment as the chief editor of the *Taixu dashi quanshu* (Complete Works of the Venerable Master Taixu). In 1952, at the request of Taixu's influential lay disciple Li Zikuan, Yinshun moved to Taiwan. There, at the Shandao si in Taipei, he became the editor of the journal *Haichao yin,* after the death of its editor (and his own former teacher) Daxing. With the exception of short trips elsewhere in East Asia for lectures and consultations, most notably to the Philippines, Yinshun's life has been spent teaching in central Taiwan, where he has become recognized, according to Robert Gimello, as "the foremost leader of Chinese Buddhism's intellectual resurgence."[25] Writes Whalen Lai:

> Master Yinshun became the foremost modern scholar-monk in China. And it has been a long time since China has seen that opportune conjunction of monk and scholar in one person of such caliber—almost three hundred years if we count from the time of the Four Great Masters of the late Ming.... Master Yinshun's accomplishments rest on those of the reformer monk Venerable Taixu. It was Venerable Taixu who brought Buddhism out of the cloisters into the modern world, who revived the Mahāyāna commitment to working in the world, who directed Buddhist reflection to current social issues, and who, during the national emergency facing China at the time, encouraged Buddhists, even monks, to participate actively in national defense. Frail of body but not of mind, Master Yinshun heeded this call during the war years but returned to his vocation after the war. Although Venerable Taixu may have been the first modern Buddhist monk to compose scholarly works, he was more an activist and a pamphleteer. Judged by the sheer weight of their scholarly work, it is not Venerable Taixu but his protégé Master Yinshun who is truly the monk-scholar of our generation.[26]

In the revitalization of Buddhism in Taiwan, Yinshun's unique role has been that of a master scholar and an advocate for a "worldly" or "humanistic Buddhism" *(renjian fojiao)*. First, as Yinshun has himself acknowledged, his temperament has always been suitable to a life of reflection and scholarship. He was never the frenetic organizer and social activist that Taixu was. In fact, he once wrote, "it has become a part of my nature to love tranquillity and shun activity."[27] As he admitted in his autobiography, "I lack the spirit of a founder of the school *(zushi)* and have no ability for organization. And I certainly do not glory in having a lot of people around me."[28] In short, Yinshun has stressed the value of solitude and quiet research both for himself and his students.[29] As a result he has become known for the range and originality of his scholarship and the number of important works on Buddhism he has produced, including the *Zhongguo Chan zong shi* (A History of Chinese Chan Buddhism), for which he received an honorary doctorate of humanities from Taishō University in Japan in 1973, *Cheng fo zhi dao* (The Way to Buddhahood), *Yindu fojiao* (Indian Buddhism), *Jingtu yu chan* (Pure Land and Chan), *Fo zai renjian* (The Buddha in the Human Realm), *Qili qiji de renjian fojiao* (A Doctrinally Harmonized and Timely Humanistic Buddhism), and *Youxin fahai liushi nian* (Sixty Years of My Mind's Wanderings in the Sea of Dharma). He continues to serve as the "Guiding Master" *(daoshi)* of the internationally respected Fa-Kuang Institute of Buddhist Studies (Faguang fojiao wenhua yanjiu suo) in Taipei.

Second, Yinshun has opposed sectarianism within the sangha. He has argued that doctrinal differences within Buddhism are merely different rivers flowing toward the same ocean of enlightenment. As he maintains in *Cheng fo zhi dao*, "To respond to the different natures [of sentient beings,] the Buddha's Dharma has different ways. There is the way of moral virtue and the way of wisdom; the difficult way and the easy way; the mundane way and the supramundane way; the way of the śrāvaka and the way of the bodhisattva; etc. Yet finally there is only one way, for all of these are only different methods for becoming a buddha."[30]

This approach is informed by Yinshun's broad ecumenical studies of Buddhist doctrine and is in harmony with his refusal, in line with Taixu's own hesitations, to be narrowly defined by a single school. Zhenhua records Yinshun as instructing his students as follows, for example:

> I have never tried to teach everyone to learn things my way. Because I went to the Wuchang Buddhist Seminary in 1934 to study the Three Treatises School [*Sanlun zong*], everyone says that I am a scholar of that school. Perhaps my innate predispositions are fairly close to the School of Void [*Kong zong*], but my studies certainly have not been limited to any sect or school. . . . It is imperative that your studies embrace many facets, lest you someday be drawn into a sectarian mentality. Each Buddhist school has its good points, and each can contribute to the perfec-

tion of the others.... So I say you should not indulge in sectarian thinking. There is only one Buddhist religion, but it was divided into schools in order to suit the innate capabilities of different people. In studying Buddhism the first thing is to "vow to learn the gateways to the Dharma, though they be innumerable."[31]

Yet as Jones points out, despite Yinshun's desire to oppose sectarianism, his early criticisms of Pure Land piety—especially in his "Jingtu xinlun" (New Treatise on the Pure Land), which consists of lectures he delivered in Hong Kong in 1951, before moving to Taiwan—alienated a great number of monks in the Taiwanese sangha.[32] Indeed, as Yang Huinan points out, when Yinshun arrived to take charge of the famous Shandao si in Taipei, the reaction was intense. "In addition to starting a whispering campaign," Yang writes, "a large number of Pure Land devotees started burning copies of 'Jingtu xinlun' and the text of another of Yinshun's lectures, 'Nian fo qianshuo' (Comments on Reciting the Buddha's Name)."[33] According to Jones, "To this day, Yinshun maintains an ambiguous position within Taiwan Buddhist circles."[34]

Third, Yinshun has continued Taixu's teachings on "the Dharma common to the five vehicles" *(wusheng gongfa)*. Accordingly, he has stressed that the disciplines that ensure better rebirths for human beings are not merely the beginner's first steps in Buddhism, which may be ignored by those who are more advanced, but are, rather, the very "foundation of the holy Dharma for transcending the world."[35] Yinshun argues that those bodhisattvas who seek to comprehend the distinctive Dharma of the Great Vehicle, and who resolve to attain a mind of wisdom and to achieve buddhahood, must recognize that the human, divine, śrāvaka, and pratyekabuddha vehicles are all good but imperfect, and that what is good is never abandoned but only deepened. Therefore, precisely because they understand that helping oneself and helping others cannot be distinguished from each other, bodhisattvas both abide in the disciplines and take the great vows of compassion to enter the world again and again to save all sentient beings, responding to the particular needs of all those confused and suffering beings whom they encounter.

Fourth, Yinshun further extended Taixu's "Buddhism for human life" *(rensheng fojiao)* through an emphasis on a "Buddhism in the human realm" *(renjian fojiao)*.³⁶ In advocating a "Buddhism for human life," Taixu targeted Buddhist rituals for the dead and the popular concern with spirits *(gui)*. Yinshun acknowledged that Taixu's stated preference for the term *"rensheng fojiao"* over *"renjian fojiao"* was grounded in the nature of his particular criticisms. However, Yinshun thought his teacher had insufficiently denounced the adoration of divinities. Thus Yinshun's primary concern was to undermine all mistaken understandings of the Buddhist heritage that allowed buddhas to be worshipped like gods in their heavens.³⁷ As he remarked, "Śākyamuni Buddha was neither a god nor a demon, neither a son nor a messenger of a god. Śākyamuni frankly stated: 'All buddhas and world-honored ones arise from within this world and not from those of gods. This is true not only of Śākyamuni Buddha; all buddhas arise from the human realm and not from a heaven.'"³⁸

Xingyun (original name: Li Guoshen)

Xingyun was born in 1927 in Jiangsu province, in the small city of Jiangdu, not far from Yangzhou and at the southwestern corner of the "Cradle of Monks," an area proud of its Buddhist heritage.³⁹ At the age of twelve, he expressed his intention to join the sangha. At first his family would not agree, but seeing the firmness of his resolve, his mother finally gave her permission. He was tonsured at Qixia Shan by Master Zhikai of the Dajue si in Yixing and given the Dharma name "Wuche." Later he chose for himself the name "Xingyun" (which literally means "a nebula of stars") because, as he said, he sought to add his own small ray of light to the constellation of bright stars radiating the Dharma.

After his initial monastic training at Qixia Shan, a large mountain monastery near Nanjing, he was fully ordained in 1941 and continued his studies at the Qixia Vinaya School. He attended the nearby Jiao Shan Buddhist Seminary, graduated in 1947, attended Taixu's "Chinese Buddhist Association's Personnel Training Class" (Zhongguo fojiao huiwu renyuan xunlian ban), and was subsequently recog-

VENERABLE MASTER XINGYUN
Source: Foguang Shan, Kaohsiung County, Taiwan.

nized as the forty-eighth lineage holder in the Linji tradition of Chan Buddhism. Acutely aware of the resistance to Taixu's ideas by many of the older members of the sangha, Xingyun said that most of the younger monks felt like one of his classmates who once exclaimed, "Should the Venerable Master Taixu ask me to tread boiling water or walk through fire, I wouldn't even ask why."[40]

Two years later, after serving as the principal of a primary school, the editor of a Buddhist magazine, and the abbot of the Huazang si in Nanjing, Xingyun left the mainland for Taiwan. In May 1967, building on his reputation as a charismatic teacher with a growing number of disciples, he established Foguang Shan (Buddha's Light Mountain), a large and impressive monastery in Kaohsiung (Gaoxiong) county in southern Taiwan. The monastery, which covers more than 120 acres in a hilly bamboo forest, is home to almost a thousand monks and nuns from different countries and has become an international pilgrimage site. Concerned about the daily distractions to the residential monastic community caused by the large number of visitors, Xingyun closed the monastery to the public (except on special occasions) in 1997, thirty years after its founding and twelve years after retiring as abbot.

Because of the Buddhist master's deep commitment to global mission, and in keeping with Taixu's aim to evangelize the West, more than a hundred Foguang Shan branch centers and temples have been established throughout the world. Among the most outstanding is Xilai si ("Coming to the West Temple") in Hacienda Heights, a suburb of Los Angeles.[41] Opened in 1988, it was constructed at a cost of more than 25 million dollars. The Buddhist organization also operates Hsi Lai University, located on its own campus nearby. Offering both undergraduate and graduate degrees in Buddhist Studies, the university's goal is to "make a substantial contribution toward satisfying the need for qualified Buddhist leadership in the West."[42]

Xingyun considers the university yet another affirmation of the four basic objectives of Foguang Shan: (1) to propagate Buddhist doctrine through cultural activities, (2) to train Dharma propagators through education, (3) to benefit society through social, educational, and health programs, and (4) to purify human minds through Buddhist practice.[43] To meet these goals, Foguang Shan publishes Buddhist literature, holds scholarly conferences, operates schools, colleges, orphanages, and senior citizen homes, administers free medical clinics and emergency relief programs, sponsors religious television programs, and organizes pilgrimages to important Buddhist sites around the world. Xingyun himself has written and edited numerous scholarly and popular works, and has hosted "Master Xingyun's Account of Chan," his own long-running television program in Taiwan.[44] As David W. Chappell has commented, Xingyun may justifiably be called "the leader of the most vigorous, innovative, and expansive Chinese Buddhist movement of the post-war generation."[45]

In the foreword to the Chan master's published lectures, the *Xingyun dashi jiangyan ji*, the editors declare, "The Venerable Master Taixu was the advocate of a Buddhism for human life, but Xingyun is the one who has put a Buddhism for human life into practice."[46] Xingyun has acknowledged that Taixu was his inspiration, once writing that "ever since I started propagating the Dharma, I have been following the teachings of Master Taixu. I emphasize the preaching of the original spirit of Buddhism and pay special attention to the preaching of a humanistic and living Buddhism. Buddhism is not a religion of empty talk. We have to start by improving people's lives."[47] He maintains that this is important because far too many people think that Mahāyāna is concerned primarily with the dead, when actually "saving those who are alive is much more important than saving the dead."[48] Because of this misunderstanding, Xingyun continues, "modern Buddhism is lifeless, like a withered tree. . . . There is no enthusiasm for work, no enthusiasm for practice, no enthusiasm when coming into contact with people, no enthusiasm to propagate Buddhism."[49]

The humanistic Buddhism that is Xingyun's response to this situation can be characterized by five central themes: (a) comprehensive happiness, (b) confident optimism, (c) compassionate service, (d) cooperative mission, and (e) consistent standards. First, with regard to happiness, Xingyun observes that people often mistakenly think that Buddhism requires them to give up material goods and to suffer in order to progress spiritually. On the contrary, he claims, Buddhism is about seeking happiness. All the blessings of life in this world can be enjoyed, and bodhisattvas do not distance themselves from them. Rather than deny such blessings, bodhisattvas transform them, as did the enlightened householder Vimalakīrti. Indeed, states Xingyun, "Having money is not a sin.... Money is basically neutral; its becoming good or bad depends on whether or not it is used correctly."[50]

Moreover, he writes, in Mahāyāna the belief is "that the more money one has, the better it is. The higher the position one attains, the better it is. As long as it does not make one greedy, and as long as it is beneficial for the spreading of Buddhism, money and position are very useful."[51] Although some Buddhists charge that Xingyun's position represents a gospel of wealth incompatible with the religion's core teachings, he defends his views as both scriptural and practical.

Second, in addition to leading people toward a comprehensive happiness, says Xingyun, humanistic Buddhism requires that we be confidently optimistic about spiritual progress within this world, that we possess a "pleasant optimistic rationality" *(leguan xiyue de shuoli)*.[52] As he comments, "If we keep practicing diligently, it will not be difficult for us to reach the stage of perfect equanimity. Today a lot of people feel that the end of the world is coming soon. I think this is an overly pessimistic and irresponsible type of mentality. We Buddhists, if we are really concerned about the destiny of humankind, should practice what the Buddha taught. Then our world will not only become a heaven, it will also turn into a Pure Land or a Lotusworld."[53] Indeed, he asks rhetorically, "Where is the Pure Land for a Chan practitioner? It is in performing lowly tasks. It is in the love for and salvation of others. It is also in the transformation of one's surroundings. Simply stated, the Pure Land is within us and is not found outside our minds."[54]

Third, humanistic Buddhism means compassionate service in the world. Mahāyāna does not require seclusion or isolation from others, avers Xingyun; it is about "coming closer and closer to them ... [and] experiencing oneness with them."[55] Buddhism teaches that because we are one with all other sentient beings, their needs become our needs. Responding to each situation with wisdom and compassion, bodhisattvas engage all of life's problems. Writes the master: "How can we benefit others? How can we bring happiness to others? The establishment of orphanages, senior citizens' homes, schools, hospitals, Buddhist museums, libraries, cultural centers, celebration parties, Sunday schools, language classes and all sorts of social activities such as performing marriage and funeral ceremonies are all beneficial to the general public.... If we do not take the responsibility, who will?"[56]

Taking responsibility naturally means participation in political affairs. On this topic Xingyun writes, "Venerable Master Taixu's view that one should 'participate in politics without seeking a political office' is the most objective, relevant, and wise perspective. Taixu thought that while Buddhists should not fervently seek to attain practical [political] power in order to accomplish things, they should care deeply about national issues.... Buddhism and politics are both matters of the people and are very closely related."[57] Xingyun is frequently criticized for such views. As Fu Zhiying admits, "Some people criticize him as a 'political monk' *(zhengzhi heshang)* because he has served on the Central Advisory Committee of the Guomindang and has supported Guomindang candidates in elections.... Xingyun's personal response to their criticisms is to say, 'Although I have left *home*, I have never left *my country*.'"[58]

During the campaign for the first popularly elected president of the Republic of China on Taiwan in 1995–1996, Xingyun openly supported Chen Li'an, a Buddhist candidate and former Guomindang member running as an independent, and thereby raised for many people the specter of religious affiliation as a divisive issue.[59] In 1997, Xingyun accepted an appointment as a commissioner of the Republic of China's Overseas Chinese Affairs Commission. In 1998, he and others associated with the Xilai si in California came under scrutiny for possible illegal campaign donations to the Democratic Party in the United States, although the Buddhist master has strongly denied any intentional wrongdoing of those affiliated with Foguang Shan.

Fourth, Xingyun has asserted that a central requirement of humanistic Buddhism is ecumenical cooperation in global mission. In a keynote speech at the Sixteenth General Conference of the World Fellowship of Buddhists, which convened at Xilai si at the time of its opening in November 1988, Xingyun called for a new measure of Buddhist cooperation and unity worldwide:

Buddhism diversified from one teaching to eighteen different sects after the Buddha's parinirvāṇa, due to the differences of disciples' personality, opinion and emphasis. In their long developmental history of more than two thousand and five hundred years, the Buddhist sects were gradually integrated into two main divisions, i.e., the Theravāda and the Mahāyāna traditions, or the Southern and Northern schools.... The traditions and customs vary from place to place. Each tradition has its own unique ways of explaining the [Buddhist] practices. [Yet] in principle, they all hold on to the same tradition.... [Thus] there should be no such saying as either great or small vehicle in Buddhism. What makes them different are the backgrounds, the thoughts of each period, and the cultural and environmental factors. Therefore all Buddhists should dispel the prejudices among themselves irrespective of their tradition, and work together single-mindedly for the propagation and unity of Buddhism.[60]

As a witness to such cooperation and a stimulus to global mission, Xingyun has proposed constructing monasteries of both Theravāda and Mahāyāna traditions in all countries, mutual exchange programs for teachers and students, inclusive conferences for intra-Buddhist dialogue, a joint project for reediting the Tripiṭaka, and the reestablishment of the ordination of nuns where this tradition no longer exists. In a Triple Platform Ordination ceremony in 1988, he ordained more than thirty women from Sri Lanka, Malaysia, Korea, Nepal, Bhutan, Australia, Canada, and the United States, challenging them to revive the Buddhist tradition of nuns in their home countries. The most recent Triple Platform Ordination ceremony at Foguang Shan in April 2000 was equally international.

Fifth, with regard to standardization, Xingyun has moved to accomplish what the Chinese Buddhist Association in the Republic of China has not been able to do. The association has no authority to strictly enforce comprehensive regulations of Buddhist practice. It can suspend membership but has no power to discipline, through laicization, monks and nuns who are guilty of serious misconduct. Therefore, Xingyun has sought to provide a clearer basis for unity through greater uniformity. For example, procedures for determining monastic ranks and responsibilities have been set forth and monastic clothing has been standardized to reflect one's status.

Few of Xingyun's reform proposals have failed to generate controversy within an increasingly pluralistic sangha. As his biographer notes, "At times, like Master Taixu's blackboard, which was once feared as wizardry, Xingyun's innovations and reforms have been called monstrous."[61] Yet his loyal followers have typically concluded that "in China the Venerable Master Taixu advocated the ideal of a Buddhism for human life. This was only an ideal for half a century until Xingyun put it into practice. In Christianity there are the reforms of Martin Luther, but Xingyun is the great master of Buddhist reform."[62]

Shengyan (original name: Zhang Caiwei)

Perhaps the best known Chinese Buddhist master in North America, Shengyan was born in 1930 in a small farming village in Nantong county, in southern Jiangsu province. Due to poor nourishment, he was often ill as a child and was slow in developing both physically and verbally. Not able to begin his education until the age of seven, he completed only the fourth grade before leaving school to help his family. At the time, the abbot of Guangjiao si, a Chan temple on Lang Shan in northern Jiangsu, had asked one of the Zhang family's neighbors to assist in recruiting candidates for the sangha. It was through this neighbor's efforts that, in 1943, quite to the surprise of his family, the young boy left home to become a Buddhist monk at the Guangjiao si. Shengyan later recalled:

> The local monastery I entered, like most others in China, was called a Chan temple. But, in fact the theory and practice of Chan was almost never discussed there. As young monks, most of us did not have any clear idea of what Chan practice really was. Our training simply consisted of the rigorous discipline prescribed for monks—everyday activities such as washing clothes, working in the fields, cooking and performing daily services. We also studied major sūtras such as the *Amitābha*, the *Lotus*,

VENERABLE MASTER SHENGYAN
Source: Nongchan si, Taipei County, Taiwan.

and the *Diamond Sūtras.* Daily chores, however, were not a problem for me; the worst thing was memorizing sūtras. . . .

I was thirteen years old and knew nothing about the history of Buddhism, yet I felt that Buddhism was on the way to extinction. Most Chinese had little understanding of the Dharma. Teachers were very rare, and what I knew came only from memorizing the scriptures. Chinese Buddhism did not provide a systematic education for monks. A monk's training was usually completed gradually and imperceptibly through the experience of everyday life. There was simply no planned education.[63]

Because of Communist activities in northern Jiangsu, most of the monks in Shengyan's monastery moved to the Shanghai area in October 1944. According to Shengyan, he and his colleagues made their living in Shanghai by performing services for the dead. "It was depressing," he wrote, "to see monks and nuns performing perfunctory rituals instead of teaching Buddhism. I did this for two years."[64]

Shengyan eventually left his monastery community to enroll at a modern seminary recently founded by a student of the reformer Taixu. Most of the teachers at the school were Taixu's students and shared their master's disapproval of sectarianism. Thus Shengyan received a broad introduction to the history and doctrines of all of Buddhism's major schools, as well as to the physical exercises of Taiqiquan and Shaolin boxing. In terms of practice, the seminary emphasized ritual repentance, so it was disappointing to the young monk that it offered little instruction on methods for meditation.

In 1949, Shengyan was conscripted into the Nationalist Army, which soon transported him to Taiwan. During his ten years of army service, in which he served as a radio communications specialist, he continued to meditate, read, and struggle with religious issues. When leaves permitted him to attend retreats, he sought further instruction from Buddhist teachers. The most important of these was the master Lingyuan, whom Shengyan considered his first real master.[65] From Lingyuan, a direct descendant of the great Chan master Xuyun, he later received the Dharma transmission in the Linji lineage. He also met with other notable teachers when possible, such as Yinshun and his student Yanpei, both of whom encouraged his studies and gave him books. Shengyan began to publish some of his own reflections on Buddhism, so that by 1957 editors of all the important Buddhist periodicals published in Taipei knew his name.[66]

Shengyan completed his military commitment in January 1960 and once again was formally tonsured, this time by Taixu's well-known student Dongchu (1907–1977), who had once served as abbot of the Dinghui si on Jiao Shan. From Dongchu, Shengyan received the Dharma transmission in the Caodong lineage. Thus he is heir to both Chan traditions. Shengyan later recalled that his stay with Dongchu "turned out to be one of the most difficult periods of my life. He constantly harassed me. It reminded me of the treatment that Milarepa received from his guru Marpa. . . . Whatever I did was wrong even if he had just told me to do it. Although it was hard to think of this treatment as compassionate, it really was. If I hadn't been trained with this kind of discipline, I would not have accomplished much."[67] After almost two years of study and practice in an intense master-disciple relationship with Dongchu, Shengyan left to begin a six-year solitary retreat in the mountains of southern Taiwan, prostrating, meditating, reading, and writing books.

Concluding after the retreat that he was still not adequately prepared for propagating the Dharma in the modern world, Shengyan left Taiwan in 1969, at the age of thirty-nine, to pursue advanced doctoral studies in Buddhist literature in Japan. In 1975 he graduated from Risshō University in Tokyo, becoming the first Chinese Buddhist master to earn a doctoral degree. Rather than restrict his subsequent work to Taiwan, he finally accepted the counsel of one of his masters in Japan, Bantetsugu Roshi, a disciple of Harada Roshi, to go to America to teach. When Shengyan objected that he didn't know English, Bantetsugu Roshi quipped, "Zen doesn't rely on words. Why worry about words?"[68]

Accordingly, Shengyan began to divide his time between Taiwan and the United States. In Taiwan, he has served as an adjunct professor at two universities; as abbot of Nongchan si; as president of the Chinese Buddhist Cultural Institute (Zhonghua fojiao wenhua guan), founded by Dongchu; and as president of the Chung-Hwa Institute of Buddhist Studies (Zhonghua fojiao yanjiu suo), which he himself founded in 1985.[69] In the U.S., after serving as the abbot of Dajue si, he founded the New York Chan Meditation Center (Niuyue chan zhongxin). Having lectured widely in American universities, Shengyan continues to travel frequently between the U.S. and Taiwan, where in April 1998 he announced authorization for the establishment of Dharma Drum College of Humanities and Social Science.

Educated under several of Taixu's students, Shengyan may be said to share a number of the Chinese reformer's goals. First, he has stressed the importance of both monastic and lay Buddhist education, seeking to improve the woefully inadequate system for transmitting the Dharma that he encountered as a young monk. As a popular lecturer and respected *shifu* (master) in the Chan tradition, he has become known for aptly guiding each student's practice according to his or her particular background and spiritual needs. A recognized authority on Mahāyāna history and doctrine, he is a founding member of the International Association of Buddhist Studies and a prolific writer of more than a hundred books on Buddhism in Chinese, Japanese, and English. In addition to the academic programs at the Chung-Hwa Institute of Buddhist Studies, the organization has hosted several important international conferences in recent years. The announced goals of the conferences have been:

> (1) To inform outstanding international scholars that the Buddhist community in Taiwan, being the exponent of Chinese Buddhist tradition, is set on the pursuit of scholarly research and study of Buddhism; (2) to motivate cultural and scholarly societies both in Taiwan and in those countries in contact with Chinese culture to recognize the universal profound importance of Buddhist studies; [and] (3) to expose young Buddhist students in Taiwan to the refreshing current of recent scholarly Buddhist studies worldwide . . . as well as provide incentive for intensified efforts on their part to swiftly attain the world standard level.[70]

Second, Shengyan has underscored the significance of the basic Buddhist precepts for bodhisattvas' practice in the midst of human life. According to the Chan master, the basic precepts that the Buddha established define the parameters for ethical values and moral activity, and are interdependent with his doctrinal teachings. "The doctrines and precepts of Buddhism cannot be separated," he writes. "Right doctrines were delivered in light of false ideas and right precepts were enumerated in view of harmful rules. In the Buddhist precepts there are the doctrines, and in the doctrines the Buddhist precepts."[71] Responding to common misperceptions of Chan on this point, he also asserts:

> The ultimate is beyond all human rules and laws. It cannot be judged by worldly standards. Thoroughly enlightened people spontaneously help sentient beings in accordance with causes and conditions. Their actions are not bound by the moral codes of society.... But the misinterpretation of this truth has caused great harm. Some people think that Chan advertises moral indifference, that Chan practitioners in general are free to ignore ethical principles.... [On the contrary,] a Chan master may seem carefree, but behind superficial appearances there is a solid foundation. It is only upon a solid foundation that one can draw on a truly liberated spirit unbounded by rules.[72]

In July 1992, at the Second Chung-Hwa International Buddhist Conference, Shengyan reviewed the challenges presented to Buddhists in applying the ancient Vinaya codes to the modern world and stressed their continuing relevance. He stated in his keynote address:

> I wish to point out that although the traditional Buddhist precepts are being confronted with a variety of problems and issues requiring our reflection and investigation, we must remain firm in the belief that we may try to make adjustments, but never for a moment think of doing away with them. This is because the very purpose of the Śrāvaka Precepts lies in purifying our physical, verbal, and mental behavior. Through the abstention from greed and hatred and the cultivation of right views, both our physical and our verbal actions are cleansed. And with the precepts serving as regulating norms, the two actions of the physical and the verbal are safely guarded against all evil forces.... In short, for the Buddha's teachings to effectively benefit humankind, the precepts are absolutely indispensable. As the Buddha himself has taught, only by

"keeping Vinaya purely and strictly" can we hope to have "Dharma residing in the world."

On the other hand, if we go along with those who claim that Buddhists in today's world no longer need the restraint of Vinaya, we may perhaps succeed in creating the false image of "freedom and emancipation," but we may also induce a real crisis for the survival and development of Buddhism. Some of you present at this conference may still recall what happened to the Japanese lineages of Buddhism in the United States in 1984–1985, when there seemed to be so many sexual scandals involving Zen masters. Several "roshis" disappeared from the scene as a result; though a number of other "roshis" unabashedly held on to their positions, yet enormous harm was already done to Buddhism as a whole. Also, in 1990, the designated successor to a renowned Tibetan lama died of AIDS owing to homosexuality. As a result, a Buddhist order that had once boasted of 100-odd meditation centers in the United States fell to pieces in no time. All these examples serve to show the consequences of not paying heed to fundamental rules of monastic discipline. It would indeed behoove us to bear these lessons in mind.[73]

Third, Shengyan, like Taixu, has emphasized the establishment of a pure land on earth. This theme has gained special prominence in Shengyan's work with the establishment in 1989 of Dharma Drum Mountain (Fagu Shan) near Jinshan township in Taipei county. The first stage of construction for relocating the Chung-Hwa Institute of Buddhist Studies is scheduled for completion in late 2000. Dharma Drum Mountain, which is aimed at "uplifting human nature and establishing a pure land on earth," will be a large and impressive complex.[74] Shengyan has explicitly linked its construction with the concerns of a line of Buddhist reformers that goes back through Taixu to Yang Wenhui:

> The modern layman Yang Wenhui promoted the printing of the Buddhist scriptures, distributing Buddhist literature and establishing a school in order to educate both monastics and lay Buddhists for propagating the Dharma. His student Taixu began to promote a "Buddhism for human life" [*rensheng fojiao*]. Taixu's student Yinshun continued this by advancing a "humanistic Buddhism" [*renjian fojiao*]. My *shifu*, the Ven-

erable Master Dongchu, published the magazine *Humanity* [Rensheng]. And then, in Taiwan, I myself founded Dharma Drum Mountain, whose goal is the "establishment of a pure land on earth" [*jianshe renjian jingtu*]. These are all measures for preserving the wisdom of Buddhism that is in great peril and activities for recovering the original design of Śākyamuni Buddha.[75]

Indeed, acknowledging their different ways of spreading the Dharma, Shengyan has expressed his admiration for the unflagging spirit of Taixu in the face of constant disappointment and frustration. Noting that Taixu was rejected by traditionalists for being too radical and by extreme modernists for being too traditional, the monk states:

> One can either say that Taixu's life was very successful or that it was a complete failure. . . . He wanted to reform Buddhism and reorganize its religious associations. Thus everyone was apprehensive about him and jealous of him to the point of hating him. He wanted to establish academic institutions to educate monastics, but his own disciples that he taught did not fully accept, understand, or agree with him, even to the point of betraying and opposing him. Because of this Taixu's educational efforts failed, and they failed at the hands of his disciples. Taixu's work to rescue Buddhist monks and temples also failed. . . .
>
> Taixu's energy was limited, while the illnesses of the age were many and serious. His whole life from the age of twenty-two was directed only to healing the sicknesses of his time. But patients have to cooperate with physicians to be cured. If they are sick but reject the advice and medicines of their physician, the doctor can do nothing about it. Some people claim that Taixu was merely a modern pathologist, not a physiologist of Buddhism, saying that he could only determine the illnesses of Buddhism but couldn't cure them. In fact, Taixu was an outstanding pathologist and eminent physiologist. . . .
>
> Although few of his ideals have been realized, it is because of him that modern Buddhism maintains many of its hopes for security and new life. Although his reorganization of Buddhism failed, the establishment of the Buddhist Association [of the Republic of China] is due to him. Although his efforts in petitioning authorities on behalf of the sangha's activities failed, Chinese monasteries and temples were not con-

fiscated by the government and monks and nuns were not compelled to return to lay life but were protected because of him. Although his contributions to monastic education failed, the lifeline of private academic institutes for modern monastic education that are still supported can be traced to his advocacy for monastic education.... As far as we and our age are concerned, what Taixu has done for us and for our age is of boundless benefit and grace.... I am not one who espouses or implements in practice Taixu's particular theories, yet I am one who reveres his spirit.... He was an extraordinarily mature and successful religious leader, and he was also an honorable, great, and lofty failure. His spirit was successful, while what he actually tried to accomplish did not succeed.[76]

Zhengyan (original name: Wang Jinyun)

Zhengyan was born in May 1937 in the small town of Qingshui, near the Taizhong harbor in central Taiwan. She was adopted and reared by her father's brother and his wife in the nearby town of Fengyuan. Her adoptive father, to whom she was very close and with whom she helped manage the family's small chain of theaters in Taizhong county, died in 1960, when she was twenty-three. It was at that time, as she contemplated the fate of her father's soul, that she first began to express an interest in religion and the possibility of becoming a Buddhist nun. She studied Christianity, being very impressed by the sacrificial witness of Dr. and Mrs. David Landsborough, English missionaries with the Presbyterian Church in Taiwan who founded the Zhanghua Christian Hospital. However, Buddhism seemed to offer a more compelling and rational religion. She later recalled:

> As a young girl in need of religion, I had reached towards Christianity. ... At the time, there was a Christian minister in Zhanghua who was also a physician working in a hospital. It was said that he had removed a part of his own skin and the skin of his wife, to transplant it onto the burned body of a child. He was a foreigner and a white man, but I admired him for what he had done.

VENERABLE MASTER ZHENGYAN

Source: Buddhist Tzu Chi Philantropic Foundation (Fojiao Ciji shan shiye jijin hui) Hualian County, Taiwan.

Knowing that I was studying Christianity, several Christians offered me the Bible and many booklets. I read them carefully but found them lacking many things. And then I read the scriptures of Buddhism and felt an instant fulfillment: in Buddhism, there is logical explanation, scientific proof, and philosophical reasoning.

I stopped searching but was not totally satisfied with Buddhism. In the eyes of many, Buddhism is a passive religion and an escape from reality. Buddhism is also viewed as the superstitious belief of the ignorant poor, who lived in backward nations and belonged to the lower class of society.

And that was when I decided to bring Buddhism back to its original form, as Buddha had wanted it to be twenty-five hundred years previously. I promised that my followers and I would prove to the world that Buddhism is a positive and active way of living and that we Buddhists would continue with our good deeds to help the suffering masses and bring joy to those living in sorrow.[77]

Zhengyan was befriended by a nun from the nearby Ciyun si who helped her reflect on her difficult struggle between wanting to help her family and wanting to pursue a religious life. Certain that her adoptive mother would never understand her desire to become a nun, Zhengyan decided to run away from home. Convinced that, beyond becoming wives and mothers, Taiwanese women had many unrecognized gifts for improving the world, she made her way to a small temple near Taipei. As she asserted in a conversation with her friend, "A woman's world is not within the boundary of her home. Equal to men, women are also entitled to serve society, the nation, and all humankind."[78] Although soon located by her anxious mother and persuaded to return home, within a year she ran away once again, finding anonymity on the eastern side of the central mountain range at a temple near Hualian. There she shaved her own head and began to live as a nun.

In February 1963, Zhengyan learned that the Linji si in Taipei was preparing for an ordination ceremony. When she went to Taipei to register, however, the Dharma master in charge of the ceremony asked the name of her tonsure master. When it became clear that without a master she could not be ordained, she prepared disappointedly to return to Hualian. However, according to Qiu Xiuzhi's account, before leaving the city she stopped to purchase a set of the *Taixu dashi quanshu,* edited by the respected Dharma master Yinshun. Suddenly, near the bookstore, much to her surprise, the renowned Yinshun walked out and stood waiting for a rainstorm to pass.

The young nun was afraid to approach Yinshun directly, so she hurriedly asked a monk to appeal to him on her behalf. The monk replied that the venerable master did not like to accept disciples and had tonsured only four disciples in his entire career, but nevertheless agreed to explain to Yinshun the young woman's desire to be ordained as a nun. Responding that masters ought to be quite familiar with persons whom they tonsure, Yinshun was unwilling to accept her as a disciple. Yet after speaking with her for a while, he finally declared, "I sense that our karmic connection as master and disciple is very special! Since you have become a nun, you must live at all times for Buddhism and for all sentient beings."[79] Yinshun then bestowed on her the Dharma name "Zhengyan" and the style name "Huizhang." The novice raced back to the Linji si to participate in the thirty-two-day ordination ceremony. Subsequently, she returned to Hualian, a newly ordained nun at the age of twenty-six.

By the end of the following year, Zhengyan was living in a small wooden hut behind the Puming si in the township of Xiulin, had already attracted her first five disciples, and was becoming widely recognized in the Hualian area. She and her nuns became known for their refusal to accept alms and their insistence on self-sufficiency, holding strictly to the historic monastic rule of the Chan master Baizhang (749–814), "A day without work, a day without eating." They were known for discouraging popular religious practices such as offering meat, burning paper money, fortune-telling, and praying for material blessings—all of which, according to Zhengyan, had nothing to do with Buddhism.

In addition, the nuns were known for helping people in need in whatever ways they could. In fact, they were intent on showing that Christianity was not the only compassionate religious force in Taiwanese society. As Hengqing has commented, Zhengyan's now famous "'Buddhist Compassion Relief Tzu Chi Foundation' (Fojiao Ciji gongde hui) was born from this aim to put into practice Buddhism's spirit of compassionate service to save the world."[80]

Founded in Hualian, Taiwan, in March 1966, the Tzu Chi (Ciji) organization was initially the undertaking of Zhengyan, her five disciples, and thirty women followers who vowed to contribute fifty cents a day to help the poor. In 1969, the main shrine hall of their new temple, the Pure Abode of Still Thoughts (Jingsi jingshe), was completed, and their ministries began to expand. Today, the sizable Buddhist foundation has assets of several billion New Taiwanese dollars. It supports many forms of relief work and social service around the world, with branch offices in more than twenty countries and a global membership more than four million. Writes Zhengyan:

> We follow Great Master Yinshun's instructions to work "for Buddhism, for all beings." With love, compassion, joy and total dedication, we strive for the realization of a pure, undefiled land of Tzu Chi.... We incorporate the [four] missions of charity, medicine, education and culture in one master plan, with principles of sincerity, integrity, honesty and trustfulness. We believe in the equality of all beings, for every one has a latent Buddha-nature. The beauty and wonder of Buddhism will be revealed through the door of compassion; and through the door of merits, the rich will give and be blessed, and the poor will receive and be saved.[81]

In terms of its mission of charity, Tzu Chi's extensive programs of assistance and emergency relief work have aided people not only in Taiwan but in the United States, the People's Republic of China, the Philippines, Bangladesh, Cambodia, Thailand, Mongolia, Ethiopia, Rwanda, and other countries. Its mission in the field of medicine includes the Tzu Chi Hospital, opened in Hualian in 1986, several branch hospitals that form part of a planned island-wide health care network, and special programs in bone marrow donation and spinal-cord injury rehabilitation. In education, the organization established the Tzu Chi Junior College of Nursing in 1989 and the Tzu Chi College of Medicine in 1992. These colleges are the first two units of Tzu Chi University, which will eventually include colleges of liberal arts, management, religion, and fine arts. The foundation's cultural mission involves a broad range of activities in publishing, broadcasting, and public service. It supports lay education, offers daily radio programs in Taiwan, publishes books and magazines in several languages, and promotes environmental protection efforts.

Through all four of these basic missions, Zhengyan emphasizes learning by doing. Tzu Chi reflects her ethical form of piety and her earliest concerns to modernize Buddhism by calling it back to its founder's intentions. She is committed to showing people that Buddhists are not passive but are actively trying to transform the world into a pure land. As Zhengyan has remarked, "If we don't practice the teachings of the sūtras, the distance between humans and the Buddha will still be immeasurably large. One who learns Buddhism should understand it thoroughly and practice it personally.... One can benefit only from rigorously practicing what one has learned."[82] She writes elsewhere:

> Arhats are those who cultivate Buddhism for their own salvation. We want to learn from the Buddha who aims at saving all sentient beings and not from the Arhats who only take care of themselves.... Many people who are learning Buddhism today think: "I need to find time to hear more lectures on the sūtras and expose myself to more discussions of the Dharma." These people go wherever there are Dharma masters lecturing on the sūtras.... They only know that "listening to the sūtras will earn *kuśalam* (karma merit)," and not necessarily have any clues as to the true wisdom in life.... When you go to support some spirituality group by attending its lectures on the sūtras, does it benefit your own spirituality? If you just follow other people to gatherings without enhancing the Dharma in your inner spirit, how does this help you cultivate Buddhism? ... Researching the words in the sūtras is not a useful learning method. Instead, we should try to appreciate the original goal of the Buddha deeply, and to understand the essence of the Dharma personally.[83]

Although Zhengyan has been called "the Mother Teresa of Asia," has received numerous humanitarian awards, and has been nominated for the Nobel Peace Prize, she has also been sharply criticized. As Qiu Xiuzhi indicates, some people have charged that she maintains inappropriately close ties to wealthy business leaders who contribute to

Tzu Chi projects. Although Zhengyan formally prohibits her disciples from participating in politics and has rejected attempts to draw the Tzu Chi organization into political campaigns, some critics claim that in her constant use of the Taiwanese language (her mother tongue) rather than Mandarin Chinese (the official language of the Republic of China) she is making a political statement that favors Taiwanese independence.

Other people criticize Zhengyan for giving so much money to help people in countries overseas when the needs in Taiwan remain so great. Still others complain that Tzu Chi frequently sends financial aid to people without sufficiently investigating what other funding agencies (governmental and nongovernmental) ought to be responsible. It is also said that aid is committed only where there is publicity and that Zhengyan's support for projects in the People's Republic of China is tantamount to treason.[84] Zhengyan acknowledges that the way of the bodhisattva is often complex. However, "nothing will be done," she says, "if we just stand and wait for a helping hand to reach down from among the clouds."[85]

All four of these Buddhist masters—Yinshun, Xingyun, Shengyan, and Zhengyan—may be said to be identified with the progressive faction in the Taiwanese sangha and to be building on aspects of the modern reforms that Taixu sought to implement. In his or her own way, each has emphasized a restated form of Buddhism, one that both recovers the religion's original spirit and responds to the needs of the contemporary world with devotion and selflessness. None of the four is one of Taixu's tonsure disciples, and none self-consciously presents himself—or herself—primarily as a transmitter of Taixu's teachings.

As a group, however, these four contemporary teachers reflect Taixu's increased attention to the basic moral precepts of Buddhism and to "the Dharma common to the five vehicles." They have discouraged concern with the dead, stressed the significance of life in the human realm, and spoken optimistically of the potential for spiritual progress. They have sought to advance Buddhism through scholarship and educational reforms, ecumenism and global mission, and engagement with all the various social, political, economic, ecological, and religious forces in the modern world in order to create a pure land on earth.

Perhaps it is only one measure of the effectiveness of their leadership in revitalizing Buddhism in Taiwan that Taixu's hope to wrest from the Christians their assumed role as the primary advocates of religiously informed social action has, according to many people, begun to come true. Taixu entreated the Chinese Buddhist community in his day to learn from the Christian church's communal spirit and ways of organizing for accomplishing goals in mission. In a parallel way, in April 1998, the forty-fifth annual meeting of the General Assembly of the Presbyterian Church in Taiwan, representing the largest Christian body on the island, adopted a resolution calling for local congregations to organize quick response teams *(shehui guanhuai xiaozu)* for emergency relief work and social service. The minister offering the resolution on behalf of the General Assembly's Church and Society Committee cited as a primary reason for the recommendation the church's relative inability to respond to various social needs as quickly and effectively as Tzu Chi and other Buddhist organizations.[86]

A "CLASSICAL" FIGURE IN MODERN RELIGION

Historian of religion Joseph M. Kitagawa has suggested that, with regard to modern religious history, it is possible to delineate three fundamental features, or trends, exhibited by virtually all major religious traditions in the world. The first he describes as a modern preoccupation with the meaning of human existence (religious anthropology). In the modern period, questions about the nature of ultimate reality (theology) and the nature of the universe (cosmology) remain important to religious thought and action. However, their significance is directly related to the development of perspectives on the meaning of human life. The dominant contemporary religious question is that of human fulfillment in a complex social world in which individual people most commonly feel threatened by alienation and meaninglessness.

Very closely related to this emphasis on the meaning of human existence, according to Kitagawa, is a second characteristic, namely, a "this-worldly soteriology." In modern world religions, goals associated with the attainment of a beatific life in a paradisaical realm beyond this world of time and space typically have a diminished significance. Indeed, heavens and hells are usually interpreted existentially. Salvation, or enlightenment, is defined most characteristically as the full achievement of human potential and harmony within the communal order of this life. Writes Kitagawa:

> The loss of other realms of existence has compelled modern world religions to find the meaning of human destiny in this world—in culture, society, and human personality. Never has there been any period in the history of the human race when the relation of religion or faith to sociopolitical, economic, and cultural spheres has been taken so seriously as it is today. This does not mean that today we are witnessing another example of the phenomenon of the "ecclesiastification of culture," as in medieval Europe, or of the "secularization of religion," as in the days of rationalism. What we find now is an increasing realization on the part of modern world religions that, just as religious man must undergo the experience of personal transformation or metanoia, culture and society must be renewed and revitalized in order to fulfill their vocation in the midst of the ambiguities and upheavals of this world. Thus, even in Theravāda Buddhism, which has been regarded by some as one of the most otherworldly of the religions, advocates of a soteriology centered on this world argue that Buddhist leaders must pursue "not a will-o'-the-wisp Nirvāṇa secluded in the cells of their monasteries, but a Nirvāṇa attained here and now by a life of self-forgetful activity...." Likewise, leaders of contemporary Judaism, Christianity, Islam, and Hinduism are deeply involved ... in various spheres of social, educational, political, and cultural activities because of their conviction that these areas of life are the very arena of salvation.[87]

The third feature that Kitagawa describes as common to the modern world religions is that of a search for "freedom" rather than the preservation of "order." That is to say, in the modern period individual people have asserted their autonomy primarily from the "givenness" of cosmic and social order. They have sought to transcend their limitations, to "make themselves," and to establish a new personal and social world responsive to their own sense of purpose and value. In the terms of Jonathan Smith, rather than transmitting "locative views," which emphasize cosmic patterns of order, modern religions have characteristically illuminated paths of escape from all such confining patterns.[88] Of course, as a consequence, a typically central dilemma for modern religious leaders is that of relating individual expressions of spirituality to structures for the community—of relating human freedom, creativity, and innovation to common and unifying understandings of transformational truth.

Taixu's work exemplified these three characteristics of modern religion within the context of Chinese Buddhism in the Republican period. He underscored the significance of human existence, emphasized the attainment of buddhahood within this world, and rejected the givenness of the social order in favor of building a pure land on earth. Thus parallels can be found both within the larger Buddhist world and within other religious communities of his day. For example, Taixu's efforts can be compared to those of late nineteenth- and early twentieth-century advocates of the liberal Christian Social Gospel and of Reform Judaism. First of all, both the Christian Social Gospel leaders and the Jewish reformers can be identified as "ethical pietists." Their teachings emphasized religious actions. These leaders typically stressed salvation through the doing of religion, and they evaluated visionary attainment in terms of demonstrated ethical performance. As Charles Braden once commented, the modern liberal, whether Christian or Jewish, "is not without interest in religion as beauty, or religion as truth in the intellectual sense, but he is surest of all of its ethical character. . . . [Moreover,] salvation, either individual or social, is not a gift to be accepted passively or at the expense only of accepting some belief. It is to be won and hardly won by the application of the highest degree of self-effort."[89]

Second, in addition to being ethical pietists, leaders of both the Christian Social Gospel movement and of Reform Judaism concurred in a simplification of the ethical dimension of their respective traditions. They attempted to simplify their traditions by focusing on norms for social responsibility, while judging other types of ethical norms to be of only secondary importance. Norms for cultic performance, self-cultivation, and institutional maintenance were all evaluated in relation to norms for morality. As Nathan Glazer once commented:

> The tendency developed among the German Reformers to emphasize the progressive nature of Jewish law, the fact that it had, indeed, developed and changed continually in response to different conditions. However, there was no question that the course of development they were proposing quite reversed the history of the law up to that time, for until then it had developed in the direction of ever greater complexity, and what the Reformers were proposing was a radical simplification. . . . One could also find among the German Reformers the position that the law was simply outgrown and that Judaism should base itself on the prophetic and not the legal portions of the Bible. And since a number of prophets had indeed emphasized social justice . . . and had attacked priestly rites, they seemed well suited to serve as forerunners of Reform Judaism.[90]

This simplification was accomplished by defining the very "essence" of their religion as social responsibility, and by linking the salvation of the individual to the perfection and redemption of the entire social order. Christians and Jews in these communities were taught to pursue forms of spirituality in which religious sacraments and devotionalism were de-emphasized in favor of voluntary moral action that promoted the greatest common good.[91] Because of the obvious parallels between the type of ethical piety advanced by Taixu and that advocated by these Christian and Jewish reformers, Yu-yue Tsu once called Taixu "the Fosdick of Chinese Liberal Buddhism," invoking the name of Harry Emerson Fosdick (1878–1969), the great popularizer of liberal Protestantism in North America during the same period.[92]

Beyond these comparisons with expressions of western religion, Taixu's teachings can also be compared with those of other reformers in Asia advocating a socially engaged form of Buddhism: B. R. Ambedkar (1891–1956) of India, Buddhadasa Bhikkhu (b. 1906–1993) of Thailand, Thich Nhat Hanh (b. 1926) of Vietnam, A. T. Ariyaratne (b. 1931) of Sri Lanka, Sulak Sivaraksa (b. 1933) of Thailand, the Fourteenth Dalai Lama, Tenzin Gyatso (b. 1935) of Tibet, and many others. Without any attempt to offer a complete "phenomenology of Buddhist liberation movements," it might be said succinctly that the efforts of Taixu and those of other engaged Buddhist leaders in Asian countries share at least five basic commonalities: [93]

1. They have typically advanced an inner-worldly asceticism, in Weber's sense of the term.[94] The religious goal has not been to adjust to the world or to flee from it, but to remake it. Spiritual liberation, it has been asserted, is experienced in the very act of reshaping unjust and oppressive social, economic, and political realities.

2. In one way or another, they have all emphasized a rationalistic approach to religion. Mysticism, emotionalism, ceremonialism, and devotionalism have all been devalued. Buddhism is commonly presented as a reasonable system of thought and action that is compatible with key elements of modern physics and cosmology.

3. Engaged Buddhist leaders have typically presented their work as part of a restoration movement. That is, they have usually characterized their efforts as the recovery of an original and ideal balance in doctrine and practice. Their aim has been to trace their tradition's roots, to find its essence. They have emphasized going back to go forward, finding the old to establish the new.

4. Such Buddhist activists have generally been ecumenists interested in global mission. They have often argued that the solution to local and regional Buddhist problems lies in part in ecumenical Buddhist cooperation and fellowship on a global scale. Moreover, they have challenged the Sangha to realize its mission to spread the Dharma to all people.

5. As Sallie King has observed, virtually all engaged Buddhists have struggled with the dynamic interplay between Buddhist identity and Buddhist negation. That is, while organizing movements that are specifically Buddhist and distinguishing their religion from all others, such leaders have, typically, not only conveyed a tolerant inclusivism but declared "that Buddhism, as a cultural artifact, is a means and not an end, a way to something else, a finger pointing at the moon, a less-than-ultimate that makes available the ultimate."[95] They have highly valued Buddhism as a conveyance but recognized that it is only a conveyance.

Taixu's work is in harmony with all five of these basic themes. What many people have found most intriguing about Taixu may in fact be the creative tensions in his position. For example, as a modern intellectual influenced by ideas from both the East and the West, and troubled by the growth of secularism, he was convinced of the need to present his religious tradition, both at home and abroad, as the supremely scientific and rational religion, while at the same time recognizing that Buddhism was grounded in intuitions and faith commitments that science could not prove. "It is my conviction," he said, "that he who loses religion through science can learn how to find it again through Buddhism."[96]

Further, Taixu's focus on morality represented a simplification of his religious tradition. Ironically, in its requirement for engagement with the bewildering range of social, economic, and political issues within the global community, it also entailed a significant complication of the bodhisattva's path. "It is only through morality that men will be able to relieve the world of this distressing condition," Taixu claimed. "But this morality must be a *world morality*. Nothing racial or provincial in its scope will do."[97]

As a Chinese patriot caught up in the contentious and violent drama of the Republican period, Taixu was on the one hand a political realist, while on the other hand he was a utopian dreamer. "If we only have faith in ourselves," he asserted, "we will be able to change society and even the universe."[98]

Finally, as a religious leader in an age of intense debate about the future of all religion, Taixu was at once deeply committed to the vitality and development of institutional Buddhism and, at the same time, capable of looking beyond it. "Forms and ceremonies are but incidental," he insisted. "It is the truth that matters."[99]

Although Taixu saw himself as a reformer with exceptionally insightful ideas but no ability for leading people, he is, paradoxically, remembered largely as a master who, while not a profoundly creative thinker, was a uniquely articulate and forceful spiritual guide. Despite his many critics, his personal limitations, and his own sense of failure, his legacy lives on within contemporary East Asian Buddhist communities. The continuing appreciation of his contribution to the revival of Chinese Buddhism in the twentieth century shows that his way of presenting the Dharma became paradigmatic for many members of the Sangha. Indeed, because Taixu's life and thought so clearly represent a definite "type" of spirituality within the Chinese Buddhist community, Taixu can be recognized in Joachim Wach's sense as a "classical" religious figure.[100]

Any religious tradition that is to survive in the modern world over an extended period of time as a vital and dynamic spiritual force must provide its adherents with compelling understandings of the visionary and ethical dimensions of truth and with a variety of viable forms of piety. Taixu's unique portrayal of one expression of Chinese Buddhist faith and life forced other people to decision and commitment, either in enthusiastic agreement or in sharp dissent. Indeed, Taixu's greatest contribution to the Buddhist revival in the Republican period lay in energetically modeling a particular form of religious piety— one that, by increasing spiritual options and stimulating active debate, enlivened the Buddhist community both in his time and into the future.

NOTES

INTRODUCTION: IN SEARCH OF A NEW BUDDHISM

1. Taixu, "Wo de fojiao geming shibai shi" (The History of My Failed Buddhist Revolution), in *Taixu dashi quanshu* (The Complete Works of the Venerable Master Taixu), 20 vols. (Taipei, 1956), 19.57.8: 61–63 (hereafter cited as "Complete Works). In all citations to this work, which is organized by topic and type of material, the first number refers to the *bian* (volume), the second to the *ce* (book), and the third to the document number, followed by the page numbers after the colon.

2. Holmes Welch, *The Buddhist Revival in China* (Cambridge: Harvard University Press, 1968), 51, 269.

3. Joachim Wach, *Types of Religious Experience: Christian and Non-Christian* (Chicago: University of Chicago Press, 1951), 48–57.

4. See John Herman Randall, Jr., *The Making of the Modern Mind* (New York: Columbia University Press, 1926), and Joseph M. Kitagawa, "Primitive, Classical, and Modern Religions: A Perspective on Understanding the History of Religions," in *The History of Religions: Essays on the Problem of Understanding,* ed. J. M. Kitagawa, with the collaboration of Mircea Eliade and Charles Long (Chicago: University of Chicago Press, 1967), 39–65.

5. A portion of this chapter is taken from or paraphrases (with permission) Don A. Pittman, "The Visionary and The Ethical: Exploring an Approach to Comparative Religious Ethics," *Shenxue yu jiaohui* (Theology and Church) 21/2 (Spring 1996): 269–279.

6. For a similarly broad definition of ethics, see Robin W. Lovin and Frank E. Reynolds, eds., *Cosmogony and Ethical Order: New Studies in Comparative Ethics* (Chicago:

University of Chicago Press, 1985), 1–35. Consult also Morton White, *What Is and What Ought to Be Done: An Essay on Ethics and Epistemology* (New York: Oxford University Press, 1981).

7. Frank R. Millican, "Tai Hsü and Modern Buddhism," *Chinese Recorder* 54/6 (June 1923): 327.

CHAPTER 1: DEFENDING THE DHARMA IN A REVOLUTIONARY AGE

1. As Paul A. Cohen argues, many historical reconstructions of the late Qing period oversimplify developments by utilizing a "Western impact/Chinese response" framework without proper acknowledgment of internal elements of dynastic decline. See his article, "Ch'ing China: Confrontation with the West, 1850–1900," in *Modern East Asia: Essays in Interpretation,* ed. James B. Crowley (New York: Harcourt, Brace & World, 1970), 29–61.

2. Joseph R. Levenson, *Confucian China and Its Modern Fate: A Trilogy,* first combined edition, vol. 1, *The Problem of Intellectual Continuity* (Berkeley: University of California Press, 1968), xxx.

3. On the tributary system and its ideological foundations, consult John K. Fairbank, *The Chinese World Order: Traditional China's Foreign Relations* (Cambridge: Harvard University Press, 1968).

4. The exception was Lord Macartney, sent by George III in 1793. See John K. Fairbank, *Trade and Diplomacy on the China Coast: The Opening of the Treaty Ports, 1842–1854* (Cambridge: Harvard University Press, 1953), 31.

5. Immanuel C. Y. Hsü, *The Rise of Modern China,* 3rd ed. (Oxford: Oxford University Press, 1983), 133–134.

6. See Jerome B. Grieder, *Intellectuals and the State in Modern China: A Narrative History* (New York: The Free Press, 1981), 55.

7. Consult Max Weber, *The Protestant Ethic and the Spirit of Capitalism,* trans. Talcott Parsons (New York: Charles Scribner's Sons, 1958).

8. See Paul A. Cohen, *China and Christianity: The Missionary Movement and the Growth of Chinese Antiforeignism, 1860–1870* (Cambridge: Harvard University Press, 1963).

9. Consult Elizabeth Perry, *Rebels and Revolutionaries in North China, 1845–1945* (Stanford, Calif.: Stanford University Press, 1980), and Franz H. Michael, in collaboration with Chung-li Chang, *The Taiping Rebellion: History and Documents,* 3 vols. (Seattle: University of Washington Press, 1966).

10. See Mary Clabaugh Wright, *The Last Stand of Chinese Conservatism: The T'ung-Chih Restoration, 1862–1874* (Stanford, Calif.: Stanford University Press, 1957).

11. Consult Levenson, *Confucian China and Its Modern Fate*, 1: 59–78.

12. Consult Philip A. Kuhn, *Rebellion and Its Enemies in Late Imperial China: Militarization and Social Structure, 1796–1864* (Cambridge: Harvard University Press, 1970), 189–225, and Frederick Wakeman, Jr., *The Fall of Imperial China* (New York: The Free Press, 1975), 163–172.

13. For a study of the reform, see Luke S. K. Kwong, *A Mosaic of the Hundred Days: Personalities, Politics, and Ideas of 1898* (Cambridge: Harvard University Press, 1984).

14. Most historians have asserted that Cixi herself supported the Boxers. Consult, for example, Immanuel C. Y. Hsü, "Late Ch'ing Foreign Relations, 1866–1905," in *The Cambridge History of China, Late Ch'ing, 1800–1911*, vol. 11, *Late Ch'ing, 1800–1911, Part 2*, ed. John K. Fairbank and Kwang-ching Liu, 70–141 (Cambridge: Cambridge University Press, 1980). For an alternate interpretation, compare Sterling Seagrave, *Dragon Lady: The Life and Legend of the Last Empress of China* (New York: Alfred A. Knopf, 1992).

15. For a translation of the Tongmeng hui's manifesto, see Ssu-yü Teng and John K. Fairbank, *China's Response to the West: A Documentary Survey, 1839–1923* (Cambridge: Harvard University Press, 1954), 227–229.

16. Unless otherwise noted, in referring to the ages of persons I have followed the western system rather than the traditional Chinese system, which calculates *sui* ("years") according to a lunar calendar. In the Chinese system, a person is born at one *sui* and gains a year at each Chinese lunar new year.

17. James E. Sheridan, *China In Disintegration: The Republican Era in Chinese History, 1912–1949* (New York: The Free Press, 1975), 55.

18. See Derek J. Waller, *The Government and Politics of Communist China* (New York: Anchor Books, 1971), 7.

19. This was the title of Wu Yue's April 1907 article in *Min Bao* (The People's Report), cited in Grieder, *Intellectuals and the State in Modern China*, 199.

20. In 1902, Liang Qichao began publishing a periodical entitled *Xinmin congbao* (New People's Periodical), which revealed the nature of the debate between the radical revolutionaries and the somewhat more conservative reformers like Liang. See Liang Ch'i-ch'ao, *Intellectual Trends in the Ch'ing Period* (Ch'ing-tai hsüeh-shu kai-lun), translated with introduction and notes by Immanuel C. Y. Hsü (Cambridge: Harvard University Press, 1959), 102. Hu Shi notes that Liang often signed his articles in the magazine, "One of the Renovated People of China." See Hu Shih, *The Chinese Renaissance* (Chicago: University of Chicago Press, 1934), 37.

21. Grieder, *Intellectuals and the State in Modern China*, 136.

22. Chen Duxiu, "Qinggao qingnian" (A Call to Youth), from *Xin qingnian* (New Youth) 1/1 (September 1915); translated by Chow Tse-tsung in his *The May Fourth Movement: Intellectual Revolution in Modern China* (Cambridge: Harvard University

Press, 1960), 46. Complete English translation of the article can be found in Teng and Fairbank, *China's Response to the West*, 240–246.

23. James Reeve Pusey, *China and Charles Darwin* (Cambridge: Council on East Asian Studies, Harvard University Press, 1983), 193.

24. Consult Hu Shi (Hu Shih), *Sishi zishu* (My Autobiography at Age Forty), (Taipei, 1959), 49–50.

25. On the career of the greatest translator of the period, see Benjamin Schwartz, *In Search of Wealth and Power: Yen Fu and the West* (Cambridge: The Belknap Press of Harvard University, 1964).

26. According to Hsü, in the period 1903–1919, 41.51 percent of the Chinese students who went abroad for higher education studied in Japan; 33.85 percent in the United States, and 24.64 percent in Europe. Consult his *The Rise of Modern China*, 496.

27. John K. Fairbank, Edwin O. Reischauer, and Albert M. Craig, *East Asia: Tradition and Transformation* (Boston: Houghton Mifflin Company, 1973), 770–771.

28. Quoted in ibid., 771.

29. See Guy S. Alitto, *The Last Confucian: Liang Shu-ming and the Chinese Dilemma of Modernity* (Berkeley: University of California Press, 1979).

30. Liang Shuming, *Dong Xi wenhua ji qi zhexue* (Eastern and Western Cultures and Their Philosophies), (Shanghai, 1922).

31. Quoted in Hsü, *The Rise of Modern China*, 509.

32. Chow, *The May Fourth Movement*, 320.

33. Quoted in ibid., 321.

34. Chen Duxiu, "Jidujiao yu Zhongguo ren" (Christianity and the Chinese People), translated by Tsu Yu-yue in *Chinese Recorder* 51/7 (July 1920), 453–458. The article was originally published in *Xin qingnian* (New Youth) 7/3 (February 1920).

35. Quoted in Hu Shih, *The Chinese Renaissance*, 90.

36. Ibid., 91.

37. Chow, *The May Fourth Movement*, 324.

38. Levenson, *Confucian China and Its Modern Fate*, 1: 123.

39. C. S. Chang (Zhang Jiasen or Zhang Junmai), "The Anti-Religion Movement," *Chinese Recorder* 55/8 (August 1923), 463.

40. Chen Duxiu, "Jidujiao yu Zhongguo ren" (Christianity and the Chinese People), 458.

41. Liang, *Intellectual Trends in the Ch'ing Period*, 116–117. A portion of this chapter is taken from or paraphrases (with permission) Don A. Pittman, "Will a New Bud-

dhism Appear? Liang Ch'i-ch'ao's Question and the Beginnings of the Chinese Sangha's Modernization," *Ching Feng* 41/2 (June 1998): 119–147.

42. See William Ayers, *Chang Chih-tung and Educational Reform in China* (Cambridge: Harvard University Press, 1971), 161–162. For a brief description of the proposal by a Buddhist writer, see Dongchu, *Zhongguo fojiao jindai shi* (A History of Modern Chinese Buddhism), 2 vols. (Taipei, 1974), 1: 73–75.

43. Liang, *Intellectual Trends in the Ch'ing Period,* 116–117.

44. Chün-fang Yü remarks that "if there had been no revival of monastic Buddhism in the late sixteenth and early seventeenth centuries, lay Buddhism would not have emerged." See Chün-fang Yü, *The Renewal of Buddhism in China* (New York: Columbia University Press, 1981), 65.

45. Ibid., 75.

46. Edward T. Ch'ien, *Chiao Hung and the Restructuring of Neo-Confucianism in the Late Ming* (New York: Columbia University Press, 1986), 22–24.

47. For a study of the sect, see Judith A. Berling, *The Syncretic Religion of Lin Chao-en* (New York: Columbia University Press, 1980).

48. On Chinese sectarian religions and their relationship to Buddhism, see Daniel L. Overmyer, *Folk Buddhist Religion: Dissenting Sects in Late Traditional China* (Cambridge: Harvard University Press, 1976); Susan Naquin, *Millenarian Rebellion in China: The Eight Trigrams Uprising of 1813* (New Haven: Yale University Press, 1976); and Jean Chesneaux, *Secret Societies in China: In the Nineteenth and Twentieth Centuries* (Ann Arbor: University of Michigan Press, 1971).

49. Dongchu, *Zhongguo fojiao jindai shi* (A History of Modern Chinese Buddhism), 1: 26.

50. Ibid., 1: 39.

51. Translated by Kenneth K. S. Ch'en in his *Buddhism in China: A Historical Survey* (Princeton: Princeton University Press, 1972), 453–454. For a classic study of Chinese Buddhism in relation to issues of economic productivity, consult also Jacques Gernet, *Buddhism in Chinese Society: An Economic History from the Fifth to the Tenth Centuries,* trans. Franciscus Verellen (New York: Columbia University Press, 1995).

52. Responding to an essay on the nature of God by Joseph Edkins, Hong stated: "The likeness of the Father may not be looked upon by earthly men. Christ and myself were begotten by the Father, and because I was in the Father's bosom, I have seen God. . . . The Elder Brother and I have personally seen the Father's sage face; The Father, the Son, and the Elder and Younger Brothers are not uncertain. The Father and the Elder Brother have brought me to sit in the Heavenly Court; the good guests shall enjoy happiness in ten thousand forms." Translated in Michael, *The Taiping Rebellion,* 3: 1205.

53. Ibid., 2: 186.

54. Dongchu, *Zhongguo fojiao jindai shi* (A History of Modern Chinese Buddhism), 1: 67.

55. Chan Kim-kwong, "Buddhists' Understanding of Christianity in Late Ming China: Implications for Interfaith Dialogue," *Ching Feng* 37/3 (September 1994), 168–192.

56. Quoted in Stephen Neill, *A History of Christian Missions* (London: Penguin Books, 1982), 189–190.

57. Consult George Minamiki, *The Chinese Rites Controversy from Its Beginning to Modern Times* (Chicago: Loyola University Press, 1985), and Kenneth Scott Latourette, *A History of Christian Missions in China* (New York: Macmillan, 1929), 131–155.

58. Neill, *A History of Christian Missions*, 282–283.

59. Ibid., 333–334. This early call for missionaries to identify with the common people is interesting in view of the 1925 report of Harry A. Franck, which noted that although the early pioneer missionaries "roughed it" and "underwent the real hardships of living with and as the Chinese," few did so anymore. He comments, "The overwhelming majority of foreigners, particularly of Americans, 'in mission work' in China, live in what is a palace among the dwellings of those they are seeking to benefit and a mansion alongside the simple cottage they would probably have occupied at home, or compared to the dwellings of a great many contributors to foreign missions. Instead of adapting themselves to the land they hope to 'evangelize,' . . . the missionaries 'in the field' and the boards at home alike seem to vie with each other and their rivals in building up enormous establishments, often out of all keeping with the community in which they are situated,—great three-story foreign houses with every modern convenience and many of the luxuries, infinitely better than the wealthiest merchant or the chief magistrate in their district can, in vast roomy compounds compared to which the Chinese round about are living forty deep." See Franck's *Roving Through Southern China* (New York: The Century Co., 1925), 584–585.

60. The largest society was the China Inland Mission, reporting in 1905 a total of 335 unordained men, 294 missionary women, 220 missionary wives, and 1,282 native workers. See Arthur H. Smith, *The Uplift of China* (New York: Young People's Missionary Movement of the United States and Canada, 1908), Appendix I: Statistics of Protestant Missions in China, 258. Smith's figures were compiled by direct correspondence with mission boards.

61. Ralph R. Covell, *Confucius, The Buddha, and Christ: A History of the Gospel in Chinese* (Maryknoll, N.Y.: Orbis Books, 1986), 94–95. On this subject, consult also Winifred Glüer, "The Encounter Between Christianity and Chinese Buddhism During the Nineteenth Century and the First Half of the Twentieth Century," *Ching Feng* 11/3 (1968): 39–57.

62. Timothy Richard, *The New Testament of Higher Buddhism* (Edinburgh: T. and T. Clark, 1910), 39. Yang Wenhui helped Richard with the translation of the *Dasheng qixin lun* (The Awakening of Faith in Mahāyāna), thinking that it would contribute to the goal of spreading Buddhism worldwide. However, when he saw that the final product reflected an obvious Christian bias and discovered that Richard basically viewed the scripture as a Christian text in Buddhist nomenclature, he refused to assist other westerners in similar undertakings. For example, Richard translated the Buddhist term *"rulai"* (Tathāgata) as "Messiah" and the "incarnate God." "Buddha" is sometimes translated as "God," sometimes as "archetype," and *"pusa"* (bodhisattva) is translated as "apostle." See *The Awakening of Faith in the Mahāyāna Doctrine: The New Buddhism,* trans. Timothy Richard (Shanghai: Christian Literature Society, 1907). Consult also Timothy Richard, *An Epistle to All Buddhists* (Shanghai, 1916) and *Forty-Five Years in China: Reminiscences by Timothy Richard* (New York: Frederick A. Stokes, 1916). Noting the criticisms that Richard received from scholars and from his fellow Christian ministers, Winifred Glüer has concluded from a missional point of view, "The tragedy of Richard's interpretation of Buddhism was that it proved too benevolent even to the Buddhists themselves who did not feel urged to commit themselves to Christ because of their reliance on the Chinese philosophical tradition with its emphasis on humanism and rationality." Consult Glüer, "The Encounter Between Christianity and Chinese Buddhism," 50. For a comparative study of the methods of Hudson Taylor and Timothy Richard, see Paul A. Cohen, "Missionary Approaches: Hudson Taylor and Timothy Richard," *Papers on China,* vol. 11, 29–62 (Cambridge: Harvard University East Asian Research Center, 1957).

63. Timothy Richard, "The Influence of Buddhism in China," *Chinese Recorder* 21/2 (February 1890): 63–64.

64. Consult Whalen Lai, "Chinese Buddhism and Christian Charities: A Comparative History," *Buddhist-Christian Studies* 12 (1992): 5–33. Lai comments that the nineteenth-century encounter between western Protestant Christians and Burmese Buddhists monks was a classic example of what happened elsewhere in Asia. He notes that in the process of destroying Burma's simple economy and traditional way of life, the British colonialists caustically criticized all Buddhist monks as "lax, unlearned, and uncaring." Writes Lai, "Once the learned educator, the monk was suddenly relabeled the ignoramus. With new sciences being taught in the missionary schools, time-honored beliefs were dubbed superstitions. For those who acquired a knowledge of 'Original Buddhism,' these monks were not even deemed Buddhist. With copies of the Western work ethic in place, the quiet life of the monk was now caricatured as an excuse for not doing anything useful. Was the monk necessarily less caring than the missionary? Probably not. It is just that, having weathered the storms of the Industrial Revolution, modern Christian institutions of charity could far better address the new social needs. The rural monastery was geared only to helping the few; it was not meant to handle the urban unemployed. Most Buddhist temples were never meant to be downtown missions; they were traditionally located on the edges

of villages and towns anyway. Traditionally, monks do not come to you; you go to visit monks" (27–28).

65. K. F. A. (Charles) Gützlaff, "Journal of a Voyage along the Coast of China from the Province of Canton to Leaoutung in Mantschou-Tartary, 1832–1833," *Chinese Repository* 2 (1833–1834): 49.

66. Ernest J. Eitel, *Buddhism, Its Historical, Theoretical, and Popular Aspects*, 3rd ed. (Hong Kong: Lane, Crawford & Co., 1884), 33.

67. Ibid., 95–96 and 145.

68. Joseph Edkins, *Chinese Buddhism: A Volume of Sketches, Historical, Descriptive, and Critical* (London: Kegan Paul, Trench, Trübner, & Co., 1893), 412 and 420.

69. Smith, *The Uplift of China*, 107–108.

70. See Chao Yang Buwei, *Autobiography of a Chinese Woman* (Westport, Conn.: Greenwood Press, 1970), 82–88. For a review of the contributions of Yang Wenhui, see *Fojiao mingren zhuan* (A Record of Famous Buddhists), (Taipei, 1987), 403–406.

71. Welch, *The Buddhist Revival in China*, 20–21.

72. Dongchu, *Zhongguo fojiao jindai shi* (A History of Modern Chinese Buddhism), 1: 41–42.

73. The Maha Bodhi Society was originally called the Bodhgaya Mahabodhi Society. Its announced purpose was "to revive Buddhism in India, to disseminate Buddhist literature, to publish Buddhist tracts in the Indian vernaculars, to educate the illiterate millions of Indian people, to maintain Bhikkhus at Bodhgaya, Benares, Kusinara, Savatthi and Calcutta, to build Dharmasalas at these places, [and] to send Buddhist missionaries abroad." To accomplish these goals, the Maha Bodhi Society asked every Buddhist to contribute one-twentieth of his daily income to the Maha Bodhi Fund. See *The Maha Bodhi and the United Buddhist World: The Journal of the Maha Bodhi Society* 10/10 (February 1902): cover page.

74. Dharmapala's presentation on modern Buddhism at the World's Parliament of Religions stressed its scientific and ethical bases. Offering counsel to Christians who wished to propagate their own religious tradition in Asia, he suggested, "The platform you have built up must be entirely reconstructed if Christianity is to make progress in the East. You must send men full of unselfishness. They must have a spirit of self-sacrifice, a sense of charity, a spirit of tolerance.... I warn you that if you want to establish Christianity in the East it can only be done on the principles of Christ's love and meekness. Let the missionaries study all the religions; let them be a type of meekness and lowliness and they will find a welcome in all lands." Quoted in John Henry Barrows, ed., *The World's Parliament of Religions*, 2 vols. (Chicago: Parliament Publishing Company, 1893), 2: 1093. See also John R. McRae, "Oriental Verities on the American Frontier: The 1893 World's Parliament of Religions and the Thought

of Masao Abe," *Buddhist-Christian Studies* 11 (1991): 7–36, which includes photographs of Dharmapala at the Chicago conference.

75. Otto Franke, "Eine neue Buddhistische propaganda," *T'oung Pao* 5 (1894): 301–303. Franke reported that the crowd which gathered included both laypeople and monastics, including one monk from Tiantai Shan in Zhejiang and one from Emei Shan in Sichuan. Sanskrit romanization altered.

76. Ibid., 303–304.

77. Whalen Lai, "Chinese Buddhist and Christian Charities: A Comparative History," *Buddhist-Christian Studies* 12 (1992): 20. As Lai observes, this fear of government reprisal and property confiscation meant that Yang Wenhui would have better luck obtaining help for educational ventures from other gentry Buddhists like himself than from monks. He writes, "Privatized in their faith and in their land dealings with the state, Buddhist temples guarded their property as jealously as any worldling. They passed it down only to their own lineages. This [also] prevented the reformer monk Taixu from rallying and uniting the sangha for a more socially active form of Buddhism that could respond to the challenge of Christianity" (ibid.).

78. Yinshun, *Taixu dashi nianpu* (A Chronological Biography of the Venerable Master Taixu), (Taipei, 1973), 38 (hereafter cited as "Chronological Biography").

79. Cai Shangsi and Fang Xing, comps., *Tan Sitong quanji* (The Complete Works of Tan Sitong), (Beijing, 1981), 60, cited in Chan Sin-wai, *Buddhism in Late Ch'ing Political Thought* (Hong Kong: Chinese University Press, 1985), 69.

80. Yang named the estate after the famous monastery built in honor of the Buddha by a wealthy merchant named Anāthapiṇḍika in the Jetavana Grove at Sāvatthi.

81. For a German translation of the thirty-five articles of the statutes of the Jetavana Hermitage, see Otto Franke, "Ein Buddhistischer Reformversuch in China," *T'oung Pao,* Ser. 2 (1909): 567–602.

82. On Dixian, consult Dongchu, *Zhongguo fojiao jindai shi* (A History of Modern Chinese Buddhism), 2: 757–761, as well as *Fojiao mingren zhuan* (A Record of Famous Buddhists), 411–415. On Su Manshu, see Henry McAleavy, *Su Man-shu (1884–1918): A Sino-Japanese Genius* (London: The China Society, 1960). Yinshun notes that there is some question about whether Su Manshu was in residence during Taixu's studies. See Yinshun, *Taixu dashi nianpu* (Chronological Biography), 37–38.

83. For a brief description of Zhiguang's career, see Dongchu, *Zhongguo fojiao jindai shi* (A History of Modern Chinese Buddhism), 2: 848–850; on Ouyang Jingwu, consult ibid., 2: 660–667; on Mei Guangxi, see ibid., 2: 650–660.

84. See Yinshun, *Taixu dashi nianpu* (Chronological Biography), 38; Ch'en, *Buddhism in China,* 448; and Wing-tsit Chan, *Religious Trends in Modern China* (New York: Columbia University Press, 1953), 59–60.

85. Consult Lewis Hodous, *Buddhism and Buddhists in China* (New York: Macmillan, 1924), 63–71.

86. James B. Pratt, "A Report on the Present Condition of Buddhism," *Chinese Social and Political Science Review* 8 (1924): 15–16. See also idem, *The Pilgrimage of Buddhism and a Buddhist Pilgrimage* (New York: Macmillan, 1928).

87. For a report on Sichuan and Emei Shan in 1899, see Archibald John Little, *Mount Omi and Beyond: A Record of Travel on the Thibetan Border* (London: William Heinemann, 1901). For a later report on Sichuan, reflecting field studies from 1919–1926, including diagrams of Buddhist temples on Emei Shan and photographs, see David Crockett Graham, *Religion in Szechuan Province, China,* Smithsonian Miscellaneous Collections 80/4 (1928): 1–83, plus 25 plates.

88. Pratt, "A Report on the Present Condition of Buddhism," 12–13.

89. Johannes Prip-Møller, *Chinese Buddhist Monasteries: Their Plan and Its Function as a Setting for Buddhist Monastic Life* (Copenhagen: G. E. C. Gad, 1937), viii. See also Wolfram Eberhard, "Temple-Building Activities in Medieval and Modern China: An Experimental Study," *Monumenta Serica* 23 (1964): 264–318.

90. Holmes Welch, "Buddhism in China Today," in *The Cultural, Political, and Religious Significance of Buddhism in the Modern World,* ed. Heinrich Dumoulin (New York: Macmillan, 1976), 165. With regard to figures for monks and nuns in the Republican period, see the statistics said to have been compiled in 1930 by the Chinese Buddhist Association at the request of its president, Yuanying, and included as Appendix 1 in Holmes Welch, *The Practice of Chinese Buddhism, 1900–1950* (Cambridge: Harvard University Press, 1967), 411–420. The basic findings were published in the Chinese Ministry of Information, comp., *The China Handbook 1937–45: A Comprehensive Survey of Major Developments in China in Eight Years of War* (New York: Macmillan, 1947), 26. A more complete report can be found in *Shenbao nianjian* (Shenbao Yearbook), (Shanghai, June 1936), 1278–1279.

91. A similar estimate of monks is made by the monk Huizhu in Taixu's journal, *Haichao yin* (Sound of the Sea Tide) 16/3 (1935): 27. Lewis Hodous, noting the difficulty in obtaining reliable figures, estimates "conservatively" in 1924 that there were approximately 400,000 monks and 10,000 nuns, with the number on the increase (see his *Buddhism and Buddhists in China,* 66). The number 10,000 is surely a misprint for the 100,000 intended: 10,000 is too far below other estimates from the period to be reasonable and also conflicts with Karl Ludvig Reichelt's subsequent reference to Hodous. Reichelt stated in 1928 that there were approximately 1 million members of the sangha, with nuns representing slightly more than 100,000, and cited investigations conducted by Hodous two years earlier (see Reichelt, *Truth and Tradition in Chinese Buddhism: A Study of Chinese Mahāyāna Buddhism,* trans. Kathrina Van Wagenen Bugge [Shanghai: Commercial Press, 1927], 298). For a description of the tonsure

ritual, with photographs of a ceremony in Taiwan, see Welch, *The Practice of Chinese Buddhism, 1900–1950,* 269–275.

92. See Earl Herbert Cressy, "A Study in Indigenous Religions," in *Layman's Foreign Missionary Inquiry, Fact-Finders Reports,* vol. 5, Supplementary Series, part 2, ed. Orville A. Petty (New York: Harper, 1933), 710.

93. D. S. Dye's May 1931 report in *West China Missionary News.* Quoted in Cressy, "A Study in Indigenous Religions," 711.

94. Welch, *The Buddhist Revival in China,* 241. Consult Loren E. Noren, "The Life and Work of Karl Ludvig Reichelt," *Ching Feng* 10/3 (1967): 6–33.

95. Karl Ludvig Reichelt, "Trends in China's Non-Christian Religions," *Chinese Recorder* 65 (December 1934): 759–760.

96. Yu-yue Tsu, "Present Tendencies in Chinese Buddhism," *Journal of Religion* 1 (September 1921): 500–501. For charters of several of these organizations, consult *Fojiao yuebao* (Buddhist Monthly), No. 1 (May 1913). See also Taixu, "Fojiao hongshi hui jianzhang" (Regulations of the Buddhist Society of the Great Vow), in *Taixu dashi quanshu* (Complete Works), 9.34.27: 451–454, and "Weichi fojiao tongmeng hui xuanyan" (Public Announcement of the League for the Support of Buddhism), in ibid., 19.61.137: 1005–1009.

97. Tsu, "Present Tendencies in Chinese Buddhism," 501.

98. Yinshun, *Taixu dashi nianpu* (Chronological Biography), 61. With regard to the number of provincial and local branches, Welch offers somewhat less impressive figures: "nineteen branches at the provincial level and well over a hundred at the local level." See Welch, *The Buddhist Revival in China,* 38.

99. At the time of the 1913 meeting of the Chinese General Buddhist Association, Yekai had just retired as abbot of the Tianning si in Zhangzhou. On the career of the respected Chan master from Jiangsu, see Dongchu, *Zhongguo fojiao jindai shi* (A History of Modern Chinese Buddhism), 2: 742–744.

100. In his study of the finances of monasteries in the city of Hangzhou in the early 1930s, Earl Herbert Cressy notes that in the ten largest monasteries in the area, with from ten to 230 monks, the total yearly income from all sources ranged between $20,000 and $80,000 (in Mexican dollars, the value of which, in 1931–1932, was approximately fifty cents in U.S. currency), with a median annual income of $35,000. The fee for an elaborate plenary mass for the dead *(shuilu fahui)* that extended to seven days in the monastery ranged from $500 to $1,000, with total yearly income from this source ranging from $20,000 to $50,000. In a second group of fifteen monasteries, with from three to thirty monks, the total income range was from $3,000 to $20,000. The minimum fee for a mass for the dead in one of these monasteries was $50, but they could run as high as $400. A third group consisted of twenty-two

small monasteries with from one to ten monks. Monks from this group generally performed inexpensive rites for the dead outside the monasteries. "For one known as Bei Jin," Cressy writes, "the price is $7 for the participation of from five to seven monks. For one known as Bei Zang, extending over three days, the fee is $12. For the 'Hungry Ghosts,' the fee is $3.50 for the participation of five monks for one day." Although one monastery in the city owned as much as 1,129 *mou*, or nearly 200 acres, the median for all monasteries in Hangchow was 9 *mou*. See Cressy, "A Study in Indigenous Religions," 697–702. Welch reports that the price for a plenary mass for the dead in the period was between $1,200 and $5,000 (Chinese currency), with as much as half the amount representing profit for the monastery (see Welch, *The Practice of Chinese Buddhism, 1900–1950*, 191). For a study of Buddhist rites for the dead, see J. J. M. de Groot, "Buddhist Masses for the Dead at Amoy: An Ethnological Essay," in *Actes du Sixième Congrès International des Orientalistes, tenu en 1883 à Leiden* (Leiden: E. J. Brill, 1885), 1–120.

101. Welch calculates that approximately 1 to 2 percent of the population in 1930 consisted of committed lay Buddhist devotees, based on the previously cited figures compiled by the Chinese Buddhist Association in that year (Welch, "Buddhism in China Today," 164). Editors of *The China Handbook* estimated that the number of Buddhist laymen and laywomen who had taken the five vows (not to kill, steal, lie, drink intoxicating beverages, or commit sexual immorality) was five times the number of monastic followers, or approximately 3.7 million out of a total population in China of 455 million, which would suggest a figure even lower than 1 percent. See Chinese Ministry of Information, comp., *The China Handbook, 1937–45*, 1, 26.

102. Consult Lewis Hodous, "The Chinese Church of the Five Religions," *Journal of Religion* 4 (1924): 71–76, as well as Paul De Witt Twinem, "Modern Syncretic Religious Societies in China: I," *Journal of Religion* 5/5 (September 1925): 463–482, and "Modern Syncretic Religious Societies in China: II," *Journal of Religion* 5/6 (November 1925): 595–606. As an illustration of the popularity of syncretic traditions, Twinem quotes the national membership of the United Goodness Society as being at least 10,000 persons, with a chapter "in nearly every province, city, and district." Hodous reports that within two years of its founding by Liu Mingseng in 1921, in Shandong, "the Chinese Church of the Five Religions" claimed seventy-five societies in eleven provinces with a membership in the tens of thousands. Such traditions continue to flourish in contemporary Taiwan.

103. The general literacy statistic is from *The Chinese Yearbook, 1926 (Shanghai)*, 426. Welch notes that most nuns were illiterate, due to fewer educational opportunities for Chinese women, whereas the majority of monks had completed a primary school education prior to joining the order. Only a few had advanced beyond that point, but illiteracy was rare. See Welch, *The Practice of Chinese Buddhism, 1900–1950*, 257–258.

104. Chen-hua (Zhenhua), *In Search of the Dharma: Memoirs of a Modern Chinese Buddhist Pilgrim,* ed. with an introduction by Chün-fang Yü, trans. Denis C. Mair (Albany: State University of New York Press, 1992), 48, 59.

105. For a discussion of monastic education and a description of some of the important institutions, see Dongchu, *Zhongguo fojiao jindai shi* (A History of Modern Chinese Buddhism), 1: 197–236. For a listing of seventy-one different seminaries started during the Republican period, see Welch, *The Buddhist Revival in China,* Appendix 2, 285–287.

106. Dongchu, *Zhongguo fojiao jindai shi* (A History of Modern Chinese Buddhism), 1: 216–220.

107. See Otto Franke, "Die Propaganda des japanischen Buddhismus in China," in *Ostasiatische Neubildungen* (Hamburg: C. Boysen, 1911), 160–161; see also Yinshun, *Taixu dashi nianpu* (Chronological Biography), 35–36.

108. With reference to the 1915 law, see Tsu, "Present Tendencies in Chinese Buddhism," 502.

109. Tsu offers a vivid description of the untoward circumstances of the ancient Longhua si in the western suburbs of Shanghai. See ibid, 502–504.

110. Consult "Chinese Buddhists Against Confiscation of Church Land," *The Young East* 4/4 (September 1928), 143.

111. Chen-hua, *In Search of the Dharma,* 22.

112. Latourette, *A History of Christian Missions in China,* 831.

113. Consult Chiang Kai-shek, "My Religious Faith," in *The China Reader: Republican China,* ed. Franz Schurmann and Orville Schell (New York: Random House, 1967), 154–157. The remarks were originally delivered as a radio broadcast on Easter eve, April 16, 1938, entitled "Why I Believe in Jesus." The text was first published in *President Chiang Kai-shek's Selected Speeches and Messages* (Taipei: China Cultural Service), 20–24.

114. On Reichelt's efforts, see Noren, "The Life and Work of Karl Ludvig Reichelt"; Notto R. Thelle, "Karl Ludvig Reichelt, 1877–1952: Christian Pilgrim of Tao Fong Shan," in *Mission Legacies: Biographical Studies of Leaders of the Modern Missionary Movement,* ed. Gerald H. Anderson et al. (Maryknoll, N.Y.: Orbis Books, 1996), 216–224; and Hakan Eilert, *Boundlessness: Studies in Karl Ludvig Reichelt's Missionary Thinking with Special Regard to the Buddhist-Christian Encounter* (Rinkobing, Aros: Eksp., DBK, 1974).

115. Wing-tsit Chan quotes Yu-yue Tsu's article on "New Tendencies in Chinese Religions" in *Wen She* (Literary Society Magazine) 2/7 (May 1927): 44. See Chan, *Religious Trends in Modern China,* 56.

116. See Robert Payne, *Forever China* (New York: Dodd, Mead, and Co., 1945), 274.

117. Consult Frank E. Manuel and Fritzie P. Manuel, *Utopian Thought in the Western World* (Cambridge: Harvard University Press, 1979), 1–29.

118. Wei-huan, "Buddhism in Modern China," *T'ien Hsia Monthly* 9/2 (September 1939): 147.

119. Manuel and Manuel, *Utopian Thought in the Western World,* 27.

CHAPTER 2: THE SOUND OF THE TIDE FOR A NEW CHINA

1. Millican, "Tai Hsü and Modern Buddhism," 327.

2. Yinshun, *Taixu dashi nianpu* (Chronological Biography), 24.

3. See Taixu, "Taixu zizhuan" (The Autobiography of Taixu), in *Taixu dashi quanshu* (Complete Works), 19.58.18: 174–179 (cited hereafter as "Autobiography"). Welch locates the Xiao (Smaller) Jiuhua si in southern Zhejiang province. Cf. Welch, *The Buddhist Revival in China,* 16. Taixu's autobiography makes it clear that it was located near the Grand Canal south of Suzhou, near Lake Tai along the Jiangsu-Zhejiang border.

4. Yinshun, *Taixu dashi nianpu* (Chronological Biography), 24. Taixu acknowledges in his autobiography that his grandmother did not sharply differentiate between Daoism and Buddhism. See Taixu, "Taixu zizhuan" (Autobiography) in *Taixu dashi quanshu* (Complete Works), 19.58.18: 170.

5. *Fojiao mingren zhuan* (A Record of Famous Buddhists), 425.

6. See Reginald F. Johnston, "A Poet Monk of Modern China," *Journal of the North China Branch of the Royal Asiatic Society* 43 (1932): 14–30. For a brief account of his career, see also Dongchu, *Zhongguo fojiao jindai shi* (A History of Modern Chinese Buddhism), 1: 100–106. For a photograph of Jichan, the "Eight-Fingered Ascetic," see Welch, *The Buddhist Revival in China,* 36.

7. According to Shengyan, *hua tou* ("critical phrase" or "principal topic") literally means "the source of words before they are uttered" and refers to baffling questions and answers that are posed for students to contemplate, such as "Who is this reciting Buddha's name?"; "What is nothingness?"; and "Does a dog have buddha-nature or not?" Intended to arouse the "doubt sensation" (*yi qing*) and counteract ordinary ways of thinking, these *hua tou* became the bases of popular *gong an* (Jap. *koan*), or "public cases," in Chan Buddhism. Consult Shengyan, *Complete Enlightenment: Zen Comments on the Sūtra of Complete Enlightenment* (Boston: Shambhala, 1999). Robert Buswell further comments, "Chan words, such as those that appear in a *hua tou,* were thus conceived of as a form of spiritual homeopathy, using a minimal, but potent, dosage of the 'poison of words' to cure the malady of conceptualization." See Robert E. Buswell, Jr., "The 'Short-cut' Approach of K'an-hua Meditation: The Evolu-

tion of a Practical Subitism in Chinese Ch'an Buddhism," in *Sudden and Gradual: Approaches to Enlightenment in Chinese Thought,* ed. Peter N. Gregory (Honolulu: University of Hawai'i Press, 1987), 348.

8. For a brief description of Yuanying's career, consult Dongchu, *Zhongguo fojiao jindai shi* (A History of Modern Chinese Buddhism), 2: 803–805.

9. Taixu, "Taixu zizhuan" (Autobiography), in *Taixu dashi quanshu* (Complete Works), 19.58.18: 187.

10. On Daojie, consult Dongchu, *Zhongguo fojiao jindai shi* (A History of Modern Chinese Buddhism), 2: 825–827. Daojie became the abbot of the important Fayuan si in Beijing in 1909.

11. Yinshun, *Taixu dashi nianpu* (Chronological Biography), 32. See also Xuming, *Taixu dashi shengping shiji* (A Record of the Life of the Venerable Master Taixu), (Taipei, 1957), 3. Consult further Taixu, "Taixu zizhuan" (Autobiography), in *Taixu dashi quanshu* (Complete Works), 19.58.18: 188.

12. A 1920 reminiscence published in the first volume of *Haichao yin,* translated in Tsu, "Present Tendencies in Chinese Buddhism," 505.

13. Yinshun, *Taixu dashi nianpu* (Chronological Biography), 33. On Huashan, consult Dongchu, *Zhongguo fojiao jindai shi* (A History of Modern Chinese Buddhism), 2: 887–889.

14. Yinshun, *Taixu dashi nianpu* (Chronological Biography), 33–34.

15. Taixu, "Taixu zizhuan" (Autobiography), in *Taixu dashi quanshu* (Complete Works), 19.58.18: 191.

16. Both Xu Xilin and Qiu Jin were members of the revolutionary society known as the Guangfu hui, a large organization that preceded the establishment of the Tongmeng hui. See ed. Arthur W. Hummel, *Eminent Chinese of the Ch'ing Period (1644–1912),* (Taipei: SMC Publishing Inc., 1943), 1: 169–171.

17. Yinshun, *Taixu dashi nianpu* (Chronological Biography), 35.

18. From the forward to Taixu, *Lectures in Buddhism* (Paris: Les Amis du Bouddhisme, 1928), 11. The editor of the volume and the author of the foreword is recorded as "Kuen-lun." Welch suggests that this is probably Barnett Conlan, the Irish art critic who helped arrange Taixu's visit to Paris in 1928 under the sponsorship of Grace Constant Lounsbery. See Welch, *The Buddhist Revival in China,* 307. Readers should note that Welch misspells her name as "Lounsberry."

19. Taixu, "Taixu zizhuan" (Autobiography), in *Taixu dashi quanshu* (Complete Works), 19.58.18: 196.

20. See Welch, *The Buddhist Revival in China,* 9.

21. Otto Franke, "Ein Buddhistischer Reformversuch in China," 299–310.

22. For brief descriptions of Yinguang's career, consult *Fojiao mingren zhuan* (A Record of Famous Buddhists), 416–418, as well as Dongchu, *Zhongguo fojiao jindai shi* (A History of Modern Chinese Buddhism), 2: 761–765. Consult also Yinguang, *Yinguang fashi wenchao quanji* (The Complete Works of the Dharma Master Yinguang), 2 vols. (Taipei, 1975), as well as Jianzheng, *Yinguang dashi de shengping yu sixiang* (The Life and Thought of the Venerable Yinguang), (Taipei, 1989).

23. Yinshun, *Taixu dashi nianpu* (Chronological Biography), 40.

24. Ibid.

25. Ibid., 41.

26. Ibid., 44.

27. Welch, *The Buddhist Revival in China*, 298.

28. Welch notes that this edition of the Tripiṭaka, the Pinjia Hermitage edition, was completed in 1913, after four years of work, at the cost of $150,000. See his *The Buddhist Revival in China*, 18.

29. Later, in 1915, when the abbotship of Jin Shan should have gone to Zongyang on the retirement of Qingquan, he was denied the position because of objections to his political involvements and his inconsistent monastic practice. See Welch, *The Practice of Chinese Buddhism, 1900–1950*, 159.

30. Taixu, "Taixu zizhuan" (Autobiography), in *Taixu dashi quanshu* (Complete Works), 19.58.18: 200.

31. Yinshun, *Taixu dashi nianpu* (Chronological Biography), 50. Welch notes that although some have questioned whether monks actually engaged in military conflict, personal interviews tend to support Yinshun's report. See Welch, *The Buddhist Revival in China*, 299.

32. Welch, *The Buddhist Revival in China*, 19–20. Located at the junction of the Han and Yangzi rivers, Wuhan is the name of the large metropolitan center in Hubei province formed from the formerly separate cities of Hankou, Hanyang, and Wuchang.

33. For a brief account of Renshan's career, see Dongchu, *Zhongguo fojiao jindai shi* (A History of Modern Chinese Buddhism), 1: 91–93.

34. Taixu, "Wo de fojiao geming shibai shi" (The History of My Failed Buddhist Revolution), in *Taixu dashi quanshu* (Complete Works), 19.57.8: 61.

35. Howard L. Boorman, ed., *Biographical Dictionary of Republican China*, 4 vols. (New York: Columbia University Press, 1970), 3: 208.

36. Taixu, "Taixu zizhuan" (Autobiography), in *Taixu dashi quanshu* (Complete Works), 19.58.18: 202. An informant advised Welch that Shuangting served a longer sentence than Qingquan and that the terms of both monks were eventually com-

muted in a general amnesty declared by Sun Yat-sen, who also dissolved the Association for the Advancement of Buddhism. See Welch, *The Buddhist Revival in China,* 299–300.

37. Yinshun, *Taixu dashi nianpu* (Chronological Biography), 52.

38. Ibid.

39. For example, see Dongchu's account of the Jin Shan incident, which describes its polarizing effect within the Buddhist community, in *Zhongguo fojiao jindai shi* (A History of Modern Chinese Buddhism), 1: 91–99.

40. Welch, *The Buddhist Revival in China,* 33. Chinese transliteration omitted from quotation.

41. On Ouyang Jingwu's thought, consult Gotelind Müller, *Buddhismus und Moderne: Ouyang Jingwu, Taixu und das Ringen um ein zeitgemässes Selbstverständis im chinesischen Buddhismus des frühen 20. Jahrhunderts* (Stuttgart: Franz Steiner Verlag, 1993).

42. Wei-huan, "Buddhism in Modern China," 153. Wei-huan provides a translation of the charter of this Chinese Buddhist Association.

43. See Welch, *The Buddhist Revival in China,* 35.

44. Xuyun had been summoned to Shanghai from Yunnan to assist with matters. Consult Cen Xuelü, ed., *Xuyun laoheshi fahui* (Collected Teachings of the Master Xuyun), 2 vols. (Taipei, 1974), 2: 60–61. See also Cen Xuelü, *Xuyun heshang nianpu* (A Chronological Biography of the Monk Xuyun), (Taipei, 1978), 54–55. For a brief account of Xuyun's accomplishments, see Dongchu, *Zhongguo fojiao jindai shi* (A History of Modern Chinese Buddhism), 2: 787–795.

45. Dongchu, *Zhongguo fojiao jindai shi* (A History of Modern Chinese Buddhism), 1: 102.

46. See Yinshun, *Taixu dashi nianpu* (Chronological Biography), 54. Consult also *Foxue congbao* (Buddhist Miscellany), no. 3 (December 1913).

47. Cen Xuelü, *Xuyun laoheshi fahui* (Collected Teachings of the Master Xuyun), 2: 61.

48. This is Yu-yue Tsu's "free translation" of the program adopted at the inaugural meeting of the Zhongguo fojiao zonghui, as given in his "Present Tendencies in Chinese Buddhism," 500. Tsu, however, incorrectly states the date of the organization's founding. Welch notes that Tsu includes two provisions—numbers 8 and 9, dealing with the age and education of those admitted to the sangha and with prohibitions against performing funerals for financial gain—that are not mentioned in the Chinese text as printed in *Foxue congbao* (Buddhist Miscellany), no. 1 (October 1912). Welch wonders whether Tsu was summarizing a later version of the charter as amended by more radical monks, like Taixu or Renshan, who would have certainly wished the association to adopt these more controversial reformist provisions. Welch

could be correct, though I have found no corroborating evidence of Taixu's possible involvement. See Welch, *The Buddhist Revival in China*, 301.

49. Yinshun erroneously reports the date as January 8, 1913. See Yinshun, *Taixu dashi nianpu* (Chronological Biography), 56. See also the account in *Foxue congbao* (Buddhist Miscellany), no. 3 (December 1912).

50. Yinshun, *Taixu dashi nianpu* (Chronological Biography), 60.

51. See Taixu, "Weichi fojiao tongmeng hui xuanyan" (Public Announcement for the League for the Support of Buddhism), in *Taixu dashi quanshu* (Complete Works), 19.61.137: 1005–1009. See also Yinshun, *Taixu dashi nianpu* (Chronological Biography), 61.

52. Yinshun, *Taixu dashi nianpu* (Chronological Biography), 63.

53. On Yuexia's career, consult Dongchu, *Zhongguo fojiao jindai shi* (A History of Modern Chinese Buddhism), 2: 755–757. Taixu reports that he actually stayed with Zongyang in his printing offices for several months. See Taixu, "Taixu zizhuan" (Autobiography), in *Taixu dashi quanshu* (Complete Works), 19.58.18: 207.

54. Yinshun, *Taixu dashi nianpu* (Chronological Biography), 64.

55. Xuming, *Taixu dashi shengping shiji* (A Record of the Life of the Venerable Master Taixu), 8.

56. From the first volume (1920) of *Haichao yin,* as translated in Tsu, "Present Tendencies in Chinese Buddhism," 505–506. Brackets are the translator's.

57. On the practice of *biguan* (sealed confinement), consult Welch, *The Practice of Chinese Buddhism, 1900–1950,* 321–322, which includes a photograph of a ceremony inaugurating a sealed confinement. See also the account of the monk Zhenhua who, beginning in 1954, spent three years in sealed confinement in a "thatched hut" *(maopeng)* built for him by a wealthy laywoman on a mountain in northern Taiwan. In this case, Zhenhua lived as a hermit but actually traveled short distances to purchase food and supplies, and longer distances, on occasion, to visit a monastery. See Chen-hua, *In Search of the Dharma,* 235–241.

58. Karl L. Reichelt, *The Transformed Abbot,* trans. by G. M. Reichelt and A. P. Rose (London: Lutterworth Press, 1954), 154. Reichelt incorrectly dates Taixu's *biguan* from 1913.

59. Taixu, "Taixu zizhuan" (Autobiography), in *Taixu dashi quanshu* (Complete Works), 19.58.18: 210.

60. For a brief description of the career of the revolutionary and renowned classical scholar Zhang Taiyan (Zhang Binglin), see Boorman, ed., *Biographical Dictionary of Republican China,* 1: 92–98. On his perspectives on Buddhism, consult Dongchu, "Zhang Taiyan yu fojiao sixiang" (Zhang Taiyan and Buddhist Thought), chap. 20/3, in idem, *Zhongguo fojiao jindai shi* (A History of Modern Chinese Buddhism), 2:

555–559. For some of his early revolutionary articles, see also Zhang Taiyan, *Zhang Taiyan wenchao* (Selected works of Zhang Taiyan), (Shanghai, 1914). On Yan Fu, see Boorman, ed., *Biographical Dictionary of Republican China,* 4: 41–47.

61. Yinshun, *Taixu dashi nianpu* (Chronological Biography), 76.

62. Hsü, *The Rise of Modern China,* 479.

63. Tsu, "Present Tendencies in Chinese Buddhism," 502.

64. Welch, *The Buddhist Revival in China,* 138.

65. Paul Callahan, "T'ai Hsü and the New Buddhist Movement," in *Papers on China,* vol. 6 (Cambridge: Harvard University, East Asian Research Center, 1952), 152.

66. Xuming, *Taixu dashi shengping shiji* (A Record of the Life of the Venerable Master Taixu), 11. *The Sūraṅgama Sūtra* was a popular text among Chinese Buddhists, and the Sūraṅgama mantra *(Lengyan zhou)* was commonly the first item recited in morning devotions. Informants told Welch that, by 1935, Taixu was urging his students to concentrate on other, more "advanced" texts. See Welch, *The Buddhist Revival in China,* 113.

67. Shengyan, "Four Great Thinkers in Modern Chinese Buddhism," in *Buddhist Ethics and Modern Society: An International Symposium,* ed. Charles Wei-hsun Fu and Sandra Wawrytko (New York: Greenwood Press, 1991), 58.

68. Gao Yongxiao, "Taixu dashi de sixiang tixi" (The System of Thought of the Venerable Master Taixu), in *Xianggang fojiao* (Buddhism in Hong Kong), no. 286 (June 1960): 27.

69. To avoid the use of the pejorative term "Hinayāna" (Lesser Vehicle), a designation invented by Mahāyānists to belittle their opponents, I have chosen to translate *xiaosheng fojiao* here—as elsewhere when historical distinctions are being made (and where it seems in no way contradictory to the author's point)—as "Nikāya Buddhism" (Buddhism of the Schools), an imperfect but increasingly adopted way to deal with this terminological problem. See, for example, John S. Strong, *The Experience of Buddhism: Sources and Interpretations* (Belmont, Calif.: Wadsworth, 1995), 86–87.

70. Gao Yongxiao, "Taixu dashi de sixiang tixi" (The System of Thought of the Venerable Master Taixu), 27.

71. Shengyan, "Four Great Thinkers in Modern Chinese Buddhism," 59.

72. John Blofeld, *The Wheel of Life: The Autobiography of a Western Buddhist,* 2nd ed. (London: Rider & Company, 1972), 170.

73. Yinshun, *Taixu dashi nianpu* (Chronological Biography), 81.

74. Gao Yongxiao, "Taixu dashi de sixiang tixi" (The System of Thought of the Venerable Master Taixu), 27.

75. Hsiang-kuang Chou, *T'ai Hsü: His Life and Teachings* (Allahabad, India: Indo-Chinese Literature Publications, 1957), 9–10. Yinshun calls attention to the fact that, in his 1929 lecture "Sheme shi foxue" (What is Buddhism?), Taixu added a fourth category of *guo* ("fruits"), under which he projected the study of the results of faith, morality, concentration, wisdom, and so forth for laity and monastics. See Yinshun, *Taixu dashi nianpu* (Chronological Biography), 81; consult also Taixu, *Taixu dashi quanshu* (Complete Works), 1.1.6: 257–268.

76. See Yang Huinan, *Dangdai fojiao sixiang zhanwang* (A Survey of Contemporary Buddhist Thought), (Taipei, 1991), 106. Consult also Taixu, "Wo zenyang panshe yiqie fofa" (How I Divide all Buddhist Teachings), in *Taixu dashi quanshu* (Complete Works), 1.2.26: 509–520.

77. Reichelt, *The Transformed Abbot*, 155.

78. Xuming, *Taixu dashi shengping shiji* (A Record of the Life of the Venerable Master Taixu), 18.

79. Yinshun, *Taixu dashi nianpu* (Chronological Biography), 92. For Taixu's own account of his trip to Japan and Taiwan, see Taixu, "Taixu zizhuan" (Autobiography), in *Taixu dashi quanshu* (Complete Works), 19.58.18: 215–224.

80. Yinshun, *Taixu dashi nianpu* (Chronological Biography), 97.

81. Taixu, "Taixu zizhuan" (Autobiography), in *Taixu dashi quanshu* (Complete Works), 19.58.18: 226.

82. Xuming, *Taixu dashi shengping shiji* (A Record of the Life of the Venerable Master Taixu), 18.

83. Taixu, "Taixu zizhuan" (Autobiography), in *Taixu dashi quanshu* (Complete Works), 19.58.18: 226.

84. From the first volume (1920) of *Haichao yin*, translated in Tsu, "Present Tendencies in Chinese Buddhism," 506. Brackets are the translator's, with the exception of the inserted date.

85. See Taixu, "Jueshe xuanyan" (Public Announcement of the Bodhi Society), in *Taixu dashi quanshu* (Complete Works), 19.61.144: 1016–1018. The title in the index differs slightly from the actual title of the text. Millican provides a rather poor translation of the regulations in his "Tai Hsü and Modern Buddhism," 329–330.

86. Translated in Tsu, "Present Tendencies in Chinese Buddhism," 506–507. Brackets are the translator's.

87. Ibid., 505. Romanization of Sanskrit altered.

88. Editorial "Note" entitled "Buddhist Revival in China," *Eastern Buddhist* 3/1 (June 1924): 86.

89. Callahan, "T'ai Hsü and the New Buddhist Movement," 157. See Taixu, "Zhengli sengqie zhidu lun" (The Reorganization of the Sangha System), in *Taixu dashi quanshu* (Complete Works), 9.33.1: 1–185.

90. Welch, *The Buddhist Revival in China*, 52. Welch relies primarily on what he considers to be the final version of the plan, as described by Taixu's disciple Fafang (1904–1951) in "Chugoku Bukkyō no genjō" (The Present State of Chinese Buddhism), in *Nikka bukkyō kenkyukai nempō daiichinen* (First Annual Report of the Japanese-Chinese Research Society (Kyoto, 1936), 28–47.

91. Cressy, "A Study in Indigenous Religions," 682.

92. The organization was sometimes referred to as the Hankou Buddhist Society (Hankou fojiao hui). The membership statistic is cited in Boorman, ed., *Biographical Dictionary of Republican China*, 3: 209.

93. Cressy, "A Study in Indigenous Religions," 709.

94. Questions remain about all the connections between the Right Faith Buddhist Society of Hankou and the Wuchang Buddhist Institute. See Welch, *The Buddhist Revival in China*, 311–312. James B. Pratt credits the school's founding to "ex-governor Li of Guangdong," who subsequently called Taixu to be its head. Consult Pratt, "A Report on the Present Condition of Buddhism," *Chinese Social and Political Science Review* 8 (1924): 25. However, Weihuan gives full credit to Taixu. Cf. Wei-huan, "Buddhism in Modern China," 147. Weihuan also reports that Taixu and Li Kaishen founded a "Buddhist Ladies Academy" (Wuchang nü foxue yuan) in 1924 as a branch of the Wuchang Buddhist Institute (ibid., 149).

95. Pratt, "A Report on the Present Condition of Buddhism," 25.

96. Xuming, *Taixu dashi shengping shiji* (A Record of the Life of the Venerable Master Taixu), 25.

97. There is disagreement about the dates for the Bali sanzang yuan in Xi'an. Chou Hsiang-kuang states that in 1935 Taixu "established a College of Pali Tripiṭaka at Daxingshan Temple of Xi'an" (see Chou, *T'ai Hsü: His Life and Teachings*, 13). Welch gives the school's dates as 1939–1945, but admits that his dating for some the seminaries in operation in the Republican period is uncertain (*The Buddhist Revival in China*, 286). Much more reliable is the date given by Yinshun, Xuming, and Dongchu, all of whom state that the school was established in the spring of 1945. Cf. Yinshun, *Taixu dashi nianpu* (Chronological Biography), 516; Xuming, *Taixu dashi shengping shiji* (A Record of the Life of the Venerable Master Taixu), 25; and Dongchu, *Zhongguo fojiao jindai shi* (A History of Modern Chinese Buddhism), 1: 341–344. Yinshun also records the fact that the idea for establishing the school at the Xi'an temple was not proposed by Taixu until March 1941 (consult Yinshun, *Taixu dashi nianpu* [Chronological Biography], 487).

98. Yinshun, *Taixu dashi nianpu* (Chronological Biography), 123. Yongming Yanshou was the famous tenth-century advocate of a synthesis of Chan introspection and Pure Land devotionalism. For a brief description of his career, see *Fojiao mingren zhuan* (A Record of Famous Buddhists), 298–301. Consult also Albert Welter, *The Meaning of Myriad Good Deeds: A Study of Yung-ming Yen-shou and the Wan-shan Tung-kuei Chi* (New York: Peter Lang, 1994).

99. Reichelt, *The Transformed Abbot*, 81.

100. This is a statement by A. J. Brace, written to James B. Pratt and quoted in Pratt's *The Pilgrimage of Buddhism and a Buddhist Pilgrimage* (New York: Macmillan, 1928), 383–384. Paragraph structure mine.

101. On Buddhist social service, both Kenneth Ch'en and Chün-fang Yü comment on the institution of *bei tian* ("fields of compassion"), which since Tang times provided that tracts of land be set aside by monasteries specifically for social relief, such as medical treatment for the ill and the care of the elderly. See Ch'en, *Buddhism in China*, 295–296, and Yü, *The Renewal of Buddhism in China*, 25–26. Consult also Lai, "Chinese Buddhist and Christian Charities."

102. Reichelt, *The Transformed Abbot*, 83.

103. Welch, *The Buddhist Revival in China*, 79–80.

104. For a description of the work of the many local Buddhist organizations springing up in the early 1920s, see Tai Ping-heng, "Modern Chinese Buddhism," *Chinese Recorder* 56 (1925): 89–95.

105. John Blofeld, *The Jewel in the Lotus: An Outline of Present Day Buddhism in China* (1948; Westport: Hyperion Press, 1975), 58–59.

106. Welch, *The Buddhist Revival in China*, 322.

107. Reichelt, *The Transformed Abbot*, 83.

108. Consult C. B. Day, *Chinese Peasant Cults* (Shanghai: Kelly and Walsh, 1946), 198.

CHAPTER 3: AN ECUMENICAL VISION FOR GLOBAL MISSION

1. Xuming, *Taixu dashi shengping shiji* (A Record of the Life of the Venerable Master Taixu), 22.

2. Welch, *The Buddhist Revival in China*, 55.

3. Huiyuan (344–416) was the most famous disciple of Daoan of Xiangyang (312–385). A representative of "gentry Buddhism," the Buddhism that developed among the upper classes in south China during the Eastern Jin dynasty (317–420), Huiyuan is remembered for his interest in meditation and is recognized as the first patriarch of the Pure Land school in China. See *Fojiao mingren zhuan* (A Record of Famous Buddhists), 36–41.

4. Taixu, "Taixu zizhuan" (Autobiography), in *Taixu dashi quanshu* (Complete Works), 19.58.18: 272–274. Taixu notes that he did not anticipate a complete rebuilding of the ancient monastery but only a limited restoration. He also reports that as the lecture series got underway on Lu Shan, western Christian missionaries and Chinese Christians in the area were concerned enough to monitor their activities, so that he frequently had to respond to criticisms of Buddhist thought and practice from missionaries who attended his lectures.

5. Reichelt, "A Conference of Chinese Buddhist Leaders," *Chinese Recorder* 54 (November 1923): 667. Reichelt notes that the subject of his lecture was the introductory part of the Gospel of John, Chapter One, verses 1–18, which refers to "the Word," or "Dao." In the lecture, "I tried to show," he wrote, "how this Dao had been eternally working from the very beginning, giving life and light, form and glory to all living beings, and how as a light (Vers. 4) it shineth in the darkness and the darkness comprehendeth it not. Nevertheless beams from this light . . . meet us everywhere . . . so that everywhere we find altars to 'an unknown God.' But God in his abundant love and mercy did not stop with this. He let that everlasting Dao come near to us . . . to be manifested and appear on earth in a man, in a 'son of man' *(renzi)*" (ibid., 668).

6. Ibid., 669.

7. Dongchu, *Zhongguo fojiao jindai shi* (A History of Modern Chinese Buddhism), 1: 282.

8. See Taixu, "Taixu zizhuan" (Autobiography), in *Taixu dashi quanshu* (Complete Works), 19.58.18: 276. Although the information does not come from Taixu's autobiography, Yinshun erroneously includes the Norwegian Lutheran missionary Karl Reichelt (Ai Xiangde) among the number of self-professed Buddhists who attended the conference. Consult Yinshun, *Taixu dashi nianpu* (Chronological Biography), 180.

9. Dongchu, *Zhongguo fojiao jindai shi* (A History of Modern Chinese Buddhism), 1: 282.

10. For a lengthy account of Changxing's distinguished career, see Dongchu, *Zhongguo fojiao jindai shi* (A History of Modern Chinese Buddhism), 2: 850–879.

11. Yinshun, *Taixu dashi nianpu* (Chronological Biography), 180.

12. Dongchu, *Zhongguo fojiao jindai shi* (A History of Modern Chinese Buddhism), 1: 290. The text of Taixu's address is included on pages 286–290.

13. Ibid., 1: 282–283. Emphasis mine.

14. The text of the constitution is included in ibid., 279.

15. Yinshun, *Taixu dashi nianpu* (Chronological Biography), 198. See a short essay that Taixu composed in Beijing at the time, "Zhonghua fojiao lianhe hui dang ruhe zuzhi ye" (How Shall the Chinese Buddhist Federation Be Properly Organized?), in *Taixu dashi quanshu* (Complete Works), 9.34.13: 373–374.

16. In his autobiography, Taixu states that the 1925 conference in Tokyo had a seven-day agenda. See Taixu, "Taixu zizhuan" (Autobiography), in *Taixu dashi quanshu* (Complete Works), 19.58.18: 294. Yinshun, however, points out that this statement is in error and that the conference formally ended on the afternoon of November 3. Cf. Yinshun, *Taixu dashi nianpu* (Chronological Biography), 206.

17. Dongchu concurs with the statement by Taixu in his autobiography that he and Daojie shared the responsibilities of chairing the delegation; see Dongchu, *Zhongguo fojiao jindai shi* (A History of Modern Chinese Buddhism), 1: 294; "Taixu zizhuan" (Autobiography), in *Taixu dashi quanshu* (Complete Works), 19.58.18: 293). Welch states, however, that "the official head of the Chinese delegation and Chinese vice-chairman of the conference was Daojie, under whom Taixu had studied twenty years before" (*The Buddhist Revival in China,* 332–333). According to Yinshun, the Chinese delegation was comprised of twenty-six persons (see Yinshun, *Taixu dashi nianpu* (Chronological Biography), 204), whereas Dongchu gives the number as twenty-eight, and Welch cites the official Japanese conference report on the delegation as giving the number twenty. Consult Welch, *The Buddhist Revivial in China,* 333, and Bukkyō Rengo-kai, ed., *Tōa Bukkyō takai kiyō* (Summary of the East Asian Buddhist Conference), (Tokyo, 1926). Taixu claims in his autobiography that more than ten thousand people turned out to welcome the Chinese delegation upon their arrival in Tokyo. See Taixu, "Taixu zizhuan" (Autobiography), in *Taixu dashi quanshu* (Complete Works), 19.58.18: 293.

18. *Eastern Buddhist* 3/4 (December 1925): 388. Paragraph structure mine.

19. Taixu, "A Statement to Asiatic Buddhists," *Young East* 1/6 (November 8, 1925): 180.

20. Ibid.

21. Welch cites the opinion of an informant who was a member of the Chinese delegation, to the effect that the conference was essentially a Japanese propaganda event. Indeed, the person charged, "Japan's mouth had long been watering for China." See his *The Buddhist Revival in China,* 167.

22. Taixu, "A Statement to Asiatic Buddhists," 179.

23. *Eastern Buddhist* 3/4 (December 1925): 387. Also noted was the fact that the educational section of the conference adopted a resolution on the fundamental principles of Buddhism: "(1) the denial of God as creator of the world; (2) universal brotherhood with no racial discrimination; (3) impartial love for all beings; (4) idealism against materialistic tendencies; and (5) salvation based on self-enlightenment." Ibid.

24. Yinshun, *Taixu dashi nianpu* (Chronological Biography), 210.

25. See the announcement entitled "Standing Committee of the Far Eastern Buddhist Conference," *Young East* 1/6 (November 8, 1925): 176.

26. Xuming, *Taixu dashi shengping shiji* (A Record of the Life of the Venerable Master Taixu), 23.

27. Welch, *The Buddhist Revival in China*, 57. Welch gives no justification for his assertion that Reginald Johnston and Liang Qichao "had refused to attend the conference in 1923." In fact, Reichelt states that "Telegrams and letters of regret at enforced absence came from Mr. Liang Qichao, Mr. R. F. Johnston in Beijing, and others" ("A Conference of Chinese Buddhist Leaders," 667). Of course, Reichelt could simply be reporting information given to him by Taixu's disciples.

28. Yinshun, *Taixu dashi nianpu* (Chronological Biography), 226.

29. The May Thirtieth Incident of 1925 involved a massive nationwide protest against the Japanese owners of a cotton mill in Shanghai who killed and injured Chinese workers who were striking for better wages and working conditions, as well as against the British-dominated municipal court in the city, which not only failed to prosecute the Japanese owners but arrested protesting Chinese workers for disturbing the peace. See Hsü, *The Rise of Modern China*, 533–534.

30. Consult Welch, *The Buddhist Revival in China*, 58.

31. Yinshun, *Taixu dashi nianpu* (Chronological Biography), 216.

32. Reichelt commented further that the obvious pain felt by Taixu and other Buddhist leaders because of the ignorance and insensitivity of Christian missionaries in China led Reichelt to pray, "Lord Jesus, take away from me and my fellow workers that spirit of arrogance which throws such shame on thy precious name." See Reichelt, "A Conference of Chinese Buddhist Leaders," 669.

33. The term "portability" is suggested by Lewis R. Lancaster, "The Portable and Fixed Buddhism: The Question of the Future of Buddhism," in *1990 Foguang Shan guoji fojiao xueshu huiyi lunwen ji* (1990 Anthology of the Foguang Shan International Buddhist Conference), 26–35 (Kaohsiung, Taiwan, 1992).

34. Clarence H. Hamilton, "An Hour with T'ai Shu, Master of the Law," *The Open Court* 42 (1928), 165–167.

35. Yinshun, *Taixu dashi nianpu* (Chronological Biography), 257.

36. See ibid., 257–258. Welch comments that the Chinese Buddhist Study Association "turned out to be nothing more than a sort of 'Sunday Evening Club,' whose ten to twenty members met once a week at the Wanshou si in Nanjing and listened to a lecture on the sūtras given by Taixu when he was available, or by others when he was not. Sometimes up to several dozen nonmembers would also come to listen. During the Sino-Japanese War the group moved to Chongqing, where it held Sunday lectures at the Chang'an si." See Welch, *The Buddhist Revival in China*, 65.

37. *Eastern Buddhist* 3/4 (December 1925): 391. Professor Petzold especially thought that the focus of such research should be the comprehensive Tendai (Tiantai) school

of Mahāyāna. Lest anyone think that Taixu picked up the idea for an international Buddhist institute at the Tokyo conference, Yinshun notes that the reformer had already made such a proposal prior to his attendance. See Yinshun, *Taixu dashi nianpu* (Chronological Biography), 205.

38. *Eastern Buddhist* 4/1 (September 1926): 81–82.

39. Manzhi and Mochan, eds., *Taixu dashi huanyou ji* (A Record of the Venerable Master Taixu's World Travel), (Taipei, 1978), 167 (hereafter cited as "World Travel").

40. Ibid., 19.

41. Yinshun, *Taixu dashi nianpu* (Chronological Biography), 268.

42. Manzhi and Mochan, eds., *Taixu dashi huanyou ji* (World Travel), 131–133.

43. Ibid. Welch cites an anonymous reviewer who remarked about this list, "The names of several orientalists are cited, not without confusing the names of those who have joined with those whom they hope to have join." (See *Bulletin de l'Association Française des Amis de l'Orient*, no. 7, 93–94.) Although the founding meeting in Paris of the World Buddhist Institute took place on October 20, 1928, those who were reported in attendance at the first actual meeting of the organization, on January 3, 1929, included none of the scholars listed. Welch comments cynically, though perhaps not without some justification, that "Taixu seems simply to have been up to his old trick of borrowing prestigious names without authorization from their owners." See Welch, *The Buddhist Revival in China*, 307.

44. Consult the notice of Miss Lounsbery's death in A. A. G. Bennett, "A Short Biography of Miss Grace Constant Lounsbery," *Maha Bodhi* 73/3–4 (March–April 1965): 83–84.

45. Based on the recollections of an informant and the previously mentioned journal entry in the *Bulletin de l'Association Française des Amis de l'Orient* (see note 43 above), Welch concluded that Taixu's lectures in France were a thorough disappointment to those who invited him. See Welch, *The Buddhist Revival in China*, 60–62. Grace Constant Lounsbery, it is true, wrote a letter to Taixu a year after his visit to Paris in which she remarked, "If we are to have the pleasure of welcoming you again, it is most necessary to bring a Chinese versed in Buddhism who speaks French and English correctly—so much that we wished to ask or hear from you was lost through interpreters not learned in Buddhism" (*Chinese Buddhist* 1/4 [January 1931]: 156). Yet however pertinent Welch's conclusions are to a realistic appraisal of Taixu's accomplishments, he is perhaps too harsh in his evaluation of the Buddhist master's trip to France. His judgment seems to be primarily based on disappointments expressed about this one speech, despite the fact that Taixu delivered several lectures in Paris and held a number of other formal and informal meetings there, as elsewhere.

46. Manzhi and Mochan, eds., *Taixu dashi huanyou ji* (World Travel), 205–206. For a translation or paraphrase of the Chinese master's lectures in France (probably a trans-

lation from a French transcription into English, since it is not entirely faithful to the Chinese text), see Taixu, *Lectures in Buddhism*. This passage roughly corresponds to the section of that text on pp. 24–26.

47. Manzhi and Mochan, eds., *Taixu dashi huanyou ji* (World Travel), 91.

48. See ibid., 190–198. For Taixu's further development of this perspective, also consult his "Shehui guan" (A View of Society), in ibid., 209–233.

49. Yinshun, *Taixu dashi nianpu* (Chronological Biography), 278.

50. Taixu, "Der Buddhismus in Geschichte und Gegenwart," *Sinica* 3 (1928): 196.

51. Manzhi and Mochan, eds., *Taixu dashi huanyou ji* (World Travel), 134.

52. Richard Wilhelm, "Chinesischer Bildersaal: Der Grossabt Schï Tai Hü," *Sinica* 4 (1929): 16.

53. Chen Huanzhang was a disciple of Kang Youwei. In 1913, he founded the Confucian Association in order to promote Confucianism as the state religion of China.

54. *The New York Times,* Wednesday, March 6, 1929, 18.

55. Ibid.

56. Welch, *The Buddhist Revival in China,* 62. See also *Buddhism in England* 3/7 (January 1929): 127.

57. Manzhi and Mochan, eds., *Taixu dashi huanyou ji* (World Travel), 139–140. Obvious typesetting errors are corrected, and the paragraph structure is mine.

58. Ibid., 137. Interestingly, the Maha Bodhi Society in Britain refused to cooperate in the establishment of the London Buddhist Joint Committee, perhaps because of the broad representative powers that the new organization claimed.

59. Ibid., 138.

60. Consult *Buddhism in England* 3/7 (January 1929): 162. Quoted in Welch, *The Buddhist Revival in China,* 59.

61. Dongchu, *Zhongguo fojiao jindai shi* (A History of Modern Chinese Buddhism), 2: 805.

62. Yinshun, *Taixu dashi nianpu* (Chronological Biography), 290. Chou Hsiang-kuang is obviously incorrect in stating that Taixu inaugurated the Chinese Buddhism Association in 1929 and that he was its first president, because Taixu had not yet returned from his trip to Europe and the United States. See Chou, *T'ai Hsü: His Life and Teachings,* 17.

63. Dongchu, *Zhongguo fojiao jindai shi* (A History of Modern Chinese Buddhism), 2: 808.

64. Yinshun, *Taixu dashi nianpu* (Chronological Biography), 322–323.

65. Ibid., 325.

66. *Xiandai sengqie* (Modern Sangha) 4/2 (June 1931): 180. Cited in Welch, *The Buddhist Revival in China*, 43.

67. Yinshun, *Taixu dashi nianpu* (Chronological Biography), 326. Welch avers that Wang Yiting had "gone over to the opposition." This may have been partially true. However, although the relationship between Taixu and Yuanying was severely damaged, Wang Yiting appears to have been able to maintain a relationship with the reformer. Perhaps Taixu ultimately understood that, given the trying circumstances and the internal political stalemate that the association was facing, Wang was only trying to find a mediating position. Vis-à-vis Taixu's relationship with Yuanying, it is also interesting that after Yuanying suffered a stroke in March 1946, Taixu went to call on him. See Yinshun, *Taixu dashi nianpu* (Chronological Biography), 523, 526.

68. Karl L. Reichelt, "Present Situation in Buddhism," in *China Christian Year Book, 1932–1933* (Shanghai: Christian Literature Society, 1933), 109–110.

69. John K. Fairbank et al., *East Asia: Tradition and Transformation* (Boston: Houghton Mifflin Company, 1978), 799.

70. W. Y. Chen, "The Ancient Religions in China Today," *China Christian Year Book, 1936–1937* (Shanghai: Christian Literature Society, 1937), 109; Chen indicates that the full text of the letter was published in *Fojiao xinwen* (Buddhist News), July 16, 1937.

71. W. Y. Chen claims that the cable was sent on July 22, 1937, whereas according to Yinshun, the date was July 16. See Chen, "The Ancient Religions in China Today," 109; and Yinshun, *Taixu dashi nianpu* (Chronological Biography), 418.

72. Yinshun, *Taixu dashi nianpu* (Chronological Biography), 415–416. The text of the plan is included in Taixu, "Fojiao heping guoji de tiyi" (A Proposal for Buddhists Bringing Peace to the Nations), in *Taixu dashi quanshu* (Complete Works), 10.35.52: 296–303. Taixu hoped to establish a society that would bring together Buddhists from all over the world to study ways to foster peace and cooperation among all peoples. He made a special plea to the Japanese in the plan, stating: "Chinese and Japanese Buddhism have special intimate connections because of having the same culture. Japanese have in the past studied Chinese Buddhism, just as Chinese now often translate Japanese Buddhist studies. Given the conflict and tense diplomatic relations that exist between Japan and China, if Chinese and Japanese Buddhists are able to respond out of the peaceful spirit of Buddhism, they will be able to turn around Japan's ambition of invading China, so that the Chinese people may restore their self-determination and they and the Japanese may all be truly equal and amicable friends" (ibid., 302).

73. Taixu, "Zhi Riben fojiaotu dian" (A Cable to Japanese Buddhists), in *Taixu dashi quanshu* (Complete Works), 15.48.64: 327.

74. Yinshun, *Taixu dashi nianpu* (Chronological Biography), 418–419.

75. Chou, *T'ai Hsü: His Life and Teachings,* 17–18.

76. Chen, "The Ancient Religions in China Today," 108–109.

77. Hsü, *The Rise of Modern China,* 584–585. Wang Kemin's name was corrected.

78. Taixu, "Wo de fojiao geming shibai shi" (The History of My Failed Buddhist Revolution), in *Taixu dashi quanshu* (Complete Works), 19.57.8: 62–63.

79. "Buddhist Leader Returns," *China at War* 4/6 (July 1940): 34. See also Yinshun, *Taixu dashi nianpu* (Chronological Biography), 446–471.

80. Yinshun, *Taixu dashi nianpu* (Chronological Biography), 450. Yinshun's figure, which might easily be taken as an exaggeration, is in fact supported by the previously cited report in *China at War,* which states that the reformer was greeted in Rangoon by "more than 10,000 people" ("Buddhist Leader Returns," *China at War* 4/6 [July 1940]: 35).

81. Yinshun, *Taixu dashi nianpu* (Chronological Biography), 448.

82. See H. G. Quaritch Wales, "Buddhism as a Japanese Propaganda Instrument," with a commentary by Lin Yutang, *Free World* 5/5 (May 1943): 428–432. Wales writes: "In the countries of Southeastern Asia, the Japanese had to go about their cultural penetration in a more diplomatic manner, at least before military conquest. They endeavored to establish happy relations by sending their so-called International Buddhist Missionaries on good-will missions of a tentative character" (429).

83. Yinshun, *Taixu dashi nianpu* (Chronological Biography), 448–449.

84. See Welch, *The Buddhist Revival in China,* 63.

85. See a lengthy report of one of Taixu's conversations in India in Yinshun, *Taixu dashi nianpu* (Chronological Biography), 459–462. The Chinese master does refer to Japan but frequently speaks of the war of resistance without specifically mentioning the Japanese. There is almost the sense in Taixu's rhetoric that the Japanese are the unfortunate victims of a western imperialistic materialism that has overcome them.

86. "Buddhist Leader Returns," *China at War* 4/6 (July 1940): 35.

87. Ibid.

88. Taixu, "Chuguo fangwen jingguo ji shijie san da wenhua zhi tiaohe" (Journeying Abroad and the Harmonization of the World's Three Great Cultures), in *Taixu dashi quanshu* (Complete Works), 18.56.167: 628.

89. For an account of the meeting between Taixu and Malalasekera, see Yinshun, *Taixu dashi nianpu* (Chronological Biography), 466–467.

90. Xuming, *Taixu dashi shengping shiji* (A Record of the Life of the Venerable Master Taixu), 28.

91. Welch, *The Buddhist Revival in China,* 64.

92. Blofeld, *The Wheel of Life,* 177–179.

93. Yinshun, *Taixu dashi nianpu* (Chronological Biography), 487.

94. Welch, *The Buddhist Revival in China,* 46.

95. Yinshun, *Taixu dashi nianpu* (Chronological Biography), 497. The date of the association's establishment is given as June 1943 in Chinese Ministry of Information, comp., *The China Handbook, 1937–45,* 592. The latter date is probably incorrect because a *Time* magazine article of June 14, 1943, entitled "Chungking Meeting," about the National Christian Council of China's first meeting since 1937, acknowledges that earlier that same month in which the conference convened, "one vehicle of interfaith cooperation among China's religions was already functioning in the All-China Inter-religious Association." The article is accompanied by photographs of Taixu, Bai Chongxi, W. Y. Chen, and Paul Yu Bin, although Taixu and W. Y. Chen are mistakenly cross-identified in the caption. Consult *Time* 52 (June, 14, 1943): 50.

96. Both the cited *Time* article and the report in *The China Handbook, 1937–45* include Methodist Bishop W. Y. Chen, although Yinshun does not mention him. *The China Handbook* also lists the executive supervisors at the time as Chen Mingshu, Tang Kesan, and J. L. Huang (Huang Renlin), and the secretary-general as Wei Limin.

97. Chinese Ministry of Information, comp., *The China Handbook, 1937–45,* 592.

98. Welch, *The Buddhist Revival in China,* 148. See also Blofeld, *Jewel in the Lotus,* 23, 48. Dongchu devotes a short section of his history of modern Chinese Buddhism to Feng Yuxiang's efforts to destroy Buddhism; see his *Zhongguo fojiao jindai shi* (A History of Modern Chinese Buddhism), 1: 345–346. Consult also the editorial, "Views of a Christian Leader in the Chinese Army," *Chinese Recorder* 54 (June 1923), which includes a picture of the general.

99. Kitagawa reported that the organization was still active in Taiwan in 1962, when he visited the island. See Joseph M. Kitagawa, "Buddhism in Taiwan Today," *France-Aise* (Tokyo) 18/174 (Juillet-Août, 1962): 441.

100. Consult Boorman, ed., *Biographical Dictionary of Republican China,* 4: 67, and Kang Junbi, "Jingdao benhui gu lishizhang Yu shuji shishi shi zhounian" (A Memorial for the Association of Chinese Religious Believers' First Chairman of the Board of Directors, Cardinal Yu, on the Tenth Anniversary of his Death), in *Yu Bin shuji shishi shi zhounian jinian wenji* (Memorial Volume on the Tenth Anniversary of the Death of Cardinal Yu Bin), (Taipei: Fu Jen Catholic University, 1988), 89. Further research is needed on the question of the organization's character and status, especially after Yu Bin's death in 1978.

101. See "Asian Religious Leaders Tour U.S.A. on Behalf of Religious Freedom," *The National Catholic Reporter* (November 6, 1977). Consult also "Taiwan Cardinal Yu-Pin Warns U.S. Against Dangers Tied to Recognition of One China," *St. Louis*

Review (October 28, 1977), 3. Despite the fact that the Presbyterian Church in Taiwan has historically advocated Taiwanese self-determination and opposed the Guomindang's takeover of the island after World War II, Chen Xizun, who served for many years as the minister of the Shuanglian Church in Taipei, was an outspoken supporter of the Guomindang.

102. Taixu, "Zhongguo zongjiaotu lianyi hui zanci" (Commendations for the Association of Chinese Religious Believers), in *Taixu dashi quanshu* (Complete Works), 13.41.32: 342–345.

103. Chinese Ministry of Information, comp., *The China Handbook, 1937–45* 620.

104. According to the records of the School History Office and Chinese Catholic Museum of Fu Jen University in Taipei (Furen daxue xiaoshi shi ji wenwu guan), there are two dates recorded for the organization's founding: July 2, 1941, and October 21, 1944. Perhaps the latter was the first functional date for an institute established on paper three years earlier. I have found no evidence that the Philosophy of Life Institute's lecture series and other activities continued beyond Cardinal Yu Bin's death in 1978.

105. Yinshun, *Taixu dashi nianpu* (Chronological Biography), 519. On Zhangjia Hutukhtu's career, see Dongchu, *Zhongguo fojiao jindai shi* (A History of Modern Chinese Buddhism), 1: 386–390. On Li Zikuan, consult ibid., 535–540.

106. Taixu, *Taixu dashi quanshu* (Complete Works), 9.34.26: 445–446.

107. Yinshun, *Taixu dashi nianpu* (Chronological Biography), 520.

108. See Taixu, "Fojiao buyao zu zhengdang" (Buddhism Does Not Want to Organize a Political Party), in *Taixu dashi quanshu* (Complete Works), 10.35.32: 184–187. Taixu wrote several other articles on this subject, such as the one in February 1947, just a month prior to his death, entitled "Guanyu fotu zu dang wenti" (On the Question of Buddhists Organizing a Political Party). See Yinshun, *Taixu dashi nianpu* (Chronological Biography), 536.

109. Welch, *The Buddhist Revival in China,* 47.

110. Reichelt portrays Taixu as a "broken man" at the end of his life, an exaggerated portrayal for which I find little justification. In my judgment, Reichelt reaches this conclusion not because so many of Taixu's reformist ideas remained unrealized, but primarily because, in Reichelt's eyes, Taixu "remained a stranger to the power and blessing of [Christian] faith and prayer." See Reichelt, *The Transformed Abbot,* 157.

111. Yinshun, *Taixu dashi nianpu* (Chronological Biography), 538.

112. On Shanyin's career, see Dongchu, *Zhongguo fojiao jindai shi* (A History of Modern Chinese Buddhism), 2: 830–834.

113. Yinshun, *Taixu dashi nianpu* (Chronological Biography), 539. Relic photographs are provided in the text. For eulogies written by Li Zikuan and Xuyun, as

well as memorial songs composed by monks and laymen, consult "Zhuidao zhi ye" (Commemoration Page), in *Xianggang fojiao* (Buddhism in Hong Kong), 286 (June 1960): 35–38.

114. Yinshun, *Taixu dashi nianpu* (Chronological Biography), 542–543. In France, Taixu's death was announced in the next issue of the *Bulletin des Amis du Bouddhisme: La Pensée Bouddhique,* acknowledging the Chinese master's influence on Grace Constant Lounsbery and other important members of the society who supported his work. See *La Pensée Bouddhique* 2/11 (July 1947): 23.

115. Xuming, *Taixu dashi shengping shiji* (A Record of the Life of the Venerable Master Taixu), 1.

116. Welch, *The Buddhist Revival of China,* 71.

CHAPTER 4: MAHĀYĀNA AND THE MODERN WORLD

1. Tsu, "Present Tendencies in Chinese Buddhism," 501.

2. As Chün-fang Yü notes, especially in smaller hereditary temples that had no temple land, monks were encouraged to spend much time performing funeral services for which they received extra personal stipends. "Lured by fame and money," she writes, "young monks who were once serious about their religious cultivation became only interested in worldly pursuits and ended up moral and physical wrecks. Temple managers who were eager to drum up business treated the monks like money-making machines. Professional female agents served as intermediaries between patrons and monks. They set up three categories of monks who were classified not on the basis of knowledge or cultivation, but purely on that of physical appearances and singing voice. Probably for the same crude commercial reasons, scriptural chanting in the regions near Shanghai came to be interspersed with the singing of popular melodies of a decidedly secular nature. The performance of funeral services degenerated into popular entertainment." See her introduction to Chen-hua, *In Search of the Dharma,* 15. For Chen-hua's account of his own experience at the small Dongyue Temple (Dongyue miao) in Nanjing, see ibid., 77–91.

3. Tsu, "Present Tendencies in Chinese Buddhism," 504.

4. Consult Yinshun, *Taixu dashi nianpu* (Chronological Biography), 57.

5. Millican, "Tai Hsü and Modern Buddhism," 326.

6. Taixu, "Wushen lun" (On Atheism), in *Taixu dashi quanshu* (Complete Works), 13.41.27: 291.

7. According to James B. Pratt, Taixu's public acceptance of many traditional forms of Buddhist cultic observance and self-cultivation, even if personally he was not appreciative of them, marked the basic difference between him and the more radical and abrasive Ouyang Jingwu. See Pratt, "A Report on the Present Condition of Buddhism," 23–27.

8. The printed index alone of Taixu's writings in his *Taixu dashi quanshu* (Complete Works) is 138 pages long, with the collection containing 1,438 separate documents with a total length in excess of 16,400 pages of Chinese text. Moreover, the set does not include a number of Taixu's works.

9. Whalen Lai so characterizes Taixu in his introduction to Yin-shun, *The Way to Buddhahood: Instructions from a Modern Chinese Master*, trans. Wing H. Yeung (Boston: Wisdom Publications, 1998), xx.

10. Yu-yue Tsu, "Trends of Thought and Religion in China Today," *The Open Court* 47 (1933): 452.

11. Taixu, "Fofa zai shijian bu li shijian jue" (The Dharma in this World Concerns a This-Worldly Enlightenment), in *Taixu dashi quanshu* (Complete Works), 18.55.66: 263.

12. Taixu, *Foxue de jianglai* (The Future of Buddhism), (Hong Kong, 1935), 13–14.

13. Ibid., 15.

14. Ibid.

15. See Taixu, "Xiyang wenhua yu dongyang wenhua" (Western Culture and Eastern Culture), in *Taixu dashi quanshu* (Complete Works), 13.40.4: 23–30.

16. Consult Max Weber, "Asceticism and the Spirit of Capitalism," chapter 5 in his *The Protestant Ethic and the Spirit of Capitalism,* trans., Talcott Parsons (New York: Charles Scribner's Sons, 1958), 155–183.

17. Taixu, *Lectures in Buddhism,* 43.

18. Yinshun, *Taixu dashi nianpu* (Chronological Biography), 459–460.

19. Taixu, *Foxue de jianglai* (The Future of Buddhism), 6.

20. Taixu, *Lectures in Buddhism,* 29, 32.

21. Ibid., 27.

22. Ibid., 48–50. Obvious grammatical errors corrected and paragraph structure altered.

23. Quoted in Tsu, "Trends of Thought and Religion in China Today," 450–451. See also James B. Pratt, "Buddhism and Scientific Thinking," *Journal of Religion* 14/1 (January 1934): 13–24.

24. Chan, *Religious Trends in Modern China,* 89.

25. Frank R. Millican, "Buddhism in the Light of Modern Thought as Interpreted by the Monk Tai Hsü," *Chinese Recorder* 57 (February 1926): 92–93. Chinese characters printed in the original text have been omitted.

26. For Taixu's 1928 lecture "Rensheng fojiao de shuoming" (An Explanation of a Buddhism for Human Life), see *Taixu dashi quanshu* (Complete Works), 2.5.17:

205–216. For his 1946 lecture "Rensheng de fojiao" (A Buddhism for Human Life), see ibid., 2.5.17: 238–242.

27. Hong Jinlian, *Taixu dashi fojiao xiandaihua zhi yanjiu* (Research into the Venerable Master Taixu's Modernization of Buddhism), (Taipei, 1995), 137ff. (hereafter cited as "Modernization").

28. See Taixu, "Duiyu zhongguo fojiao geming seng de xunci" (Instructions to Chinese Buddhism's Revolutionary Monks), in *Taixu dashi quanshu* (Complete Works), 9.34.47: 598.

29. See ibid., 598–603.

30. Hong, *Taixu dashi fojiao xiandaihua zhi yanjiu* (Modernization), 153.

31. On Liang's perspectives on religion and culture, see Alitto, *The Last Confucian*.

32. Liang Shuming, *Dong Xi wenhua ji qi zhexue* (Eastern and Western Cultures and Their Philosophies), (1922; Taipei reprint, 1960), 202, 210–211.

33. Taixu, "Lun Liang Shuming dong xi wenhua ji qi zhexue" (On Liang Shuming's Eastern and Western Cultures and Their Philosophies) in *Taixu dashi quanshu* (Complete Works), 16.50.38: 306.

34. Taixu, "Foxue zhi rensheng daode" (Buddhism's Human Morality), in *Taixu dashi quanshu* (Complete Works), 2.5.10: 162.

35. Yin-shun, *The Way to Buddhahood,* x–xii. For the Chinese original, see Yinshun, *Cheng fo zhi dao* (Taipei, 1994), 3–4.

36. Burton Watson, trans., *The Vimalakīrti Sūtra* (New York: Columbia University Press, 1997), 128–129.

37. Taixu, "Ai zhi chongbai" (In Praise of Love), in *Taixu dashi quanshu* (Complete Works), 13.51.30: 333–334. This text represents a transcribed lecture that Taixu gave in 1926 in Shanghai, originally entitled "Ai zhi yanjiu" (Research on Love). Yinshun notes the title change, which is based on language that Taixu uses at the conclusion of the lecture. The text was first published in *Haichao yin* and can be found under its original title in *Haichao yin wenku* (Collected Essays from Haichao yin) 1/3 (Shanghai, 1931): 1–5.

38. Taixu, "Lun Liang Shuming dong xi wenhua ji qi zhexue" (On Liang Shuming's Eastern and Western Cultures and Their Philosophies) in *Taixu dashi quanshu* (Complete Works), 16.50.38: 304.

39. Taixu, "Rensheng fojiao de shuoming" (An Explanation of a Buddhism for Human Life), in *Taixu dashi quanshu* (Complete Works), 2.5.17: 206.

40. I have employed the now rather frequently used term "communitarian" to convey the meaning of what Taixu refers to in the above text as a *"zuzhi de qunzhonghua"* (literally, "an organized form of 'groupification'"). See ibid., 208.

41. Taixu, "Rensheng fojiao kaiti" (An Introduction to a Buddhism for Human Life), in *Taixu dashi quanshu* (Complete Works), 2.5.18: 220.

42. See Taixu, "Zongjiao goucheng zhi yuansu" (Elements in the Structure of Religions), in *Taixu dashi quanshu* (Complete Works), 13.41.25: 269–274.

43. Taixu, "Zongjiao duiyu xiandai renlei de gongxian" (The Contribution of Religion to Modern Human Beings), in *Taixu dashi quanshu* (Complete Works), 13.41.26: 279.

44. Ibid., 276–277, 279.

45. Ibid., 280–281.

46. See White, *What Is and What Ought to Be Done*, 123.

47. See Paul Tillich, *Systematic Theology*, 3 vols. (Chicago: University of Chicago Press, 1951–1963), especially vol. 3, Part 4/3, "The Divine Spirit and the Ambiguities of Life."

48. Taixu, "You ren zhi chengfo zhi lu" (The Path through the Human Realm to Becoming Buddhas), in *Taixu dashi quanshu* (Complete Works), 18.55.103: 413.

49. Taixu, "Chengfo jiushi yu geming jiuguo" (Becoming a Buddha to Save the World and Participating in a Revolution to Save the Country), in *Taixu dashi quanshu* (Complete Works), 15.48.37: 189. According to this text, the other four of the eight stages of the Buddha's career include his descent to this world in birth, his great renunciation in leaving the householder life, his period of austerities prior to enlightenment, and, finally, parinirvāṇa.

50. Ibid., 189–190. Paragraph structure mine.

51. Taixu, "Ziyou shiguan" (A Historical Perspective on Freedom), in *Taixu dashi quanshu* (Complete Works), 14.47.4: 247–347. Taixu advocates a globalized form of education, a socialized form of economics, and an internationalized form of government.

52. Welch, *The Buddhist Revival in China*, 157.

53. Taixu, "Taixu zizhuan" (Autobiography), in *Taixu dashi quanshu* (Complete Works), 19.58.18: 194.

54. Welch, *The Buddhist Revival in China*, 157. See *Fohua xin qingnian hui* (Buddhist New Youth Society) 2/2 (1924): 26.

55. Quoted in Arif Dirlik, "The Ideological Foundations of the New Life Movement: A Study in Counterrevolution," *Journal of Asian Studies* 34/4 (August 1975): 957–958. Brackets in the quotation are those of the translator. For a westerner's summary of the movement's goals at the time, see George W. Shepherd, "The New Life Movement," in *The China Christian Year Book, 1936–1937* (Shanghai: Christian Literature Society, 1937), 67–77.

56. Dirlik, "The Ideological Foundations of the New Life Movement," 976–978.

57. Taixu, "The Meaning of Buddhism," trans. Frank R. Millican, *Chinese Recorder* 65/11 (November 1934): 690.

58. Ibid.

59. See Taixu, "Pusa xing yu xin shenghuo yundong" (The Acts of a Bodhisattva and the New Life Movement), in *Taixu dashi quanshu* (Complete Works), 13.42.70: 713–716.

60. A copy of the 1928 photograph of Taixu and Chiang Kai-shek is included in an interesting collection of photographs of the Buddhist reformer published in the journal *Xianggang fojiao* (Buddhism in Hong Kong), 286 (June 1960): 17–23.

61. See Prip-Møller, *Chinese Buddhist Monasteries,* 366.

62. Taixu, "Pusa de zhengzhi" (The Politics of a Bodhisattva), in *Taixu dashi quanshu* (Complete Works), 13.44.101: 1041.

63. See Taixu, "Renqun zhengzhi yu fojiao sengzhi" (The Government of the People and the Government of the Buddhist Sangha), in *Taixu dashi quanshu* (Complete Works), 13.44.102: 1056.

64. Taixu, "Yi fofa piping shehui zhuyi" (Using the Buddhist Dharma to Criticize Socialism), in *Taixu dashi quanshu* (Complete Works), 13.44.110: 1210–1211.

65. Taixu, "Yi fofa jiejue xianshi kunnan" (Using Buddhism to Solve the Problems of this World), in *Taixu dashi quanshu* (Complete Works), 13.44.106: 1160. Unfortunately, Taixu's complementary "Gao pinruo jieji" (To the Poor and Weak Classes), which forms the second section of this text, was omitted in the printing of *Taixu dashi quanshu.* However, it can be found in *Haichao yin wenku* (Collected Essays from Haichao yin) 1/8 (Shanghai, 1931): 4–8.

66. See Taixu, "Sengqie yu zhengzhi" (The Sangha and Politics), in *Taixu dashi quanshu* (Complete Works), 10.35.31: 180.

67. Taixu, "Fojiao buyao zu zhengdang" (Buddhism Does Not Want to Organize a Political Party), in *Taixu dashi quanshu* (Complete Works), 10.35.32: 186–187.

68. Taixu, "Lianheguo zhansheng hou zhi pinghe shijie" (A Peaceful World After the Allied Victory), in *Taixu dashi quanshu* (Complete Works), 15.48.56: 295. A much condensed English version of this essay, citing an original Chinese version in *The New China Monthly* (August 1943), was published under the title, "A Peaceful World After Allied Victory," in *China at War* 11/6 (December 1943): 20–22. The latter journal, which identified Taixu as president of the Chinese Buddhist Association, was published by the China Information Committee, Chongqing, China, and distributed in the U.S. by the Chinese News Service.

69. Taixu, "A Statement to Asiatic Buddhists," 181.

70. Taixu, "Lianheguo zhansheng hou zhi pinghe shijie" (A Peaceful World After the Allied Victory), in *Taixu dashi quanshu* (Complete Works), 15.48.56: 288.

71. Taixu, "A Peaceful World After Allied Victory," 20–21.

72. Ibid., 21.

73. Ibid.

74. Taixu, "Lianheguo zhansheng hou zhi pinghe shijie" (A Peaceful World After the Allied Victory), in *Taixu dashi quanshu* (Complete Works), 15.48.56: 300.

75. Ibid., 307. Taixu suggested that voting representatives to the World Congress be selected according to the following plan: "For every political unit with less than ten million population, there should be one representative; one for every thirty million people after the first ten million; one for every fifty million after the first one hundred million people; one for every seventy million after the first two hundred million people, and one for every one hundred million people for numbers above three hundred and fifty million. [Therefore] each nation would have at least one representative and no more than nine." Ibid., 307–308.

76. Taixu, "A Peaceful World After Allied Victory," 22.

77. Taixu, *Lectures in Buddhism*, 34.

78. Ibid.

79. Ibid., 32.

80. C. Yates McDaniel, "Buddhism Makes Its Peace with the New Order," *Asia* 35/9 (September 1935): 541.

CHAPTER 5: A CREATIVE RECOVERY OF TRADITION

1. See James Legge, trans., *The Chinese Classics* (Hong Kong: Hong University Press, 1960); Arthur Waley, trans., *The Analects of Confucius* (London: George Allen & Unwin, Ltd., 1938); and Tu Wei-ming, *Centrality and Commonality: An Essay on Chung-yung* (Honolulu: The University Press of Hawai'i, 1976).

2. Consult Donald J. Munro, *The Concept of Man in Early China* (Stanford, Calif.: Stanford University Press, 1969), 49–83.

3. See Hu Shih (Hu Shi), *The Development of the Logical Method in Ancient China*, with an introduction by Hyman Kublin, 2nd ed. (Shanghai, 1922; New York: Paragon Book Reprint Corp., 1963).

4. Even for Confucians like Xunzi, who maintained that names are fundamentally a matter of human convention, consensus is reached *in illo tempore* and remains absolutely binding unless changed by government action in accord with the Mandate of Heaven.

5. The quotation is a famous line from *The Heart Sūtra*. For an English translation with commentary, see Edward Conze, trans., *Buddhist Wisdom Books, Containing The Diamond Sūtra and The Heart Sūtra* (London: George Allen & Unwin, Ltd., 1958).

6. For a discussion of the locative view of the cosmos as one of two basic structures of human symbolization and experience, consult Jonathan Z. Smith, "The Influence of Symbols upon Social Change: A Place on Which to Stand," in idem, *Map Is Not Territory: Studies in the History of Religions* (Leiden: E. J. Brill, 1978), 129–146.

7. Richard H. Robinson and Willard L. Johnson, *The Buddhist Religion: A Historical Introduction*, 4th ed. (Belmont, Calif.: Wadsworth, 1996), 100.

8. See Jan Yün-hua, "The Bodhisattva Idea in Chinese Literature: Typology and Significance," in *The Bodhisattva Doctrine in Buddhism*, ed. Leslie S. Kawamura (Waterloo, Ontario: Wilfrid Laurier University Press, 1981), 148.

9. See Lewis R. Lancaster, "The Bodhisattva Concept: A Study of the Chinese Buddhist Canon," in *The Bodhisattva Doctrine in Buddhism*, ed. Kawamura, 155.

10. Consult Bhikṣu Maha Sthavira Sangharakshita, *A Survey of Buddhism*, 5th ed. (Boulder, Colo.: Shambhala Publications, 1980), 389.

11. See Peter N. Gregory, *Tsung-mi and the Sinification of Buddhism* (Princeton, N.J.: Princeton University Press, 1991), 101.

12. Taixu, *Pusa xue chu* (The Bodhisattva's Context for Learning), (Taipei, 1957), 18. Published as a small book for distribution, the text is also found in Taixu, *Taixu dashi quanshu* (Complete Works), 9:33.8: 251–327, and is hereafter cited as "Context for Learning."

13. Luis O. Gómez, "From the Extraordinary to the Ordinary: Images of the Bodhisattva in East Asia," in *The Christ and the Bodhisattva*, ed. Donald S. Lopez, Jr., and Steven C. Rockefeller (Albany: State University of New York, 1987), 150–151.

14. Sangharakshita, *A Survey of Buddhism*, 397.

15. Consult Welch, *The Practice of Chinese Buddhism, 1900–1950*, 395–400.

16. See Yü's introduction to Chen-hua, *In Search of the Dharma*, 18.

17. Ch'en, *Buddhism in China*, 460.

18. Quoted in Chen-hua, *In Search of the Dharma*, 109–110.

19. Taixu, *Pusa xue chu* (Context for Learning), 1–2.

20. Ibid., 2.

21. Taixu, *Foxue de jianglai* (The Future of Buddhism), 18.

22. Taixu, "The Meaning of Buddhism," 694.

23. Taixu, *Pusa xue chu* (Context for Learning), 2.

24. Taixu, "Xinxin" (Faith), in *Taixu dashi quanshu* (Complete Works), 10:35.42: 238.

25. Taixu, *Lectures in Buddhism*, 27–28.

26. Taixu, "Xuefo de xiashou fangbian" (Means for Starting to Study Buddhism), in *Taixu dashi quanshu* (Complete Works), 10:35.43: 243. Even when the Chinese master discusses the Three Jewels in the traditional order (Buddha, Dharma, Sangha), he typically emphasizes the Dharma as the preeminent refuge. Appreciative of Buddhist idealism, in his article entitled "Faith," Taixu presents a fourfold refuge based on the *Dasheng qixin lun*. In that text, he notes, bodhisattvas are instructed that they should express faith first and foremost in the "basis" of all things, i.e., in the Bhūtatathatā (genuine thusness; Ch., *zhenru*). See Taixu, "Xinxin" (Faith), in *Taixu dashi quanshu* (Complete Works), 10:35.42: 240–241.

27. Taixu, "Fo shi women de shanyou" (The Buddha Is Our Good Friend), in *Taixu dashi quanshu* (Complete Works), 18:56.180: 689.

28. Taixu, *Pusa xue chu* (Context for Learning), 5.

29. Taixu, "You ren zhi chengfo zhi lu" (The Road from the Human Level to Becoming a Buddha), in *Taixu dashi quanshu* (Complete Works), 18:55.103: 412–413.

30. Taixu, *Pusa xue chu* (Context for Learning), 5.

31. Sangharakshita, *A Survey of Buddhism*, 406–407.

32. Müller, *Buddhismus und Moderne*, 162–175.

33. Welch, *The Buddhist Revival in China*, 52. On Taixu's thoughts of returning to lay life during the 1920s, see ibid., 305. For a mention of one such instance from 1928, consult Yinshun, *Taixu dashi nianpu* (Chronological Biography), 249–250.

34. For a report about three prominent literati who were recruited through Taixu's preaching to join the monastic order, consult Tsu, "Present Tendencies in Chinese Buddhism," 508–510. One of them wrote, "World salvation requires the Law of Buddha. But this cannot be accomplished without my earnestly and speedily proclaiming the Law among men. To do this, the best way is for me to strengthen my will, study the doctrine and thus prepare myself to give my personal testimony of faith. Hence the primary step of entering the Order. My now doing this, namely, leaving family and society and learning the Law of Buddha is to prepare myself for the task of saving the world with the Law. It is not dissimilar to my previous action of leaving home and studying Military Art to prepare myself for the task of saving my own country. The difference is that previously my aim was the salvation of my country and people, while now my aim is the salvation of all living creatures" (ibid., 509).

35. *Haichao yin* once published a letter to the Chinese master from an educated woman seeking spiritual advice on the question of monastic versus lay life. She wrote: "At present, Buddhism has deteriorated and reached the lowest ebb. The main

reason is the corruption of monastic orders, male and female. The monks and nuns do not know how to save themselves, not to think of their saving others. Not one out of a hundred can keep the discipline and read the sūtras. This is indeed most sad. So I think we cannot hope for improvement of the condition unless there come forward monks and nuns, of genuine motive for saving the world, with deep knowledge of the Law and respect for the Order, (1) to purify the monastic life and (2) to propagate the religion. But how few are such choice spirits, like your reverend self, and others.... If only more would take up the monastic vow! But some say that one may serve Buddha without laying aside family and social life. In my opinion, at the present time, to purify monastic life and propagate the religion, it is absolutely necessary to shave off the hair and enter the Order. I am therefore greatly surprised to read in one of the numbers of the Magazine that you, reverend Sir, wrote, 'The best way is to practice *bodhi* without forsaking the world [becoming a monk].' Now, you, reverend Sir, are yourself a monk; why then advise others against becoming monks? There must be a reason. Will you instruct me?" See her inquiry translated in Tsu, "Present Tendencies in Chinese Buddhism," 509–510. Brackets in the quotation are Tsu's.

36. See, for example, Taixu, *Pusa xue chu* (Context for Learning), 13.

37. Ibid., 19 and 28.

38. Ibid., 8.

39. Reichelt, "Trends in China's Non-Christian Religions," *Chinese Recorder* 65 (December 1934), 763. Reichelt wrote five years earlier on this, "The secret of his [Taixu's] influence is, in addition to his great personal qualifications, his remarkable ability to gather around himself the best and most powerful types among the lay devotees. Through him they are linked up with the ordained and consecrated men who are naturally the real ruling representatives of Buddhism in China. However, as only a small fraction of the monks live up to their high calling, the sincere devotees think that they must step in and take the lead. In this, Taixu partly supports them, requiring only that a few of the best priests, the elite of the monks must work with them. 'If this is not done,' says Taixu, 'the old foundation is taken away, the connecting link is removed.'" See "Present-Day Buddhism in China," *Chinese Recorder* 60 (October 1929), 649.

40. Dongchu, *Zhongguo fojiao jindai shi* (A History of Modern Chinese Buddhism), 1: 216–220.

41. Taixu, "Zunzhong sengjie huansu ren" (Respecting Monastics who Return to the Laity), in *Taixu dashi quanshu* (Complete Works), 9:34.55: 627.

42. Ibid., 627–628. See also the sections on those who wish to leave the sangha and those who, having left the sangha, wish to return to the monastic life, in Taixu's early 1915 plan entitled "Zhengli sengqie zhidu lun" (On Reorganizing the Monastic System), in *Taixu dashi quanshu* (Complete Works), 9:33.1: 102–108.

43. Taixu, "Buneng shou sengjie huansu wu wu seng" (Those Who are Unable to Keep the Monastic Precepts Must Not Debase the Sangha), in *Taixu dashi quanshu* (Complete Works), 9:34.56: 629–630.

44. Taixu, *Taixu dashi Guangdong yanjiang ji chubian* (Lectures in Guangdong by the Venerable Master Taixu: First Edition), (Guangdong, 1935), 18 (hereafter cited as "Guangdong Lectures")

45. Hong Jinlian, *Taixu dashi fojiao xiandaihua zhi yanjiu* (Modernization), 159.

46. Taixu, *Taixu dashi guangdong yanjiang ji chubian* (Guangdong Lectures), 19. Emphasis mine.

47. See Taixu, *Pusa xue chu* (Context for Learning), 7.

48. Taixu's position on women seems to represent something of a mediating compromise, as Gotelind Müller points out ("Die Rolle der Frau," in *Buddhismus und Moderne,* 176–181). On the one hand, Taixu supports the traditional leadership role of monks over nuns and the common view that women will eventually be transformed into men according to good karmic merit. He does not understand this to pose a question of inequality but only to be a natural development compatible with the lack of sexual activity in pure lands. On the other hand, he strongly affirms the important role of women both inside the home and in the broader society of the modern world. Recognizing that enlightened women are mentioned in Mahāyāna scripture and that such attainment remains a possibility in this lifetime for all human beings, he encourages modern women to attain their full potential in the bodhisattva path. He writes, "Women are able to fulfill their responsibilities, i.e., to become bodhisattvas—since bodhisattvas are those who, when they themselves are enlightened, enlighten others; when they themselves stand up, help others to stand; when they themselves are correct, help to correct others; so they are not idols made of mud or wood—and everywhere they able to benefit society, the nation, the people, and all humankind." See Taixu, "Zenyang zuo xiandai nüzi" (How to Be a Modern Woman), in *Taixu dashi quanshu* (Complete Works), 13.44.121.1324–1332. Consult also Taixu, "Da Zhu Zhonghan wen" (Answers to Questions from Zhu Zhonghan), in ibid., 17:52.187: 333–342, as well as Taixu, "Fünü xuefo zhi guifan" (The Scope of Women's Study of Buddhism), in Taixu, *Jushi xue fo zhi chengxu* (The Course of the Laity's Study of Buddhism), (Taipei, 1978), 55–58.

49. D. T. Suzuki, *Outlines of Mahāyāna Buddhism* (New York: Schocken Books, Inc., 1963), 306.

50. Taixu, "Zongjiao goucheng zhi yuansu" (Elements in the Structure of Religion), in *Taixu dashi quanshu* (Complete Works), 13:41.25: 269–270.

51. See Taixu, "Wo de zongjiao jingyan" (My Religious Experiences), in *Taixu dashi quanshu* (Complete Works), 13:41.33: 346–350. For a summary discussion of his experiences, see Hong Jinlian, *Taixu dashi fojiao xiandaihua zhi yanjiu* (Modernization), 148–149.

52. Taixu, "Taixu zizhuan" (Autobiography), in *Taixu dashi quanshu* (Complete Works), 19:58.18: 188. For a slighty different account of this critical religious experience, see Taixu, "Wo de zongjiao jingyan" (My Religious Experiences), in *Taixu dashi quanshu* (Complete Works), 13:41.33: 347. Consult also Yinshun, *Taixu dashi nianpu* (Chronological Biography), 32–33.

53. Taixu, "Wo de zongjiao jingyan" (My Religious Experiences), in *Taixu dashi quanshu* (Complete Works), 13:41.33: 350.

54. Taixu, *Pusa xue chu* (Context for Learning), 7.

55. Taixu, "Wo de zongjiao jingyan" (My Religious Experiences), in *Taixu dashi quanshu* (Complete Works), 13:41.33: 350.

56. Har Dayal, *The Bodhisattva Doctrine in Buddhist Sanskrit Literature* (Delhi: Motilal Banarsidass, 1932), 65.

57. Taixu, *Pusa xue chu* (Context for Learning), 19.

58. Ibid.

59. Ibid., 20.

60. Ibid.

61. Ibid., 21.

62. Ibid., 9. Dayal notes that it is probable that the prohibition of alcoholic beverages was at first intended only for monks, though it was subsequently extended to the laity. See his *The Bodhisattva Doctrine in Buddhist Sanskrit Literature,* 198.

63. Taixu, *Pusa xue chu* (Context for Learning), 22.

64. Ibid., 23.

65. Taixu, *Taixu dashi guangdong yanjiang ji chubian* (Guangdong Lectures), 17.

66. Taixu, *Pusa xue chu* (Context for Learning), 23–24.

67. Ibid., 25.

68. Callahan, "T'ai Hsü and the New Buddhist Movement," 160.

69. Taixu, *Pusa xue chu* (Context for Learning), 2–3.

70. Ibid., 4.

71. Ibid., 28.

72. Taixu, "Jianshe renjian jingtu lun" (On Establishing a Pure Land on Earth), in *Taixu dashi quanshu* (Complete Works), 14:47.5: 426.

73. Ibid., 427.

74. Ibid., 428–429.

75. See Taixu, "Zenyang lai jianshe renjian fojiao" (How to Establish a Humanistic Buddhism), in *Taixu dashi quanshu* (Complete Works), 14:47.6: 431–456. The trans-

lation here of *"renjian"* as "humanistic" was first suggested to me by the authorized English translations of the term in the writings of the Venerable Xingyun (b. 1927), the founder of Foguang Shan (Buddha Light Mountain) in Kaohsiung County, southern Taiwan. See, for example, Xingyun, "Ruhe jianshe xiandai fojiao" (How to Construct a Modern Buddhism), in *1990 Foguang Shan guoji fojiao xueshu huiyi lunwen ji* (1990 Anthology of the Foguang Shan International Buddhist Conference), Chinese version, 2–6; English version, 7–13 (Kaohsiung, 1992).

76. Consult Taixu, "Ji ren chengfo de zhen xianshi lun" (True Realism Concerning Humans Becoming Buddhas), in *Taixu dashi quanshu* (Complete Works), 14:47.7: 457–464.

77. Given Taixu's own rational and "scientific" religious outlook, it may seem odd that he was always concerned to include the Tantric component of Buddhism in his various schemes. Yet this was a part of his commitment to ecumenical inclusivism.

78. A *li* is equal to approximately 0.33 mile.

79. A *mu* is equal to 733.5 square yards; 6.6 *mu* equal 1 acre.

80. Taixu, "A Statement to Asiatic Buddhists," 179–180.

81. Tsu, "Present Tendencies in Chinese Buddhism," 507–508.

82. See Taixu, "Zhengli sengqie zhidu lun" (On Reorganizing the Monastic System), in *Taixu dashi quanshu* (Complete Works), 9:33.1: 8. See also his distribution chart of monastics in ibid., 65–67.

83. Ibid., 26–46.

84. Ibid., 46–51. For Taixu's perspective on economic reform and the need for a central Buddhist bank, see, for example, "You jingji lilun shuodao sengsi jingji jianshe" (On Establishing the Monastic Economy from the Perspective of Economic Theory), in *Taixu dashi quanshu* (Complete Works), 10:35.34: 191–193.

85. For a report on the age at which monks in monasteries were typically tonsured and ordained in the Republican period, consult Welch, *The Practice of Chinese Buddhism, 1900–1950,* 248–258.

86. Taixu, "Zhengli sengqie zhidu lun" (On Reorganizing the Monastic System), in *Taixu dashi quanshu* (Complete Works), 9:33.1: 179.

87. Ibid., 171–174. For a picture of Taixu in one of the new twenty-five striped monastic vestments that he designed, see Welch, *The Buddhist Revival in China,* 53.

88. See Taixu, "Sengzhi jinlun" (A Current Discussion of the Monastic System), in *Taixu dashi quanshu* (Complete Works), 9:33.4: 195–199.

89. Consult Taixu, "Jianseng dagang" (An Outline for Building Up the Sangha), in *Taixu dashi quanshu* (Complete Works), 9:33.5: 205.

90. Ibid., 206.

91. Ibid., 207–210.

92. See Taixu, "Jianli zhongguo xiandai fojiao zhuchi seng dagang" (An Outline for the Work of a Modern Chinese Buddhist Abbot), in *Taixu dashi quanshu* (Complete Works), 9:33.6: 213–217.

93. Consult Taixu, "Seng jiaoyu zhi mudi yu chengxu" (The Purpose and Procedures for Monastic Education), in *Taixu dashi quanshu* (Complete Works), 9:34.31: 479, in which, in 1931, Taixu reiterated his scheme for reducing the numbers of monastics to twenty thousand.

94. See Taixu, "Zhengli sengqie zhidu lun" (On Reorganizing the Monastic System), in *Taixu dashi quanshu* (Complete Works), 9:33.1: 7.

95. Consult Taixu, "Jianshe xiandai zhongguo fojiao tan" (A Discussion of the Establishment of a Modern Chinese Buddhism), in *Taixu dashi quanshu* (Complete Works), 9:33.7: 265.

96. Welch, *The Buddhist Revival in China*, 52.

97. Consult Taixu, "Fojiao yingban zhi jiaoyu yu seng jiaoyu" (The General and Monastic Education That Buddhism Ought to Offer), in *Taixu dashi quanshu* (Complete Works), 9:34.32: 481–482.

98. Welch, *The Buddhist Revival in China*, 106.

99. Taixu, "Xianzai xuyao de seng jiaoyu" (The Monastic Education Needed Today), in *Taixu dashi quanshu* (Complete Works), 9:34.35: 498. The title in the index differs slightly from the actual title of the text.

100. Ibid., 500.

101. Taixu, *Pusa xue chu* (Context for Learning), 29.

102. "Taixu's great aim," wrote Reichelt, "is to preserve an organic connection with the Chinese Buddhism of the past and at the same time to free it from the entanglements of superstitions and obscure practices, which have loaded it down and brought it under the scorn of so many educated people." See his "Trends in China's Non-Christian Religions," 763.

103. See Millican, "The Present Situation Among the Buddhists," *Chinese Recorder* 59 (September 1928): 600.

104. Private letters from Mrs. F. R. Millican to James B. Pratt, January 12 and March 4, 1929, in the Pratt Collection, Williams College Library. Cited in Welch, *The Buddhist Revival in China*, 220.

105. Yu-yue Tsu, "Buddhism and Modern Social-Economic Problems," *Journal of Religion* 14/1 (January 1934): 40–41.

106. Reichelt, "Present Situation in Buddhism," 105–106.

107. Yinguang, "Fu Yue Xianjiao jushi shu" (Reply to Layman Yue Xianjiao), in *Yinguang fashi wenchao quanji* (The Complete Works of the Dharma Master Yinguang), 1: 101–102.

108. Frank R. Millican, "Recent Developments in Religious Thought," in *The China Christian Year Book, 1929* (Shanghai: Christian Literature Society, 1929), 126–127. For Yinguang's letter to Dixian, to which Millican refers, see Yinguang, "Zhi Dixian fashi wenji shu" (Letter to Dharma Master Dixian Inquiring About His Illness), in *Yinguang fashi wenchao quanji* (The Complete Works of the Dharma Master Yinguang), 1: 70–71.

109. Pratt, "A Report on the Present Condition of Buddhism," 24, 26. Emphasis mine.

110. For the report on the more radical element among the reformers, see W. Y. Chen, "The Ancient Religions of China Today," 101–102.

111. Taixu, "Wangsheng jingtu lun jiang yao" (A Lecture on Key Points of the Rebirth Treatise), in *Taixu dashi quanshu* (Complete Works), 7.30.38: 2,709. The title listed in the index differs slightly from the title of the actual text.

112. Ibid., 2,675.

113. Callahan, "T'ai Hsü and the New Buddhist Movement," 178.

114. Hu Shih, "The Civilizations of the East and West," in *Whither Mankind: A Panorama of Modern Civilization,* ed. Charles A. Beard (New York: Longmans, Green and Co., 1928), 30–31. Original romanization retained.

115. Hu Shih, "The Task of Confucianism," in *Modern Trends in World Religions,* ed. Albert Eustace Haydon (Chicago: University of Chicago Press, 1934), 248.

116. Quoted in Frank R. Millican, "Humanism in China," *Chinese Recorder* 65/11 (November 1934): 682.

117. Hu Shih, "The Task of Confucianism," 249.

118. See Hu Shih, "My Credo and Its Evolution," in *Living Philosophies,* ed. Albert Einstein et al. (New York: Simon and Schuster, 1931), 241.

119. Reichelt, "A Conference of Chinese Buddhist Leaders," 667–669.

120. Consult Philip West, *Yenching University and Sino-Western Relations, 1916–1952* (Cambridge: Harvard University Press, 1976). A portion of this chapter's section on the Christian challenge to Buddhism in China is taken from or paraphrases (with permission) Don A. Pittman, "The Modern Buddhist Reformer T'ai-hsü on Christianity," *Buddhist-Christian Studies* 13 (1993): 71–83.

121. Millican, "T'ai Hsü and Modern Buddhism," 333.

122. Taixu, "Wushen lun" (On Atheism), in *Taixu dashi quanshu* (Complete Works), 13.41.27: 284–295.

123. See Zhang Taiyan, "Wushen lun" (On Atheism), in *Zhangshi congshu* (Collected Works of Zhang Taiyan), 2: 864–869. See also Whalen Lai, "The Buddhist-Christian Dialogue in China," in *Religious Issues and Interreligious Dialogues: An Analysis and Sourcebook of Developments Since 1945,* ed. Charles Wei-hsun Fu and Gerhard E. Spiegler (New York: Greenwood Press, 1989), 613–631.

124. Taixu, "Wushen lun" (On Atheism), in *Taixu dashi quanshu* (Complete Works), 13.41.27: 289.

125. Taixu, "The Meaning of Chen Ju and Ju Lai," *Chinese Recorder* 55/2 (February 1924): 120.

126. Taixu, "Buddhism and the Modern Mind," *Chinese Recorder* 65/7 (July 1934): 437.

127. Chan, *Religious Trends in Modern China,* 125. According to Chan, it was synthesis that motivated Taixu. He writes, "In his Wuchang Buddhist Institute, lectures were given on practically all Buddhist schools. He himself promoted all sects, although he bore the label of Weishi. He says that synthesis has distinguished the development of thought in Chinese history. He attempted to carry it a step further. . . . Although he did not go far enough, he did go a step in the right direction and thus enhanced the Chinese spirit of synthesis" (ibid., 125–126).

128. Lai, "The Buddhist-Christian Dialogue in China," 619.

129. Clarence H. Hamilton, "Buddhistic Idealism in Wei Shih Er Shih Lwen," in *Essays in Philosophy by Seventeen Doctors of Philosophy of the University of Chicago,* ed. Thomas Vernor Smith and William Kelley Wright (Chicago: Open Court, 1929), 99.

130. Chan, *Religious Trends in Modern China,* 120. Chan offers in chapter 3 a general description of Taixu's version of Buddhist idealistic philosophy in comparison to those of Ouyang Jingwu and Xiong Shili. See also Taixu, *Faxiang weishi xue* (Dharma-Character Idealistic Philosophy), (Shanghai, 1938).

131. Taixu, "Buddhism and the Modern Mind," 438–439.

132. Millican, "Tai Hsü and Modern Buddhism," 332–333.

133. Taixu, *Lectures in Buddhism,* 37.

134. Millican, "Tai Hsü and Modern Buddhism," 331.

135. Quoted in Reichelt, "A Conference of Chinese Buddhist Leaders," 668.

136. Taixu, "Zhongguo xu yejiao yu Ou Mei xu fojiao" (China Needs Christianity and Europe and America Need Buddhism), in *Taixu dashi quanshu* (Complete Works), 13.41.31: 338.

137. See Taixu, "Shanghai fofa sengyuan fayuan zhi xin jianshe" (The New Establishment of the Shanghai Monastic Dharma Garden), in *Taixu dashi quanshu* (Complete Works), 9.34.38: 520.

138. See Yinshun, *Taixu dashi nianpu* (Chronological Biography), 234. Consult also Taixu, "Taixu zizhuan" (Autobiography), in *Taixu dashi quanshu* (Complete Works), 19.58.18: 304–305.

139. Taixu, "Zhongguo xu yejiao yu Ou Mei xu fojiao" (China Needs Christianity and Europe and America Need Buddhism), in *Taixu dashi quanshu* (Complete Works), 13.41.31: 338–339.

140. Quoted in Hamilton, "An Hour with T'ai Shu, Master of the Law," 168–169.

141. Reichelt, "Present Situation in Buddhism," 111.

142. Taixu, "Wushen lun" (On Atheism), in *Taixu dashi quanshu* (Complete Works), 13.41.27: 286.

143. Ibid., 286.

144. Ibid., 294.

145. Ibid., 295. Taixu's reference is to the *Zhuangzi*, section 26, "External Things." Consult Burton Watson, trans., *The Complete Works of Chuang Tzu* (New York: Columbia University Press, 1968), 302.

146. Taixu, "Xin jiu wenti de genben jiejue" (The Fundamental Solution to the Issue of the New and the Old), in *Taixu dashi quanshu* (Complete Works), 13.40.6: 34.

147. See Lai, "Why Is There Not a Buddho-Christian Dialogue in China?" *Buddhist-Christian Studies* 6 (1986): 81–96.

148. John Dunne, *The Way of All the Earth* (New York: Sheldon Press/Macmillan, 1972), vii.

CHAPTER 6: TAIXU'S LEGACY

1. For a list of Taixu's tonsure disciples and grandson disciples, see Yinshun, *Taixu dashi nianpu* (Chronological Biography), 15–17. For a brief description of the tonsure family relationships, see Welch, *The Practice of Chinese Buddhism, 1900–1950*, 276–281.

2. Holmes Welch, *Buddhism Under Mao* (Cambridge: Harvard University Press, 1972), 1.

3. Richard C. Bush, Jr., *Religion in Communist China* (Nashville: Abingdon, 1970), 302–303.

4. Taixu, "The Meaning of Buddhism," 690.

5. Juzan, "An Account of My Work Over the Past Year," translated in Welch, *Buddhism Under Mao*, 395–396.

6. Holmes Welch, "Buddhism in China Today," 176.

7. Welch, *Buddhism Under Mao*, 85–86.

8. Quoted in Bush, *Religion in Communist China*, 303.

9. Quoted in ibid., 306.

10. Welch, *Buddhism Under Mao*, 143–144.

11. Julian F. Pas, "Introduction: Chinese Religion in Transition," in *The Turning of the Tide: Religion in China Today*, ed. Julian F. Pas (Oxford: Oxford University Press, 1989).

12. See Kenneth Dean, *Taoist Ritual and Popular Cults of Southeast China* (Princeton, N.J.: Princeton University Press, 1993), 211.

13. In January 1988, Donald MacInnis interviewed the abbot of the Nanputuo si in Xiamen (Amoy). The abbot admitted that, while he was aware of Taixu's educational efforts during the Republican period, he himself was illiterate. In fact, he said, many older monks actively opposed Taixu and argued that sitting meditation was sufficient practice. It was advice he himself apparently accepted. See Donald E. MacInnis, *Religion in China Today: Policy and Practice* (Maryknoll, N.Y.: Orbis Books, 1989), 135–136.

14. I have only seen a reference to the unpublished 1996 University of Beijing dissertation by Zhou Xuenong, entitled "Taixu fashi de 'renjian fojiao' sixiang yanjiu" (A Study of the Ideas of the Venerable Master Taixu's Humanistic Buddhism).

15. Bartholomew P. M. Tsui, "Recent Developments in Buddhism in Hong Kong," in *The Turning of the Tide*, ed. Pas, 299–311.

16. Ibid., 300. In a report for the Sixteenth General Conference of the World Fellowship of Buddhists in 1988, it is claimed that at the time there were 300 monks and 200 nuns in Hong Kong, along with a lay Buddhist community of more than 650,000. Consult *Shijie fojiaotu youyi hui di shiliu jie dahui: jinian tekan* (The Sixteenth General Conference of the World Fellowship of Buddhists: Souvenir Program), 142–143.

17. See Taixu, "Cong Xianggang de ganxiang shuodao Xianggang de fojiao" (Commenting on Buddhism in Hong Kong on the Basis of Impressions of Hong Kong), in *Xianggang fojiao* (Buddhism in Hong Kong) 286 (June 1960): 14–17.

18. Tsui, "Recent Developments in Buddhism in Hong Kong," 304.

19. See *Shijie fojiaotu youyi hui di shiliu jie dahui: jinian tekan* (The Sixteenth General Conference of the World Fellowship of Buddhists: Souvenir Program), 143–144.

20. For example, in the spring and summer of 1997, the dramatic presentation "Taixu dashi" (Venerable Master Taixu), sponsored by the Golden Lotus Theater Group, successfully toured all the major cities of Taiwan. Following the narrative of Yinshun's chronological biography, the play depicted the Chinese master's entire career in 65 scenes. The program booklet prepared for the event included photo-

graphs of Taixu, other important masters of the period, and places the monk had visited in Taiwan. The production that I attended in May 1997 nearly sold out the large cultural center auditorium in the central Taiwan city of Taizhong.

21. See Zhu Baotang, "Buddhist Organizations in Taiwan," *Chinese Culture* 10/2 (June 1969): 120.

22. Charles Brewer Jones, *Buddhism in Taiwan: Religion and State, 1660–1990* (Honolulu: University of Hawai'i Press, 1999), 135.

23. Yinshun, *Wo zhi zongjiao guan* (My View of Religion), 304, quoted in Zhaohui, *Renjian fojiao de bozhong zhe* (The Sower of the Seeds of a Humanistic Buddhism), (Taipei, 1995), 10–11. Parenthetical remarks in the quotation are Yinshun's. See also his articles "Shangdi ai shiren?" (God Loves Humans?) and "Shangdi ai shiren de zai taolun" (A Second Discussion on God's Love for Humans), both in *Dasheng wenku, 7: Fojiao yu yejiao de bijiao* (Mahāyāna Studies, Vol. 7: Comparing Buddhism and Christianity), ed. Zhang Mantao (Taipei, 1971), 163–244.

24. Taixu claimed that his ordination brother Yushan was his first real friend in the sangha. See Yinshun, *Taixu dashi nianpu* (Chronological Biography), 32.

25. Robert M. Gimello, foreword to Yin-shun, *The Way to Buddhahood*, trans. Wing H. Yeung, vii.

26. Whalen Lai, introduction to Yin-shun, *The Way to Buddhahood*, trans. Wing H. Yeung, xvii, xx.

27. From an article by Yinshun entitled "Idle Remarks on Fuyan Retreat," quoted in Chen-hua, *In Search of the Dharma*, 249.

28. See Yinshun, *Pingfan de yisheng* (An Ordinary Life), (Taipei, 1994), 145.

29. Zhenhua reported that when Yinshun finally accepted him as a student in 1957, the master's teaching method was simply to assign him and the other older students readings and ask them to take notes on their contents. Every month or two, Yinshun would read their notes and record the date in his own hand. See Chen-hua, *In Search of the Dharma*, 250.

30. Yinshun, *Cheng fo zhi dao* (The Way to Buddhahood), (Taipei, 1994), 1.

31. Chen-hua, *In Search of the Dharma*, 249–250. Brackets in the quotation are those of the translator.

32. See Yinshun, "Jingtu xinlun" (New Treatise on the Pure Land), in idem, *Jingtu yu chan* (Pure Land and Chan), (Taipei, 1995), 1–75.

33. Yang Huinan, *Dangdai fojiao sixiang zhanwang* (A Survey of Contemporary Buddhist Thought), 22–23.

34. Jones, *Buddhism in Taiwan*, 133.

35. Yinshun, *Cheng fo zhi dao* (The Way to Buddhahood), 63.

36. For comparative analyses of their approaches, see Jiang Canteng, "Cong 'rensheng fojiao' dao 'renjian fojiao'" (From a "Buddhism for human life" to a "Buddhism for the human realm"), in idem, *Taiwan fojiao yu xiandai shehui* (Taiwanese Buddhism and Contemporary Society), (Taipei, 1992), 169–188; and Yang Huinan, "Cong 'rensheng fojiao' dao 'renjian fojiao'" (From a "Buddhism for human life" to a "Buddhism for the human realm"), in idem, *Dangdai fojiao sixiang zhanwang* (A Survey of Contemporary Buddhist Thought), 75–125.

37. Yinshun, *Fo zai renjian* (The Buddha in the Human Realm), (Taipei 1971), 18–19.

38. Ibid., 23.

39. Noting the dominance of the religion in the area, Welch states in *The Practice of Chinese Buddhism, 1900–1950* that "the soil of northern Jiangsu was soaked in Buddhism. Here had been the earliest Buddhist community mentioned in Chinese historical records; the first Buddha image; the earliest temple" (257). See also the map of East Central China inside the back covers of his *The Buddhist Revival in China* and *Buddhism Under Mao*.

40. Fu Zhiying, *Chuan deng: Xingyun dashi zhuan* (Handing Down the Light: A Biography of Venerable Master Xingyun), (Taipei 1995), 39.

41. Although the organization specifically translates the name "Xilai" as "Coming to the West," the temple has been incorporated in California as the "International Buddhist Progress Society." See "The History of Fo Kuang Shan Hsi Lai Temple," an English-language brochure distributed by the organization, available from the Hsi Lai Temple in Hacienda Heights, California.

42. *Hsi Lai University General Catalog, 1991–1993*, 9, available from Hsi Lai University in Rosemead, California.

43. See an English-language guide to the Foguang Shan Monastery entitled *Fo Kuang Shan Monastery: Promoting Humanistic Buddhism, Building A Pure Land on Earth*, available from Fo Kuang Shan Monastery in Kaohsiung county, Taiwan.

44. In addition to edited materials, Xingyun's many published writings include his four-volume series on Chan Buddhism, *Xingyun Chan hua* (Xingyun's Chan Talks), which have been translated into English (Taipei, 1987–1989); his four-volume series of public lectures, *Xingyun dashi jiangyan ji* (The Collected Lectures of the Venerable Master Xingyun) (Taipei, 1987); and numerous monographs. Recent English-language materials include Hsing Yün (Xingyun), *Being Good: Buddhist Ethics for Everyday Life*, trans. Tom Graham (New York: Weatherhill, 1998) and Hsing Yün (Xingyun), *Only a Great Rain: A Guide to Chinese Buddhist Meditation*, trans. Tom Graham, introduction by John McRae (Boston: Wisdom Publications, 1999).

45. David W. Chappell, back cover of Hsing Yün (Xingyun)'s book, *The Lion's Roar: Actualizing Buddhism in Daily Life and Building the Pure Land in Our Midst* (New York: Peter Lang, 1991).

46. See Xingyun, *Xingyun dashi jiangyan ji* (The Collected Lectures of the Venerable Master Xingyun), 3: 1.

47. Hsing Yün (Xingyun), *The Prospect for Buddhist Youth* (Fojiao qingnian de zhanwang), (Kaohsiung, 1987), 25–26.

48. Hsing Yün (Xingyun), *How to Be a Fo Kuang Buddhist,* Vol. 1 (Zenyang zuo ge foguang ren, 1), (Kaohsiung, 1987), 13.

49. Hsing Yün (Xingyun), *The Young Buddhist's Path to Success* (Fojiao qingnian chenggong liye zhi dao), (Kaohsiung, 1987), 30.

50. Xingyun, *Ruhe jianshe renjian de fojiao* (How to Establish a Humanistic Buddhism), (Kaohsiung, 1989), 9.

51. Xingyun, *Two Talks on Buddhism* (Foxue jiangzuo), (Kaohsiung, 1987), 53.

52. Xingyun, "Ruhe jianshe xiandai fojiao" (How to Establish a Modern Buddhism), in *1990 Foguang Shan guoji fojiao xueshu huiyi lunwen ji* (1990 Anthology of the Foguang Shan International Buddhist Conference), (Kaohsiung, 1992), 3–4.

53. Hsing Yün (Xingyun), *The Prospect for Buddhist Youth,* 6–7.

54. Hsing Yün (Xingyun), *The Lion's Roar,* 136.

55. Xingyun, *Ruhe jianshe renjian de fojiao* (How to Establish a Humanistic Buddhism), 3.

56. Hsing Yün (Xingyun), *The Prospect for Buddhist Youth,* 25–26.

57. Xingyun, "Fojiao de zhengzhi guan" (Buddhism's View of Politics), in idem, *Xingyun dashi jiangyan ji,* 3: 391.

58. Fu Zhiying, "Fojiaojie de chuangyi dashi: Xingyun" (A Creative Venerable Master of the Buddhist World: Xingyun), in Lu Keng, ed., *Renjian fojiao de Xingyun* (Humanistic Buddhism's Xingyun), (Kaohsiung, 1991), 50.

59. The other two leading candidates at the time, Lee Denghui of the Nationalist Party (Guomindang), who eventually won the election, and Peng Mingmin of the Democratic Progressive Party (Minjindang), were both Presbyterian Christians. The press reported that Peng personally sought to dissuade Xingyun from openly supporting Chen. See Christopher Bodeen, "Chen Still Wooing Buddhist Votes," *The China Post,* November 21, 1995.

60. See "Xingyun dashi zhuti yanshuo" (Keynote Speech of the Venerable Master Xingyun), in *Shijie fojiaotu youyi hui di shiliu jie dahui: jinian tekan* (The Sixteenth General Conference of the World Fellowship of Buddhists: Souvenir Program), 97–98, 100.

61. Chi-ying Fu (Fu Zhiying), *Handing Down the Light: The Biography of Venerable Master Hsing Yün,* trans. Amy Lui-ma (Hacienda Heights, Calif.: Hsi Lai University Press, 1996), 122.

62. Lu Keng, "Xinhuai tianxia de gaoseng: ji Xingyun dashi zheige heshang" (An Eminent Monk Who Cherishes the World: Recollections of the Venerable Master Xingyun), in Lu Keng, ed., *Renjian fojiao de Xingyun* (Humanistic Buddhism's Xingyun), 29.

63. Shengyan, *Getting the Buddha Mind* (Elmhurst, N.Y.: Dharma Drum Publications, 1982), 23–24.

64. Ibid., 24

65. For a 1978 picture of Shengyan with Master Lingyuan, see Shengyan, *Shengyan fashi xuesi licheng* (The Course of My Education and Thought), (Taipei, 1993), 63.

66. Ibid., 42.

67. Shengyan, *Getting the Buddha Mind,* 30–31.

68. Ibid., 34.

69. While indicating the *pinyin* romanization in parentheses, I have chosen to retain the Institute's own romanization of its name as "Chung-Hwa" because all its English-language materials use this spelling.

70. Shengyan, "Opening Speech" (Shengyan fashi kaimu ci), in *The Second Chung-Hwa International Buddhist Studies Conference: Program Booklet* (Taipei, July 18–21, 1992), 18. Obvious grammatical and spelling errors in the official English translation corrected.

71. Shengyan, *Shengyan fashi xuesi licheng* (The Course of My Education and Thought), 72.

72. Shengyan, *Faith in Mind: A Guide to Chan Practice* (Elmhurst, N.Y.: Dharma Drum Publications, 1987), 124–125.

73. Shengyan, "Traditional Buddhist Precepts and the Modern World" (Chuantong jielü yu xiandai shijie), in *The Second Chung-Hwa International Buddhist Studies Conference,* 32–33. Grammatical and spelling errors in the official English translation are corrected.

74. See the promotional brochure *Renjian jingtu de fagu shan* (The Pure Land on Earth That Is Dharma Drum Mountain), (Taipei: Dharma Drum Cultural and Religious Foundation, no date).

75. Shengyan, *Shengyan fashi xuesi licheng* (The Course of My Education and Thought), 44.

76. Shengyan, *Xuefo zhijin* (The Ferry for Learning Buddhism), (Taipei, 1995), 261, 263–266. Paragraph structure mine.

77. Quoted in Yu-ing Ching, *Master of Love and Mercy: Cheng Yen* (Nevada City: Blue Dolphin Publishing, Inc., 1995), 271.

78. Ibid., 174.

79. Qiu Xiuzhi, *Da ai: Zhengyan fashi yu ciji shijie* (Great Love: Dharma Master Zhengyan and the World of Ciji), (Taipei, 1996), 40.

80. Hengqing, *Puti dao shang de shan nüren* (Women of Virtue on the Path of Enlightenment), (Taipei, 1995), 180. While indicating the *pinyin* romanization in parentheses, I retain the organization's romanization of its own name as "Tzu Chi" because all its English-language publications use this spelling.

81. Cheng-yen (Zhengyan), "Tzu Chi Resolutions," trans. Y. L. Lee, in *Tzu Chi Quarterly* 1/1 (Spring 1994), 3.

82. Cheng-yen (Zhengyan), "The Difficulty in Reading Buddhist Sūtras," trans. Andy Chen, *Tzu Chi Quarterly* 3/3 (Fall 1996): 14.

83. Cheng-yen (Zhengyan), "The Thirty-Seven Dharma Principles of Enlightenment Which Lead to Buddhahood," trans. E. E. Ho and W. L. Rathje, *Tzu Chi Quarterly* 2/3 (Fall/Winter 1995), 9. The term "Dharma" has been capitalized.

84. Qiu Xiuzhi, *Da ai* (Great Love), 7–8.

85. Ching, *Master of Love and Mercy,* 187.

86. See resolution 8, in *Taiwan jidu zhanglao jiaohui, de 45 jie zonghui tongchang nianhui yishi shouce* (The Program Booklet of the Forty-Fifth Annual Meeting of the General Assembly of the Presbyterian Church in Taiwan), (Taipei, 1998), 6. I attended the assembly as a voting missionary delegate. The written explanation of the resolution in the booklet contains no explicit reference to Buddhism, although Tzu Chi was prominently mentioned in the verbal explanation for the resolution, which was subsequently adopted by the assembly.

87. Kitagawa, "Primitive, Classical, and Modern Religions," 61–62.

88. See Jonathan Z. Smith, "The Influence of Symbols upon Social Change," in idem, *Map Is Not Territory,* 129–146.

89. Charles S. Braden, "How Liberal Christianity Conceives of Salvation," *Journal of Religion* 17/1 (January 1937): 15.

90. Nathan Glazer, *American Judaism* (Chicago: University of Chicago Press, 1957), 31. Consult also W. Gunther Plaut, *The Rise of Reform Judaism* (New York: World Union for Progressive Judaism, 1963) and David Philipson, *The Reform Movement in Judaism* (New York: Ktav, 1969). For expressions of the Christian Social Gospel movement, see Walter Rauschenbusch, *Christianity and the Social Crisis* (New York: Hodder and Stoughton, 1907); *A Theology for the Social Gospel* (New York: Macmillan, 1917); and *Social Principles of Jesus* (New York: Association Press, 1919).

91. With specific reference to American Judaism, see the discussion of the influences of "protestantism, pluralism, moralism, and voluntaryism" in Joseph L. Blau, *Judaism in America: From Curiosity to Third Faith* (Chicago: University of Chicago Press, 1976), 1–20.

92. Tsu, "Buddhism and Modern Social-Economic Problems," 41.

93. For such a survey of themes articulated by engaged Buddhist leaders, see "The Shapes and Sources of Engaged Buddhism," in Christopher S. Queen and Sallie B. King, eds., *Engaged Buddhism: Buddhist Liberation Movements in Asia* (Albany: State University of New York Press, 1996), 1–44. Consult also Fred Eppsteiner, ed., *The Path of Compassion: Writings on Socially Engaged Buddhism* (Berkeley: Parallax Press, 1988), and Arnold Kotler, ed., *Engaged Buddhist Reader* (Berkeley: Parallax Press, 1996).

94. See Max Weber, *The Sociology of Religion,* trans. Ephraim Fischoff (Boston: Beacon, 1964).

95. See Sallie B. King, "Buddhist Social Activism," in Queen and King, eds., *Engaged Buddhism,* 422.

96. Quoted in Hamilton, "An Hour with T'ai Shu," 167.

97. Taixu, "Buddhism and the Modern Mind," 438. Emphasis mine.

98. Ibid., 439. Grammar is corrected.

99. Quoted in Hamilton, "An Hour with T'ai Shu," 165.

100. See Wach, *Types of Religious Experience,* 48–57.

GLOSSARY OF CHINESE CHARACTERS

ai 愛
Ai li yuan 愛儷園
aiyu 愛語
Bai Chongxi (Pai Ch'ung-hsi) 白宗禧
bai shoutao 白手套
baihua 白話
Bailian jiao 白蓮教
Baiyun Shan 白雲山
Baiyun zong 白雲宗
Baizhang (Pai-chang), Ven. 百丈法師
Bali sanzang yuan 巴利三藏院
Baoliansi 寶蓮寺
bei yuan 悲願
benneng 本能
bian 編
bianjue 遍覺
biguan 閉關
biqiu 比丘
biqiu jie 比丘戒
biqiuni 比丘尼
Bolin si 柏林寺
Bolin si jiaoli yuan 柏林寺教理院
boshi xuewei 博士學位

buli wenzi 不立文字
bushi 布施
Cai Yuanpei (Ts'ai Yüan-p'ei) 蔡元培
caichan geming 財產革命
can chan hui 參禪會
Caodong 曹洞
ce 冊
Chan tang 禪堂
Chan zong 禪宗
chanding 禪定
Changjue (Ch'ang-chüeh), Ven. 常覺法師
Changxing (Ch'ang-hsing), Ven. 常惺法師
Changyuan (Ch'ang-yüan), Ven. 昌圓法師
chanshi 禪師
Chen Dingmo (Ch'en Ting-mo) 陳定謨
Chen Duxiu (Ch'en Tu-hsiu) 陳獨秀
Chen Huanzhang (Ch'en Huan-chang) 陳煥章

Chen Li'an 陳履安
Chen Wenyuan (Ch'en Wen-yüan) 陳文淵
Chen Xizun (Ch'en Hsi-tsun, or C. C. Ch'en) 陳溪圳
Chen Yuanbai (Ch'en Yüan-pai) 陳元白
cheng fo 成佛
chengdeng zhengjue 成等正覺
chi 恥
Chiang Kai-shek 蔣介石
chijiao yuan 持教院
chijie 持戒
Chisong (Ch'ih-sung), Ven. 持松法師
chu dalei yin 出大雷音
ci 慈
Cien zong 慈恩宗
Cihang (Tz'u-hang), Ven. 慈航法師
Cixi (Tz'u-hsi) 慈禧
Ciyun si 慈雲寺
da sheng 大乘
da yi wang 大醫王
Dajue si 大覺寺
Dalin si 大林寺
danao Jin Shan 大鬧金山
dangren 黨人
dao (way; district) 道
Dao Feng Shan 道風山
Daoan (Tao-an), Ven. 道安法師
daochang 道場
daode wenhua 道德文化
Daode xue she 道德學社
Daojie (Tao-chieh), Ven. 道階法師
daoshi 導師
daoyou 道友
Dasheng fojiao 大乘佛教
dashi (Venerable Master) 大師

dashi xuewei (Venerable Scholar) 大士學位
Datong shu 大同書
datong zhi shi 大同之世
Daxing (Ta-hsing), Ven. 大醒法師
Daxingshan si 大興善寺
de seng 德僧
De Wang (Te Wang, or Demchukdong-grub) 德王
Deyi (Te-i), Ven. 得一法師
Dinghui si 定慧寺
Dixian (Ti-hsien), Ven. 諦閑法師
Dongchu (Tung-ch'u), Ven. 東初法師
Dongya fojiao dahui 東亞佛教大會
du zhongsheng 度眾生
Edo Sentaro 江戶千太郎
Emei Shan 峨嵋山
fa men 法門
fa yuan 法院
Fafang (Fa-fang), Ven. 法舫法師
Fagu Shan 法鼓山
Faguang fojiao wenhua yanjiu suo 法光佛教文化研究所
Fahua zong 法華宗
fangbian 方便
fashi 法師
faxiang weishi xue 法相唯識學
Faxing zong 法性宗
Fayuan si 法源寺
Fazun (Fa-tsun), Ven. 法尊法師
Fei zongjiao da tongmeng 非宗教大同盟
Feng Yuxiang (Feng Yü-hsiang) 馮玉祥 (or 馮御香)
fo 佛
fo sheng 佛乘
focha 佛剎

fofa 佛法
fofa de panshe 佛法的判攝
fofa sengyuan 佛法僧園
Foguang Shan 佛光山
foguo 佛國
foguo zhuyi 佛國主義
fohua zhuyi 佛化主義
Fojiao Ciji gongde hui 佛教慈濟功德會
Fojiao Ciji shan shiye jijin hui 佛教慈濟善事業基金會
Fojiao fangwen tuan 佛教訪問團
fojiao geming 佛教革命
Fojiao gonghui 佛教公會
Fojiao hongshi hui 佛教宏誓會
Fojiao jinde hui 佛教進德會
Fojiao jingshe 佛教精舍
Fojiao qingnian xuehui 佛教青年學會
Fojiao wenhua she 佛教文化社
Fojiao xiejin hui 佛教協進會
Fojiao yanjiu hui 佛教研究會
Fojiao yanjiu she 佛教研究社
fojiao yinhang 佛教銀行
Fojiaotu guoji heping hui 佛教徒國際和平會
foseng zhuyi 佛僧主義
fotu 佛土
foxue hui 佛學會
Foxue yanjiu she 佛學研究社
Furen daxue 輔仁大學
Gao baiyi shu 告白衣書
Gao fozi shu 告佛子書
gaodeng jaioli 高等教理
geming 革命
Geming Jun 革命軍
gong an 公案
gongchan zhuyi 共產主義

Gongchandang 共產黨
guan xing 觀行
Guangji si 廣濟寺
Guangjiao si 廣教寺
Guangxu (Kuang-hsü) 光緒
Guanli simiao tiaoli 管理寺廟條例
Guanyin ge 觀音閣
Guanzong si 觀宗寺
gui 鬼
gui yuan 歸元
guiju 規矩
guiyi sanbao 皈依三寶
guo 國
Guomindang 國民黨
Haichao si 海潮寺
Haichao yin 海潮音
Han 漢
Han Zang jiaoli yuan 漢藏教理院
Hankou fojiao zhengxin hui 漢口佛教正信會
Hong Xiuquan (Hung Hsiu-ch'üan) 洪秀全
Hongfa xueyuan 宏法學院
Hongsan (Hung-san), Ven. 弘傘法師
Hongyi (Hung-i), Ven. 弘一法師
Hu Ruilin (Hu Jui-lin) 胡瑞霖
Hu Shi (Hu Shih) 胡適
hua tou 話頭
huadao dazhong 化道大眾
Hualin si 華林寺
Huang Qinglan (Huang Ch'ing-lan) 黃慶瀾
Huang Zongyang (Huang Tsung-yang) 黃宗仰
Huangjiao si 黃教寺
Huashan (Hua-shan), Ven. 華山法師
Huayan daxue 華嚴大學

Huayan zong 華嚴宗
Huazang si 華藏寺
Huiyuan (Hui-yüan), Ven. 慧遠法師
Huizhang 慧璋
huo li 活力
Inada Ensai 稻田圓成
Itō Kendō 伊藤賢道
ji 濟
jian wang 漸忘
jian yuan 監院
Jiandu simiao tiaoli 監督寺廟條例
Jiang Fangzhen (Chiang Fang-chen) 蔣方震
jiang mo 降魔
Jiang Zhe fojiao lianhe hui 江浙佛教聯合會
jiao 教
Jiao Shan 焦山
Jiao Shan foxue yuan 焦山佛學院
jiaohu tang 角虎堂
jiaohua 教化
Jiaxiang zong 嘉祥宗
Jichan (Chi-ch'an), Ven. 寄禪法師 (or Eight Fingers, Bazhi Toutuo) 八指頭陀
jichan zhuyi 集產主義
Jiedai si 接待寺
Jiezhu si 戒珠寺
jiji 積極
jin 進
Jin Ping Mei 金瓶梅
Jin Shan 金山
jing 精
jing chun 精純
jing xin 淨心
Jing'an si 靜安寺

Jingci si 淨慈寺
Jingfan yuan 淨梵院
jingjin 精進
Jingling kejing chu 金陵刻經處
Jingsi jingshe 靜思淨舍
jingtu 淨土
Jingtu xinlun 淨土新論
Jingtu zong 淨土宗
Jishan (Chi-shan), Ven. 寂山法師
jiuhu jun 救護軍
Jue she 覺社
Jueshe congshu 覺社叢書
junzi 君子
jushi 居士
Juzan (Chü-tsan), Ven. 巨贊法師
Kaiyuan si 開元寺
Kaiyuan zong 開元宗
Kang Youwei (K'ang Yu-wei) 康有為
Kangxi (K'ang-hsi) 康熙
kexue de foxue 科學的佛學
Kimura Taiken 木村泰賢
kong 空
kong zong 空宗
kongsanmei 空三昧
Laiguo (Lai-kuo), Ven. 來果法師
Lama jiao 喇嘛教
Lang Shan 狼山
leguan xiyue de shuoli 樂觀喜悅的說理
li (doctrines, principles, relational ideals) 理
li (measurement of distance) 里
li (propriety) 禮
Li Dazhao (Li Ta-chao) 李大釗
li fo 禮佛
Li Guoshen (Li Kuo-shen) 李國深

Li Kaishen (Li K'ai-shen) 李開侁
Li Rongxi (Li Jung-hsi) 李榮熙
Li Yinchen (Li Yin-ch'en) 李隱塵
Li Yuanhong (Li Yüan-hung) 黎元洪
Li Zikuan (Li Tzu-k'uan) 李子寬
lian 廉
Lian zong 蓮宗
Liang Hongzhi (Liang Hung-chih) 梁鴻志
Liang Qichao (Liang Ch'i-ch'ao) 梁啓超
Liang Shangtong (Liang Shang-t'ung) 梁尚同
Liang Shuming (Liang Shu-ming) 梁漱溟
lianshe 蓮社
Liaochen (Liao-ch'en), Ven. 了塵法師
Lin Shu 林紓
Lin Zhaoen (Lin Chao-en) 林兆恩
Lindu si 林渡寺
Lingdu si 靈渡寺
Lingyuan (Ling-yüan), Ven. 靈源法師
Linji si 臨濟寺
Linji Yixuan (Lin-chi I-hsüan), Ven. 臨濟義玄法師
liu du 六度
Liuyun si 留雲寺
lixing 利行
Longhua si 龍華寺
Lü Peilin (Lü P'ei-lin) 呂沛林
Lu Shan 盧山
Lu Shan zong 盧山宗
Lu Xun (Lu Hsün) 魯迅
lü yi 律儀
Lü zong 律宗
lüfa 律法

Luo Jialing (Lo Chia-ling) 羅迦陵
lüshi 律師
Manzhouguo 滿洲國
Mao Zedong (Mao Tse-tung) 毛澤東
Mei Guangxi (Mei Kuang-hsi) 梅光羲
Mi zong 密宗
Mile tuan 彌勒團
Minbao 民報
Minnan foxue yuan 閩南佛學院
minquan 民權
minsheng 民生
Minzhi (Min-chih), Ven. 敏智法師
minzu 民族
minzu zhuyi 民族主義
Mizuno Baigyō 水野梅曉
Mo Jipeng (Mo Chi-p'eng) 莫紀彭
mofa 末法
Mohe jiangyuan 摩訶講園
mu 畝
Nanjio Bunyiu 南條文雄
Nanshan zong 南山宗
Neizheng bu 內政部
Nian 捻
nian fo 念佛
nian fo hui 念佛會
Nian fo qianshuo 念佛淺說
Ningbo seng jiaoyu hui 寧波僧教育會
Niuyue chan zhongxin 紐約禪中心
Nongchan si 農禪寺
Ouyang Jingwu (Ou-yang Ching-wu) 歐陽竟無
Pan Dawei (P'an Ta-wei) 潘達微
Pilu si 毗盧寺
Puming si 普明寺
pusa 菩薩
pusa jie 菩薩戒

pusa seng 菩薩僧
pusa sheng 菩薩乘
puti 菩提
puti saduo 菩提薩埵
putong jiaoli 普通教理
Putuo Shan 普陀山
Puyi (P'u-i) 溥儀
Qianlong (Ch'ien-lung) 乾隆
Qichang (Ch'i-ch'ang), Ven. 歧昌法師
Qing 清
qingjie 清潔
Qingliang si 清涼寺
Qingliang zong 清涼宗
Qingnian (Ch'ing-nien), Ven. 清念法師 (or Yushan) 昱山
Qingquan (Ch'ing-ch'üan), Ven. 青權法師
Qiu Jin (Ch'iu Chin) 秋瑾
Qixia Shan 棲霞山
Qiyun (Ch'i-yün), Ven. 棲雲法師
Qu Wenliu (Ch'ü Wen-liu) 屈文六
Quan xue pian 勸學篇
Quanguo fojiao daibiao huiyi 全國佛教代表會議
Quanguo jiaoyu huiyi 全國教育會議
Quanlang (Ch'üan-lang), Ven. 全朗法師
Quanya fohua jiaoyu she 全亞佛化教育社
Quefei (Ch'üeh-fei), Ven. 卻非法師
ren 仁
renjian fojiao 人間佛教
renjian gaishan 人間改善
renjian jingtu 人間淨土
renru 忍辱
Renshan (Jen-shan), Ven. 仁山法師
Rensheng 人生

rensheng de foxue 人生的佛學
rensheng fojiao 人生佛教
rensheng gaishan 人生改善
Rensheng zhexue yanjiu hui 人生哲學研究會
Renxue 仁學
saduo 薩埵
Saeki Teien 佐伯定胤
san bao 三寶
san jiao 三教
sanfo zhuyi 三佛主義
Sanlun zong 三論宗
sanmin zhuyi 三民主義
sanmin zhuyi de wenhua 三民主義的文化
seng 僧
Seng jiaoyu hui 僧教育會
seng jun 僧軍
Sengqie huansu fotu hui 僧伽還俗佛徒會
Sengzhao (Seng-chao), Ven. 僧肇法師
shami 沙彌
shamini 沙彌尼
shan shu 善書
Shandao si 善導寺
shangdi 上帝
Shanghaishi fojiao qingnian hui 上海市佛教青年會
Shanyin (Shan-yin), Ven. 善因法師
shanzhang 山長
shao ba 燒疤
Shaoshi zong 少室宗
Shehui bu 社會部
shehui guanhuai xiaozu 社會關懷小組
shehui zhuyi 社會主義
shen 神
sheng (conveyance) 乘

sheng (province) 省
shengwen sheng 聲聞乘
Shengyan (Sheng-yen), Ven. 聖嚴法師
shi beixin 失悲心
shi cixin 失慈心
shi de 十德
shi di 十地
shi lirenxin 失利人心
Shi Mingke (Shih Ming-k'o) 石鳴珂
shi shan 十善
shi xin wei 十信位
shi xing 十行
shi zhihuixin 失智慧心
shi zhu 十住
Shida (Shih-ta), Ven. 士達法師
shifang conglin 十方叢林
shifu 師父
Shijie daibiao dahui 世界代表大會
shijie de foxue 世界的佛學
Shijie fohua daxue 世界佛化大學
Shijie fojiao lianhe hui 世界佛教聯合會
Shijie fojiaotu youyi hui 世界佛教徒友誼會
Shijie foxue yuan 世界佛學院 (or 世界佛學苑)
Shijie hongwanzi hui 世界紅卍字會
Shijie xuanchuan dui 世界宣傳隊
shijie zhuyi 世界主義
Shirob Jaltso, Ven. 喜饒嘉措法師
shizheng de foxue 實證的佛學
Shizi lin 獅子林
Shizi Shan 獅子山
shou jie 受戒
shouzuo 首座
Shuangting (Shuang-t'ing), Ven. 霜亭法師

Shuangxi si 雙溪寺
Shuihu zhuan 水滸傳
shuilu fahui 水陸法會
si hong shiyuan 四弘誓願
si qiang 四強
si shefa 四攝法
sifen jieben 四分戒本
Simiao guanli tiaoli 寺廟管理條例
Soong Meiling (Soong Mei-ling) 宋美齡
Su Manshu (Su Man-shu) 蘇曼殊
Sun Yat-sen 孫逸仙
ta sheng chu fa 他勝處法
Tai Shuangqiu (T'ai Shuang-ch'iu) 邰爽秋
Taiping 太平
Taiping Tianguo 太平天國
Taixu (T'ai-hsü), Ven. 太虛法師
Tan Sitong (T'an Ssu-t'ung) 譚嗣同
Tan Yunshan (T'an Yün-shan) 譚雲山
Tang 唐
Tanxu (T'an-hsü), Ven. 倓虛法師
ti 體
Tian Wang 天王
Tianning foxue yuan 天寧佛學院
Tiantai zong 天台宗
Tiantong si 天童寺
Tianyan lun 天演論
Tieyan (T'ieh-yen), Ven. 鐵　法師
Tongmeng hui 同盟會
Tongshan she 同善社
tongshi 同事
Tongzhi zhongxing 同治中興
Wang Jinyun (Wang Chin-yün) 王錦雲
Wang Kemin (Wang K'o-min) 王克敏
Wang Senpu (Wang Sen-p'u) 王森甫
Wang Yiting (Wang I-t'ing) 王一亭

Weichi fojiao tongmeng hui 維持佛教同盟會
Weifang (Wei-fang), Ven. 葦舫法師
Weihuan (Wei-huan), Ven. 惟幻法師
Weishi zong 唯識宗
Weixin 唯心
wenyan 文言
wu jie 五戒
wu sheng 五乘
wu wei 無為
wu wo 無我
wu za 無雜
Wu Zhihui (Wu Chih-hui) 吳稚輝
wu zhuo 五濁
Wuchang foxue yuan 武昌佛學院
Wuchang nü foxue yuan 武昌女佛學院
Wushan she 悟善社
wusheng gongfa 五乘共法
Wutai Shan 五臺山
wutuobang 烏託邦
Xi Wang Mu 西王母
xian (county) 縣
xian (immortal) 仙
xian (manifestation) 現
xiandai 現代
Xiandai foxue 現代佛學
Xianggang fojiao lianhe hui 香港佛教聯合會
xianshi zhuyi 現實主義
Xianshou zong 賢首宗
Xiao Jiuhua si 小九華寺
xiaoji 消極
Xiaosheng fojiao 小乘佛教
Xie Zhuchen (Hsieh Chu-ch'en) 謝鑄陳
Xifang si 西方寺

Xilai si 西來寺
Xilin tang 錫麟堂
xin 信
xin fojiao 新佛教
xin min 新民
xin seng 新僧
xin shenghuo yundong 新生活運動
xin wenhua yundong 新文化運動
xing 行
xing jie 性戒
xingjiao yuan 行教院
Xingxiu (Hsing-hsiu), Ven. 性修法師
Xingyun (Hsing-yün), Ven. 星雲法師 (original Dharma name: Wuche) 悟徹
Xinmin congbao 新民叢報
Xinmin shuo 新民說
xinzhi 心志
xiu lin 修林
xiu zheng 修證
Xiyou ji 西遊記
Xizhu si 西竺寺
Xu Xilin (Hsü Hsi-lin) 徐錫麟
xuanjiao yuan 宣教院
Xuantong (Hsüan-t'ung) 宣統
xue seng 學僧
xuejian 學監
xueli geming 學理革命
Xuming (Hsü-ming), Ven. 續明法師
Xuyun (Hsü-yün), Ven. 虛雲法師
Yan Fu (Yen Fu) 嚴復
Yan Shaofu (Yen Shao-fu) 嚴少孚
Yang Wenhui (Yang Wen-hui) 楊文會 (or Yang Renshan) 楊仁山
Yang Xiuqing (Yang Hsiu-ch'ing) 楊秀清
Yanpei (Yen-p'ei), Ven. 演培法師

Yanqing si 延慶寺
Yekai (Yeh-k'ai), Ven. 冶開法師
yi (heal) 醫
yi (justice, righteousness) 義
yi qing 疑情
Yiguan Dao 一貫道
Yinguang (Yin-kuang), Ven. 印光法師
Yinping (Yin-p'ing), Ven. 蔭屏法師
Yinshun (Yin-shun), Ven. 印順法師
Yinshun wenjiao jijin hui 印順文教基金會
yong 用
Yongfeng si 永豐寺
Yongming Yanshou (Yung-ming Yen-shou), Ven. 永明延壽法師
Yu Bin (Paul Yü-pin) 于斌
Yuan 元
Yuan Shikai (Yüan Shih-k'ai) 袁世凱
yuanjue sheng 緣覺乘
yuanqi 緣起
Yuanying (Yüan-ying), Ven. 圓瑛法師
Yudanyue zhou 鬱單越洲
Yuebin (Yüeh-pin), Ven. 月賓法師
Yuexia (Yüeh-hsia), Ven. 月霞法師
Yufo si 玉佛寺
Yuhuang dian 玉皇殿
Yunhua tang 雲華堂
Yunnan daxue 雲南大學
yuqieshi 瑜伽師
Yuwang si 育王寺 (or Ayuwang Si) 阿育王寺
yuzhou guan 宇宙觀
Zeng Guofan (Tseng Kuo-fan) 曾國藩
Zeng Jize (Tseng Chi-tse) 曾紀澤
Zhang Caiwei (Chang Ts'ai-wei) 張采薇
Zhang Jiasen (Chang Chia-sen; C. S. or Carsun Chang) 張嘉森 (or Zhang Junmai) 張君勱
Zhang Luqin (Chang Lu-ch'in) 張鹿芹
Zhang Taiyan (Chang T'ai-yen) 章太炎 (or Zhang Binglin) 章炳麟
Zhang Zhidong (Chang Chih-tung) 張之洞
Zhang Zuolin (Chang Tso-lin) 張作霖
Zhangjia (Chang-chia Hutukhtu), Ven. 章嘉活佛
zhanglao seng 長老僧
Zhao Puchu (Chao P'u-ch'u) 趙樸初
Zhao Yang Buwei (Chao Yang Pu-wei) 趙楊布偉
zhe jie 遮戒
zheng xin 正心
zhengli guogu 整理國故
Zhengli sengqie zhidu lun 整理僧伽制度論
Zhengyan (Cheng-yen), Ven. 證嚴法師
zhengzhi heshang 政治和尚
Zhenhua (Chen-hua), Ven. 真華法師
zhenru 真如
Zhenyan zong 真言宗
zhi 智
zhi ben 治本
zhi biao 治標
zhi seng 職僧
zhiguan 止觀
Zhiguang (Chih-kuang), Ven. 智光法師
Zhihuan jingshe 祇洹精舍
zhihui 智慧
Zhikai (Chih-k'ai), Ven. 志開法師
Zhina neixue yuan 支那內學院
Zhiyue lu 指月錄

Zhong Xi wenhua xiehui 中錫文化協會
Zhongguo 中國
Zhongguo fojiao hui 中國佛教會
Zhongguo fojiao huiwu renyuan xunlian ban 中國佛教會務人員訓練班
Zhongguo fojiao xiehui 中國佛教協會
Zhongguo fojiao yiyuan 中國佛教醫院
Zhongguo fojiao zhengli weiyuan hui 中國佛教整理委員會
Zhongguo foxue hui 中國佛學會
Zhongguo wenyi fuxing 中國文藝復興
Zhongguo zhengli weiyuan hui 中國整理委員會
Zhongguo zongjiaotu lianyi hui 中國宗教徒聯誼會
Zhonghua fohua jiaoyu she 中華佛化教育社
Zhonghua fojiao lianhe hui 中華佛教聯合會
Zhonghua fojiao wenhua guan 中華佛教文化館
Zhonghua fojiao yanjiu suo 中華佛教研究所
Zhonghua fojiao zonghui 中華佛教總會
Zhonghua huangwanzi hui 中華黃卍字會
Zhongxue wei ti, Xixue wei yong 中學為體，西學為用
Zhou Enlai (Chou En-lai) 周恩來
Zhu'an (Chu-an), Ven. 竺庵法師
zhuan falun 轉法輪
Zhuangnian (Chuang-nien), Ven. 奘年法師
zhuchi 住持
ziran 自然
zong 宗
zongjiao 宗教
zongjiao hui 宗教會
Zongli Yamen 總理衙門
Zongyang (Tsung-yang), Ven. 宗仰法師
Zou Rong (Tsou Jung) 鄒容
zuo shizi hou 作獅子吼
zushi 祖師
zusun miao 祖孫廟
zuzhi geming 組織革命

SELECTED BIBLIOGRAPHY

I. WORKS BY TAIXU
A. In Chinese

Taixu 太虛. *Foxue de jianglai* 佛學的將來 (The Future of Buddhism). Hong Kong, 1935.

———. *Taixu dashi Guangdong yanjiang ji chubian* 太虛大師廣東演講集初編 (Lectures in Guangdong by the Venerable Master Taixu: First Edition). Guangdong, 1935.

———. *Faxiang weishi xue* 法相唯識學 (Dharma-Character Idealistic Philosophy). Shanghai, 1938.

———. *Huguo yanlun ji* 護國言論集 (Collected Speeches on Protecting the Country). Hong Kong, 1939.

———. *Taixu dashi quanshu* 太虛大師全書 (The Complete Works of the Venerable Master Taixu), 20 vols. Taipei, 1956.

———. *Pusa xue chu* 菩薩學處 (The Bodhisattva's Context for Learning). Taipei, 1957.

———. *Zhengdun sengqie zhidu lun* 整頓僧伽制度論 (On Reorganizing the Monastic System). Taipei, 1958.

———. *Jushi xue fo zhi chengxu* 居士學佛之程序 (The Course of the Laity's Study of Buddhism). Taipei, 1978.

———. *Zhexue* 哲學 (Philosophy). Taipei, 1978.

———. *Fahua jing jiaoshi* 法華經教釋 (A Commentary on the Lotus Sūtra). Kaohsiung, 1979.

———. *Fojiao ge zongpai yuanliu* 佛教各宗派源流 (The Origin of Each Buddhist School). Wuchang, no date.

B. In Translation

Taixu (T'ai-hsü). "The Meaning of Chen Ju and Ju Lai." *Chinese Recorder* 55/2 (February 1924): 119–120.

———. "A Statement to Asiatic Buddhists." *Young East* 1/6 (November 8, 1925): 177–182.

———. "Der Buddhismus in Geschichte und Gegenwart." *Sinica* 3 (1928): 189–196.

———. *Lectures in Buddhism*. Paris: Les Amis du Bouddhisme, 1928.

———. "Buddhism and the Modern Mind." Translated by Frank R. Millican. *Chinese Recorder* 65/7 (July 1934): 435–440.

———. "The Meaning of Buddhism." Translated by Frank R. Millican. *Chinese Recorder* 65/11 (November 1934): 689–695.

———. "A Peaceful World After Allied Victory." *China At War* 11/6 (December 1943): 20–22.

II. BUDDHIST TEXTS

(in the Taishō Tripiṭaka)

Cheng weishi lun 成唯識論. Translated by Xuanzang 玄奘. T vol. 31, no. 1585.

Dafoding shoulengyan jing 大佛首楞嚴經 (Sūraṅgama Sūtra). T vol. 19, no. 945.

Dasheng qixin lun 大乘起信論. T vol. 32, no. 1666.

Gaoseng zhuan 高僧傳. By Huijiao 慧皎. T vol. 50, no. 2059.

Jingang banruo boluomi jing 金剛般若波羅蜜經 (Diamond Sūtra). T vol. 8, no. 235.

Lengqie abaduoluo bao jing 楞伽阿跋多羅寶經 (Laṅkāvatāra Sūtra). Translated by Gunabhadra. T vol. 16, no. 670.

Miaofa lianhua jing 妙法蓮華經 (Lotus Sūtra). T vol. 9, no. 262.

Weimojie suoshuo jing 維摩詰所説經 (Vimalakīrti-nirdeśa Sūtra). Translated by Kumārajīva. T vol. 14, no. 475.

Wuliangshou jing youbotishe yuansheng jie 無量壽經優波提舍願生偈 (Rebirth Treatise). By Vasubandhu. T vol. 26, no. 1524.

III. OTHER CHINESE OR JAPANESE SOURCES

Bukkyō Rengo-kai 佛教聯合會, ed. *Tōa Bukkyō taikai kiyō* 東亞佛教大會記要 (Summary of the East Asian Buddhist Conference). Tokyo, 1926.

Cen Xuelü 岑學呂, *Xuyun heshang nianpu* 虛雲和尚年譜 (Chronological Biography of the Monk Xuyun). Taipei, 1978.

———, ed. *Xuyun laoheshang fahui* 虛雲老和尚法彙 (Collected Teachings of the Venerable Monk Xuyun). 2 vols. Taipei, 1974.

Dongchu 東初. *Zhongguo fojiao jindai shi* 中國佛教近代史 (History of Modern Chinese Buddhism). 2 vols. Taipei, 1974.

———. *Dongchu laoren quanji* 東初老人全集 (The Complete Works of the Elder Master Dongchu). 4 vols. Taipei, 1985.

Fafang 法舫. "Chugoku Bukkyō no genjō" 中國佛教の現狀 (The Present State of Chinese Buddhism). In *Nikka bukkyō kenkyukai nempō daiichinen* (First Annual Report of the Japanese-Chinese Research Society). Kyoto, 1936: 28–47.

Fojiao mingren zhuan 佛教名人傳 (A Record of Famous Buddhists). Taipei, 1987.

Fojiao yuebao 佛教月報 (Buddhist Monthly).

Foxue congbao 佛學叢報 (Buddhist Miscellany).

Fu Zhiying 符芝瑛. *Chuan deng: Xingyun dashi zhuan* 傳燈：星雲大師傳 (Handing Down the Light: A Biography of Venerable Master Xingyun). Taipei, 1995.

Gao Yongxiao 高永霄. "Taixu dashi de sixiang tixi" 太虛大師的思想體系 (The System of Thought of the Venerable Master Taixu). *Xianggang fojiao* (Buddhism in Hong Kong), no. 286 (June 1960): 24–30.

Guo Peng 郭朋. *Yinshun foxue sixiang yanjiu* 印順佛學思想研究 (A Study of the Buddhist Thought of Yinshun). Taipei, 1992.

———. *Taixu dashi sixiang yanjiu* 太虛大師思想研究 (A Study of the Thought of the Venerable Master Taixu). Taipei, 1996.

Haichao yin wenku 海潮音文庫 (Collected Essays from *Haichao yin*). Shanghai, 1931.

Hengqing 恆清. *Puti dao shang de shan nüren* 菩提道上的善女人 (Women of Virtue on the Path of Enlightenment). Taipei, 1995.

Hong Jinlian 洪金蓮. *Taixu dashi fojiao xiandaihua zhi yanjiu* 太虛大師佛教現代化之研究 (Research into the Venerable Master Taixu's Modernization of Buddhism). Taipei, 1995.

Hu Shih 胡適. *Sishi zishu* 四十自述 (My Autobiography at Age Forty). Shanghai, 1933; Taipei reprint, 1959.

Jianzheng 見正. *Yinguang dashi de shengping yu sixiang* 印光大師的生平與思想 (The Life and Thought of the Venerable Master Yinguang). Taipei, 1989.

Jiang Canteng 江燦騰. *Renjian jingtu de zhuixun* 人間淨土的追尋 (The Pursuit of a Pure Land on Earth). Taipei, 1989.

———. *Taiwan fojiao yu xiandai shehui* 臺灣佛教與現代社會 (Taiwanese Buddhism and Contemporary Society). Taipei, 1992.

Liang Shuming 梁漱溟. *Dong Xi wenhua ji qi zhexue* 東西文化及其哲學 (Eastern and Western Cultures and Their Philosophies). Shanghai, 1922; Taipei reprint, 1960.

Lin Ziqing 林子青. *Hongyi dashi nianpu* 弘一大師年譜 (Chronological Biography of the Venerable Master Hongyi). Taipei, 1978.

Lu Keng 陸鏗, ed. *Renjian fojiao de Xingyun* 人間佛教的星雲 (Humanistic Buddhism's Xingyun). Kaohsiung, 1991.

Lu Zhenting 陸震廷. *Renjian fojiao yu Xingyun dashi* 人間佛教與星雲大師 (Humanistic Buddhism and the Venerable Master Xingyun). Tainan, 1992.

Manzhi 滿智 and Mochan 墨禪, eds., *Taixu dashi huanyou ji* 太虛大師寰游記 (A Record of the Venerable Master Taixu's World Travel). Taipei, 1978.

Qiu Xiuzhi 丘秀芷. *Da ai: Zhengyan fashi yu ciji shijie*: 大愛：證嚴法師與慈濟世界 (Great Love: Dharma Master Zhengyan and the World of Ciji). Taipei, 1996.

Shengyan 聖嚴. *Shengyan fashih xuesi licheng* 聖嚴法師學思歷程 (The Course of My Education and Thought). Taipei, 1993.

———. *Fagu shan de fangxiang* 法鼓山的方向 (The Future of Dharma Drum Mountain). Taipei, 1995.

———. *Fojiao rumen* 佛教入門 (The Gateway to Buddhism). Taipei, 1995.

———. *Xuefo zhijin* 學佛知津 (The Ferry for Learning Buddhism). Taipei, 1995.

Shijie fojiaotu youyi hui di shiliu jie dahui: jinian tekan 世界佛教徒友誼會第十六屆大會：紀念特刊 (The Sixteenth General Conference of the World Fellowship of Buddhists: Souvenir Program). Hacienda Heights, Calif., 1988.

Xingyun 星雲. *Xingyun dashi jiangyan ji* 星雲大師講演集 (The Collected Lectures of the Venerable Master Xingyun). 4 vols. Taipei, 1987.

———. *Ruhe jianshe renjian de fojiao* 如何建設人間的佛教 (How to Establish a Humanistic Buddhism). Kaohsiung, 1989.

———. "Ruhe jianshe xiandai fojiao" 如何建設現代佛教 (How to Construct a Modern Buddhism). In *1990 Foguang Shan guoji fojiao xueshu huiyi lunwen ji* 佛光山國際佛教學術會議論文集 (1990 Anthology of the Foguang Shan International Buddhist Conference), Chinese version, 2–6; English version, 7–13. Kaohsiung, 1992.

———. *Xingyun Chan hua* 星雲禪話 (Xingyun's Chan Talks). 4 vols. Taipei, 1987–1989.

Xianggang fojiao 香港佛教 (Buddhism in Hong Kong).

Xuming 續明. *Taixu dashi shengping shiji* 太虛大師生平事蹟 (A Record of the Life of the Venerable Master Taixu). Taipei, 1957.

Yang Huinan 楊惠南. *Dangdai fojiao sixiang zhanwang* 當代佛教思想展望 (A Survey of Contemporary Buddhist Thought). Taipei, 1991.

Yinguang 印光. *Yinguang fashi wenchao quanji* 印光法師文鈔全集 (The Complete Works of the Dharma Master Yinguang). 2 vols. Taipei, 1975.

Yinshun 印順. *Taixu dashi nianpu* 太虛大師年譜 (A Chronological Biography of the Venerable Master Taixu). Taipei, 1973; originally published in Hong Kong in 1950.

———. *Fo zai renjian* 佛在人間 (The Buddha in the Human Realm). Taipei, 1971.

———. "Shangdi ai shiren?" 上帝愛世人？ (God Loves Humans?) In *Dasheng wenku*, 7, *Fojiao yu yejiao de bijiao* 大乘文庫 7, 佛教與耶教的比較 (Mahāyāna Studies, Vol. 7: Comparing Buddhism and Christianity), ed. Zhang Mantao, 163–195. Taipei, 1971.

———. "Shangdi ai shiren de zai taolun" 上帝愛世人的再討論 (A Second Discussion on God's Love for Humans). In *Dasheng wenku*, 7, *Fojiao yu yejiao de bijiao* 大乘文庫 7, 佛教與耶教的比較 (Mahāyāna Studies, Vol. 7: Comparing Buddhism and Christianity), ed. Zhang Mantao, 197–244. Taipei, 1971.

———. *Yindu zhi fojiao* 印度之佛教 (Indian Buddhism). Taipei, 1985.

———. *Cheng fo zhi dao* 成佛之道 (The Way to Buddhahood). Taipei, 1994.

———. *Pingfan de yisheng* 平凡的一生 (An Ordinary Life). Taipei, 1994.

———. *Jingtu yu chan* 淨土與禪 (Pure Land and Chan). Taipei, 1995.

Zhaohui 昭慧. *Renjian fojiao de bozhong zhe* 人間佛教的播種者 (The Sower of the Seeds of a Humanistic Buddhism). Taipei, 1995.

Zhengyan 證嚴. *Zhengyan fashi shuo gushi* 證嚴法師說故事 (Stories by Dharma Master Zhengyan). Taipei, 1996.

IV. OTHER WESTERN LANGUAGE SOURCES

Alitto, Guy S. *The Last Confucian: Liang Shu-ming and the Chinese Dilemma of Modernity*. Berkeley: University of California Press, 1979.

Awakening of Faith in the Mahāyāna Doctrine: The New Buddhism. Translated by Timothy Richard. Shanghai: Christian Literature Society, 1907.

Ayers, William. *Chang Chih-tung and Educational Reform in China*. Cambridge: Harvard University Press, 1971.

Barrows, John Henry, ed. *The World's Parliament of Religions*. 2 vols. Chicago: Parliament Publishing Company, 1893.

Bellah, Robert N. *Religion and Progress in Modern Asia*. New York: The Free Press, 1965.

Bennett, A. A. G. "A Short Biography of Miss Grace Constant Lounsbery." *Maha Bodhi* 73/3–4 (March–April 1965): 83–84.

Berling, Judith A. *The Syncretic Religion of Lin Chao-en*. New York: Columbia University Press, 1980.

Blofeld, John. *The Jewel in the Lotus: An Outline of Present Day Buddhism in China*. London: Sidgwick & Jackson, 1948; Westport: Hyperion Press, 1975.

———. *The Wheel of Life: The Autobiography of a Western Buddhist*. 2nd ed. London: Rider & Company, 1972.

Boorman, Howard L., ed. *Biographical Dictionary of Republican China*. 4 vols. New York: Columbia University Press, 1970.

Braden, Charles S. "How Liberal Christianity Conceives of Salvation." *Journal of Religion* 17 (January 1937): 12–29.

"Buddhist Leader Returns." *China at War* 4 (July 1940): 34–35.

Bush, Richard C., Jr. *Religion in Communist China*. Nashville: Abingdon Press, 1970.

Buswell, Robert E., Jr. "The 'Short-cut' Approach of K'an-hua Meditation: The Evolution of a Practical Subitism in Chinese Ch'an Buddhism." In *Sudden and Gradual: Approaches to Enlightenment in Chinese Thought*, ed. Peter N. Gregory. Honolulu: University of Hawai'i Press, 1987.

Callahan, Paul. "T'ai Hsü and the New Buddhist Movement." In *Papers on China*, vol. 6, 149–188. Cambridge: Harvard University East Asian Research Center, 1952.

Chan Kim-kwong. "Buddhists' Understanding of Christianity in Late Ming China: Implications for Interfaith Dialogue," *Ching Feng* 37/3 (September 1994), 168–192.

Chan Sin-wai. *Buddhism in Late Ch'ing Political Thought*. Hong Kong: The Chinese University Press, 1985.

Chan Wing-tsit. *Religious Trends in Modern China*. New York: Columbia University Press, 1953.

Chang, C. S (Carsun), (Zhang Jiasen or Zhang Jumai). "The Anti-Religion Movement." *Chinese Recorder* 55/8 (August 1923): 459–467.

———. *The Development of Neo-Confucian Thought*. New York: Bookman Associates, 1962.

Chang Hao. *Chinese Intellectuals in Crisis: Search for Order and Meaning (1890–1911)*. Berkeley: University of California Press, 1987.

Chao Yang Buwei. *Autobiography of a Chinese Woman*. New York, 1947.

Chen Duxiu. "Christianity and the Chinese People" (Jidujiao yu zhongguo ren). Translated by Yu-yue Tsu. *Chinese Recorder* 51 (July 1920): 453–458.

Chen, W. Y. "The Ancient Religions in China Today." In *The China Christian Year Book, 1936–1937*, 98–111. Shanghai: Christian Literature Society, 1937.

Chen-hua. *In Search of the Dharma: Memoirs of a Modern Chinese Buddhist Pilgrim*. Edited with an introduction by Chün-fang Yü and translated by Denis C. Mair. Albany: State University of New York Press, 1992.

Ch'en, Kenneth K. S. *Buddhism in China: A Historical Survey*. Princeton: Princeton University Press, 1972.

———. *The Chinese Transformation of Buddhism*. Princeton: Princeton University Press, 1973.

Cheng-yen (Zhengyan). "Tzu Chi Resolutions." Translated by Y. L. Lee. *Tzu Chi Quarterly* 1/1 (Spring 1994): 3.

---. "The Thirty-Seven Dharma Principles of Enlightenment Which Lead to Buddhahood." Translated by E. E. Ho and W. L. Rathje. *Tzu Chi Quarterly* 2/3 (Fall/Winter 1995): 5–9.

---. "The Difficulty in Reading Buddhist Sūtras." Translated by Andy Chen. *Tzu Chi Quarterly* 3/3 (Fall 1996): 13–14.

Chesneaux, Jean. *Secret Societies in China: In the Nineteenth and Twentieth Centuries*. Ann Arbor: University of Michigan Press, 1971.

---, ed. *Popular Movements and Secret Societies in China, 1840–1950*. Stanford: Stanford University Press, 1972.

Ch'ien, Edward T. "The Neo-Confucian Confrontation with Buddhism: A Structural and Historical Analysis." *Journal of Chinese Philosophy* 9 (1982): 307–328.

---. *Chiao Hung and the Restructuring of Neo-Confucianism in the Late Ming*. New York: Columbia University Press, 1986.

Chinese Ministry of Information, comp. *The China Handbook 1937–45: A Comprehensive Survey of Major Developments in China in Eight Years of War*, revised and enlarged with 1946 supplement. New York: Macmillan, 1947.

Ching Yu-ing. *Master of Love and Mercy: Cheng Yen*. Nevada City: Blue Dolphin Publishing, Inc., 1995.

Chou Hsiang-kuang. *T'ai Hsü: His Life and Teachings*. Allahabad, India: Indo-Chinese Literature Publications, 1957.

Chow Tse-tsung. *The May Fourth Movement: Intellectual Revolution in Modern China*. Cambridge: Harvard University Press, 1960.

Chu Pao-tang. "Buddhist Organizations in Taiwan." In *Chinese Culture* 10/2 (June 1969): 98–132.

Cohen, Paul A. "Missionary Approaches: Hudson Taylor and Timothy Richard." In *Papers on China*, vol. 11, 29–62. Cambridge: Harvard University East Asian Research Center, 1957.

---. *China and Christianity: The Missionary Movement and the Growth of Chinese Antiforeignism, 1860–1870*. Cambridge: Harvard University Press, 1963.

---. "Ch'ing China: Confrontation with the West, 1850–1900." In *Modern East Asia: Essays in Interpretation*, ed. James B. Crowley, 29–61. New York: Harcourt, Brace & World, 1970.

Covell, Ralph R. *Confucius, The Buddha, and Christ: A History of the Gospel in Chinese*. Maryknoll, N.Y.: Orbis Books, 1986.

Cressy, Earl Herbert. "A Study in Indigenous Religions." In *Layman's Foreign Missionary Inquiry, Fact-Finders Reports*, vol. 5, Supplementary Series, part 2, ed. Orville A. Petty, 655–717. New York: Harper, 1933.

Day, C. B. "A Unique Buddhist-Taoist Union Prayer Conference." *Chinese Recorder* 56 (June 1925): 366–369.

———. *Chinese Peasant Cults.* Shanghai: Kelly and Walsh, 1946.

Dayal, Har. *The Bodhisattva Doctrine in Buddhist Sanskrit Literature.* Delhi: Motilal Banarsidass, 1932.

de Groot, J. J. M. "Buddhist Masses for the Dead at Amoy: An Ethnological Essay." In *Actes du Sixième Congrès International des Orientalistes, tenu en 1883 à Leiden*, 1–120. Leiden: E. J. Brill, 1885.

de Vargas, Ph. "The Religious Problem in the Chinese Renaissance." *International Review of Missions* 15 (1926): 3–20.

Dean, Kenneth. *Taoist Ritual and Popular Cults of Southeast China.* Princeton: Princeton University Press, 1993.

Demiéville, Paul. "Le Bouddhisme et la Guerre: Post-scriptum à l' 'Historie des Moines Guerriers du Japon' de G. Renondeau." *Mélanges Paris Universitaire Institut des hautes études chinoises* 1 (1957): 347–385.

Dirlik, Arif. "The Ideological Foundations of the New Life Movement: A Study in Counterrevolution." *Journal of Asian Studies* 34/4 (August 1975): 945–980.

Eber, Irene. "Thought on Renaissance in Modern China: Problems of Definition." In *Studia Asiatica: Essays in Asian Studies in Felicitation of the Seventy-fifth Anniversary of Professor Ch'en Shou-yi,* ed. Laurence G. Thompson, 189–218. San Francisco: Chinese Materials Center, 1975.

Eberhard, Wolfram. "Temple-Building Activities in Medieval and Modern China: An Experimental Study." *Monumenta Serica* 23 (1964): 264–318.

Edkins, Joseph. *Chinese Buddhism: A Volume of Sketches, Historical, Descriptive, and Critical.* London: Kegan Paul, Trench, Trübner, & Co., 1893.

Eilert, Hakan. *Boundlessness: Studies in Karl Ludvig Reichelt's Missionary Thinking with Special Regard to the Buddhist-Christian Encounter.* Ringkobing, Aros; Eksp., DBK, 1974.

Eitel, Ernest J. *Buddhism, Its Historical, Theoretical, and Popular Aspects.* 3rd ed. Hong Kong: Lane, Crawford & Co., 1884.

Eppsteiner, Fred., ed. *The Path of Compassion: Writings on Socially Engaged Buddhism.* Berkeley: Parallax Press, 1985.

Fairbank, John K. *Trade and Diplomacy on the China Coast: The Opening of the Treaty Ports, 1842–1854.* Cambridge: Harvard University Press, 1953.

———. *The Chinese World Order: Traditional China's Foreign Relations.* Cambridge: Harvard University Press, 1968.

Fairbank, John K., Edwin O. Reischauer, and Albert M. Craig. *East Asia: Tradition and Transformation.* Boston: Houghton Mifflin Company, 1973.

Franck, Harry A. *Roving Through Southern China*. New York: The Century Co., 1925.

Franke, Otto. "Eine neue Buddhistische propaganda." *T'oung Pao* 5 (1894): 299–310.

———. "Ein Buddhistischer Reformversuch in China." *T'oung Pao* Ser. 2 (1909): 567–602.

———. "Die Propaganda des japanischen Buddhismus in China." In Otto Franke, *Ostasiatische Neubildungen*, 158–165. Hamburg: C. Boysen, 1911.

Fu Chi-ying. *Handing Down the Light: The Biography of Venerable Master Hsing Yun*. Translated by Amy Lui-ma. Hacienda Heights, Calif.: Hsi Lai University Press, 1996.

Gernet, Jacques. *Buddhism in Chinese Society: An Economic History from the Fifth to the Tenth Centuries*. Translated by Franciscus Verellen. New York: Columbia University Press, 1995.

Glüer, Winifred. "The Encounter Between Christianity and Chinese Buddhism During the Nineteenth Century and the First Half of the Twentieth Century." *Ching Feng* 11/3 (1968): 39–57.

Graham, David Crockett. *Religion in Szechuan Province, China*. Smithsonian Miscellaneous Collections 80/4 (1928): 1–83, plus 25 plates.

Gregory, Peter N. *Tsung-mi and the Sinification of Buddhism*. Princeton, N.J.: Princeton University Press, 1991.

Grieder, Jerome B. *Intellectuals and the State in Modern China: A Narrative History*. New York: The Free Press, 1981.

Gützlaff, Charles. "Journal of a Voyage along the Coast of China from the Province of Canton to Leaoutung in Mantschou-Tartary, 1832–1833." *Chinese Repository* 2 (1833–1834): 49–60.

Hamilton, Clarence H. "Religion and the New Culture Movement in China." *Journal of Religion* 1 (May 1921): 225–232.

———. "An Hour with T'ai Shu, Master of the Law." *The Open Court* 42 (1928): 162–169.

———. "Buddhistic Idealism in Wei Shih Er Shih Lwen." In *Essays in Philosophy*, ed. Thomas V. Smith and William K. Wright. Chicago: The Open Court, 1929, 99–115.

———. "Buddhism." In *China*, ed. H. F. McNair, 290–300. Berkeley: University of California Press, 1946.

Hodous, Lewis. *Buddhism and Buddhists in China*. New York: Macmillan, 1924.

———. "The Chinese Church of the Five Religions." *Journal of Religion* 4 (1924): 71–76.

Hsiao Kung-chuan. *A Modern China and a New World: K'ang Yu-wei, Reformer and Utopian, 1858–1927*. Seattle: University of Washington Press, 1975.

Hsing Yün (Xingyun). *How to Be a Fo Kuang Buddhist* (Zenyang zuo ge foguang ren). 2 vols. Kaohsiung, 1987.

———. *Only a Great Rain: A Guide to Chinese Buddhist Meditation.* Translated by Tom Graham, introduction by John McRae. Boston: Wisdom Publications, 1999.

———. *The Prospect for Buddhist Youth* (Fojiao qingnian de zhanwang). Kaohsiung, 1987.

———. *Two Talks on Buddhism* (Foxue jiangzuo). Kaohsiung, 1987.

———. *The Young Buddhist's Path to Success* (Fojiao qingnian chenggong liye zhi dao). Kaohsiung, 1987.

———. *The Lion's Roar: Actualizing Buddhism in Daily Life and Building the Pure Land in Our Midst.* Translated by Yung Kai and Chen Xin. New York: Peter Lang, 1991.

———. *Being Good: Buddhist Ethics for Everyday Life.* Translated by Tom Graham. New York: Weatherhill, 1998.

Hsü, Immanuel C. Y. "Late Ch'ing Foreign Relations, 1866–1905." In *The Cambridge History of China,* vol. 11, *Late Ch'ing, 1800–1911, Part 2,* ed. John K. Fairbank and Kwang-ching Liu, 70–141. Cambridge: Cambridge University Press, 1980.

———. *The Rise of Modern China.* 3rd ed. Oxford: Oxford University Press, 1983.

Hu Shih. "The Civilizations of the East and West." In *Whither Mankind: A Panorama of Modern Civilization,* ed. Charles A. Beard, 25–41. New York: Longmans, Green and Co., 1928.

———. "My Credo and Its Evolution." In *Living Philosophies,* ed. Albert Einstein et al., 235–263. New York: Simon and Schuster, 1931.

———. *The Chinese Renaissance.* Chicago: University of Chicago Press, 1934.

———. "The Task of Confucianism." In *Modern Trends in World Religions,* ed. Albert Eustace Haydon. Chicago: University of Chicago Press, 1934.

———. *The Development of the Logical Method in Ancient China.* With an introduction by Hyman Kublin. 2nd ed. Shanghai, 1922; New York: Paragon Book Reprint Corp., 1963.

Hummel, Arthur W., ed. *Eminent Chinese of the Ch'ing Period (1644–1912).* Taipei: SMC Publishing Inc., 1943.

Hurvitz, L. "Toward a Comprehensive History of Chinese Buddhism." *Journal of the American Oriental Society* 89 (1969): 763–773.

Jen Yu-ren. *The Taiping Revolutionary Movement.* New Haven: Yale University Press, 1973.

Johnston, Reginald F. "A Poet Monk of Modern China." *Journal of the North China Branch of the Royal Asiatic Society* 43 (1932): 14–30.

Jones, Charles Brewer. *Buddhism in Taiwan: Religion and the State, 1660–1990*. Honolulu: University of Hawai'i Press, 1999.

K'ang Yu-wei. *Ta T'ung Shu: The One-World Philosophy of K'ang Yu-wei*. Translated with introduction and notes by Laurence G. Thompson. London: George Allen and Unwin, 1958.

Kawamura, Leslie S., ed. *The Bodhisattva Doctrine in Buddhism*. Waterloo, Ontario: Wilfrid Laurier University Press, 1981.

Kitagawa, Joseph M. "Buddhism in Taiwan Today." *France-Aise* (Tokyo) 18 (Juillet-Août, 1962): 439–444.

———. "Primitive, Classical, and Modern Religions: A Perspective on Understanding the History of Religions." In *The History of Religions: Essays on the Problem of Understanding*, ed. J. M. Kitagawa, with the collaboration of Mircea Eliade and Charles Long, 39–65. Chicago: University of Chicago Press, 1967.

Kotler, Arnold, ed. *Engaged Buddhist Reader*. Berkeley: Parallax Press, 1996.

Kuhn, Philip A. *Rebellion and Its Enemies in Late Imperial China: Militarization and Social Structure, 1796–1864*. Cambridge: Harvard University Press, 1970.

———. "The Taiping Rebellion." In *The Cambridge History of China*, vol. 10, *Late Ch'ing, 1800–1911, Part 1*, ed. John K. Fairbank, 264–317. Cambridge: Cambridge University Press, 1978.

Kwong, Luke S. K. *A Mosaic of the Hundred Days: Personalities, Politics, and Ideas of 1898*. Cambridge: Harvard University Press, 1984.

Lai, Whalen. "Why Is There Not a Buddho-Christian Dialogue in China?" *Buddhist-Christian Studies* 6 (1986): 81–96.

———. "The Buddhist-Christian Dialogue in China." In *Religious Issues and Interreligious Dialogues: An Analysis and Sourcebook of Developments Since 1945*, ed. Charles Wei-hsun Fu and Gerhard E. Spiegler, 613–631. New York: Greenwood Press, 1989.

———. "Chinese Buddhism and Christian Charities: A Comparative History." *Buddhist-Christian Studies* 12 (1992): 5–33.

Lancashire, D. "Some Views on Christianity Expressed by the Buddhist Abbot T'ai Hsü." *Quarterly Notes on Christianity and Chinese Religion* 3 (1959): 15–19.

Lancaster, Lewis R. "The Portable and Fixed Buddhism: The Question of the Future of Buddhism." In *1990 Foguang shan guoji fojiao xueshu huiyi lunwen ji* (1990 Anthology of Fo Kuang Shan International Buddhist Conference), 26–35. Kaohsiung, Taiwan: Fo Kuang Shan Foundation, 1992.

Latourette, Kenneth Scott. *A History of Christian Missions in China*. New York: Macmillan, 1929.

Levenson, Joseph R. *Confucian China and Its Modern Fate: A Trilogy*, first combined edition. Berkeley: University of California Press, 1968.
Liang Ch'i-ch'ao. *Intellectual Trends in the Ch'ing Period* (Ch'ing-tai hsüeh-shu kai-lun). Translated with introduction and notes by Immanuel C. Y. Hsü. Cambridge: Harvard University Press, 1959.
Little, Archibald John. *Mount Omi and Beyond: A Record of Travel on the Thibetan Border.* London: William Heinemann, 1901.
Lopez, Donald S., Jr., and Steven C. Rockefeller, eds. *The Christ and the Bodhisattva.* Albany: State University of New York Press, 1987.
Lovin, Robin W., and Frank E. Reynolds, eds. *Cosmogony and Ethical Order: New Studies in Comparative Ethics.* Chicago: University of Chicago Press, 1985.
McAleavy, Henry. *Su Man-shu (1884–1918): A Sino-Japanese Genius.* London: The China Society, 1960.
McDaniel, C. Yates. "Buddhism Makes Its Peace with the New Order." *Asia* 35 (September 1935): 536–541.
MacInnis, Donald E. *Religion in China Today: Policy and Practice.* Maryknoll: Orbis Books, 1989.
McRae, John R. "Oriental Verities on the American Frontier: The 1893 World's Parliament of Religions and the Thought of Masao Abe." *Buddhist-Christian Studies* 11 (1991): 7–36.
Manuel, Frank E., and Fritzie P. Manuel. *Utopian Thought in the Western World.* Cambridge: Harvard University Press, 1979.
Michael, Franz H., in collaboration with Chung-li Chang. *The Taiping Rebellion: History and Documents.* 3 vols. Seattle: University of Washington Press, 1966.
Millican, Frank R. "Tai Hsü and Modern Buddhism." *Chinese Recorder* 54/6 (June 1923): 326–334.
———. "Buddhism in the Light of Modern Thought as Interpreted by the Monk Tai Hsü." *Chinese Recorder* 57 (February 1926): 91–94.
———. "Philosophical and Religious Thought in China." In *The China Christian Year Book, 1926*, 423–469. Shanghai: Christian Literature Society, 1926.
———. "The Present Situation Among the Buddhists." *Chinese Recorder* 59 (September 1928): 599–601.
———. "Recent Developments in Religious Thought." In *The China Christian Year Book, 1929*, 109–141. Shanghai: Christian Literature Society, 1929.
———. "Buddhist Activities in Shanghai." *Chinese Recorder* 65 (April 1934): 221–227.
———. "Humanism in China." *Chinese Recorder* 65/11 (November 1934): 677–683.

Minamiki, George. *The Chinese Rites Controversy from Its Beginning to Modern Times.* Chicago: Loyola University Press, 1985.

Müller, Gotelind. *Buddhismus und Moderne: Ouyang Jingwu, Taixu und das Ringen um ein zeitgemässes Selbstverständisim im chinesischen Buddhismus des frühen 20. Jahrhunderts.* Stuttgart: Franz Steiner Verlag, 1993.

Naquin, Susan. *Millenarian Rebellion in China: The Eight Trigrams Uprising of 1813.* New Haven: Yale University Press, 1976.

Neill, Stephen. *A History of Christian Missions.* London: Penguin Books, 1982.

Noren, Loren E. "The Life and Work of Karl Ludvig Reichelt." *Ching Feng* 10/3 (1967): 6–33.

Overmyer, Daniel L. *Folk Buddhist Religion: Dissenting Sects in Late Traditional China.* Cambridge: Harvard University Press, 1976.

Pas, Julian F., ed. *The Turning of the Tide: Religion in China Today.* Oxford: Oxford University Press, 1989.

Payne, Robert. *Forever China.* New York: Dodd, Mead, and Co., 1945.

Perry, Elizabeth. *Rebels and Revolutionaries in North China, 1845–1945.* Stanford, Calif.: Stanford University Press, 1980.

Pittman, Don A., "The Modern Buddhist Reformer T'ai-hsü on Christianity." *Buddhist-Christian Studies* 13 (1993): 82–108.

———. "The Visionary and The Ethical: Exploring an Approach to Comparative Religious Ethics." *Shenxue yu jiaohui* (Theology and Church) 21/2 (Spring 1996): 269–279.

———. "Will a New Buddhism Appear? Liang Ch'i-ch'ao's Question and the Beginnings of the Chinese Sangha's Modernization." *Ching Feng* 41/2 (June 1998): 119–147.

Pratt, James B. "A Report on the Present Condition of Buddhism." *Chinese Social and Political Science Review* 8 (1924): 1–32.

———. *The Pilgrimage of Buddhism and a Buddhist Pilgrimage.* New York: Macmillan, 1928.

———. "Buddhism and Scientific Thinking." *Journal of Religion* 14/1 (January 1934): 13–24.

Prip-Møller, Johannes. *Chinese Buddhist Monasteries: Their Plan and Its Function as a Setting for Buddhist Monastic Life.* Copenhagen: G. E. C. Gad, 1937.

Pusey, James Reeve. *China and Charles Darwin.* Cambridge: Council on East Asian Studies, Harvard University Press, 1983.

Queen, Christopher S., and Sallie B. King, eds. *Engaged Buddhism: Buddhist Liberation Movements in Asia.* Albany: State University of New York Press, 1996.

Randall, John Herman, Jr. *The Making of the Modern Mind.* New York: Columbia University Press, 1926.
Rawlinson, Frank. "Modern Revolution and Religion in China." *International Review of Missions* 18 (1929): 161–178.
Reichelt, Karl Ludvig. "Special Work Among the Buddhists." *Chinese Recorder* 51 (July 1920): 491–497.
———. "A Conference of Chinese Buddhist Leaders." *Chinese Recorder* 54 (November, 1923): 667–669.
———. *Truth and Tradition in Chinese Buddhism: A Study of Chinese Mahayana Buddhism.* Translated by Kathrina Van Wagenen Bugge. Shanghai: Commercial Press, 1927.
———. "Present-Day Buddhism in China." *Chinese Recorder* 60 (October 1929): 647–651.
———. "Present Situation in Buddhism." In *China Christian Year Book, 1932–1933,* 100–112. Shanghai: Christian Literature Society, 1933.
———. "Trends in China's Non-Christian Religions." *Chinese Recorder* 65 (December 1934): 758–768.
———. "Buddhism in China at the Present Time and the New Challenge to the Christian Church." *International Review of Missions* 26 (1937): 153–166.
———. *The Transformed Abbot.* Translated by G. M. Reichelt and A. P. Rose. London: Lutterworth Press, 1954.
Richard, Timothy. "The Influence of Buddhism in China." *Chinese Recorder* 21/2 (February 1890): 49–64.
———. *The New Testament of Higher Buddhism.* Edinburgh: T. and T. Clark, 1910.
———. *An Epistle to All Buddhists.* Shanghai, 1916.
———. *Forty-Five Years in China: Reminiscences by Timothy Richard.* New York: Frederick A. Stokes, 1916.
———, trans. *The Awakening of Faith in the Mahāyāna Doctrine: The New Buddhism.* Shanghai: Christian Literature Society, 1907.
Robinson, Richard H., and Willard L. Johnson. *The Buddhist Religion: A Historical Introduction,* 4th ed. Belmont, Calif.: Wadsworth, 1996.
Sangharakshita. *A Survey of Buddhism.* 5th ed. Boulder: Shambhala Publications, 1980.
Saunders, Kenneth J. "Sketches of Buddhism as a Living Religion." *Journal of Religion* 2 (1922): 418–431.
Schwartz, Benjamin. *In Search of Wealth and Power: Yen Fu and the West.* Cambridge: The Belknap Press of Harvard University, 1964.
Seagrave, Sterling. *Dragon Lady: The Life and Legend of the Last Empress of China.* New York: Alfred A. Knopf, 1992.

Shengyan. *Getting the Buddha Mind*. Elmhurst, N.Y.: Dharma Drum Publications, 1982.
———. *Faith in Mind: A Guide to Ch'an Practice*. Elmhurst N.Y.: Dharma Drum Publications, 1987.
———. *The Infinite Mirror*. New York: New York Dharma Drum Publications, 1990.
———. "Four Great Thinkers in Modern Chinese Buddhism." In *Buddhist Ethics and Modern Society: An International Symposium*, ed. Charles Wei-hsun Fu and Sandra A. Wawrytko. New York: Greeenwood, 1991, 55–67.
———. *Complete Enlightenment: Translation and Commentary on the Sūtra of Complete Enlightenment*. Boston: Shambhala, 1999.
Shepherd, George W. "The New Life Movement." In *The China Christian Year Book, 1936–1937*, 67–77. Shanghai: Christian Literature Society, 1937.
Sheridan, James E. *China in Disintegration: The Republican Era in Chinese History, 1912–1949*. New York: The Free Press, 1975.
Smith, Arthur H. "A Buddhist Temple Converted into a Christian Church." *Chinese Recorder* 9 (1878): 466–469.
———. *The Uplift of China*. New York: Young People's Missionary Movement of the United States and Canada, 1908.
Smith, Jonathan Z. *Map Is Not Territory: Studies in the History of Religions*. Leiden: E. J. Brill, 1978.
Suzuki, D. T. *Outlines of Mahāyāna Buddhism*. New York: Schocken Books, Inc., 1963.
Tai Ping-heng. "Modern Chinese Buddhism." *Chinese Recorder* 56 (1925): 89–95.
Teng Ssu-yü and John K. Fairbank. *China's Response to the West: A Documentary Survey, 1839–1923*. Cambridge: Harvard University Press, 1954.
Tsu Yu-yue. "Present Tendencies in Chinese Buddhism." *Journal of Religion* 1 (September 1921): 497–512.
———. "Trends of Thought and Religion in China Today." *The Open Court* 47 (1933): 433–452.
———. "Buddhism and Modern Social-Economic Problems." *Journal of Religion* 14/1 (January 1934): 35–43.
Twinem, Paul De Witt. "Modern Syncretic Religious Societies in China: I." *Journal of Religion* 5/5 (September 1925): 463–482.
———. "Modern Syncretic Religious Societies in China: II." *Journal of Religion* 5/6 (November 1925): 595–606.
"Views of a Christian Leader in the Chinese Army." *Chinese Recorder* 54 (June 1923): 334–338.
Wach, Joachim. *Types of Religious Experience: Christian and Non-Christian*. Chicago: University of Chicago Press, 1951.

Wakeman, Frederick, Jr. *The Fall of Imperial China*. New York: The Free Press, 1975.

Wales, H. G. Quaritch. "Buddhism as a Japanese Propaganda Instrument," with a commentary by Lin Yutang. *Free World* 5/5 (May 1943): 428–432.

Wei-huan. "Buddhism in Modern China." *T'ien Hsia Monthly* 9/2 (September 1939): 140–155.

Welch, Holmes. "The Foreign Relations of Buddhism in Modern China." *Journal of the Royal Asiatic Society* 6 (1966): 73–99.

———. *The Practice of Chinese Buddhism, 1900–1950*. Cambridge: Harvard University Press, 1967.

———. *The Buddhist Revival in China*. Cambridge: Harvard University Press, 1968.

———. *Buddhism Under Mao*. Cambridge: Harvard University Press, 1972.

———. "Buddhism in China Today." In *The Cultural, Political, and Religious Significance of Buddhism in the Modern World*, ed. Heinrich Dumoulin, 164–185. New York: Macmillan, 1976.

Welter, Albert. *The Meaning of Myriad Good Deeds: A Study of Yung-ming Yen-shou and the Wan-shan Tung-kuei Chi*. New York: Peter Lang, 1994.

West, Philip. *Yenching University and Sino-Western Relations, 1916–1952*. Cambridge: Harvard University Press, 1976.

White, Morton. *What Is and What Ought To Be Done: An Essay on Ethics and Epistemology*. New York: Oxford University Press, 1981.

Wilhelm, Richard. "Chinesischer Bildersaal: Der Grossabt Schï Tai Hü." *Sinica* 4 (1929): 16.

Woodbridge, Samuel I. *China's Only Hope: An Appeal by Her Greatest Viceroy, Chang Chih-tung, with the Sanction of the Present Emperor, Kwang Sü*. Edinburgh: Oliphant, Anderson & Ferrier, 1901.

Wright, Mary Clabaugh. *The Last Stand of Chinese Conservatism: The T'ung-Chih Restoration, 1862–1874*. Stanford: Stanford University Press, 1957.

Yin-shun. *The Way to Buddhahood: Instructions from a Modern Chinese Master*. Translated by Wing H. Yeung with a foreword by Robert M. Gimello and introduction by Whalen Lai. Boston: Wisdom Publications, 1998.

Yü Chün-fang. "Chu-hung and Lay Buddhism in the Late Ming." In *The Unfolding of Neo-Confucianism*, ed. Wm. Theodore de Bary and the Conference on Seventeenth-Century Chinese Thought, 93–140. New York: Columbia University Press, 1970.

———. *The Renewal of Buddhism in China*. New York: Columbia University Press, 1981.

INDEX

Abhidharma literature, 173, 201
Academy for Spreading the Dharma (Hongfa xueyuan), 56
Alitto, Guy S., 24
All-Asia Buddhist Education Association (Quanya fohua jiaoyu she), 115
Ambedkar, B.R., 296
Amis du Bouddhisme, Les, 123
Amitābha Buddha, 2, 30, 92, 100, 134, 203, 222, 237–240
Anarchism, 81, 109, 182
Apprehension of Goodness Society (Wushan she), 53
Ariyaratne, A.T., 296
Association for the Advancement of Buddhism (Fojiao xiejin hui), 51, 74–76, 78, 315n. 36
Association for the Education of Monks (Seng jiaoyu hui), 71
Association Française des Amis de l'Orient, 122
Association Franco-Chinoise, 122
Association of Chinese Religious Believers (Zhongguo zongjiaotu lianyi hui), 145–146, 251, 328nn. 95–101
Association of Former Buddhist Monastics Who Returned to Lay Life (Sengqie huansu fotu hui), 210
Avataṃsaka Sūtra. *See* Huayan Sutra

Awakening of Faith in Mahayana (Dasheng qixin lun), 41, 44, 83, 94

Bai Chongxi, 145–146
Baiyun Shan (Guangzhou), 71
Baizhang, Ven., 288
Bakunin, Mikhail, 72
Bali sanzang yuan. *See* Pali Tripiṭaka Institute
Bantetsugu Roshi, 280
Baohua Shan (Nanjing), 54–55
Baolian si (Hong Kong), 261
bei tian (fields of compassion), 320n. 101
biguan. See sealed confinement
Blofeld, John, 87, 102, 143
Bodhi Society (Jue she), 90–94
bodhicitta (thought of enlightenment), 67, 197–198, 212, 217
Bodhisattvas: basic precepts of, 53, 88, 216, 340n. 62; meritorious actions of, 88, 173, 176, 216–217; practice of the Six Perfections *(liu du)* by, 10, 166, 199, 217–221; serious offenses of, 215–216; universal vows of, 205, 214–215, 221
Bolin Buddhist Institute (Bolin si jiaoli yuan), 99
Bolin si (Beijing), 99
Boorman, Howard, 75, 146

379

Boxer Rebellion, 17, 301n. 14
Brace, A.J., 100
Brahmajāla Sūtra, 92
Buddhadasa, Ven. 296
Buddhism: dual practice of Chan and Pure Land in, 99, 201; five vehicles *(wu sheng)* doctrine in, 87, 171–173, 199–200, 204, 269; for human life *(rensheng fojiao) (see under* Taixu); humanist criticisms of, in China 170–171; humanistic *(renjian fojiao)*, 226, 263, 267, 270, 273, 283, 340n. 75; in Hong Kong, 261–262; interdependence of monastic and householder forms in, 30, 303n. 44; lay associations in, 30–31, 33; lay believers in, 310n. 101; negation of, by adherents, 297; Nikaya schools of, 87–88, 124–125, 175, 200, 317; in People's Republic of China, 11, 154, 255–260; rites for the dead in, 28, 49, 52, 79, 96, 259, 279, 309n. 100, 315n. 48, 330n. 2; socially engaged forms of, 11, 295–297; in Taiwan, 11, 154, 262–292; Theravāda tradition of, 199, 276, 293; Vajrayāna tradition of, 88
Buddhist bank *(fojiao yinhang)*, 231
Buddhist Compassion Relief Tzu Chi Foundation (Fojiao Ciji gongde hui), 288–291
Buddhist Confederation (Fojiao gonghui), 50
Buddhist Culture Society (Fojiao wenhua she), 150
Buddhist Ladies Academy (Wuchang nü foxue yuan), 319n. 94
Buddhist Lodge (London), 125, 129
Buddhist Moral Endeavor Society (Fojiao jinde hui), 50
Buddhist Research Association (Fojiao yanjiu hui), 45
Buddhist Research Society (Fojiao yanjiu she), 50
Buddhist Society of the Great Vow (Fojiao hongshi hui), 51, 79

Buddhist vihāra *(fofa sengyuan)*, 231
Buddhist Youth Association of Shanghai (Shanghaishi fojiao qingnian hui), 150
Burma Society, 129
Bush, Richard, 256
Bushwell, Robert E., 312n. 7

Cai Yuanpei, 23, 25–26
Callahan, Paul, 85, 95, 220, 240
can chan hui (meeting for meditation), 93
Capitalism, 15, 109, 192–193
Chan Kim-kwong, 35
Chan, Wing-tsit, 167, 246–247, 344n. 127
Chan zong (Chan school), 32, 55, 86–87, 92, 95, 175, 227, 230–231, 246, 274, 277, 281–282, 288; Caodong lineage of, 280; Linji lineage of, 32, 55, 272, 279
Chang, Carsun (or C.S. Chang). *See* Zhang Jiasen
Changjue, Ven., 266
Changxing, Ven., 107–108
Changyuan, Ven., 148
Chappell, David W., 273
Chen Dingmo, 140
Chen Duxiu, 19, 22, 25, 27
Chen Huanzhang, 127, 325n. 53
Ch'en, Kenneth, 202
Chen Li'an, 275
Chen Mingshu, 328n. 96
Chen Wenyuan (W. Y. Chen), 135, 137, 145, 328nn. 95, 96
Chen Xizun (C. C. Chen), 146, 329n. 101
Chen Yuanbai, 97
Cheng weishi lun, 84
Chen-hua, Ven. *See* Zhenhua, Ven.
Chiang Kai-shek, 19, 20, 59, 117–118, 135, 137–138, 140–142, 149, 183, 185, 311n. 113, 334n. 60
Ch'ien, Edward, 31
China Inland Mission, 37, 41, 304n. 60
China Institute (Frankfurt), 126
Chinese Buddhist Association (Zhongguo fojiao hui, Nanjing, 1912), 50, 77

Chinese Buddhist Association (Zhongguo fojiao hui, Shanghai, 1929), 47, 52, 66, 130–133, 135, 137, 139, 148; reconstituted Chinese Buddhist Association (Nanjing, 1947), 150, 262–263, 276, 284
Chinese Buddhist Association (Zhongguo fojiao xiehui; Bejing, 1953), 258–259
Chinese Buddhist Association (Zhonghua fojiao hui, Beijing, 1917), 52
Chinese Buddhist Cultural Institute (Zhonghua fojiao wenhua guan), 280
Chinese Buddhist Education Association (Zhonghua fohua jiaoyu she), 115
Chinese Buddhist Federation (Zhonghua fojiao lianhe hui), 108–109, 113
Chinese Buddhist Goodwill Mission (Fojiao fangwen tuan), 139–143
Chinese Buddhist Hospital (Zhongguo fojiao yiyuan), 150
Chinese Buddhist Study Association (Zhongguo foxue hui), 118, 323n. 36
Chinese Church of the Five Religions. See Temple of Five Religions (Wujiao Dao yuan)
Chinese General Buddhist Association (Zhonghua fojiao zonghui, Shanghai, 1912), 50–52, 58, 77–78, 80, 85, 103, 309n. 99, 315n. 48
Chinese Metaphysical Institute. See Metaphysical Institute
Chinese United League (Tongmeng hui), 17, 68
Chinese Yellow Swastika Society (Zhonghua huangwanzi hui), 51, 137
Chinese-Ceylonese Culture Association (Zhong Xi wenhua xiehui), 142
Chisong, Ven., 109
Chou Hsiang-kuang, 88, 137, 325n. 62
Chow, Tse-tsung, 25
Christianity, 25, 116, 223, 241, 251, 265, 285, 287, 293; criticisms of in China, 11, 25–28; in Europe and North America, 125–126, 154, 164, 249–250; growth of in Republican China, 15, 35–37, 58–59, 243; and missionaries' criticisms of Chinese Buddhism, 37–40; Social Gospel Movement in, 11, 243, 294; Taixu's views of (see under Taixu)
Chung-Hwa Institute of Buddhist Studies (Zhonghua fojiao yanjiu suo), 280–281, 283
Cihang, Ven., 139
Cixi, Empress Dowager, 16, 301n. 14
Ciyun si: Fengyuan, Taiwan, 287; Nan'an, 145
Committee for the Reorganization of Chinese Buddhism (Zhongguo fojiao zhengli weiyuan hui), 145, 148–150
Communist Party (Gongchandang), 19–21, 26, 48, 52, 135, 149–150, 182–184, 186–187, 189, 191, 249, 257, 259, 266
Confucianism, 23, 25, 29, 31, 35, 53, 164, 170–171, 196–197, 213, 217, 223, 238, 265, 325n. 53, 335n. 4
Conlan, Barnett, 313n. 18
Consciousness-Only school. See Weishi zong
Court of the Dao (Dao yuan), 53
Covell, Ralph R., 38
Cressy, Earl Herbert., 48, 96–97, 309n. 100
Cultural Revolution, 256–257, 259

Dajue si: Yixing, Jiangsu, 270; New York, 281
Dalai Lama (Tenzin Gyatso), 296
Dalin si (Jiangxi), 106, 248
Dao Feng Shan (Hong Kong), 59
Daoan, Ven., 197, 320n. 3
Daoism, 25, 29, 31, 33–35, 40, 46, 48, 53, 85, 164, 213, 223, 242, 265
Daojie, Ven., 67, 70, 109, 322n. 17
Darwin, Charles, 22–23
Daxing, Ven., 266–267
Daxingshan si (Xi'an), 99, 319n. 97
Dayal, Har, 214, 340n. 62

Dayu Shan (Hong Kong), 261
De Wang (Demchukdonggrub), 138
Dean, Kenneth, 260
Democratic League, 189
Democratic Socialist Party, 150, 189
Dewey, John, 23
Deyi, Ven., 56
Dharma: common to the five vehicles *(wusheng gongfa)*, 88, 171–173, 269, 291; final age of *(mofa)*, 10, 202
Dharma Drum College of Humanities and Social Science, 281
Dharma Drum Mountain. *See* Fagu Shan
Dharma Master *(fashi)*, 55, 232
Dharmapala, Anagarika, 42–44, 58, 70, 306n. 74
Diamond Sūtra (Jingang jing), 41, 279
Dinghui si (Zhenjiang), 45, 280
Dirlik, Arif, 183
Dixian, Ven., 45, 55, 56, 74, 77, 114, 152, 238
Dongchu, Ven., 32, 35, 42, 56, 107, 108, 118, 131, 209, 280, 284
Dye, D. S., 48

East Asian Buddhist Conference (Dongya fojiao dahui), 108, 119, 322n. 17
Eastern Buddhist, 94, 109, 112
Edkins, Joseph, 40, 43, 303n. 52
Edo Sentaro, 106
education: Buddhist parochial, 234–235; monastic, 10, 54–56, 235–236, 310n. 103; secular, 191–192, 302n. 26
Eight Fingers (Bazhi Toutuo), Ven. *See* Jichan, Ven.
Eitel, Ernest J., 39–40
Engaged Buddhism. *See under* Buddhism
ethical naturalism, as form of moral reasoning, 179
evolution, 22–23

Fafang, Ven., 266
Fagu Shan (Dharma Drum Mountain, Taipei), 283–284

Fairbank, John K., 24, 135
Fa-Kuang Institute of Buddhist Studies (Faguang fojiao wenhua yanjiu suo), 268
Fayuan si (Beijing), 70, 79
Fazun, Ven., 259
Fellowship of Faiths, 127
Feng Yuxiang, 58, 145–146
Five precepts. *See under* Bodhisattvas
Five vehicles. *See under* Buddhism
Foguang Shan (Kaohsiung), 272, 348n. 44
Fojiao congbao (Buddhist Miscellany), 50
Fojiao yuebao (Buddhist Monthly), 50, 80–81
Fosdick, Harry Emerson, 295
Foucher, Alfred, 122
Franck, Harry A., 304n. 59
Franke, Otto, 44, 70, 307n. 75
Fu Zhiying, 275

Gao Yongxiao, 86–88
German Research Academy for Chinese Culture, 126
Gimello, Robert, 267
Glazer, Nathan, 295
Glüer, Winifred, 305n. 62
Golden Lotus Theater Group, 346n. 20
Golden Swastika First-aid Corps. *See* Chinese Yellow Swastika Society
Gómez, Luis, 200
Granet, Marcel, 122
Great Federation of Anti-Religionists (Fei zongjiao da tongmeng), 26
Gregory, Peter, 199
Grieder, Jerome, 21
Grousset, René, 122
Guangfu hui. *See* Restoration Society
Guangji si (Beijing), 108
Guangjiao si (Jiangsu), 277
Guangxu, Emperor, 16, 17, 63
Guanyin ge (Zhenjiang), 74
Guanyin si (Beijing), 51
Guanzong si (Ningbo), 45, 56
Guomindang. *See* Nationalist Party
Gützlaff, Karl F.A. (Charles), 36

Haichao si (Hangzhou), 151
Haichao yin (Sound of the Sea Tide), 83, 93–95, 100, 171, 230, 262, 266
Hamilton, Clarence H., 115–117, 247
Han Zang jiaoli yuan. *See* Sino-Tibetan Buddhist Institute
Harada Roshi, 280
Hardoon Gardens (Ai li yuan), 73
Hardoon, Mrs. Silas (Luo Jialing), 73
Hengqing, Ven., 288
hereditary temples *(zusun miao)*, 47, 54
Higashi-Honganji sect, 57, 135
Hitler, Adolf, 125
Hodous, Lewis, 45, 308n. 91
Hong Jinlian, 169–170, 211
Hong Kong Buddhist Association (Xianggang fojiao lianhe hui, Hong Kong, 1931), 261
Hong Xiuquan, 34, 303n. 52
Hongsan, Ven., 109
Hongyi, Ven., 152
horned tiger hall *(jiaohu tang)*, 99
Hsi Lai University, 272
Hsü, Immanuel C.Y., 15, 84, 138
Hu Ruilin, 109, 113
Hu Shi, 22–23, 26, 196, 240–242
Hu Shuhua, 148
hua tou (critical phrase) method in Chan Buddhism, 66, 312n. 7
Hualin si (Guangzhou), 71
Hualin, Ven., 102
Huang, J. L. (Huang Renlin), 328n. 96
Huang Qinglan, 148
Huang Zongyang. *See* Zongyang, Ven.
Huangjiao si (Beijing), 32
Huashan, Ven., 67–68, 70
Huayan (Avataṃsaka) Sūtra (Huayan jing), 205, 213
Huayan University (Huayan daxue), 56
Huayan zong (Huayan [or Xianshou] school), 55, 86–87, 227, 231, 246
Huayu Primary School (Huayu xiaoxue), 70
Huazang si (Nanjing), 272
Huiyuan, Ven., 106, 320n. 3

humanistic Buddhism. *See under* Buddhism
Humphreys, Christmas, 129

Inada Ensai, 106
Institute for Religious Adherence (chijiao yuan), 231
International Buddhist Peace Society (Fojiaotu guoji heping hui), 135
International Buddhist Progess Society. *See* Foguang Shan
Itō Kendō, 57

Jan Yün-hua, 198
Jātaka Tales, 199
Japanese Buddhist Association, 135–136
Japanese Students' Association (London), 129
Jetavana Hermitage (Zhihuan jingshe), 44, 70, 74, 77
Jiang Fangzhen, 30
Jiangsu-Zhejiang Buddhist Federation (Jiang Zhe fojiao lianhe hui), 130–131
Jiao Shan Buddhist Seminary (Jiao Shan foxue yuan), 270
Jiao Shan (Zhenjiang), 45, 280
Jichan, Ven., 50, 66–69, 73, 77–80, 130, 154, 158
Jiedai si (Ningbo), 70
Jiezhu si (Shaoxing), 74
Jin Shan (Zhenjiang), 63, 70; "invasion of" (danao Jin Shan), 74–77, 81, 184
Jing'an si (Shanghai), 51, 80
Jingci si (Hangzhou), 99
Jingfan yuan (Hangzhou), 93–94
Jingtu zong (Pure Land school), 10, 30, 55, 86, 100, 175, 202, 231, 234, 237–240, 246, 258, 263, 269, 274, 320n. 98
Jinling Scriptural Press (Jinling kejing chu), 41, 42, 44, 50, 70
Jishan, Ven., 75–76
Jiuhua Shan (Anhui), 63
Johnston, Reginald F., 114, 323n. 27
Jones, Charles Brewer, 263, 269

Judaism, Reform Movement in, 11, 294–295
Jueshe congshu (Enlightenment Magazine), 93
Juzan, Ven., 257–259, 261

Kaiyuan si (Shaoxing), 74
Kang Junbi, 146
Kang Youwei, 19, 25, 67
Kangxi, Emperor, 35
Kimura Taiken, 108
Kitagawa, Joseph M., 3, 146, 292
Kropotkin, Peter, 72
Kubokawa Kyokiyo, 113

Lai, Whalen, 39, 44, 246, 254, 267, 305n. 64, 307n. 77
Laiguo, Ven., 152
Laloy, Louis, 122
Lamaism (Lama jiao), 32
Lancaster, Lewis, 115, 199
Land Reform Law (1950), 256
Landsborough, Dr. and Mrs. David, 285
Lang Shan (Jiangsu), 277
Latourette, Kenneth Scott, 58
League for the Support of Buddhism (Weichi fojiao tongmeng hui), 51, 80
League of Neighbors, 127
Legge, James, 196
Levenson, Joseph, 14, 26
Lévi, Sylvain, 122
Li Dazhao, 19
Li Kaicheng, 97
Li Kaishen, 319n. 94
Li Rongxi, 259
Li Yinchen, 97
Li Yuanhong, 25
Li Zikuan, 148, 150, 266
Liang Hancao, 148
Liang Hongzhi, 138
Liang Qichao, 24, 28–30, 68, 114, 301n. 20, 323n. 27
Liang Shangtong, 72
Liang Shuming, 24, 25, 170–171, 174, 208
Liaochen, Ven., 107

Lin Shu, 23
Lin Zhaoen, 31
Lindu si (Hong Kong), 261
Lingdu si (Hong Kong), 261
Lingyuan, Ven., 279
Linji si (Taipei), 287
Linji, Ven., 252
Liu Minseng, 310n. 102
Liuyun si (Shanghai), 78
London Buddhist Joint Committee, 129, 325n. 58
Longhua si (Shanghai), 43–44, 58
Lotus Sūtra (Fahua jing), 66, 87, 199–200, 227, 277
Lounsbery, Grace Constant, 123, 324nn. 44, 45, 330n. 114
Lu Shan (Jiangxi), 106–107, 135, 242, 248
Lu Xun, 24
Lü zong (Vinaya school), 86, 231, 235

Ma Jinxun, 113
MacInnis, Donald, 346n. 13
Maha Bodhi Society, 42–43, 125, 306n. 73, 325n. 58
Maitreya, 32, 151, 227
Maitreya Society, 31
Malalasekera, G.P., 142–143
Manchukuo (Manzhouguo), 135
Mao Zedong, 20, 21, 135, 183–184, 255, 257, 259–261
March, A. C., 129
Marshall, George C., 149
Marx, Karl, 22, 72, 184, 186, 251–252, 255
May Fourth Movement, 98
May Thirtieth Incident of 1925, 114, 323n. 29
McDaniel, C. Yates, 195
Meditation Master *(chanshi)*, 232
Mei Guangxi, 45
Metaphysical Institute (Zhina neixue yuan), 54
Miaoji, Ven., 102
Millican, Frank R., 11, 62, 155, 167–168, 237–238, 243, 248

Minzhi, Ven., 56
Mizuno Baigyō, 57, 108, 112–113
Mo Jipeng, 72
monastic community. *See* sangha
monastic education. *See under* education
monastic troops *(seng jun)*, 73
morality books *(shan shu)*, 31
Morrison, Robert, 36
Moslem Rebellion, 16
Müller, Gotelind, 207
Müller, Max, 42
Musée Guimet, 122–123

Nāgārjuna, 201
Nanjio Bunyiu, 42, 112
National Conference of Buddhist Representatives (Quanguo fojiao daibiao huiyi), 131
National Conference on Education (Quanguo jiaoyu huiyi), 130
Nationalist Party (Guomindang), 18, 19, 20, 21, 26, 48, 52, 57, 58, 81, 114, 118, 130, 138, 140–142, 144–146, 149–151, 182–185, 189, 260, 275, 329n. 101
Nazism, 125, 138
Neill, Stephen, 36
New Culture Movement (Xin wenhua yundong), 22–25, 169
New Life Movement (Xin shenghuo yundong), 20, 183
New York Chan Meditation Center (Niuyue Chan zhongxin), 281
Nhat Hanh, Thich, 296
nian fo (reciting name of Buddha), 30, 42, 92–93, 96, 202–203, 238
Nian Rebellion, 16
Nikāya. *See under* Buddhism
Ningbo Sangha Educational Association (Ningbo seng jiaoyu hui), 69
Nongchan si (Taipei), 280

Opium War, 13, 15, 36
ordination *(shou jie)*, 54, 209, 276
Ouyang Jingwu, 45, 50, 54, 77, 79, 98, 114, 208, 239, 247, 330n. 7

Pali Tripiṭaka Institute (Bali sanzang yuan), 99, 319n. 97
Pan Dawei, 72–73
Pas, Julian, 260
Petzold, Bruno, 109, 119, 323n. 37
Philosophy of Life Institute (Rensheng zhexue yanjiu hui), 148, 251, 329n. 104
Pilu si (Nanjing), 51, 74, 132
Political Consultative Conference, 149
Prajñā school. *See* Sanlun zong
Prajñāpāramitā literature, 67, 201, 213, 227
Pratt, James B., 45–47, 98, 239, 330n. 7
pratyekabuddhas, 87, 171–172, 199–200, 204, 269
Presbyterian Church in Taiwan, 285, 292, 329n. 101, 349n. 59, 351n. 86
Prip-Møller, Johannes, 45, 47, 185
Proudhon, Pierre-Joseph, 72
Przyluski, Jean, 123
public monasteries *(shifang conglin)*, 47, 54, 65
Puming si (Hualian), 288
Pure Abode of Still Thoughts (Jingsi jingshe, Hualian), 289
pure land *(jingtu):* definition of, 222; in devotional practice, 30, 32–33, 92–93, 99, 201–202; in this world *(renjian jingtu)*, 180–181, 221–222, 274, 283–284, 290, 292, 294
Pure Land school. *See* Jingtu zong
Pusey, James Reeve, 22
Putuo Shan (Zhejiang), 39, 65, 73, 81–83, 89, 91, 227, 266
Puyi (Emperor Xuantong), 13, 17, 19, 135

Qianlong, Emperor, 33
Qichang, Ven., 66, 67
Qingliang si (Shanghai), 80
Qingnian, Ven. *See* Yushan
Qingquan, Ven., 75–76, 314nn. 29, 36
Qiu Jin, 68
Qiu Xiuzhi, 288, 290
Qixia Shan (Nanjing), 270

Qiyun, Ven., 68–72
Qu Wenliu, 148
Quanlang, Ven., 148
Quefei, Ven., 73

Randall, John, 3
Rape of Nanjing, 137
Rebirth Treatise (Wuliangshou jing youbotishe yuansheng jie), 239
Record of Pointing at the Moon (Zhiyue lu), 66
Record of the Lives of Eminent Monks (Gaoseng zhuan), 66
Reform Judaism. *See* Judaism
Regulations for the Control of Monasteries and Temples (Guanli simiao tiaoli, 1915), 52, 57, 84, 90
Regulations for the Control of Monasteries and Temples (Simiao guanli tiaoli, January 1929), 131
Regulations for the Supervision of Monasteries and Temples (Jiandu simiao tiaoli, December 1929), 58, 131
Reichelt, Karl Ludvig, 48, 82–83, 89, 99, 103, 106–107, 115, 133, 150, 209, 238, 242, 248, 251, 308n. 91, 321n. 5, 323nn. 27, 32, 329n. 110, 338n. 39
religion: modern trends of, 3, 292–295; secular humanist criticisms of, 25–26; syncretistic forms of, 31–32, 310n. 102; visionary and ethical dimensions of, 3–7
Renou, Louis, 123
Renshan, Ven., 74–76, 89, 132, 315n. 48
Reorganization of the Sangha System (Zhengli sengqie zhidu lun), 90, 95, 230–236, 259
Restoration Society (Guangfu hui), 313n. 16
Ricci, Matteo, 35
Richard, Timothy, 38, 42, 44, 305n. 62
Right Faith Buddhist Society of Hankou (Hankou fojiao zhengxin hui), 97, 102, 114, 137
Rites Controversy, 36

Roosevelt, Frankin D., 192
Russell, Bertrand, 23, 124

Saeki Teien, 108
sangha (monastic community): literacy rates within, 54, 310n. 103; size of, in Republican China 95–96, 231–233, 309n. 100
Sangharakshita, Ven., 201, 207
Sanlun zong (Three Treatise [Prajñā or Mādhyamika] School), 86–87, 231, 266, 268
sealed confinement *(biguan)*, 82–83, 85, 87, 89–90, 95, 316n. 57
Sengzhao, Ven., 197
Shandao si (Taipei), 266, 269
Shanyin, Ven., 151
Shengyan, Ven., 11, 86–87, 263, 277–285, 291, 312n. 7
Sheridan, James, 18
Shi Mingke, 259
Shida, Ven., 65–66
Shirob Jaltso, Ven., 257–258, 260
Shizi lin (Guangzhou), 71
Shuangting, Ven., 75–76, 314n. 36
Shuangxi si (Guangzhou), 71–73
Sino-Japanese Wars: (1894–1895), 16; (1937–1945), 21, 130, 135, 151, 180–181
Sino-Tibetan Buddhist Institute (Han Zang jiaoli yuan), 99, 137
Six Perfections. *See under* Bodhisattvas
Six Sages True Dao Union Society (Liu shen zhen Dao tongyi hui), 53
Smith, Arthur H., 40
Smith, Jonathan Z., 197, 294
Social Gospel, liberal Christian. *See under* Christianity
Socialism, 81, 84, 109, 182, 185–186
Socialist Party, 74–75
Société Théosophique de France, 123
Soong Meiling, 59, 117
South Fujian Buddhist Seminary (Minnan foxue yuan), 56, 99, 257, 259, 266

Śrāvakas, 87, 171–172, 199–200, 204, 268, 269, 282
Study of Morality Society (Daode xue she), 53
Su Manshu, 45, 307n. 82
Sulak Sivaraksa, 296
Sun Yat-sen, 17, 18, 19, 68, 73, 74, 77, 125, 169, 184, 185, 315n. 36
Sūraṅgama Sūtra (Lengyan jing), 41, 66, 70, 83, 317n. 66
Suzuki, D. T., 112, 212

Tai Pingheng, 320n. 104
Tai Shuangqiu, 130–131
Taiping Rebellion, 1, 16, 34–35, 40–41, 45
Taixu, Ven.: on a Buddhism for human life *(rensheng fojiao)*, 169–181, 202; on Christianity, 242–252; criticisms of, by conservative Buddhists and secular humanists, 236–242, 346n. 13; on dual practice of Chan and Pure Land, 99–100, 201–202; early life and education of, 63–72, 213–214; on establishing a pure land on earth, 180, 221–229; founding of the Bodhi Society by, 91–94; founding of World Buddhist Federation by, 106–114; founding of Wuchang Buddhist Institute by, 96–99; on global society of post-World War II era, 190–195; on his own failures, 138–139; on "invasion of Jin Shan" incident, 74–77; leadership of interfaith organizations by, 145–148; methods of evangelism of, 99–104, 133–135; mission to Europe and the United States by, 118–130; mission to South Asia by, 139–143; on the modern world's moral crisis, 159–165; on monastic career, 207–209; on monastics returning to lay life, 209–210; on political involvement, 149–150, 182–190; on the portability of Chinese Buddhism, 114–118, 157; on practice of the precepts and six perfections, 216–221; program of prison visitation by, 103–104, 150; on the religionless future, 250–254; on reorganizing the sangha system, 95–96, 229–236; on a scientific Buddhism, 165–168; sealed confinement *(biguan)* of, 81–89; on styles of moral reasoning, 177–179; on types of cultures, 162–165; utopian tendencies of, 12, 60, 96, 157–158, 181, 229, 297; on women, 212, 339n. 48; work with the Chinese Buddhist Association (Shanghai, 1929) by, 77–81, 130–133, 145, 148–150
Takakusu Junjirō, 112
Tan Sitong, 29, 44, 68
Tan Yushan, 140
Tang Kesan, 328n. 96
Tantric Master (yuqieshi), 232
Tantric school. *See* Zhenyan zong
Tanxu, Ven., 152
Taylor, James Hudson, 37
Temple of Five Religions (Wujiao Dao yuan), 53, 310n. 102
Theravāda. *See under* Buddhism
Three principles of the people (sanmin zhuyi), 17, 69, 169, 184
Three Teachings Sect (San jiao), 31
Three Treatise (or Prajñā) School. *See* Sanlun zong
Threefold Movement, 127
Tianning Buddhist Institute (Tianning foxue yuan), 56
Tianning si (Zhangzhou), 309n. 99
Tiantai zong (Tiantai school), 55, 86–87, 175, 231, 246
Tiantong si (Ningbo), 62, 65–67, 73, 266
Tieyan, Ven., 74
Tillich, Paul, 179
Tongmeng hui. *See* Chinese United League
Tongzhi Restoration, 16
Tonsure family, 47, 54, 341n. 85
Treaty of Nanjing, 15, 36
Triad Society, 32

Truman, Harry, 149
Tsu, Yu-yue, 51, 78, 85, 94, 153–154, 230–231, 237, 295, 315n. 48
Tsui, Bartholomew, 261
Tu Wei-ming, 196
Twenty-one Demands, 84
Tzu Chi Foundation. *See* Buddhist Compassion Relief Tzu Chi Foundation (Fojiao Ciji gongde hui)

Union of East and West, 127
United Goodness Society (Tongshan she), 53, 310n. 102
Uttarakuru (Yudanyue zhou), 223

Vairocana, 227
Vasubandhu, 239
Venerable Master *(dashi)*, 232
Venerable Scholar degree *(dashi xuewei)*, 236
Vimalakīrti Sūtra (Weimojie suoshuo jing), 173, 221, 274
Vinaya codes, 282–283
Vinaya Master *(lüshi)*, 232
Vinaya school. *See* Lü zong
von Solf, W.H., 113, 119

Wach, Joachim, 3, 298
Wales, H. G. Quaritch, 327n. 82
Waley, Arthur, 196
Waller, Derek, 19
Wang Kemin, 138
Wang Senpu, 97
Wang Yiting, 90, 109, 113, 115, 132–133, 326n. 67
Watanabe Kaikyoku, 113
Way of Unity (Yiguan Dao), 53
Weber, Max, 162
Wei Limin, 328n. 96
Weifang, Ven., 139
Weihuan, Ven., 77, 139
Weishi zong (Consciousness-Only school), 7, 45, 54, 86–87, 91, 99, 231, 246, 266
Welch, Holmes, 2, 41, 47–48, 74, 77, 85, 95, 106, 113–114, 127, 140, 143, 145–146, 150, 152, 182, 207, 234–235, 256, 258–259, 309n. 98, 310n. 101, 315n. 48, 323n. 36, 324n. 43, 326n. 67
West, Philip, 243
White Cloud Mountain. *See* Baiyun Shan
White Cloud Sect, 32
White Lotus Sect, 32
Wilhelm, Richard, 126–127
World Buddhist Federation (Shijie fojiao lianhe hui), 106–115, 142
World Buddhist Institute (Shijie foxue yuan), 99, 118–119, 121–123, 125–130
World Buddhist New Youth Society (Shijie fohua xin qingnian hui), 115
World Buddhist University (Shijie fohua daxue), 118, 120
World Congress (Shijie daibiao dahui), 194, 335n. 75
World Fellowship of Buddhists (Shijie fojiaotu youyi hui), 142–143, 250, 261–262, 275
World Propaganda Team (Shijie xuanchuan dui), 115
World Red Swastika Association (Shijie hongwanzi hui), 137
World's Parliament of Religions (Chicago, 1893), 42
World's Student Christian Federation, 26
Wright, Mary Clabaugh, 16
Wu Yue, 21
Wu Zhihui, 25
Wuchang Buddhist Institute (Wuchang foxue yuan), 56, 96–99, 104, 114, 239, 242, 266, 268, 319n. 94
Wuming, Ven. 146
Wutai Shan (Shanxi), 46

Xiandai fojiao (Modern Buddhism), 258–259
Xiao Jiuhua si (Jiangsu), 65, 68, 312n. 3
Xie, S. T., 146
Xie Zhuchen, 132–133

Xifang si (Jiangsu), 67, 71, 213
Xilai si (Hacienda Heights, California), 272
Xilin tang (Putuo Shan), 81
Xingxiu, Ven., 107
Xingyun, Ven., 11, 263, 270–277, 291
Xizhu si (Shanghai), 150
Xu Xilin, 68
Xuantong, Emperor. *See* Puyi
Xuming, Ven., 81, 86, 89–90, 105–106, 113, 142, 151, 266
Xuyun, Ven., 55, 77–78, 148, 152, 279, 315n. 44

Yan Fu, 23, 68, 83
Yan Shaofu, 106
Yang Huinan, 88, 269
Yang Wenhui (Yang Renshan), 40–45, 50, 70, 74, 77, 283, 305n. 62
Yang Xiuqing, 34
Yanpei, Ven., 280
Yanqing si (Ningbo), 51, 79, 150
Yekai, Ven., 51, 309n. 99
Yinguang, Ven., 2, 71, 82, 114, 152, 201–202, 237–238
Yinping, Ven., 75–76
Yinshun, Ven., 11, 65, 67–69, 71–73, 76, 84, 118, 122, 131, 133, 140, 145, 149, 151, 158, 170, 172–173, 204, 261, 263–270, 279, 283, 288–289, 291, 324n. 37, 347n. 29
Yogācāra. *See* Weishi zong
Yongfeng si (Ningbo), 66
Yongming Yanshou, Ven., 99
Young Buddhist Study Association (Fojiao qingnian xuehui), 50–51
Young East, 58
Young Men's Buddhist Association, 102
Young Men's Christian Association, 132
Youth Party, 150, 189
Yu Bin (Paul Yu Bin), 145–146, 148, 251
Yü Chün-fang, 30, 201, 330n. 2

Yuan Shikai, 17–19, 25, 52, 57, 78, 80–81, 84–85
Yuanying, Ven., 66–67, 69–70, 77, 89, 130–133, 148, 258, 263, 266, 326n. 67
Yuebin, Ven., 71–72
Yuexia, Ven., 56, 81
Yufo si (Shanghai), 74, 150
Yunhua tang (Zhanghua, Taiwan), 90
Yunnan University (Yunnan daxue), 142
Yushan, Ven., 266
Yuwang si (or Ayuwang si, Asoka Monastery, Ningbo), 65

Zeng Guofan, 35, 41–42
Zeng Jize, 42
Zhang Binglin. *See* Zhang Taiyan
Zhang Jiasen (or Zhang Junmai), 24, 26–27
Zhang Taiyan, 68, 83, 90, 115, 170, 244
Zhang Zhidong, 16, 29
Zhang Zuolin, 117
Zhangjia Hutukhtu, 148
Zhao Puchu, 257–258
Zhao Yang Buwei. 41
Zhengli sengqie zhidu lun. See Reorganization of the Sangha System
Zhengyan, Ven., 263, 285–292
Zhenhua, Ven., 54–55, 58, 202, 268, 316n. 57, 347n. 29
Zhenyan zong (Tantric school), 55, 86–87, 92, 175, 227, 231, 234, 341n. 77
Zhiguang, Ven., 45
Zhikai, Ven., 270
Zhou Enlai, 20
Zhou Xuenong, 346n. 14
Zhu Baotang, 262
Zhu'an, Ven., 108
Zhuangnian, Ven., 66, 70, 73
Zongyang, Ven. (Huang Zongyang), 73, 81, 314n. 29
Zou Rong, 68

ABOUT THE AUTHOR

Don A. Pittman received his Ph.D. from the University of Chicago. From 1994 to 2000, he lived in Southern Taiwan and was professor of history of religions and chair of the Department of Theological Studies at Tainan Theological College and Seminary and served as a member of the regional faculty of the South East Asia Graduate School of Theology, Manila. He is now dean and professor of history of religions at Phillips Theological Seminary in Tulsa, Oklahoma.